D0831870

AN ARTFUL LIFE

ALSO BY PIERRE ASSOULINE

Gaston Gallimard: A Half-Century of French Publishing

PIERRE ASSOULINE

AN ARTFUL LIFE

· · ·

A BIOGRAPHY OF
D. H. KAHNWEILER,
1884-1979

TRANSLATED FROM THE FRENCH
BY CHARLES RUAS

Fromm International Publishing Corporation
NEW YORK

This translation is for Rob Wynne—C.R.

Published in 1991 by Fromm International Publishing Corporation
by arrangement with Grove Weidenfeld,
a division of Wheatland Corporation
Published in Canada by General Publishing Company, Ltd.
Copyright © 1988 by Editions Balland
Translation copyright © 1990 by Charles Ruas
Originally published in French as
L'homme de l'art: D.H. Kahnweiler, 1884-1979
by Editions André Balland, Paris, in 1988
This translation has been slightly abridged from the original
French edition

All rights reserved. No part of this book may be reproduced
or utilized in any form or by any means, electronic or
mechanical, including photocopying, recording, or by any
information storage and retrieval system, without permission
in writing from the Publisher. Inquiries should be addressed to
Fromm International Publishing Corporation,
560 Lexington Avenue, New York, NY 10022.

Designed by Helene Berinsky

Manufactured in the United States of America

Printed on acid-free paper

First U.S. Edition 1990

First Paperback Edition 1991

Cover printed by Keith Press, Inc., Knoxville, TN
Printed and bound by R.R. Donnelley & Sons Co.,
Harrisonburg, VA

Library of Congress Cataloging-in-Publication Data
Assouline, Pierre.
[L'homme de l'art. English]
An artful life : a biography of D.H. Kahnweiler, 1884-1979 /
Pierre Assouline ; translated from the French by Charles Ruas. —
1st pbk. ed.
p.   cm.
Translation of : L'homme de l'art.
Includes bibliographical references (p.   ) and index.
ISBN 0-88064-131-2 (pbk. : acid-free paper) : $14.95
1. Kahnweiler, Daniel Henry, 1884-1979. 2. Art dealers—France-
-Biography. I. Title.
N8660.K3A9513 1991
709'.2—dc20   [B]   91-16439

ISBN 0-88064-131-2

To Major Ronnie Yadgaroff

CONTENTS

. . .

ACKNOWLEDGMENTS

. . .

⊏⊐ I dedicate this work to my beloved grandmothers, Cécile and Marie.

This book was written with the invaluable assistance of numerous people. I must express my gratitude to Louise Leiris, Michel Leiris, and Maurice Jardot. Without their cooperation, openness of mind, and constant support this work would be less original and less substantial. By entrusting me with their recollections and opening the gallery archives to me, with complete license to immerse myself in the material and pursue any direction, they have given me a rare and precious experience for a biographer: the sense of being in touch with the essential truth about a unique man.

I also had the constant help of Bernard Lirman, Quentin Laurens, Jeannette Druy, and Jeanne Chenuet. They know how much this book owes to them.

There would be many more errors and flaws in this work without the rigorous criticism and assistance of Pierre Boncenne, Stéphane Khémis, and Robert Maillard.

If it were not for the daily support of my best friend, Angela, and the understanding of my little chums Meryl and Kate, I could not have brought this difficult project to a conclusion.

Finally I must express my profound gratitude to:

Mmes. Paule Chavasse, Sarah Halperyn, Frances Honegger-

Trevezant, Marianne Howald, Sigrid Kupferman, Denise Laurens, Marie-Anne Lescourret, Jeanine Pezet, S. Schneidermann, Myriam Sicouri-Roos, and Andrea Von Strumm.

Messrs. Joseph Barry, Francis Berthier, Adam Biro, Daniel Bourgeois, Edward Burns, François Chapon, Georges-Emmanuel Clancier, Daniel Cordier, Marc Dachy, Pierre Daix, Oscar Ghez, Peter Hurni, Vidar Jacobsen, Gustave Kahnweiler, Sulivan Kaufman, Sandor Kuthy, Charles Lapicque, Claude Laurens, André Masson, Jean Masurel, Georges Nisenbaum, Patrick-Gilles Persin, and Alfred Richet.

—Pierre Assouline

FOREWORD

■ ■ ■

◻ Why Kahnweiler? Because he was extraordinary and unique. In the course of this century there may have been other great art dealers. Perhaps these others were even more appealing, had better judgment, or were less dogmatic. But of all those from Kahnweiler's generation who launched themselves on this adventure, he remains the only one whose name is inseparable from a decisive moment in modern art, the "epic" of cubism. The most important painters are indebted to this man, the greatest art dealer of his day.

He was only twenty-three when he opened his gallery in 1907. By the time he retired he was ninety-five. He lived through the twentieth century following his own path, discreetly but with tenacity, and his life was shaped by all its tragic upheavals. He survived two world wars, which twice made him an outcast from French society: the first time because he was German, the second because he was a Jew. Between the wars he overcame the economic depression that caused enormous losses in the financial community. From the very beginning he championed a school of painting that almost no one else believed in, and he continued to do so as if there were no obstacles, until it became established and successful many decades later. For over seventy years Daniel-Heinrich Kahnweiler adhered to his principles. The measure of his success is that he lived and worked during those years in complete harmony with the values that he had made his own.

The pettiness of his associates, the betrayal by certain painters, the instability of the art market, the incredible lack of support by the government, and the insane march of history in times of crisis often combined to ruin him. But his optimism was rarely destroyed. Kahnweiler never despaired of his fellowman.

This may seem oversimplified, but Kahnweiler always took this tone when telling his life story. He gave more details, of course, but only superficial ones. By remaining on the surface of events, skimming over problems, and carefully refraining from any introspection, he was responding in the style of Martin Heidegger, who began his lectures on Aristotle: "He was born, he worked, and he died," before getting to the essential, his works.

On several occasions Kahnweiler pushed back the fateful hour when the man of action picks up his pen to write his autobiography. He did not feel ready. He was never able to resolve his old dilemma: the painters he liked best were those in his gallery, and his narrative would have immediately come under fire from his detractors as a work of self-promotion. As for the painters he did not like, and the art dealers for whom he had little respect, and the current state of the arts which (with few exceptions) he abhorred, one volume would not have been sufficient. At any rate, Kahnweiler would never have done it, preferring to be constructive rather than destructive. But what a loss!

The only means of resolving this dilemma was for me to write his biography. I did not know Kahnweiler, and I am neither connected with nor an observer of the art world. All the more reason to do it. This innocence seemed to guarantee my objectivity in undertaking a project made sensitive by its dual nature: art and money. The life of a man can be explained and understood only in relation to his milieu—in this case, the art world. The biography of Kahnweiler touches the lives of the painters, dealers, critics, collectors, and writers who marked his life. In retrospect, except for the two world wars, his period was exhilarating in terms of its diversity, intensity, and creativity.

In order to reconstruct the atmosphere of the period, to describe things said and seen at events ranging from an art dealer opening a gallery in the center of Paris at the beginning of the century up to his triumph in our own day, I conducted research in all directions. My first sources were books. Those written by painters were generally more helpful, as opposed to those by dealers, so superficial and smug, illustrated by anecdotes. Newspapers, journals of the period, art reviews, and cultural magazines were good barometers. The oral history for the "heroic" period of cubism is almost nonexistent for obvious reasons. Other accounts of the twenties are rare and require a cross-reference interpretation. Research for a biography such as this one is evaluated by the originality of the documents on which it is based.

I had access to an important archive, mostly unedited, preserved for decades in the basement of the Galerie Louise Leiris (Kahnweiler's sister-in-law), and never before examined. Aside from traditional business records (invoices, contracts, and purchases), I discovered the correspondence (both the letters and the replies) that Kahnweiler, this secretive man, carried on with thousands of people throughout the world, both business associates and friends, from 1908 right up to his death in 1979. It was known that he spent his mornings writing letters. He came from a generation that rarely used the telephone. He had a special affinity with the written and printed word and happily kept up his correspondence the way other people did their diaries. If by chance at a particular passage in a chapter the reader has the feeling of being in touch with the essence of this man, it is due to these letters. Kahnweiler can be found in them.

This does not mean that his life lacks a certain mystery—far from it. But one can find here the dimensions of the man, his contradictions, his foibles, his solid commercial sense, his infinite culture, and his aesthetic conscience—in sum, everything that made Kahnweiler an extraordinary man and without doubt the art dealer of the century.

His biography is the story of a man whose life was inspired by one idea, but one to which he dedicated himself completely.

"What would have become of us if Kahnweiler hadn't had a business sense?"

PABLO PICASSO

"It is great artists who make great dealers."

D. H. KAHNWEILER

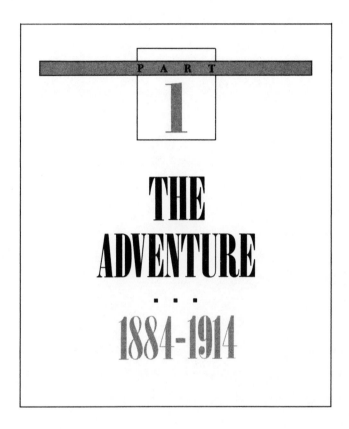

PART

1

THE
ADVENTURE
. . .
1884-1914

MANNHEIM, STUTTGART, FRANKFURT

▭ It was June 25, 1884. Nothing noteworthy occurred in Mannheim that day; it was simply business as usual in the Rhine Palatinate. The kaiser was in the last years of his reign, and his country was on the verge of becoming the fourth industrial power of the world.

The city of Mannheim—an important river port at the confluence of the Rhine and Neckar—was home to the Kahnweilers, even though the family had its roots, dating back to the sixteenth century, in the provinces. This sense of belonging to the land from time immemorial was especially important to them—as Jewish citizens they had always had to prove themselves. Originally their name was Masse (a derivation of Moses), then Manasseh (like the king of Judah). Things changed only with the revolution of 1806, the breakup of the old order under the French occupation, and the decree emancipating the Jews six years later, transforming their status from a tolerated minority to citizens with equal rights. When Napoleon decided to place himself at the head of a united Europe and the old Palatinate state allied itself with Bavaria, Daniel Manasseh decided to change his name to Daniel Kahnweiler. He was married twice. The children of his first marriage emigrated to America; those of his second marriage, most notably Heinrich, remained in Europe.[1]

It was logical, therefore, that on June 25, 1884, in Mannheim, in the home of Heinrich's son, Julius Kahnweiler, and Betty Neumann, the birth of their first child would be celebrated by bestowing on him the double name of Daniel-Heinrich.

One family, two clans, therefore two temperaments. The Kahnweilers had been importers of overseas commodities, especially coffee, and were prosperous businessmen. The Neumanns had specialized in the buying and selling of precious metals for over a century, and enjoyed a considerable fortune that they increased with great business acumen. As young men, Betty's two brothers left their country to live in London. They could best be described as bankers, speculators, entrepreneurs, or brokers. In the City they quickly acquired a position on the stock market, and they controlled gold and diamond mines in South Africa. Julius Kahnweiler was head of their Stuttgart office. To some extent he was employed by them. It was a constraining situation. He was simultaneously a businessman, an outside broker, and a half-commission man who earned his living on the commissions from the business he conducted in Germany for his brothers-in-law.

In Stuttgart, where they moved in 1889, the Kahnweilers lived comfortably in a large house with twelve rooms. They maintained a complete staff, as befitting their social position—a chauffeur to drive the Adler, housemaids, a French governess, and a cook.[2] Frau Kahnweiler supervised the education of the children: Daniel-Heinrich, his sister Augusta, nicknamed Gustie (born 1890), and the youngest, Gustave (born 1895). Julius Kahnweiler spent most of his time speculating on the stock market or gossiping with his cronies. In the morning when he was given his newspapers, the *Frankfurter Zeitung* and the *General Anzeiger,* he immediately turned to their financial sections.

They were well off, but the only problem was the source of the income: it always came from London. Julius Kahnweiler would gradually grow embittered by the situation. This became more noticeable over the years, and it would make him an angry and tyrannical man—all the more so as his wife never missed a chance to praise the success of the Neumanns, in particular the British branch.

At an early age Daniel-Heinrich had differences with his father. The discord between them would only worsen, going from complete disagreement to total indifference. He felt no affinity with his father and searched in vain for common traits before giving up once and for all. Having come to judge him at an early age, he considered his father thickheaded, violent, incapable of analyzing anything, and inept in dealing with people other than in straightforward business relations or the carrying out of his civic duties.

Young Daniel-Heinrich was a Kahnweiler in spirit but he secretly admired the Neumann side of the family. A reserved, discreet boy, he was decidedly influenced by his granduncle, the brother of his maternal grandmother, Joseph Goldscheider, known as "Amico." He was a character, somewhat of a libertine, friend of artists and writers, who loved the theater almost as much as the actresses. He had an open and inquisitive nature. He was just a touch unconventional, but not too much so, and the family considered him a sweet eccentric. He was the ideal uncle to understand Daniel-Heinrich's rebelliousness. The adolescent nephew read poems, spent hours listening to music, and took interminable walks through neighboring forests.[3] Amico was the exact opposite of the boy's perpetually angry father, who insulted his staff in front of the family as if it were the beginning of the nineteenth century.

Above all, Daniel-Heinrich despised his father for having no taste. His library was sparse, revealing no particular interests nor any intellectual development. But even worse were the paintings hanging on the walls of the dining room. Most were works by Franz von Defregger, a painter famous in Munich for his depiction of historical themes and of domestic life in the Tyrol. In this house, only a few pieces of furniture and some of the carpets were worth saving.[4]

In 1890, when the country was stunned by the dismissal of old Chancellor Bismarck by the young Kaiser Wilhelm II, Daniel-Heinrich was only six years old. He felt at home in Stuttgart; all his life he would consider himself a Stuttgartian. For him this ancient realm of the kings of Württemberg was a great big village where everyone knew one another.[5] He would always remember Stuttgart as the place where fireworks were set off over the vineyards on the hillsides in autumn, to celebrate the harvest.[6]

His first contact with the world occurred when he attended the local school, where he discovered that people can be divided into two categories: the majority (Protestants), and the minorities (Catholics and Jews). He would never forget being chased down the street by students shouting at him: *"Judenbub! Judenbub!"* ("You little Jew! You little Jew!")[7]

He was Jewish; he was also small. He didn't understand why the words "little Jew" had become a taunt and an insult. At home religion was only practiced nominally. His family ate ham; his father went to the synagogue only twice a year, for Rosh Hashanah and for Passover. And that was it.

He did not encounter any other anti-Semitism while he studied at the Realgymnasium, the secondary school of Stuttgart. Later, he would give a surprising portrait of himself then: an admired leader, a respected arbiter among his fellows, a good student who did not study hard except during the Easter or summer vacations and on the night before his examinations. He showed promise and ability.[8]

The fact that Kahnweiler always called himself a "Stuttgartian" requires some explanation. For him it was a tribute to his education and the values and principles his teachers inculcated in him. This explains how a young German-Jewish intellectual from the end of the nineteenth century could consider himself a Lutheran without betraying his origins, renouncing his faith, or changing his religion. By proudly accepting and upholding a culture he achieved a style and intellect that were absent, if not unknown, in his father's house. Once he had acquired his inflexible principles from his years at the Realgymnasium he would retain them for the rest of his life, along with an unflagging discipline in his work and in his thinking. These are all qualities which, once mastered, gave a coherence, a moral attitude, a logic to his way of being, an order to his life, but which when carried to extremes could become uncontrollable, leading inevitably to dogmatism, intransigence, and parochialism. It is by these standards that the life and work of Daniel-Heinrich Kahnweiler must be measured.

He would say that his interest in art began at the age of twelve when he visited the museum at Karlsruhe, which housed the collections of the princes of Zahringen, the margraves and grand dukes of Baden. The paintings intrigued him more than they impressed him: François Boucher and Jean-Baptiste-Siméon Chardin, Jacob Ruysdael and Rembrandt, and above all Lucas Cranach.[9]

Several years later he would visit museums more regularly, both in Germany and when touring with his parents in Holland. During this period between adolescence and manhood, he began acquiring a collection of art books, which his family and friends did not understand. His growing interest in art did not replace his earlier passions: poetry (Hölderlin, Novalis) and literature (Gerhart Hauptmann, Max Halbe, Emile Zola, Hermann Sudermann). Social realism and naturalism in fiction took him far from his own milieu.

But it was his precocious talent for languages that would enable him to travel beyond the boundaries of his province and later the borders of his country. He spoke French fluently, due to the combined influences of his teachers and of his governesses (who, if not French, were Belgian or Swiss). His English was not quite as fluent. From the age of eighteen, French was his second language: when he talked to himself, it was always in French. But for a long time he continued to dream in German.[10]

At the age of fifteen he felt the impact of philosophy for the first time when he read Nietzsche's *Thus Spake Zarathustra*, subtitled "A Book for

Everyone and No One." He understood that it was addressed to him, and he was overwhelmed by this magnificent philosophical poem. Nietzsche remained a favorite writer of Kahnweiler's for a long time, well into his old age, but always as a poet. As long as he had the use of his memory he would recite certain passages by heart.[11]

What he loved in *Zarathustra*, with its references to Goethe and Luther, Biblical themes, and the seventeenth-century French moralists, was the prophetic voice, the power of conviction, the unshakable faith, and the war it declares against the state, the academies, and all vulgarization of ideas. Zarathustra is the personification of rebellion. Kahnweiler made him the hero of his own revolt against the forces of inertia in his environment and identified with him while waiting to break away.

By the time he completed his secondary school studies, at the age of sixteen, he had already accepted that he would not attend the university. In his family this was not done. Julius Kahnweiler had fallen ill and, forced by circumstances, retired from business to live on his pension. The issue was not to earn a living, but to make a fortune. The specter of the Neumanns and their success and position in the business world was never discussed at home; still, Daniel-Heinrich was expected to become just as wealthy.[12] Even if he had no say in the matter, Daniel-Heinrich did not hide the fact that he had other ambitions: he wanted a career in music, his other grand passion, along with literature. In his wildest dreams he pictured himself as a great orchestra conductor. He wanted to interpret composers for the general public, to be the mediator between the creators and the spectators. This ambition, unattainable in music, would finally be realized in another realm.

His piano teacher's condescending attitude had turned him away once and for all from the keyboard, for which he had little talent. However, it did not prevent him from attending every concert in Stuttgart, musical score in hand, applauding wildly. As in the case of Wagner, he would defend his taste, his idea of great music, against the tide of public opinion. He understood his course in life: he would not be creative but he would represent artists and defend what he liked.[13]

His ideals were commendable and his goal was worthy of respect. But these did not add up to a career. For Daniel-Heinrich the die was cast before he was even aware of it—he would become a businessman.

Frankfurt, 1901. The Kahnweiler family could not have found a better place than this old financial center on the river Main to assure

Daniel-Heinrich an apprenticeship. His family connections procured a position for him in a large bank, where he was hopelessly bored. He would have been totally alienated from this environment if he had not made friends with another young man, also working in the Correspondence Department, who seemed to show as little enthusiasm as he did for exchange and interest rates. Hermann Rupf was Swiss, and four years older than Daniel-Heinrich. His family owned the important haberdashery firm of Hossman-Rupf in Bern, where they were known and respected.

The young men soon were on familiar terms, using the nicknames "Heini" for Kahnweiler and "Mani" for Rupf. Their colleagues at the bank agreed that the office they shared was unusual because it was the only one in the firm where the conversation was exclusively about music! Often at lunchtime a group formed around them and impassioned discussions took place: from department heads to clerks, they were all music lovers. Each person defended his favorite composer and his opinion of who was the best performer. Rupf had an advantage over them that Kahnweiler envied: he was not only a knowledgeable music lover, but he was a consummate musician. He played piano, violin, and flute.

The two young men shared a common interest in literature and art, and both were enthusiastic about hiking in the mountains, but it was music that formed the basis of their friendship. Often they would start arguing over a subject Saturday evenings outside the Frankfurt opera house and would continue the argument the next day while hiking through the wooded slopes of the Taunus, the Odenwald, or the Spessart mountains. Their friendship was a strong and enriching bond that lasted a lifetime.[14]

At seventeen the character of Daniel-Heinrich seemed fixed once and for all. The few people who knew him from his earliest days confirm that his good qualities remained unchanged, as did his faults.

A nineteenth-century man in style, conservative in dress and sober in speech, Kahnweiler developed the characteristics of the head of a large family: willfulness and imperiousness. He was extremely organized, sharp and hard when his professional dealings had to take precedence over friendship. A puritan, a bit old-fashioned, guarded against any form of flattery, his reactions were often the expression of an enormous ego. When he had thought through a problem and had come to a conclusion, he was convinced he was right, even if the whole world was against him. He was not stubborn or narrow-minded, it was just that his behavior had to make sense to himself. He was dogmatic in spirit, a flaw among his good qualities—but some people would call this being single-minded. He had no personal prejudices. When he was not listening to music he was reading. He was a cultivated man, with great breadth of learning and with a profound ability to see startling connections and relationships. His amazing capacity to gather information and form a synthesis, as well as his avid reading, can only be explained by his sense of deprivation at having to abandon his education too soon. It was as if he wanted to make up for lost time.

As a member of the bourgeoisie he spent money carefully without being ostentatious, always according to his principles. When he said that he was Protestant or Lutheran, he was not merely throwing out explanations. They represented his most basic values, including knowing the exact worth of things. Within his makeup there was a rigid Prussian; but he was both German and Jewish. In other words, a price was a price, but he knew how to adapt to different situations and how to negotiate when the need arose.

Calm by temperament, he was also capable of being angry and making scenes—for trivial reasons, according to those who knew him; according to him, it was a matter of principle. His lack of humor was the weak point of his intelligence. Humor was foreign to his nature. He enjoyed jokes and knew how to be funny, but he thought comedy was the height of intemperance and he did not have a sense of the absurd. Though his subtlety lay in his wit, he was neither funny nor a brilliant conversationalist in the social sense of the word. He liked smiling but disliked laughing; he was too disciplined to enjoy extremes. The difference between being familiar and being vulgar was tenuous according to him.[15] He even acknowledged that his dreams were very concrete. Usually the people in them spoke one of the three languages he had mastered. Sometimes they even spoke Italian or else, the height of absurdity, a language he did not understand.

All of this is not meant to create a schematic picture. Rather, it should describe a person motivated by a sense of duty, one who was slightly detached, quite appealing and attractive in spite of being very demanding in all things. On meeting the eighteen-year-old Daniel-Heinrich Kahnweiler in Frankfurt in 1902, who would have believed that he would be one of the first to have a sense of an impending revolution in modern art? Who would have believed that he would dedicate his life to defending and disseminating this revolution?

⬚

PARIS, LONDON, AND BACK

▭ He could hardly believe it—France at last! He had heard so much about it that he had already formed a mental picture. During the previous months his departure from Germany had become inevitable. Increasingly at odds with his father, Kahnweiler had jumped at the opportunity when his Neumann uncles in London had suggested sending "the intellectual" to Paris so that he might complete his training for a career as a financier. To accomplish this, they had sent a recommendation to their friend, Monsieur Tardieu, an important stockbroker in the capital.

As soon as he arrived he claimed his velocipede at the Gare de l'Est, feeling self-conscious about his German accent. He then hailed a cab which took him to the Hôtel Moderne. Once he had registered, he ran out into the streets, marveling at the nightlife all around him, then had a late dinner. He had come to Paris in search of Art and nothing else.[1] He finally felt carefree and his own man. Tardieu, who was to take him on as a trainee, had not deemed it necessary to offer any remuneration for the position, but Daniel-Heinrich's family agreed to pay for his lodgings and would forward the finances necessary for him to live free of material needs.

He already knew France through its language and literature; henceforth he would love it from within. From his first week at the office at 28 boulevard Haussmann, he quickly understood that his presence was not indispensable. He had to accomplish a minimal amount of work, show up in the morning, lunch with his colleagues at the office, attend the stock market at noon to greet his boss in the brokers' enclosure when the ritual bell rang the opening of the exchange, and reappear at three o'clock, before the bell closed the exchange in a tumultuous scene he soon gave up trying to understand.

His internship with Tardieu had at least one advantage, similar to the one at the bank in Frankfurt—among the employees there were interesting people. A glance, a handshake, and a few words exchanged were enough to establish a rapport and understanding with men as out of place as he was. Sometimes that was enough to form a strong friendship that would influence his life.

Kahnweiler was glad to meet up with his Swiss friend from Frankfurt. Hermann Rupf shared his lodgings, and they became inseparable. At Tardieu's he also met an older man who made a strong impression. Eugène Reignier worked in the treasurer's office; his interests lay in the theater, and in the great actor and manager Aurélian-Marie Lugné-Poë in particular. Reignier gave his young colleague an appreciation for Lugné-Poë, an artist who had sacrificed everything for the sake of his art. To say that Kahnweiler was under his influence is to put it mildly: he was overwhelmed by the man.

Imperceptibly, Eugène Reignier soon took the place of Joseph Goldscheider (Uncle Amico) for the young man and became his mentor. Receptive to all forms of art and always open to the new, he not only made him discover the theater but also a whole body of writing which took him far afield from his consecrated authors (Goethe and Zola) to a new intellectual realm, represented by André Gide and Paul Claudel. Reignier gave him a taste for overnight trips, showing how in just two days one could take a train to the remotest corners of France (or even elsewhere in Europe) and back. He was among those who do not hesitate to cross borders and great distances just to attend the performance of a play or a concert.

Devoted to Reignier, Kahnweiler took all his words, advice, and counsel to heart. And from him he would derive another more personal lesson: by observing Reignier day after day, he understood that this remarkable man had in fact missed out on life for not having dared to take a risk. He should have taken another path a long time ago, changed his course, quit the stock exchange, and, for example, joined his friend Lugné-Poë, if only as theater administrator. But he never dared.[2] In spite of his admiration for the man, Kahnweiler could never shake the terrible sense of failure he felt about him. It only strengthened his determination about the direction of his future life. The important thing was to live with his own values, in harmony with his own sense of himself.

He resolutely began by making a break with a milieu in which he felt alienated but which he had frequented since his arrival in Paris. The people associated with the Neumanns were rich, self-confident, and well-connected, interesting only because of the apparent ease with which they got the best of everything. Kahnweiler understood once and for all that their world was not his one night at the opera, when Baron Jacques de Gunzburg invited him to his box. On stage was *Romeo and Juliet*, but it was impossible to follow the performance, so noisy were the baron's friends. They never stopped talking, saying anything that came to mind about the music, imposing the trivial conventions of the drawing room, and going beyond the bounds of acceptable behavior by criticizing Wagner. That was the limit! He made up his mind never to see these people again.[3]

They could have said anything about literature or art, but they could not touch music: that was sacred. And to defend it, he was capable of losing his self-control and becoming unrecognizable, breaking the cool attitude that often made him seem haughty. Later, while attending a concert with two friends who criticized the military heaviness with which the German conductor interpreted Mozart's *A Little Night Music*, Kahnweiler suddenly turned on them and shouted, "Stupid asses."[4]

What was being performed in Paris in 1902? Much Beethoven, Franck, and Saint-Saëns, slightly less Schubert, Mozart, and Brahms, and then some Liszt and Schumann. The great new work was Richard Strauss's *Till Eulenspiegel* and his other symphonic poems, which aroused much heated controversy. The more Strauss was booed, the more Kahnweiler applauded, sometimes to the point of frenzy. At the Colonne concerts, he did not hesitate to voice his opinion that Colonne was an overrated conductor. At the Lamoureux concerts he praised the talents of Camille Chevillard, Lamoureux's son-in-law, whom he believed was a great conductor. True, Colonne's name was linked in the public's mind with the works of Georges Bizet and Hector Berlioz; that of Lamoureux with the Wagnerian repertory.

Kahnweiler found opera disappointing to say the least. He hardly went, believing that he had seen what he called the bad side of the nineteenth century: Halévy, Meyerbeer, Auber, and others. By contrast, he found the comic opera a hundred times better, especially the performances of Gluck, whom he deemed above all praise.

Then he saw *Pelléas et Mélisande*, and developed a passion for Claude Debussy's musical drama. He regretted not being in Paris in February in time to attend the premiere and take sides in the uproar of the crowd, the skepticism of the critics, and the enthusiasm of the young. He had missed this "historic" event by eight months, and to make up for lost time after his arrival in Paris, he attended seventeen performances of *Pelléas*.[5] For this puritanical young man who never set foot in a cabaret or a music hall and who held a sad prejudice against them, the works of Debussy stood for all that the capital had to offer in terms of beauty, pleasure, and celebration.

Pelléas was based on the dramatic poem by Maurice Maeterlinck, which helps to explain his enthusiasm. Kahnweiler enjoyed combining the things he liked, as long as they were intellectual. With Eugène Reignier, he attended the theater to applaud the performances by Réjane, Sarah Bernhardt, Jean Mounet-Sully, or Lucien Guitry. They went to dress rehearsals and to any rehearsal where Lugné-Poë was involved. To Kahnweiler, Lugné-Poë stood for everything worthwhile in the theater of his day—*The Lost Sheep* by Francis Jammes, the symbolist theater, *The Lady with the Scythe* by Saint-Pol Roux, and the early works of Henry Bataille, not to mention Alfred Jarry's *Ubu Roi*, which had caused such a scandal upon its premiere.

It was probably due to this same influence that Kahnweiler's taste in poetry ran toward the ecstatic paganism of Emile Verhaeren or the Christian humility of Francis Jammes. He was indifferent to the impact of philosopher Henri Bergson, then lecturing at the Collège de France, whom he believed to be antithetical to post-Kantism. He preferred immersing himself in the novels of Anatole France and Maurice Barrès, whom he found quintessentially "French," or else in volumes of poetry by Arthur Rimbaud, Paul Verlaine, and Stephane Mallarmé. This did not dampen his taste for popular literature, such as the novels of Charles-Louis Philippe, whom he praised to the heavens, and he considered the publication of his *Bubu of Montparnasse*[6] an event of worldwide importance.

The pleasure he derived from Paris was that the city gave him the means to be eclectic. There was such a wealth of artistry around him. He could try everything. Paris was made for a young European intellectual, who could not decide whether his direction lay in music, literature, or the theater. Kahnweiler was dazzled by the intensity of this cultural activity as he became acquainted with it through Reignier.

Politics interested him at first, but that would not be the case for long. Newspaper stories on local elections, debates in the Chamber of Deputies about private distillers of wine or cider, and even the formation of the Socialist Party held his attention. The Gallic nature of many events escaped him, but he was convinced that, given time, he would grasp the essential issues.

Being both German and Jewish, the startling discovery that young Kahnweiler would make was the pervasiveness of anti-Semitism in French society. Naturally he had heard of the Dreyfus affair when he was in Germany. But since the trial of Captain Alfred Dreyfus in 1899 at Rennes, he had believed that the problem had been resolved. The innocence of "Captain three-feet" (*drei fuss*), as he was called in the anti-Semitic pamphlets, had appeared obvious. Kahnweiler's failure to understand the persistence of the military is the most evident expression of his naiveté in the face of this society. If he had admired Emile Zola for his writing, Zola became even more of a hero as the author of "J'accuse," with his steadfast courage in fighting for the cause of the exiled man. To commemorate the first anniversary of the writer's death, Kahnweiler and his friend Rupf, carrying dried red flowers, joined the impressive crowd of people going to the Montmartre cemetery, a tribute more political than literary.

This marks the time Daniel-Heinrich Kahnweiler would become, not a militant (which was not in his nature), but a man of the left in the ethical sense of the word. His attitude represented neither a political nor an electoral stance but an adherence to principle. He supported the basic tenets of the Republic and the rights of man,[7] and these beliefs would occasionally lead him to behave in a belligerent manner. If anyone spoke to him about the "belle epoque," a recurrent cliché, he would reply that it was only so for the bourgeoisie. People of means enjoyed what passed officially for liberty, but he thought the only true liberty was the one defended by anarchists.[8] He would attend the meetings of socialist leader Jean Jaurès and draw his own conclusions.

It must be stressed that Kahnweiler had the spirit of contradiction. He did not intend to show off; he simply sought the stimulus of breaking with a consensus of opinion to allow other truths to pierce through. At the Tardieu office, he answered derisively when his young colleagues demanded that he (as a German citizen) return Alsace and Lorraine or five million francs in compensation. At the height of the Russo-Japanese War, when everyone sided with the Russians because of the loans made by France to that country, he began to defend the enemy. In the offices at boulevard Haussmann he was known as "the little Japanese."[9] Aside from his hatred of tsarism, he may have been drawn to the Empire of the Sun by its spirit of conquest. It is difficult to imagine that someone connected with the stock market would defend the Japanese invasion of Sakhalin

Island and the Liao Tung peninsula, which would prevent the repayment of the Russian loans. It was not a case of dying for Port Arthur; Kahnweiler had moments when he enjoyed playing Zarathustra. His involvement with political issues and causes inconsequential, if not alien, to him was merely practice for the struggle that would soon challenge him, the ideas for which he would sacrifice everything.

In the square in front of the stock exchange, the ringing of the noon bell released the energies of hundreds of people, who would start shouting and waving their arms in all directions. Kahnweiler would show up in the reserved section across from Monsieur Tardieu, in whose office he was now officially a clerk. He understood after several weeks that no one would ever need him from twelve until three in the afternoon. This meant that every day of the work week he had three hours free, and without hesitation he went to the Louvre, a short walk from the stock exchange. He could not imagine a better opportunity to extend the pleasure he had experienced when he discovered the paintings in the museum at Karlsruhe. Just the idea of being able to actually see paintings he had known only through books was exciting to him. Thus during his first few months in Paris, Daniel-Henry (in France, he did not insist on Heinrich but was still called "Heini") went almost every day to the Louvre with his friend Rupf. Whereas these repeated visits encouraged a collector's instinct in the young Swiss, in the young German this immersion in the history of art, this frontal assault by the best paintings, created great intellectual excitement.

Kahnweiler was fascinated by Rembrandt's *Self Portrait* and overwhelmed by his *Bathsheba*, which would be for the longest time "one of the most beautiful paintings in the world" to him; but his curiosity eventually encompassed the whole museum. He wanted to see everything, to stand for hours discussing such and such a work, and to consult other works for more than just information. When he could not understand what the artist was trying to do with a painting, such as Rembrandt's self-portrait, Kahnweiler would return to the museum to spend hours in front of it. That was the best part of his day.[10]

One day, the Louvre was no longer enough for him. He wanted to know more about contemporary painting and was advised to go to the Luxembourg Museum. The first time he did not walk down rue de Richelieu on the ringing of the noon bell he was disappointed. The Luxembourg Museum seemed to be a repository for the stale glories of official works of art: academic painting at its most inexpressive. Yet, whether upon the advice of Rupf or Reignier, he then managed to find his way to the Caillebotte Collection in the Luxembourg, which had opened to the public in 1897.

In his will, the painter Gustave Caillebotte had left his personal collection of impressionist art to the nation on the condition that it be placed on exhibit as a whole in the Luxembourg Museum. But the paintings caused a scandal. People hated them, calling them "garbage," "aborted efforts," "moral flaccitude," claiming that "these people paint by relieving themselves." These insults were also seen in print. After long negotiations between August Renoir, the appointed executor of the will, and museum officials, and abiding by the regulation limiting the number of works by each painter, the opposing parties reached a compromise about making a selection of the works. Of the sixty-five impressionist paintings left by Caillebotte, the nation accepted only thirty-eight, releasing the others and ceding the rights to the painter's heirs. But for the impressionists it was a victory of sorts. [11]

On his first visit to the Caillebotte Collection Kahnweiler was disconcerted. Certainly he saw the difference between these paintings and the other works on the walls of the Luxembourg, but he did not understand what he saw. To him it was all spots of color without meaning. He did not want to judge hastily; he promised to return. These paintings made him feel humble. He never stopped saying that this reaction taught him a lesson on how to conduct himself. After several visits when he walked straight to this room, ignoring the deplorable surroundings, he gradually grew used to these colors and acquired a taste for looking at them even without being able to understand them. For him it would never be a question of seeing a painting as an end in itself; a painting would always be the stimulus to an intellectual inquiry. [12]

Little by little he grew to discover in these paintings "an admirable world where air and light are in perpetual motion." [13] It was a painter's world of clouds and shadows, form and color, diametrically opposed to the academic paintings all around. This vivid new way of painting did not come as a shock, but as a progressive discovery to him.

It was neither their notoriety nor the volatile responses to their work that drew him to these painters. Despite the strong prejudice against it in higher circles, this art was no longer considered disreputable. Proof of this was the rumor Kahnweiler heard in the office that a painting by Claude Monet had sold for a hundred thousand francs in gold.

Kahnweiler grew to realize that the label "impressionists" was barely adequate to describe the spirit of these painters. What did they seek to accomplish, if not to fix their impression of what they saw? It was an extroverted form of art, it seemed to him, the culmination of several centuries of art turned toward outward appearances. Its practitioners attempted to capture what photography was incapable of reconstructing—light in all its finest shadings, the atmosphere surrounding objects, the very air at its purest and most ineffable.

There were paintings by Edgar Degas, Alfred Sisley, Monet, Camille Pissarro, Renoir, Paul Cézanne, and many others. The paintings by Edouard Manet were a revelation to him, as he seemed to be the first painter to use colors, and even white, for their own sake. Georges Seurat also impressed him profoundly, but for other reasons; as he stood in front of Seurat's paintings he had that rare feeling of being in the presence of something important: a turning point in the history of art. But finally it was Cézanne who impressed him the most. Here was a painter with a completely new palette of colors, who did not hesitate to break every rule of classical painting: perspective, proportion, accuracy of drawing, exact rendering . . . Of course this new school of painting had not freed itself from representation, but it was going in that direction. Cézanne sometimes worked like an architect's draftsman, an approach Kahnweiler could appreciate.

Unlike some of his friends, who liked the landscapes and still lifes of the "Master of Aix" but could not stand his figures without faces, Kahnweiler found the figures rather natural. He refused to be disturbed by the painter's distortions. At first he had seen the paintings pretty much as everyone else did, but not any longer. More than once he refused to accept his friends' description of Cézanne's paintings as a crooked table, a plate, three apples—in other words, subjects easily identified and therefore readily imitated. For him the subject of the painting was anything but that; such a description was too facile, too obvious. What interested him was the means by which the painter achieved his end. Very quickly he placed Cézanne apart from other impressionists. What he grew to understand was that, in order to express his perception, the artist constructed a surface plane in a way that created a solid reality rather than fugitive impressions of light. This understanding seemed all the more meaningful because Kahnweiler immediately placed it, as was his habit, in the cultural context of this period of experimentation in art, literature, and music.

Much later, when discussing the past, Kahnweiler would always insist that his reactions owed nothing to historical reinterpretation, that his intellectual discipline would not permit him to attribute to himself theories later formed out of his experiences of a half-century. He must be given credit for the first of his brilliant intuitions. In 1903, while standing in the Caillebotte Collection before the Cézannes, he was convinced that these paintings—which inspired many transformations to come—marked the culmination of a historical period, rather than the beginning of a new one.

After the museums, Kahnweiler explored the public Salons, always after the noontime bell. It was the second stage of his venture into contemporary art. He did not visit them to gauge the public's reactions; for him the public was of no importance and had nothing to say. Public favor given too suddenly, too soon, before the critics and historians had had their say, was a negative influence. To say that Kahnweiler always considered painting an elite art is to put it mildly. Nor was it to familiarize himself with the judges that he attended these Salons, he who took a malicious pleasure in the one-upmanship of this sort of group. Salons, for him, were the laboratories of the modern, beyond the sphere of influence of the Ecole des Beaux-Arts. The exhibitions seemed to reflect the artists' experiments and concerns more than their accomplishments and old certitudes.[14] This was the case in some Salons, and it was necessary to differentiate among them.

The Salon des Artistes Français was the one Kahnweiler liked the least, calling it "the Salon of those without taste," and he considered it only a social event. Collectors paid high prices for canvases by painters of questionable talent, painters swept aside by the surge of history: Paul Chabas, who painted aquatic nymphettes, delicious young women standing, quivering, in clear cold water at dusk; or Franck and Joseph Bail, who specialized in still lifes in the Dutch eighteenth-century manner and who painted copper pots whose shine people praised.[15]

The Salon of the National Society of Beaux-Arts was hardly worth more. There was also the Salon d'Automne, the last one to come along, which had been inaugurated in October 1903 and installed in the basement of the Petit Palais. The opening party was so Parisian, so worldly, that the artists were hardly noticed and the dealers even less so. The president of the Salon was the well-connected architect Frantz Jourdain, and Kahnweiler wondered if the art exhibit was not just a pretext for a big social event. This was a misleading first impression, however, as the organizers of the Salon d'Automne were strict and coherent in their choices and did not give a second thought about upsetting or even shocking the public.

The Salon des Indépendants, which Kahnweiler liked the best, justified the existence of the other Salons the way the Caillebotte Collection justified the Luxembourg Museum. Fernand Léger once described it as a Salon of painting for painters, open to experimentation and secure enough to stand up to people who came to mock the works, pointing at them and guffawing as if they were at the circus. Léger compared the exhibiting of a new painter in this sanctuary of painting to a drama, saying that if the bourgeoisie had any artistic awareness, they would have been tiptoeing around with respect, as if in church.[16] The Salon des Indépendants was a hothouse of modern art and the one place where different and sometimes diametrically opposed feelings for painting could meet. Kahnweiler liked the organization's rule of having neither judges nor awards. It was for the real outcasts, and the rule was simple: all paintings were admitted without any censorship, for a fee of twenty-five francs. A complaint or a denunciation at a police station had to be made to oust a canvas on the grounds of its being obscene, which happened very rarely, as a true fraternal feeling united this gathering of artists.[17]

Kahnweiler enjoyed this exhibit, which was housed in shabby storehouses in the Cours la Reine of the Jardin des Tuileries. Where once, under the ancien régime, the court used to stroll, now there were painters rejected by the major Salons. The spirit of the place with its temporary set of walls was the extreme opposite of the sumptuous surroundings of the Petit Palais and the Grand Palais. The absence of any criteria placed the worst next to the best. But Kahnweiler did not mind having to make his own choices. For him the most faithful picture ever made of the Indépendants would always be the painting by Henri Rousseau, *Liberty inviting artists to take part in the twenty-second exhibition of independent artists.* In this painting canvases are piled high in carts or carried rolled under the arm like newspapers and painters with broad-brimmed felt hats are lined up feverishly at the gate. There was the generosity of the experienced and well-known exhibitors inviting young beginners to hang their canvases next to theirs without regard to the crowds of attackers or supporters.[18]

Kahnweiler had been training himself to judge art by visiting museums, galleries, and Salons. His taste became more sure: he was overwhelmed by Vincent van Gogh, who put his whole life and his own range of colors into his canvases. Seurat intrigued him in spite of the fact that his experimentation with pointillism was a promising undertaking only for the realistic subject of his paintings. Paul Gauguin, who had recently died in the Marquesas Islands, held his interest for a while before becoming once and for all his *bête noire*. Kahnweiler understood his contribution but reproached him for having turned away from the problems of construction, as Cézanne saw them, for the sake of the picturesque, the exotic, the decorative, and the ornamental. For him Gauguin would remain the great failure, a misleading influence to be avoided.[19]

These Salons played an important role in creating a new audience. If Kahnweiler learned how to judge art, Rupf laid the groundwork for his future collection. A slightly younger visitor, André Level, experienced a true revelation: art was authentic because it moved him. The shock gave him a brilliant idea: why not create a group of friends to acquire some of these paintings? It was not an idle notion, because in February 1904 he would sign the charter of an organization called "La Peau de L'Ours" (The Bear Skin). Eleven subscribers each paid 250 francs per year, it being agreed that each could not own more than two shares. Level, as the presiding head, selected and purchased the paintings (by Gauguin, van Gogh, Pierre Bonnard, Edouard Vuillard, and others). Each member in turn could enjoy the paintings under the stated terms. But in ten years the whole collection would be placed on the auction block. These young collectors, without any means, were thus able to help artists and enjoy works that seemed undervalued to them.[20]

Kahnweiler visited museums and Salons, but he did not dare to cross the thresholds of famous galleries. In front of one of these, the Durand-Ruel Gallery, he would witness an unforgettable scene: on exhibit were Monet's thirty-seven paintings of the Thames, which he had brought over from London. In front of the window two coachmen, round faces filled with hatred and ready to explode with rage, were screaming, "Any place that shows such rubbish should have its window bashed in!"[21] Their violent reaction made him think, and he learned a lesson for the future— for a painting to be original, first of all it must shock.

Durand-Ruel was the only gallery into which he would venture, if only for a few minutes. It was very crowded, but what prevented him from going inside more freely was his belief that you had to be initiated to enter; he was convinced that one entered only to buy a painting, not to look—it was the opposite of a museum or a Salon.

Kahnweiler frequented the Salons and writers' cafés, even though he did not welcome controversy or people's familiarity. With Eugène Reignier he went to actors' hangouts; with Rupf to artists' cafés, as if they were natural continuations of the Salon des Indépendants. In one of them, he would form a friendship that would mark his life.

The Café du Dôme is on the corner of boulevards Raspail and Montparnasse, and the German community congregated there. They called themselves *domiers,* and the café was "the Cathedral" (*die Dom*).[22] The person who figured as the archbishop of this cathedral was Wilhelm Uhde, a young mentor, a father figure only ten years older than Kahnweiler. He had completed law school in Munich before studying art history in Florence and then settling down in Paris. He was in open rebellion against his Prussian middle-class family. On occasion he would sell a painting, and on Sundays at home he welcomed painters and collectors and introduced them to dealers. His portrait by Robert Delaunay (1907) shows a sedate person, with a bright attentive glance and a serene expression, wearing the sort of mustache that would become unforgettable thirty years later when worn by a bloodthirsty German corporal.

Kahnweiler admired and respected his fellow countryman, and he could identify with Uhde, who was the epitome of the enlightened collector. With Rupf and Reignier, he would form the inner circle of Kahnweiler's life, and when together, they spoke in German. There were certain things that could only be expressed in German. In poetry, for example, he believed that one could only express oneself in one's native language.[23]

In 1904, Daniel-Henry Kahnweiler was twenty years old and wanted to get married. For some time he had been living with a woman two years older than he, Léontine Alexandrine Godon, known as Lucie. She hailed from Sancerre, in the province of Berri. Julius Kahnweiler was scandalized by the relationship and refused to meet her until she and his son were legally married. This puritan indignation masked his disappointment that Daniel-Heinrich, whom he thought had been introduced to Parisian Jewish high society, had not married a Rothschild.

Kahnweiler followed his own inclination. He and Lucie began a journey, a "honeymoon" that shortly preceded their actual marriage (on November 5).

They were not concerned at the office when he announced that he was going on a trip. After all, he was not a salaried employee. The people at Tardieu's office had decided that Kahnweiler would never become a stockbroker, nor even a banker. He was not of the same material as the Neumanns. But his uncles in England also suspected something and summoned him to the London office on the pretext of improving his English, hoping in vain to set him back on the right path.

Kahnweiler and his wife arrived in London at the end of 1905, a time of political upheaval. The Liberals, with help from the Labour Party, had won the elections and would press for social reforms while King Edward VII was especially engrossed in foreign policy. But neither the issues of pensions for the elderly nor the subtleties of the Entente Cordial held any interest for the young man. He had hardly settled before he wanted to leave. He missed Paris. He felt isolated, especially since Rupf, who had joined them, finally had to return to Bern to take up the family business and devote his energies to haberdashery and notions.

For Kahnweiler, the National Gallery, the Wallace Collection, and the Victoria and Albert Museum were rich and instructive, and he spent most of his free time there. But he felt that the atmosphere of the whole country was like the office, constrained and narrow, while Paris, with its cafés and literary salons, was pure liberty—the only place in Europe where he felt completely at home. He had been convinced of this after his brief stay in Madrid, "a town which had been asleep for fifty years."[24] Naturally, when he visited the Prado, he felt El Greco did not occupy his rightful place.

In Paris the things that mattered to him were not the issues in the headlines, such as the new law separating church and state—which hardly concerned him, as his artistic milieu was naturally anti-clerical.[25] Instead, what mattered to him was the scandal that swept the opening of the Salon d'Automne when the critic Louis Vauxcelles, trying to be ironic, called it "la cage aux fauves [the cage of wild beasts],"[26] because of such painters as Henri Matisse, Albert Marquet, Georges Rouault, André Derain, and Maurice de Vlaminck, unknowingly baptizing a movement in art that he wanted to mock. And what moved Kahnweiler profoundly was the news of Cézanne's death.

People in London were still speaking about the opening of the Whitechapel Gallery four years earlier, which had the intention of bringing modern art to the working-class environment, but Kahnweiler did not hesitate to leave for Paris on weekends to attend the Salon des Indépendants, which to him revealed the greatest freedom among his contemporaries.

His uncle Sigmund Neumann, with whom he worked, could hardly have failed to notice this, but he never mentioned it, understanding the nature of the young man's imaginative life. For his part, Kahnweiler understood that, contrary to what they imagined in Stuttgart, Uncle Neumann did not head an important firm. He had only about twenty employees, being more of an administrator than an entrepreneur, but was impressively wealthy nonetheless.[27] Kahnweiler would not dream of following in his footsteps. Money and wealth were not important to him. At twenty he had no firsthand experience of deprivation of any kind, so that he was free of material need. Deprivation for him was having a cup of coffee instead of lunch to gain a few minutes to spend at the British Museum.

Then one day he decided that the charade must come to an end. These frantic stockbrokers, these tense speculators, these people obsessed by the Dow-Jones had nothing in common with him. He was too timid to set foot in a gallery but now he was brave enough to consider opening one of his own.

He decided his vocation would be that of art dealer. There followed long distance conferences between London and Stuttgart. The news hit like a bomb.[28] His father was furious, his uncles skeptical—paintings! What an idea! They wanted a private conference. Kahnweiler also wanted a chance to explain himself to them. Ironically what inspired him to take this radical step was the negative example of Eugène Reignier.

At the family meeting his Neumann uncles sat on the left facing their nephew, who stated, "I don't like your business, I know little about it, it doesn't interest me, and I'll never amount to anything there."

"We have also been turning over the question," replied the elder of the two uncles. "Now is the time to decide. We need a responsible man to take charge of our office in South Africa. A position is waiting for you in Johannesburg."

There was a silence as he thought, They propose Johannesburg when I'm burning to return to Paris. There was a complete breakdown in communication. He had to do something. "You don't understand. I want to become an art dealer in Paris."

"But you don't know anything about it."

"That's true, but I've seen a lot of paintings, and I would like to make a place for myself by representing the painters whose work I like."

"What is it that you want to sell?" his uncles asked him.[29]

It was difficult to explain a world so alien to them. They did not quite understand and they did not really approve. But he was a member of the family, and they were liberal in temperament. They believed that he would learn more by example than by being forced against his will. They knew people in London from every social level, even in the art world. Their own dealer, who sold them the Gainsboroughs, Reynolds, and Lawrences hanging in their homes (which they treated with disdain, as if they were fashion illustrations) was a reputable person by the name of Wertheimer. He was a man of common sense who knew his business, the ideal man to test the reality of Daniel Kahnweiler's vocation.

Kahnweiler's immediate understanding that he was undergoing a test was unbearable to him. Mr. Wertheimer was exactly the sort of dealer he loathed, and he did not want to be like him. He provided his clients with what they wanted, content to flatter their taste, which was the most accepted way of doing business. It was doubtful that he even had ideas about painting, and he was certainly not someone to make a discovery. Kahnweiler's ambition was to become a dealer who would introduce the public to admirable works by unknown artists in need of his support to develop their careers.

Thus, at the appointed time of the confrontation, Wertheimer, who was to ask the questions, seemed as embarrassed as the candidate in this comedy the Neumann brothers were putting them through. The dealer asked the young man, "At the National Gallery, which artists do you like?"

The young man considered how to answer—should he be defiant or conciliatory? In the latter case he needed only to mention the portrait painters of the eighteenth century, and the limit would be Rubens or Velázquez.

He chose to be provocative and answered, "The artist I like is El Greco."

The older man seemed startled.

"And Vermeer van Delft also."

In truth his favorite was Velázquez, but he preferred to go against the dealer's taste, and both El Greco and Vermeer were considered of doubtful reputation.

"Of course, of course," murmured Wertheimer. He should have known—the taste of the young. He continued by asking, "But, ultimately, you want to open a gallery. What are you going to sell? Rather, whose works would you buy?"

Again it was a question of strategy. If he mentioned the impressionists, the dealer was going to rub his eyes and yawn. In London hardly anyone knew who they were. If he mentioned Matisse and Derain, he was sure the answer would be a withering "I don't know them," which would put a chilly end to the test. Kahnweiler decided not to confront the dealer with his ignorance of contemporary art and by way of answer cited known artists.

"I would buy canvases by Vuillard and Bonnard."

"Never heard of them. I don't know their work," the old man answered imperturbably. [30]

Kahnweiler failed the test, but fortunately the old man was kindly by nature and did not hold against him what another would have considered insolent behavior. His final report must have been positive, or at least that was Kahnweiler's conclusion from the conference with his uncles that followed the interview.

"This is what we have decided," they told him. "You will go back to Paris to open a gallery since that is what you want to do. We will give you a thousand pounds, the equivalent of twenty-five thousand francs in gold, and one year's time. If after a year this gallery takes hold, it can make it on its own, and you can support yourself and your wife, you can continue with it. If not you will return to join our company."[31]

If he failed in Paris, he would go to Johannesburg, so far distant from everything he valued, ancient Europe and painting. He was condemned to succeed. Everything was relative; there had been more agonizing challenges than this. But this one was the challenge offered by his background.

At last he would be an art dealer in Paris! He wrote to notify Reignier, to ask for advice and to receive his blessing. The cautious friend began by asking questions of his friends—an architect, an art critic—and at first did everything in his power to discourage Kahnweiler. "You need a fortune to venture into that. You need connections. Not everyone can sell paintings by the great masters, which have a set market value, and the discovery of new talent is a matter of chance, a slow, risky enterprise. Established dealers will give stiff competition. It's not a business for a Kahnweiler."[32]

When he realized that his arguments made no impression, he wrote him a second time to define the ways Kahnweiler was different from others in this business.

"You have taste and intellect and your intelligence will never allow you to be mean. You have an aversion to being aggressive with people, you loathe publicity and false pretenses. You will wait until they come to you and for them to understand."[33]

He was right about the character of the man, but he overlooked the determination. If Kahnweiler had not been in England and they could have spoken in person, Reignier would have been convinced. He would have seen that the failings were nothing in the face of such determination. After a few more letters, he claimed to be convinced by Kahnweiler. But again he presented a dark picture of the future: twenty-five thousand francs was not enough. The family wanted quick results, and Paris dealers were all sharks, they would not allow him to . . . Too late, the decision had been made. It was the moment for final advice before his great leap into the unknown.

"No more bohemianism, no more ridiculous hairstyle, looking wild

. . . now everything has to be correct. I mean it. All that was fine when you wanted to get away from people, but now you have to seek them out, even those you formerly disdained. No, it will not be a path strewn with roses."[34]

In February 1907 Daniel-Henry Kahnweiler decided to return to France. On the ferry crossing the Channel he knew that his decision was irrevocable.

THE KAHNWEILER GALLERY

On the boat back to France he reread a message that had been delivered to him before boarding: "Courage. . . . Your real life, with its hard times, is about to begin."[1]

The prospect did not frighten him; on the contrary, he looked forward to finally being able to fight on his own ground with his own weapons.

His first task was to find an apartment, which was difficult during this period of social unrest. The government of Georges Clemenceau was facing a strike by the electrical workers of Paris and had to negotiate with union officials. The Kahnweilers finally found suitable accommodations at 28 rue (soon dubbed avenue) Théophile-Gautier in the Auteuil section of the sixteenth arrondissement. It was on the fifth floor and not very spacious, but from the windows there was an unobstructed view of the entire Left Bank. His next step was to find a "shop" where he could open his gallery.

It had to be located on the Right Bank, which was essential to its standing. The critic Vauxcelles, who knew the art world, often said that when a dealer moved from the Left to the Right Bank, it was a sure sign that he was prospering. This geographical designation had to be taken into consideration in a business where reputation precedes monetary value. Rue Laffitte was traditionally a street of galleries. People would say, "I'm going to rue Laffitte" when they meant that they were making a tour of the galleries. In the same way, they would say "going to the Hôtel," meaning they were attending the auctions at the Hôtel Drouot. This was the vocabulary of those in the know, who seemed to have a propensity for these shorthand references. In art as in other businesses, people wanted to know in two words if they were dealing with an initiate or not.

Kahnweiler immediately realized that rue Laffitte and rue Le Peletier were already too old-fashioned and associated with the styles and tastes of the nineteenth century. On the other hand, Bernheim-Jeune and Druet opened galleries not far from the Madeleine, and in the future this neighborhood of luxurious shops and call-girl hotels around a very solid-looking church would become the "Center."

On rue Vignon Kahnweiler found a minuscule storefront, twelve feet square, occupied by a Polish tailor with financial problems who now made one good deal by subletting his shop for six hundred francs more per year than he paid.[2] This was a detail Kahnweiler only learned afterward. Instead of planning a complete renovation he called in a decorator to transform the interior into a gallery: carpeting the floor, putting burlap on the walls, repainting the ceiling. Dispelling the feeling of a tailor's workshop was the least of his problems. He wanted to modernize, but he could not as yet install a telephone. However, he replaced the gaslights with more powerful auer ones. He hired a rather simple young man as an assistant, whose duty was to open the gallery in the morning. Thus everything was ready for business. But there was no inaugural celebration, no hors d'oeuvres, no publicity or art critics. The opening was in the Kahnweiler spirit: anyone could come in to look, whether they wanted to buy or not.

Florent Fels, the future art critic, lived with his grandmother on rue Vignon, which he recalled as a secluded section of Paris with well-established tradespeople. Despite the proximity of main thoroughfares it remained an island of relative peace and quiet. In 1900 only the clip-clop of coach horses could be heard at night until the milk carts came around at dawn.[3]

When the gallery was ready to open, Kahnweiler had to find an appropriate name; naturally, he chose to call it the Kahnweiler Gallery. This personalization of the place of business, this complete identification between the dealer and his gallery was becoming the rule at that time.

Everything was set for the start of a drama with four characters in search of their full potential: the artist, the art dealer, the critic, and the collector. While waiting, the walls were fairly dull, with a few engravings and lithographs purchased from Le Véel, a small-time dealer on rue La

Fayette. Exactly a month after Kahnweiler's return to Paris, he took advantage of the opening of the Salon des Indépendants to make some purchases. He was interested in the works of Renoir, Cézanne, Monet, and Johan Jongkind, and especially Bonnard and Vuillard, whom he thought were unfortunately overshadowed by very great predecessors and flamboyant successors. It was at the Indépendants that he became a true art dealer, not a collector or a dilettante. In his mind there was a general idea of his profession, and he was outspoken about it. It was not a question of running a business like any other business. It was not that he felt superior to his fellow art dealers, but rather that his ultimate goals were different from those of the majority of his colleagues.

His philosophy came from his background, his culture, his sensibilities, his intuition, and his values. The paintings in themselves became a means to an end. His highest priorities would be his refusal to compromise and his fidelity to individuals and ideas. His gallery would not become a warehouse. He wanted to make new discoveries. The artists of the nabis school, those "prophets" who gathered around Maurice Denis, Vuillard, and Paul Sérusier, were too old and too well-known. Kahnweiler wanted to find the young artists of his own generation, whose careers had not as yet gotten under way and who needed help. Not only did he have to seek them out, but also he had to make a choice, evaluate and select among them. The discoverer is always the one who knows how to refuse; this was his inner conviction.[4]

He wanted to make a break with the traditional image of the art dealer, which became evident on stepping inside his premises at rue Vignon. There was no overwhelming sense of luxury, nor the oppressive atmosphere of a private museum that gave a false sense of confidence. Kahnweiler would never initiate a sale. The visitor had to take the first step if he wanted to engage in a dialogue with the dealer. Unlike the person who entered the gallery, Kahnweiler wanted to be neither an art patron, nor a speculator, nor even a collector. Paintings were created to circulate without being artificially promoted. He was not one to praise paintings or formulate opinions, organize parties, or bargain over prices as in a flea market. His intention was to transform a commercial success into a moral triumph.[5]

For him, a dealer was above all an explorer, and he knew that he was working for posterity, an obsession that would enable him to keep his success in perspective and absorb the shock of his failures. This role of intermediary was adopted after considering how some of the greatest nineteenth-century painters were marginal figures because of the policies of the state, the official Salons, and the academies. What would have become of their art had they been represented by a dealer such as he imagined himself to be? By his own definition, his function as a dealer was to serve art rather than to guard it. He would never be the sort of dealer Eugène Delacroix described in his *Journal*. He wanted to become a Durand-Ruel or a Vollard; that is, a precursor, someone who bought what he liked and then imposed his taste on the public: "And the public followed them because these men were right."[6] He believed that a great art dealer should not be satisfied with merely going against contemporary taste in painting but that he should also follow his instincts when it came to old masters, such as buying El Grecos in 1900.[7]

This art dealer, convinced of success at the age of twenty-three, went to the Salon des Indépendants with a firm resolution to buy. He knew nothing about the business of selling art, knowing more about art itself than about the art market. But at the exhibition he strolled along, loving or hating what he saw without self-consciousness, and while he remained humble before the paintings, he was inspired to learn more. Often he would say, "People are always saying, 'Excuse me, but I'm not a musician,' while no one ever says, 'I'm sorry, but I'm not a painter.' "[8]

He had no frame of reference and tried to stay innocent in his reactions, trusting only his own judgment, his own taste with regard to his sense of beauty. He could have adopted the words of Henri-Pierre Roché, the writer and collector: "The beautiful contains the unknowable. The instrument of measure is a clinical thermometer. Where should it be placed?"[9]

What most appealed to Kahnweiler in this 1907 selection of works at the Indépendants were the fauvist painters. "Wild animals indeed," he said. Two painters made an especially powerful impression on him— Derain and Vlaminck. He was indifferent to decorative elements and immune to the dreadful influence of Gauguin. What distinguished these artists from others, and from the impressionists especially, was their use of color to express light—vibrant and soft with Derain, thick and violent and explosive with Vlaminck, like dynamite going off in the midst of fireworks. It was rumored that Vlaminck applied the paint directly from the tube without using a palette, and Kahnweiler hoped it was true.

He made a selection and asked the officials of the Salon for the price: "One hundred francs." He paid the hundred francs, ignoring the fact that he was expected to negotiate according to the unwritten code. This was even more true of dealers since they usually were given a discount. He only learned of these things later.[10] When he understood how naive he had been, he felt that he was like Parsifal, ignorant of evil.[11]

Kahnweiler's first purchases in paintings were not handed over to him, because in those days the artist himself delivered them. After a brief correspondence he saw them arrive one after the other at his home on rue Théophile-Gautier. It was his first encounter with artists, but these two certainly did not conform with his notion of what an artist looked like. They were neither completely bohemian, nor really the thugs for whom they might be mistaken. They were strong but not violent, and most sincere in their enthusiasm. Both men, who shared a studio in Chatou, already had solid reputations among other artists. Their pugnacious natures increased the farther away they were from the Fournaise restaurant in Chatou and the nearer they were to the terrace of the Café du Dôme in Montparnasse. These great sportsmen often left destruction in their wake. For Derain everything could always be smoothed over, since he was the son of a municipal official, a more-than-prosperous businessman. But this was not the case for Vlaminck, bicyclist and cabaret musician, belligerent and always ready for a fight, especially in an argument over painting. They were a strange but likable pair. Derain's favorite expression was "amazing," which for variation and to break his habit he sometimes changed to "amazingly." His first contact by mail with the dealer was, as he put it, "mercantile." For the *Jetée de l'Estaque* (Jetty at l'Estaque), he wanted 150 francs and not 100 francs. Kahnweiler told him that he had been misinformed and generously agreed to the sum, at the same time proposing to buy some watercolors that he had seen. He showed the two artists his gallery.

Henceforth the way to rue Vignon became familiar to them, and they dropped by often without notice, just to visit and chat with their new friend. Their works were hung next to those by Pierre Girieud and Boutet de Monvel.[12] "Hung" is hardly the word, since they were barely framed— poised on the wall would be more appropriate—according to the frugal taste of Kahnweiler, which was diametrically opposite theirs. They were as struck by his reserve and timidity as he was by their style, which had nothing in common with the elegant ascots, straight pants, and felt hats of academic painters. They were in tweeds, with caps and thick-soled workmen's shoes.[13]

A few days later a man entered the gallery wearing an even more unlikely outfit: cotton pants, sandals, a shapeless sweater, and a cap. His beard was bleached by sun and salt water. No doubt a sailor, Kahnweiler thought, who wants to buy himself a picture. The man introduced himself: "Hello, my name is Kees van Dongen. Would you like to see some of my paintings before I return to Holland?"

Even before Kahnweiler had time to reply, the artist began unrolling large canvases on the floor, stepping on them to hold them in place—without even taking off his sandals. The dealer watched and considered. He asked to see earlier works in order to understand his development. When he decided to buy, he bought everything. That was the policy he had formulated and he decided it was time to act on it. When he wanted a painter, he wanted all of him. [14]

The two men took to each other and began getting together often to discuss ideas. But very soon Kahnweiler began to realize that he did not share all of van Dongen's notions, even while wanting to put him under contract. The painter claimed that he could visualize every detail of a painting even before he began. He had a mental picture of the finished painting before putting brush to canvas. Kahnweiler disliked this attitude, not only because it seemed to him an empty boast, but also for a more fundamental reason: all of his life he would be on the side of painters who would begin a painting with only a vague idea of what they wanted to paint, as Pablo Picasso would put it. Later, Juan Gris would say that the mental picture of what he wanted to paint evolved and became more specific in the process of working. [15] This may be the reason that Kahnweiler considered van Dongen a talented colorist, but nothing more than that; he soon had a basis for comparison.

In April he became acquainted with Georges Braque, whose fauvist canvases he had seen at the Indépendants. Visiting him in his top-floor studio directly across from the Montmartre Theater, he was as surprised by the place as he was by the artist. Braque's father had a house-painting business in Le Havre, and Braque had left school in order to work for him before coming to Paris to devote himself to his art. He was an elegant man, nattily dressed in blue suits, square-toed shoes, and string ties, a dandy in his own way, and his studio reflected this style: it was clean, well-kept, and sparsely furnished.

Kahnweiler discovered Braque as his work was in the process of evolving. Coming out of fauvism, he wanted to subdue this riot of color and form; he wanted to dim the brilliance to reveal the solid substance of the underlying structure. The influence of Cézanne could be felt in his quest.

When Kahnweiler returned to see Braque, he began buying the canvases the artist had painted that year during his stay at the Hôtel Maurin in l'Estaque, a small fishing port not far from Marseilles*—even before offering to buy all the works in the studio.

* *Paysage à l'Estaque* (The Harbor at l'Estaque) from 1907 was auctioned for 5,500,000 francs (nearly one million dollars) in June 1987 at Hôtel Drouot.

Kahnweiler was proud of the canvases by Braque, Derain, Vlaminck, and van Dongen alongside the few by Paul Signac, Othon Friesz, and Charles Camoin, which clashed on the walls of the gallery. In a way he was more interested in artists than in paintings, and because of this he wanted the exclusive right to represent the artists he sought out. For the moment all agreements were verbal; there was no question of contracts. Kahnweiler had begun to broach the subject of a contract to Vlaminck, who immediately went to ask the advice of dealer Ambroise Vollard, who had represented him informally. "Do it; it will get your painting known," was the answer. "It will move your paintings, and paintings must move along, change places, travel. . . ."[16] This was astonishing advice, as unexpected as everything else about Vollard.

In the beginning, a handshake was enough to seal a mutual agreement with Derain and Braque. Gradually it became known in the small world of art galleries that their works could be found in the new gallery on rue Vignon. Now, who else, Kahnweiler began to wonder keeping in mind his still vivid first impression of the Caillebotte Collection. Seurat, van Gogh, and Cézanne were dead. His admiration for them was boundless, but he wanted to be the dealer who would discover his own "generation of artists." It was too late to become financially involved in the works of Cézanne and the others.[17] It was probably too late even for Matisse, who was only thirty-eight years old.

Kahnweiler visited Matisse often at the studio in his home on quai St. Michel, and he was so taken with the artist that their conversations would make them forget lunch. They discussed everything, talking shop of course, and always about painting. Two years earlier, Kahnweiler had seen Matisse's *Woman with Hat,* which he still remembered down to the smallest detail. He loved the way color was used to express emotion rather than representationally. He appreciated Matisse as a person and as an artist without reservation. But he had to give up the idea of representing him almost immediately. Matisse had sold some paintings to Druet and was about to sign a contract with Bernheim-Jeune, and even if it had been proposed that they share him (which was very unlikely), Kahnweiler would have refused outright; he wanted all of an artist's work for himself. Even the possibility of winning Matisse away from Bernheim-Jeune was out of the question, as the artist's prices were already too high for him.

All of his life Kahnweiler would regret this, but he was not embittered by it. Despite this failure, after one of their conversations Kahnweiler went against his own principles to do a favor for Matisse. At his request Kahnweiler agreed to take care of a transaction for an artist he did not represent. Two American collectors, the Steins, wanted to buy Matisse's *Coiffeuse* in exchange for a stated sum of money and a small Gauguin. "I would like you to buy my painting in order to resell it to them, on the understanding that the Gauguin will be the bulk of the transaction."[18]

Following the artist's wishes, the young dealer showed up at rue Madame to negotiate the sale with Michael and Sarah Stein. That was when he also met Leo and Gertrude, whose unique style had not gone unnoticed at art exhibitions. His strict principles had made him lose out on a great artist, but he had also met a remarkable woman who played a unique role in the artistic and literary life of Paris, as well as in his own career as an art dealer.

Exclusivity was the basis of his actions and the only rule he would never forsake. To his way of thinking, it made complete sense. For the painters he represented, he wanted to assume all their material worries so that they would be able to devote themselves to their art, and he wanted to be responsible for their future losses and their triumphs. In return he insisted on exclusive rights to their work. Mutual trust seemed to him a sound basis for a relationship between painter and dealer, though it was far from the rule in the art world of the period.

Vlaminck called them "financiers of the unknown."[19] Others believed that they would be offended at being relegated to the position of "managers." Often people said they lived by betting on the winning horse. These were the art dealers of the day. There were two types, salesmen and entrepreneurs. The former had business sense; the latter, a sense of adventure, a recognized distinction. Vauxcelles defined it another way: the dealers who enjoy their capital and their influence, and then the rest of them. The first create exhibits; the second build up a stock.[20]

At the beginning of the century, when Kahnweiler entered the profession, the profile of the ideal art dealer could be defined in these terms: a man with sound business sense, flair, and intuition, who was capable of artistic judgment. He would also be shrewd enough to capitalize on the qualities of his artists and plan a targeted promotion for them by placing their work in exhibitions and by writing about it in an intelligent and understandable way for the collector. A great art dealer—a rare phenomenon—is valued by posterity for his judgment, as much for what he refused as for what he accepted. This sort of definition delighted Kahnweiler, since it separated the wheat from the chaff, separated dealers who would hang anything and rent their walls to anyone from those who selected discriminately and took risks.

In 1907 Paris was the place to be if you wanted to be an artist or an art dealer. There were only a dozen reputable dealers, although their numbers were increasing slowly. Among the newcomers to the field were numerous foreigners, notably German Jews of wealthy bourgeois families.[21] When attempts were made to stereotype this new generation of art dealer, Kahnweiler would cite the example of two of the greatest men in the field, who were neither German nor Jewish: Ambroise Vollard and Paul Durand-Ruel.

This was a remarkable time and place: prices of works by young artists were going to rise, the established galleries did not want to take the risk involved in showing these works, and the audience for these works was slowly increasing. Kahnweiler established himself strategically in the midst of everything. He started with capital to meet the expenses of his establishment and also to invest in art. His gallery cost 2,400 francs a year, ten times more than the lease of a butcher shop or bakery.[22]

As Kahnweiler learned when his friend Reignier tried to discourage him from the profession, the easiest way of becoming an art dealer was to be the son of an art dealer: this was the case of Georges Wildenstein, son of Nathan; Léonce and Paul Rosenberg, sons of Alexander; Gaston and Josse, sons of Alexandre Bernheim-Jeune; Paul Durand-Ruel, son of Jean; and Georges Petit, son of Jacques.

There were other personalities, like Vollard, who had both a vocation and a penchant for taking risks, which was extremely rare. There were those, such as Clovis Sagot and Old Man Tanguy, who sold art supplies to painters, and ended up exhibiting and selling works left by their customers. Finally there were those who got started by having worked in the same business, as was the case for several young people who worked at the Goupil Gallery on boulevard Montmartre, which specialized in the sale of nineteenth-century prints and engraved reproductions. In 1896 Michel Knoedler went to New York as a salesman for the firm, a trip that convinced him to become a dealer of French art in the United States. Michel Manzi started working for the Goupil Gallery in 1881 and ten years later left the firm to start his own gallery in Paris. Finally, the last avatar of the art dealer was a would-be dealer who nevertheless belonged to the art world: Alexandre Berthier, Prince of Wagram, an important collector, twenty-four years old, who had so many connections that he naturally started acting as an agent. He had a falling-out with the Bernheim-Jeune Gallery barely a few months after joining them, and there was even talk of a lawsuit.

In his modest way Kahnweiler tried to emulate two contrasting models, Vollard and Durand-Ruel, with whom he shared not their specific taste for the works of particular painters, but their ethical stance in relation to the work of art, the artist, the market, and the public. When his friends reminded Kahnweiler that the success of these two art dealers would be difficult for a foreigner to achieve, he would console himself with the example of Charles Sedelmeyer, a great specialist in old masters, whose gallery had been located in rue de La Rochefoucauld since the Second Empire, and who was the favorite and trusted adviser to the great American collectors.

Kahnweiler had a store of historical analogies which he found edifying and which he used to confirm all his beliefs. For example, to prove his notion that the dealer is the indispensable link between artist and collector, he referred to Caravaggio, whose works he admired. The artist met one of his patrons, the Cardinal del Monte, through his dealer, Master Valentin, who was French. An eminent personage in the papal court, the cardinal welcomed the painter to his palace, lodged him there, and became his protector. Around 1590 he commissioned him to decorate the Contarelli Chapel in the Church of Saint Louis, which was a decisive moment in the artist's career.[23]

He also used his historical curiosity and sagacity in another realm— to discover examples of speculation in art. When people insisted that speculation was a phenomenon of modern art, he reminded them that the idea of investing in the art market had first occurred in the seventeenth century, when the Marquis de Coulanges stated that paintings were as valuable as gold bars. In 1772 Baron Friedrich Grimm, the shrewd observer of Parisian intellectual and artistic life, noted in a letter his amazement that "purchasing paintings for resale was an excellent way to invest one's money." Two Vanloo paintings purchased for twelve thousand pounds had just been sold for thirty thousand pounds to Catherine II of Russia.[24] These examples were not lost on a young man who knew his way in the corridors of a bank better than around an artist's studio.

Speculation was not a new phenomenon, but in the nineteenth century it had generally been practiced in the market for old masters. The year 1870 marked a major turning point: the appearance of a new breed of collector in the art world, the business tycoon.[25] An example in France was Ernest Hoschedé, the owner of a department store. His collection was so extensive (over eighty Monets, Pissarros, Corots, Courbets, and others) that when his bankruptcy necessitated the total liquidation of his possessions and his collection was auctioned off, the paintings fetched low prices, temporarily ruining the value of impressionist paintings. Above all it was in the United States that this new style of collector appeared, coinciding with the emergence of giant modern enterprises, in particular the development of the railroad. Most of the big American collectors of the end of the nineteenth century—W. H. Vanderbilt, Collis Potter Huntington, W. T. Walters, Jay Gould, W. W. Aspinwall, John Taylor Johnston, August Belmont, John Pierpont Morgan, H. O. Havemeyer—were railroad magnates, industrialists, or financiers.[26]

At the end of the nineteenth century these collectors looked to Paris, the art center and art market of the world, and French dealers looked to America for new collectors. Two important new characteristics thus came into play: the international scope of the art market and the growing importance of vested interests.

The circle of Parisian art dealers was small, disproportionate to the importance ascribed to it by intellectuals and financiers. Kahnweiler could quickly draw up a succinct list of art dealers, describing each individual with unmitigated severity.

There was Sagot, a most colorful man, who dabbled in bric-a-brac. He took an interest in young painters whom other art dealers turned away, and this drew an equally young following of collectors to his shop. He could be found there at any time, sitting at a table and poring over new art catalogues. Kahnweiler found him amusing but indiscriminate: he would show anything.

More interesting was his predecessor, with whom the art world always compared him: Julien-François Tanguy, known as Old Man Tanguy, who had died in 1894. He was the son of weavers from Britanny, had been a plasterer, had worked for the railroad, and after many adventures had ended up in Paris selling paint. When artists could not pay him he would accept their paintings as a pledge, thereby accumulating a collection of van Goghs, Pissarros, and others. For over twenty years his shop was the only place where paintings by Cézanne could be found. It was precisely because Vollard saw one in the window of Tanguy's shop in 1892 that he was instantly converted and three years later mounted the first Cézanne exhibition in his own gallery.[27] Tanguy was a real personality; at once debonair and rebellious, he was completely sincere in the defense of his impressionist friends—which was not the case for Sagot, in Kahnweiler's opinion. Whether speaking of Sagot or of Tanguy, Kahnweiler was careful not to confuse true art dealers with men of goodwill who accepted as collateral works from a thousand artists when among all of them only four or five had any value.[28] Even Berthe Weill, known as Little Old Lady Weill, belonged in this category. It is true that she should be given credit for showing new talent, but she was neither a pioneer nor someone who took risks, and she often hung on her walls whatever was brought to her without showing any critical sense. But along with Sagot, she was among the few Parisian art dealers to show Picasso before Kahnweiler. This may explain his opinion of them.

There was also Eugène Druet, who had worked as Auguste Rodin's photographer and who had opened his own gallery four years earlier on rue du Faubourg St. Honoré. He established himself rapidly, having already mounted shows of Matisse, van Dongen, the nabis and the fauves. In Kahnweiler's opinion he knew his direction and was a true art dealer.

The success of the Bernheim-Jeune Gallery on place de la Madeleine, under the direction of Gaston and Josse, eclipsed the fact that the family business, which started in the eighteenth century in Besançon, was selling art supplies. Only after their move to Paris and Brussels did the family turn to the selling of art. Besides van Gogh and Cézanne, they also represented the nabis and the post-impressionists.

Georges Petit started his gallery in 1846; it became one of the most reputable firms and had a truly international clientele. He had one-man shows of the works of Rodin, Monet, and Sisley.

These were the established galleries that Kahnweiler had to contend with. And there were others, no longer in existence but which Kahnweiler had heard of, which completed the roster of the art dealer's world.

Among these, Louis Le Barc de Boutteville had owned a gallery on rue Le Pelletier until his death ten years earlier. He had been quietly selling the works of secondary masters when suddenly he experienced a revelation that was almost religious in intensity. It occurred at the Salon des Indépendants, in front of paintings by Henri de Toulouse-Lautrec and Paul Signac. Almost immediately he sold off his old stock, refurbished his gallery, and changed his sign to "Impressionists and Symbolists." He mostly showed the nabis painters, and in the place where a restaurant usually displays the menu he listed the names: Manet, Monet, Pissarro, Sisley, Zuloaga. The average price of an oil painting was two hundred francs gold, and watercolors were a mere twenty francs.[29]

Kahnweiler was fond of these edifying stories even if the gallery of Le Barc de Boutteville was now closed. Other people in the field who also came from abroad made him think more about the profession which he was only just discovering. In Germany a few art dealers dominated: Heinrich Thannhauser, Joseph Brenner, and Paul Cassirer. The latter fascinated him by his originality and his meteoric career. After studying art history in Munich, he had started his business in 1901. One of the most active promoters of the works of van Gogh, he was active in representing French art in general and the impressionists in particular. He became the friend and German affiliate of Durand-Ruel.

There was another figure in the art world about whom Kahnweiler could not be indifferent, whose position was a hundred times superior morally and aesthetically and at an even greater level financially than either Le Barc or Cassirer. Joseph Duveen was thirty-eight, the son of a dealer in objets d'art, who wanted to become one of the greatest art dealers in the world in the volume of his sales, and who had both sound business sense and a cynicism to match any occasion. His motto defined him better than a portrait: "You can never pay too much for what is priceless." He was prepared to buy at any price because he was always sure of being able to resell.

Like his colleagues, he also had a moment of revelation, but there was nothing mystical about it. He had understood that, in the words of William Sharp, "the United States would become the Louvre of Nations before the end of this century."[30] When the three largest museums of the day were being created—the Museum of Fine Arts in Boston, the Corcoran Gallery in Washington, and the Metropolitan Museum of Art in New York—Duveen decided to become indispensable to this promising market. His goal was to create a monopoly, as if he were the only one who could procure what they needed. When asked about his success, he always used the metaphor of water levels in communicating vessels: "Europe has art to sell and America has money to spend." It was extremely simple; you had only to think about it. For years Duveen had thought only about the business of art.

Duveen sold only "rare" art and had no interest in painting after 1800. He understood his business and his clientele and knew how to work on the psychology of his Boston or New York bourgeoisie. What these wealthy industrialists wanted when they purchased a painting was not only the certificate of authenticity bestowed by the Duveen name, but also the bit of history that accompanied it. For these people, so entranced by the traditions and manners of the European aristocracy, there was nothing like an old master painting or, better still, an entire collection that would associate their names with those of famous past owners. Joseph Duveen understood this and thus he became a great art dealer, especially for the scope of his business.[31]

For Kahnweiler, however, there were only two art dealers who possessed true greatness in their reputation, stature, and impact on the future development of art.

The first, Ambroise Vollard, was the man who said, "Art cannot be bought; it can only be sold." Whatever the collector may think, everything depends on the dealer's ability to show, hide, exhibit, flatter, suggest, place a work, or promote a painting. Vollard was never interested in either intimidating or impressing a client. He was not about to make his customers believe that they were stepping into the inner sanctum of Art. When he first opened his gallery on rue Laffitte, he only knew of art what he had learned by attending public auctions. On the advice of painters such as Pissarro, he showed van Gogh, Degas, Gauguin, Renoir, and Picasso when they were still unknown. But for him, the greatest artist was unquestionably Cézanne. He identified so closely with Cézanne's painting that it became his personal mission.

Vollard quickly made a reputation for himself among painters and dealers with his habit of taking risks and his pioneering work as an editor and publisher of art books. He had an extraordinary personality, and his dinners were famous. The table was set for the occasion in the basement, where he invariably served curried chicken, the national dish of his native Réunion. He enjoyed seating the most improbable people next to each other at the table, such as Abbé Mugnier, a literary priest, next to a chorus girl, or the critic Paul Léautaud next to a poor writer he had just dragged through the mud. Other than impressionist painting he had a passion for napping. He observed the siesta time religiously and would not change his habit even for a wealthy American client. When spoken to, he would nod and drift off when a price was mentioned.[32] Vollard insisted that in his profession he earned a fortune while napping. The poet Guillaume Apollinaire, who thought the basement dinners were among the most exclusive events in Paris, used to say that when Vollard was questioned he would only answer by singing to the tune of a popular song:

> I show everything that's offered,
> Laprade, Marquet, Manzana;
> Even though their paintings aren't pink and pretty.
> I would have preferred selling Bonnats
> But I'm a dealer, I sell what you want,
> And Fortune comes marching in.[33]

Vollard was a joker, self-mocking and provocative. The wealthy collectors who crossed the Atlantic to buy Cézannes and who ended up waiting outside his door for hours while his naps dragged on found his devil-may-care attitude very insulting, but they still waited for him.

By the time Kahnweiler opened his gallery Vollard was thirty-nine years old. His most fascinating and admirable quality was the confidence with which he would refuse to buy what was before him and what was offered to him. Selectivity was his absolute criterion. When praising him, Kahnweiler would say, "Vollard's mistakes can be counted on the fingers of one hand."[34]

By 1907 Vollard had begun to change. Cézanne had died the previous year, and Vollard's warehouse was full of his works. He organized fewer shows, showed paintings only to his most faithful clients, and seemed indifferent to new artistic directions. He did not even try to hang on to the young painters his colleagues wanted to work with, whether it was Derain or Vlaminck or Picasso, and he had no understanding of their evolution. This did not prevent him from posing in 1910 for Picasso, who painted a portrait in the purest cubist style. And in 1933 and 1934, he inspired Picasso's most dazzling series of engravings, the one hundred plates of the "Vollard series."

For Kahnweiler, Vollard's greatness was only surpassed by that of Paul Durand-Ruel, who was seventy-three in 1907. Not only a precursor, Durand-Ruel held an important position in the history of the art market because he had made a break with the past.

He replaced the traditional patron of the arts with the art dealer, a friend and adviser, ever ready to help and give advice without trying to influence the artist's work. In exchange for this, he was given exclusive representation of the artist's production. He did not want to answer to the collector's taste and needs; on the contrary, he wanted to shape and direct it. When he took up the cause of the unpopular impressionists, he was in extremely difficult economic circumstances. At all cost, and against all odds, he pursued his goal. It took time, but eventually he saw himself vindicated and his taste become consecrated in the eyes of the public. He never doubted it for a moment. But his apostasy was not an easy one, as can be inferred from Pissarro's correspondence with his son Lucien. One can imagine all the maneuvers, the lies, and the pleas he made to the penniless artist to convince him that he was not overstocked with work, and to persuade him to remain in the gallery despite the lean times.[35]

Kahnweiler held him up as the ultimate model to follow; his deeds were the best justification possible for the existence of art dealers. Before him artists had lived on commissions, whether from church officials, aristocrats, or the bourgeoisie. Now paintings were no longer restricted to the wealthy. He transformed the whole system by opening the market to new collectors of moderate means. Paintings by his artists—Monet, Pissarro, André Beaudin, Renoir, Sisley, Degas, Mary Cassatt, and Berthe Morisot among them—were no longer unsaleable; nothing was unsaleable anymore.[36] Simply by buying what they could in the beginning, the dozen or so collectors enthusiastic about the impressionists had the same impact as wealthy patrons of the arts. It was a situation that Durand-Ruel had created and felt at home with. He was the son and heir to a family of merchants who, instead of dissipating the family fortune, made a success for himself in the long run. Courageous, intelligent, and daring during a period (the Second Empire) when the only purpose of art was to cover walls, he was a pioneer who transformed paintings into a marketable commodity, an innovator who organized the first exhibit of impressionist art in New York as early as 1886. Two years later he opened a gallery there. His name is linked with an artistic movement that would change history.[37]

Vollard and Durand-Ruel: one was the exact opposite of the other. One put old frames in his window whereas the other was meticulous about his displays. Kahnweiler was sorry that the former's nonchalance supplanted all his other qualities, and that the latter's correspondence with the impressionists did not delve into the problems of painting.[38] He admired both of them, but while he felt affection for Vollard, he truly respected Durand-Ruel.

The May 1907 entry in Kahnweiler's notebook listing purchases and shipping (works on loan, or delivered) read: 1. Van Dongen, watercolor; 2. Matisse, drawing; 3. Vuillard, litho; 4. Derain, engraving.[39]

Opening a gallery was a challenge even for a young man supported by his family. For someone from his background who had refused to take over a prosperous venture in South Africa, starting a business selling modern paintings or manufacturing airplanes came to the same thing. Kahnweiler felt that he was the right man in the right place behind the small desk on rue Vignon. He had all the prerequisites for a gallery director: a knowledge of the history of art, practical knowledge of contemporary painting (he willingly admitted that he could not manage a gallery that sold old masters), familiarity with business, and a personal following of clients.[40] People said of him that he was trustworthy and loyal, serious about art, and respectful of the work of painters. Painting was part of every aspect of his life. In his home in Auteuil he had the works of the artists he liked. They were hung with the same simplicity as at the gallery, with little attention paid to the placement or the frame. His main concern was simply to keep the canvas up on the wall.

He wanted to be informed, not only about France (newspapers and magazines kept him current) but on the state of painting and the foreign market. There was no dealer in Paris more European, more cosmopolitan than he.

Autodidact by nature, he had no aesthetic criteria and relied on his readings, supplemented with magazines from abroad, especially England. One of these, *The Studio*, was a monthly, established in 1893, subtitled "An Illustrated Magazine of Fine and Applied Art." It was dedicated to theories, history, and aesthetics, and was a useful international clearing house for people in the business. Another was the *Burlington* magazine, which had only been published for four years; its high level of erudition would eventually make it into an institution.

Almost immediately Kahnweiler was in contact with foreign magazines, from the most important to the most marginal, for a reason that reveals his originality: they requested reproductions of paintings. He was among the first—if not the first—to systematically photograph the paintings by his artists. It was one of his most serious and demanding tasks, "not as a nice obsession of the collector, but as a basic necessity of his business." He photographed everything except drawings because developing a photograph would be more expensive than a drawing was worth, and he would have had such quantities of them. He employed a professional photographer, Delétang, who used transparencies, though Kahnweiler preferred his own portable camera to capture, for his own use, the landscapes that inspired certain paintings or the artist caught unawares in his studio. Kahnweiler appreciated photography on its own terms, as well as its ability to document the development of painting.

The first photograph by Joseph Niepce, the invention of the daguerreotype, and the developing of photographs on paper all indicated to Kahnweiler that painting should be other than the direct reproduction of appearance. The impressionists painted what photography of the day could not capture—color, atmosphere—and they organized their very first exhibit in the studio of a photographer, Gaspard Felix Tournachon, better known as Nadar.

Systematic photographing was expensive and would become increasingly so, Kahnweiler knew; but he insisted on it, as it enabled him to have his stock at hand at all times and to show people earlier works by painters whose recent works they collected. He was also able to disseminate the works of his artists abroad. The artists were delighted with his method, since they often traveled or worked outside of the capital and could request photographs of their paintings to compare with work in progress.

Without giving advance notice artists often stopped by the gallery. Eventually collectors and critics started making the detour to rue Vignon on their way to the galleries in the neighborhood around the Madeleine.

Kahnweiler's very first client was his friend Hermann Rupf. Although he was now living in Bern, he often made trips to Paris to buy paintings, which was his passion and his mania. Rupf was typical of the new breed of collector—the perfect "gentleman," cultivated, well-traveled, and a frequenter of the museums of Europe. He loved and understood the paintings of previous centuries, but an openness of mind enabled him to look with great curiosity at an art that was new and provocative. As the first customer of the Kahnweiler Gallery he would buy *La Route* (The Road), a landscape by Derain, and a Vlaminck which he would later part with when he believed that the artist had taken a wrong direction. Each year until 1914 he would buy a Braque and a Derain.[41]

Other collectors turned up for the first time on rue Vignon, notably Olivier Sainsère, a councillor of state who collected with discernment. His apartment on nearby rue de Miromesnil revealed his taste and his daring. On the walls the impressionists were hung next to works by new painters, whom he met at studios in Montmartre and at the Clovis Sagot and Berthe Weill galleries. He had been buying Picasso's work since 1901.

To collectors, Kahnweiler seemed to be speaking a new language, using words and a tone they were not accustomed to hearing in galleries. He was not solicitous, nor did he disturb them when they came to his place. In response to a question he would discuss, show, explain anything about the works and artists he liked without ever having to prove anything. The question of money only came up afterward, awkwardly, as if it were an unseemly but necessary evil. They felt confident; the dealer was not trying to place the painting, and this must be stressed. He was convinced that a gallery did not need the masses, nor even a large public, just a few reliable followers. He was looking to the future and trying to develop a handful of courageous collectors who would stand apart from the crowd. He wanted to create the right situation for the work to be seen and to be among collectors who would have a profound feeling for it. Patient, informative, and even didactic, he often took out paintings and discussed the way to fully appreciate them. He was the opposite of Félix Fénéon, an assistant at the Bernheim-Jeune Gallery, who, when asked by a client about a still life, answered condescendingly, "But sir, it portrays fairly well-known edibles."[42]

The patience of this young old man was essential to his proselytizing, which he exerted with Rupf and even more so with Roger Dutilleul, whom he had just met, and who would remain a faithful client for decades. Ten years older, Dutilleul was of the Parisian bourgeoisie, but did not possess a personal fortune of his own. His father was an examiner at the Banque de Paris, and he was a councillor at the Audit Office, where he represented the Portland Cement Company in the Boulonnais. His art collection was contemporary with the Kahnweiler Gallery, and for certain periods it faithfully reflected Kahnweiler's taste. The one exception was Juan Gris, whom Kahnweiler could never persuade Dutilleul to include, as Dutilleul found his work too dry and professorial. He would later discuss how Kahnweiler strengthened his own inclinations, making him discover the great painters of his day when they were still unknown, and that he was more of a teacher than a dealer. "In truth I became his disciple."[43]

Dutilleul was in complete rapport with Kahnweiler and was passionate about the painters and the movements that critics associated with the dealer. Always wary of people who "admire with their ears," he shut out all rumors about artists' reputations. He was a prime example of a credo dear to the dealer: to be a collector is an act of faith and not a trade, a hobby, or even a feather in one's cap. But even while following the teachings of someone he credited with being his "mentor," he nevertheless upheld his own freedom of choice. He abhorred painters who were emotionally too controlled, who avoided spontaneity and irrationality.

His principles were unshakable. One day in an effort to convince him, Kahnweiler offered him a Gris, which Dutilleul immediately refused with the argument that it could not stand up to the Braque or the Picasso on his wall. He loved the expression of raw emotions unfiltered by culture. Vlaminck, Derain, and Braque were his first purchases from the gallery on rue Vignon.

Roger Dutilleul was a bachelor who lived with his brother, a collector of engravings, in an apartment in the Monceau section. There were paintings on all the walls of all the rooms, and as there was no space left on the walls there were piles on the floor leaning against the walls and furniture in every direction. Artists, periods, genres were all mixed up. The common factor, other than the influence of Kahnweiler in the original direction of the collection, was the format of the paintings. For reasons of space, he quickly resolved to eliminate large paintings, keeping only paintings of average size, small for the most part, even miniature, although he would eventually buy a big Léger. Passionate and filled with enthusiasm in all this confusion, he thought of his paintings as his children.

Kahnweiler found this original, withdrawn personality very sympathetic. But the character trait of Dutilleul's that pleased him the most as a dealer was his quiet attentiveness. He was never intrusive when in the artist's studio or in the dealer's gallery, so as not to disturb them in their work. He was so discreet that Picasso, who was regularly invaded by troublesome people and parasites, would insist that he come to visit the studio, and Kahnweiler had to send him notes at regular intervals to notify him of new arrivals, or even just to remind him that "I haven't seen you."[44]

Dutilleul enjoyed the company of young painters at the end of the day at the gallery, but his satisfaction was complete only if the dealer urged him to stay on so they could talk. Afterward he could re-create the mood of these gatherings with precise words and inflections. He was a man who, during the whole of his life as a collector, could never buy a painting from an artist without beginning his request with: "Sir, if you would consent to part with . . ."[45] This sums him up in a phrase, and it was so obviously French that Kahnweiler found him irresistible.

The gallery on rue Vignon was becoming a place where things began to happen and people could meet. Ardengo Soffici could be found there even as he prepared to return to Florence after seven years in Paris. Painter, writer, and above all art critic, he considered himself intimately associated with the cultural avant-garde. Kahnweiler remained in correspondence with him during his struggles for the futurists, receiving the magazines he wrote for: *La Voce, Leonardo,* and *Lacerba.* Soon English art critics such as Clive Bell and Roger Fry, closely tied to the Bloomsbury set and London-based advocates of the post-impressionist artists, would make the detour to rue Vignon. But for obvious reasons the first relations that Kahnweiler formed around him were German—two men who, despite their friend in common, did not get along with one another.

Carl Einstein was the same age as Kahnweiler and, like him, had started as a clerk in a bank in Karlsruhe. This native of Berlin was familiar with literary and artistic circles and always had numerous projects in the works. His temperament was the opposite of Kahnweiler's: extravagant, tormented, original, always in the throes of an intense inner life. When he spoke of the harmonious nature of his friend Heini, there was a note of envy in his tone, as if he had tried to achieve such inner peace without ever being able to attain it. Even his background was radically different from Kahnweiler's, since he had studied the history of art at the University of Berlin. The art dealer was nonetheless his intellectual equal and intimate, on whom he would try his ideas, and whose opinion and advice, so full of common sense, he would seek. Kahnweiler always considered him one of the best art critics of his generation and a first-rate art historian, one of the few to have confronted African art and modern art at a time when it was not done.[46] He also esteemed him highly as a poet and writer, convinced that Carl Einstein would be as important for German literature as Gertrude Stein was for American literature. He described his slender novel *Beduquin* (1906) as closer to "German literary cubism" than to the literary outpouring of expressionism.[47]

Anyone looking for Carl Einstein would often find him in the gallery on rue Vignon, which became his second home. That was also where the second person important to Kahnweiler, Wilhelm Uhde, was to be found. He was the leading figure among the German emigrés who met at the Dôme in Montparnasse. Born ten years earlier than Kahnweiler, in northern Germany, he was the grandson of a clergyman and the son of a prosecutor. This background led to law school and a position in the government, and he followed this preordained path until one day a sudden shock made him abandon it: the revelation of painting. This event occurred in Florence in 1899, and Giotto was an important factor. Uhde thus changed his goal and began studying the history of art in Munich, Breslau, and Rome before arriving in 1904 in Paris, the place where all his passions converged.[48]

For Kahnweiler he was the German ideal—clean and pure.[49] For the holy trinity of the German imagination (Luther, Goethe, and Bismarck) Uhde had substituted others: Hölderlin, Nietszche, and Jean Paul (Richter). Fundamentally European in culture, he nevertheless believed that a return to authentic German values was necessary to regenerate the people. But these were extremely different ideas from those which would be proclaimed on the eve of World War I. Uhde's faith and his convictions were those of a missionary casting down false idols; he recognized only one criterion, which he called "art of great quality." Following this high standard, he began buying paintings by Braque and Picasso as early as 1907. He wanted to influence others to collect, and despite Kahnweiler's skepticism, he insisted on showing him the works of Henri Rousseau two years before his death. Uhde's apartment gallery was open to one and all, even to the most conservative collectors, to display the works of artists he supported. Later, his castle in Franconia, where he would settle with one of his artist friends in the guise of secretary, would also be open to all.

Uhde's rapport with Kahnweiler was made up of friendship, mutual respect, and confidence. He would remember 1907 as an important date, marking the opening of the gallery on rue Vignon and the undertaking of a good hard battle—led in concert by both men.[50] As for Kahnweiler, he would always speak of Uhde with great respect and infinite gratitude, because just a few words dropped by him in 1907 transformed the course of Kahnweiler's life.

It was the beginning of summer, and one day a stranger entered the gallery, an oddly dressed and peculiar-looking young man, whose hair was jet black, shining like fibers of hard coal. His dark and mysterious glance animated his whole face. He looked at the paintings attentively and left without a word. Kahnweiler was startled to see him return the next day in the company of a large bearded man who remained equally silent, then left in turn. These aficionados didn't waste any words, to put it mildly.

Kahnweiler had forgotten the incident when Uhde suggested that he visit Pablo Picasso's studio in Montmartre. "He has a picture," he said, "that looks Assyrian, something utterly strange."[51] Two days later Kahnweiler was climbing the steps to the Butte Montmartre, driven by an instinctive curiosity and by his confidence in Uhde's judgment. But "Assyrian" meant nothing to him; he had to see for himself. A dealer risked nothing by visiting a studio. He knew nothing about Picasso, having only glimpsed his work as far as he could remember in the shops of Sagot, Vollard, and Berthe Weill, but it had not made any special impression on him. He felt that he had been surpassed by the fauvist movement; he was too casual in his use of color.

The decor of Picasso's studio at 13 rue Ravignan was difficult to describe, halfway between picturesque and poverty-stricken. Affixed to the door were bits of paper with hastily written messages: "Manolo went to see Azon"; "Toto was here"; "Derain will come by in the afternoon." It was a very interesting door. The artist himself opened it. So this young man wearing an open shirt and shorts was Picasso. He was the mysterious visitor, the silent man who had come by the other day. Kahnweiler now realized that the man who had stepped out of the coach must have been Vollard.

"Do you know what Vollard said to me on leaving your gallery?" Picasso asked. "He said, 'This is a young man whose family gave him a gallery for his first communion.' "[52]

Kahnweiler was embarrassed that a man he respected so much had expressed such an opinion. He looked around at the total disorder, the piles of drawings and stacks of canvases propped every which way, with a thick layer of dust over everything. There was neither gas nor electricity in this shabby wooden structure that would be known to posterity as the "Bateau-Lavoir," an old boat stranded on the Butte, where each studio was like a cabin in a steamship, minus the luxury.[53] Water had to be fetched by filling containers on the ground floor. Picasso, who liked to work at night, used a kerosene lamp for light.

The poet Pierre Mac Orlan, who had chosen to live in the area of Montmartre since the beginning of the century, described the Bateau-Lavoir simply as a hideous place. The studios were big matchboxes with rough plank walls, without any real furnishings, and some people used copies of *l'Intransigeant* as mattresses because it had six pages more than other newspapers. It was completely stark but no one there ever mentioned money.[54]

As far as the painting that Uhde had called the "Assyrian work," his description seemed to apply to all the canvases in the studio.

When Kahnweiler finally saw the painting it came as a complete shock; he was astounded at first and then dazzled. He felt that something admirable, extraordinary, inconceivable had occurred.[55] He was totally unprepared for this vision, and it stunned him: he was expecting more paintings in blue and rose from this artist. "Assyrian" was not the word—it was wonderful, crazy, and monstrous at the same time, and yet moving. Without a doubt this work was completely new and important. Running out of superlatives he simply said, "It's indescribable."[56]

How can something absolutely new be understood and analyzed? Kahnweiler could not help but try to conceptualize and articulate this revelation. The painting, which would be known in art history as *Les Demoiselles d'Avignon*, could not be judged solely on the basis of taste; just looking at it was not enough. It had to be perceived and deciphered in terms of how the rhythm of the forms was in contradiction with the representation of visual reality.[57]

Kahnweiler perceived two distinct halves in this large canvas, which measured 93 by 96 inches. On the left three women were painted in monochrome, in flesh colors, a color scheme which was not radically different in style from that in his paintings of the rose period. But they were unlike anything the artist had done until then, as they were no longer heightened sketches. Now the forms were powerfully modeled, as if very roughly carved out. On the right were two women, one standing, the other crouching down, drawn in parallel lines of violent colors. This portion of the painting announced a break with the past. Kahnweiler had the sudden intuition that a whole tradition had been overthrown as of that moment.[58] The fruits and the draperies around the women were not as important. At any rate, the painting appeared unfinished to him, as it did not form a coherent whole. On the left the style was still 1906, and it was the degree of shading that created forms, as before. On the right it was the style of 1907; the outline and color created forms by the direction of the paint strokes, as if they were carved out at rough angles. It was this first outburst that would transform everything. Cubism began on the right-hand side of *Les Demoiselles d'Avignon*.[59]

Kahnweiler was convinced that Picasso had a madman's daring. Instead of taking on the problems of painting one at a time, he chose to confront them all at once. He was not working on a pleasing composition, but rather making a construction on the surface of the canvas. The insurmountable problem that Picasso was trying to resolve in a desperate and futile attempt Kahnweiler summed up in a few words: it was the depiction of three-dimensional colored forms on a surface plane, in an attempt to incorporate them within the unity of the surface.[60] Certainly not everything in *Les Demoiselles d'Avignon* was revolutionary. It was understandable that it would disorient the viewer because it burst upon an art world already agitated by the fauves, who used light only as a means to highlight forms. And then there were different parts, secondary to the rhythm of the whole composition, that created such distortions.

In attempting to define what was original on the right-hand side of the canvas, Kahnweiler saw that the artist no longer even tried to imitate external reality; he sought to give its essence. The dealer did not doubt for a second that the emergence of this new style in painting dealt a final blow to fauvism. But it would not end there. He saw it as a decisive step in the history of painting, a genuine break with the past. He understood why people who saw this painting said it was insane. They were confused.[61]

"It's indefinable . . . admirable," Kahnweiler repeated to Picasso.

He was truly impressed, but he had been the only one. Since Picasso had started showing the painting to friends he had heard only sarcasm and reactions that tried to be ironic or discouraging, and which he sometimes found painful. When Kahnweiler visited his studio for the first time, Picasso was in the depths of his isolation, alone in front of his creation. His friends were not very far away, but they were uneasy and as worried as if he had been the proverbial young man on the flying trapeze—working without a safety net. "It's as if someone drank gasoline to spit fire," said Braque.[62] Derain, who believed the whole project was hopeless, told Kahnweiler, "One day Picasso will be found hanging dead behind that big painting."[63]

A muffled rumor claimed that Picasso had gone insane, and that in his studio, which poet Max Jacob used to call "The Central Laboratory of Modern Art," he concocted monstrous transformations. Uhde, whom Picasso had in despair asked to come to see his *Demoiselles*, was not so much frightened as disconcerted. He marveled at it, but needed to think about it for several weeks before he came around and could accept it.[64]

These people were not stupid; they were painters, critics, poets, collectors, and, as he knew very well, they were not in sympathy with academic painting. They were open-minded, they were his friends, but they were disturbed by the way he deformed reality in the big painting: an arm there, the breasts there, and in what a state! It could only inspire feelings of revulsion. Picasso would later confide in Kahnweiler: "In those days people said that I made the noses crooked, even in *Les Demoiselles d'Avignon*, but I had to make the nose crooked so that they could see it was a nose."[65]

In the summer of 1907 Picasso seemed to Kahnweiler to be Zarathustra incarnate, come down from his mountain retreat to bring an inspired message that almost no one could understand. At this privileged moment, the young dealer felt the way Vollard did at the sight of his first Cézanne—as if he had been punched in the stomach; the way Durand-Ruel must have felt in 1870 when he met Monet in London. The paths of aesthetic knowledge are incomprehensible.

Standing before *Les Demoiselles d'Avignon* Kahnweiler and Picasso observed one another; there was mutual understanding and a feeling of solidarity. There was no need for words. From then on Picasso knew that he was not entirely alone, and Kahnweiler knew he had made the right decision in refusing to go to South Africa to manage diamond mines. Meeting this man and seeing this painting gave a new meaning to his life. When he walked into this studio he was an art dealer; he would still be a dealer on leaving, but he would no longer be the same man.

They took each other's measure. The dealer was twenty-three years old and the artist twenty-six. The next day they would meet again. Kahnweiler bought several recent gouaches, and some small paintings that had the same new spirit as the *Demoiselles*. Among these sketches were preliminary studies for the great painting. But what of the painting itself? Picasso was not ready to sell. "It's not finished," he said.

Kahnweiler did not insist, not because he had not wanted to, but because he did not dare. He did not have the strength to confront the artist, whose suspicion was obvious. It was not manifested toward Kahnweiler alone, but toward the whole world—in particular art dealers. Even Vollard and Weill were disconcerted by Picasso's blue canvases, let alone *Les Demoiselles d'Avignon*. They shied away from the artist. Picasso was free and Kahnweiler had no rivals to contend with. Without knowing anything about the young German, Picasso was touched by his exceptional enthusiasm. Kahnweiler was one of the few people to believe in him completely and absolutely at a moment when Picasso had touched bottom. To win his consent, overcome his reticence, and assuage his suspicions, Kahnweiler had to show that in spite of his being young and inexperienced he had the strength of his conviction.[66] From that moment their fates were sealed.

As a friend Kahnweiler became part of Picasso's inner circle, making the acquaintance of poets Max Jacob and Guillaume Apollinaire; the latter lived in Auteuil, near Kahnweiler's home. They often traveled together for company and conversation, and formed a profound friendship, often interrupted by violent altercations. From the first Kahnweiler recognized that Apollinaire was a great poet, and he sincerely admired him, but he did not trust his taste in art. Apollinaire's approach to painting was sensual and intellectual, and he reacted as a friend, supporting the works of artists he liked, drawn especially toward the experimental. No matter what others said, Kahnweiler did not believe that Apollinaire was a good art critic and never missed an opportunity to let him know it, which often strained the atmosphere.[67]

The first Picassos were immediately sold to Hermann Rupf. Kahnweiler barely had time to hang them. Naturally he wanted more and developed the habit of visiting the artist regularly at the Bateau-Lavoir. He was learning to know the painter, and quickly understood that he must not disturb him in the morning because he liked to work at night. Whoever was unfortunate enough to disturb Picasso at the normal start of the day would be the recipient of his execrable mood. Another trait that was evident was the artist's reluctance to part with his paintings. He was often upset at the sale of his work when he watched it leaving his studio. Thus Kahnweiler learned early never to insist—what Picasso wanted was the rule. They were two friends of the same generation, but there was nevertheless a slight distance between them, perhaps due to the domination of the painter by his self-confidence and his burning convictions—qualities shared by Kahnweiler, but less evident in him. He felt more at his ease with Derain, Vlaminck, or Braque, while for Picasso he felt complete respect. It was while showing one of Picasso's paintings to Swiss collectors that he found himself saying, as he whistled the Valhalla theme from *Twilight of the Gods*: "One day this painting will hang in the Louvre!"

Considering his reserve and prudence this comment revealed his outlook and his motive for subscribing to the Argus of the Press, a clipping service, in order to collect all newspaper mentions of his name, his gallery, and his artists. On July 15, 1907, he began a huge black scrapbook with a newspaper article that he glued on the first page, "The Spanish Invasion: Picasso" by Felicien Fagus in *La Gazette d'Art*. He could not have imagined that sixty years later his gallery would stop subscribing to clipping services or even collecting articles on Picasso because they were so numerous.

For the moment the Kahnweiler Gallery was taking its first steps. To an outsider it seemed so makeshift that some people thought he was only improvising the role of art dealer. This was false. If he was learning in the field, at least he was doing it with his principles and code of behavior clearly established and solidly planted.

Starting with Uhde, Rupf, and Dutilleul most notably, he was beginning to form a circle of collectors. With the arrival of new paintings, Kahnweiler sent them notices, and often they would come and buy; it was that simple. He believed that it was useless to exhibit at the major Salons because the public attended most often as a group with the intention of heaping ridicule and slapping their thighs in derision.

Still, when Derain sent him suggestions as to which canvases he should show in the more experimental, less established Salon d'Automne in October, he set about the task with great diligence. Braque was also exhibiting there. The young gallery owner was not really known by the people of this prestigious organization, since all the paintings he sent ended up mislabeled as Kahmweiler, or Kohuweiler, or Rahnweiler. The great event of this Salon was a retrospective of Cézanne a year after the artist's death. In order to reach this exhibit the visitor had to pass by the works of Abel-Truchet, a painter who used the subterfuge of hyphenating his first and last names in order to be the first in the catalogue. But this year he was out of luck as he was superseded by one Aary-Max, an artist every bit as improbable.

This Cézanne retrospective of fifty-seven paintings was important for such people as Kahnweiler, Braque, and Picasso, because it gave them a perspective on how far they had come, and what remained to be done. It was thanks to this exhibition that they would get their bearings. More than one painter of the younger generation came away dazzled, even overwhelmed.

By the end of 1907, because of a legacy benefiting the town, a museum was opened for the very first time in Kahnweiler's native Mannheim. Meanwhile, on rue Vignon, innovations of a different order were under way.

THE HEROIC YEARS

☐ In the middle of an opening at the Bernheim-Jeune Gallery, four men suddenly entered the room causing quite a stir. What outfits! They wore heavy sweaters and plaid coats made from horse blankets, and on their heads some wore boxing helmets while others wore funny-looking bowler hats pulled down over their eyes.

One of the four had an elegant manner; his somewhat shorter friend wore wide-wale corduroy pants. The other two, who were much taller, were even more eccentric. The color of their neckties and their thick-soled yellow shoes made them look as if they came from the circus! Their style was far removed from the delicacy of nineteenth-century artists, with their vests and ascots. These artists were unmistakable, and so disconcerting that as André Dunoyer de Segonzac stepped forward to meet them he heard someone whisper: "That's the Kahnweiler stable!"[1]

These thoroughbreds were named Georges Braque, Pablo Picasso, André Derain, and Maurice de Vlaminck. They were the vanguard of the rue Vignon gallery. They didn't form a group or a movement, nor were they a stable; rather, they were friends, with Kahnweiler as their common denominator. It was at his gallery that they had met, become acquainted, and finally formed friendships. Kahnweiler watched over them, and they were left to work undisturbed. He told them, "You do your painting, I will look after the rest." The sale of work, collectors, exhibitions, and the rest of it he made his business. Painting was theirs; if they could give him paintings, he would provide the clients. He had no doubts about his ability. He had projected his enormous ego onto them. If he defended them, it was because they were the greatest. He intended to devote himself exclusively to artists who lived up to his idea of painting. There were other artists who lived at the Bateau-Lavoir, or who were staying there temporarily. He could, for example, easily convince his fellow countryman Otto Freundlich to let him, rather than Clovis Sagot, represent his work; but he did not like Freundlich's painting.

He was not simply being idealistic, as he did hope to earn money eventually.[2] Whether on the subject of aesthetics or of business, Kahnweiler was profoundly convinced that he alone was right.[3] As to how he recognized a true artist and why he must paint, the reply was that the artist could not do otherwise, that he was driven to it by a demon inside.[4] When pressed to explain, this most cerebral of art dealers always answered with his theories.

Yet, despite all his statements of principle, he mounted four exhibits in 1908: van Dongen (March), Camoin (April), Girieud (October), and Braque (November). He let himself be persuaded by pressure from his artists, the demands of the art market, and the mood of the times. But he swore that he would never be placed in that position again. The fauvists Girieud and Camoin were already memories, because after *Les Demoiselles d'Avignon* he would lose his taste for their violent primary colors.

The idyll with van Dongen would be short-lived; it was over by the end of the year. They separated on friendly terms. Van Dongen felt a sense of obligation toward the critic Félix Fénéon, who had been one of the first to discover his work shortly after he had arrived in Paris in 1897. In December, with Kahnweiler's approval, he joined the Bernheim-Jeune Gallery, where Fénéon worked. In the course of Kahnweiler's conversations with the painter he had discovered more differences than things in common, which perhaps had already given him an inkling of what would happen subsequently; and when van Dongen began painting society portraits, Kahnweiler felt vindicated.

This was Kahnweiler's way. Some people were surprised that he did not attend Picasso's banquet at the Bateau-Lavoir in honor of Henri Rousseau, nicknamed "the Douanier" (the customs agent). But those closest to Kahnweiler understood immediately that he did not like Rousseau very much, and he did not want his work in the gallery. They had met several times, either at the Indépendants or elsewhere, but somehow they did not get along. The dealer could recognize Rousseau's unique genius and his talent but reproached him for the style of his paintings, so stubbornly resisting the context of his times. They were paintings without culture, and Rousseau as a painter ignored the tradition of his art. It was neither great painting nor was it folk art. According to Kahnweiler, Rousseau's story was simply that of an honest painter who tried to paint in a modern style without ever succeeding. The Douanier was a tasteful man and the subjects of his paintings had great charm, but if his canvases were placed next to those of Braque, Picasso, or Derain, they could not hold up. The dealer wanted no part of such a painter.[5] His fellow countryman Wilhelm Uhde never succeeded in having him share his complete enthusiasm for Rousseau. Uhde was so devoted that he went so far as to organize an exhibition of the Douanier's work. Not one person showed up, which did not come as a surprise to Kahnweiler. Finally the reason for this fiasco was discovered; it seemed that Uhde, the sharp critic but muddled organizer, had forgotten to print the address on the invitations. This was the Douanier Rousseau's first one-man show, and the only one during his lifetime.[6]

If ever he had to choose between a charming Rousseau and a violent Vlaminck, the mild-mannered Kahnweiler would not have hesitated for a moment, which is exactly what occurred. He would often spend Sundays in the towns of Rueil and Chatou with Vlaminck and his friends. He never tired of these people, who were at the opposite extreme from a Kahnweiler in origin, culture, education, and manners. This was perhaps the reason for his strong attraction.

Vlaminck's friend Derain was another matter. Kahnweiler reacted strongly to his work and considered it painting in the grand tradition. Derain, a thoughtful man, was perhaps best represented by his spontaneous statement in a letter on the art of painting landscapes: "The telegraph wires have to be made thicker, so much passes through them!"[7]

Derain's parents wanted him to be an engineer, but just as he was about to enter the Ecole Centrale, he switched to the Académie Carrière. They disapproved, but nevertheless assisted him in every way. This was neither the background nor the temperament of Vlaminck, even though these two were as thick as thieves. According to the legend that was already beginning to form around them, they first met during a railroad accident and had been inseparable since. Their military service parted them for a while, only to strengthen their friendship. In their studio near the bridge at Chatou, when they wanted a change from painting, they would start wrestling for relaxation. The townspeople were disappointed that their local artists did not correspond to the romantic ideal. Little by little they grew to like Vlaminck, "a huge blond with periwinkle blue eyes, wearing a small bowler hat and dressed in the finest gymnastic outfit."[8] He would work among his fishermen friends, who gossiped and swilled wine, which did not exactly encourage them to keep their opinions on art to themselves, and they would say out loud what they thought of the painting on which he was working. They did not so much keep him company as become part of his work; their spontaneous opinions were what Vlaminck used to call "the workers' critique." One day one of them said, "Nature really takes a beating from you!" The painter was so struck by this comment that he paid for drinks all around and proposed that his "critic" write the introduction to the catalogue of his next exhibition.[9]

Vlaminck was born in les Halles, the old wholesale market of Paris; he grew up in Chatou and exhibited in rue Vignon. He would never forget his father's argument that he would be happier if he became a small-town bandleader. "Art! You have to be rich to become an artist!"[10]

He was rich only in his extraordinary personality and his boundless creative energy. Most of his friends went along with his various guises: the talented violinist, the bicycle racer, the loudmouthed braggart. Apollinaire was especially impressed by his wooden staff varnished in brilliant colors, which he used for many purposes, generally loudly and offensively. The poet feared the worst, and was persuaded that Vlaminck, "out of personal friendship and, let's not mince words, out of self-interest, has taken upon himself the dangerous task of killing us. Dressed in his rubber suit, and armed with his staff, he follows us everywhere, just watching for the right moment when he can treacherously deliver the mortal blow with his Croatian instrument."[11]

The person who best described him was the art critic Gustave Coquiot, who called him a diamond in the rough, a giant with a tender soul, facing the open road with a pile of canvases to paint: "He seemed very sure of himself in life, but he was racked with anxiety and suffered every possible neurosis."[12] This is probably the way Kahnweiler saw him.

By September 1908 Braque was back in Paris after having spent several months painting in the town of l'Estaque. For completely different reasons, Kahnweiler immediately became as fond of Braque as he was of Vlaminck.

Braque also gave the appearance of being a "colossus," hiding his thick curly hair beneath a Tyrolean felt hat like the personification of earnest youth. But he was also a dandy, and he practiced wrestling, gymnastics, and roller skating. In the morning he worked out with a punching bag to loosen up his hands before starting to paint.[13] It was a colorful pose, but not the most interesting aspect of this innovator who never allowed his worries and torments to be seen. The series of paintings he brought back from l'Estaque fascinated Kahnweiler. They were monochromatic, with a strong sense of composition; the dealer found them curiously similar to what Picasso had recently painted on the outskirts of Paris at La-Rue-des-Bois, although there was no communication between the two. In order to see this similarity in style and spirit, one would have had to travel between the two painters as Kahnweiler did.[14]

Braque decided to submit his paintings to the jury of the Salon d'Automne in spite of Kahnweiler's objections; the judges turned them down. But individual members of the jury had the right to sponsor, and thus gain admittance for, certain artists, and two among them, Charles Guerin and Albert Marquet, used their prerogative to get Braque included. The other judges agreed, but only to a couple of paintings. Then it was the artist's turn to refuse—all or nothing, and it was nothing. Kahnweiler immediately went into action, changed his plans, and on the spot organized an exhibition in his gallery, setting the date for November 9. He removed the paintings by Pierre Girieud and Francisco Durio, which were supposed to remain on view until November 14: this was an emergency. They were replaced by twenty-seven paintings by Braque. Kahnweiler asked Apollinaire to contribute an introduction to the catalogue overnight; Apollinaire wrote, "The incandescence of his paintings makes our understanding radiant."

Everything was ready on the ninth, but Braque was so intimidated that on his only visit to the gallery he was careful to arrive after sunset, after everyone had left, and so found the gallery empty and dark.[15] The visitors' reactions were evenly divided between indignation and sympathy, but most of all they were surprised. Kahnweiler took note of this. The degree of astonishment was how he measured the impact of an exhibition, more so than by the sale of a few paintings to faithful followers.[16] It provided the opportunity to confront the critics. His usual attitude of contempt no longer held true because this event concerned him closely. His name and gallery were associated with an artist who had been refused by the Salon.

The important critics of the day were Louis Vauxcelles, André Salmon, Waldemar George, Guillaume Apollinaire, Félix Fénéon, Roger Allard, Maurice Raynal, and Roger Marx. They could be divided into two types: professional art critics (of which Vauxcelles was the prototype) and poets who covered "art criticism" for the dailies (Apollinaire, for example), with a few, such as Allard, in both camps.

Kahnweiler's precepts in this area were almost religious. Though he understood the market value of a painter's work in relation to his critical standing, he subscribed to J. K. Huysmans's statement that art critics were cowards, men of letters who were incapable of creating a work of their own. What he held against them was their inability to get to the core of the subject. Huysmans lamented that these people flaunted their independence while revealing themselves to be dilettantes incapable of real judgment. According to Huysmans, both "enthusiasm and contempt were prerequisite for the creation of a work of art."[17] Throughout his career, Kahnweiler would verify the truth of this judgment when he saw how panic spread over the faces of certain critics before the works of an artist about whom no one had written yet. The question posed itself anew of how to judge, how to define or even approach the work. "When there is no previous model to follow, they usually avoid the issue in such a case by saying that it resembles Matisse or someone else."[18]

Why shouldn't he be hard on the critics when he had a mission to fulfill? Despite his talents as a diplomat and fine negotiator, his self-control, and his capacity to absorb setbacks, Kahnweiler could not repress a need to voice his every thought, especially when it came to art.

Outside of his immediate circle of friends—which included Apollinaire, Salmon, Raynal, Einstein, and Uhde—there were two critics in Paris who Kahnweiler felt deserved special notice, due to their character and their influence. Félix Fénéon, who was in his forties, seemed enigmatic and indecipherable to Kahnweiler, especially because of the way he looked. He was a man with a dangerous past, having participated in three revolutionary movements: impressionism, symbolism, and anarchism. In art, as in literature and politics, nothing subversive was alien to him. He was often questioned and arrested by the police, who had been updating his dossier in the General Information Files since the explosion of three bombs in 1892. After having worked on numerous dailies he quit journalism in 1906 to join the Bernheim-Jeune Gallery. He became its director two years later, gaining the power to offer contracts to young artists he considered valuable. At the same time, in his guise as a critic he could guarantee their publicity.

This evident conflict of interest hardly surprised anyone in this world, as it was so commonly done. Critics were often related by bonds of friendship, if not more, to dealers and artists. Some even turned curator to mount exhibitions, even though they might have been on the payroll of a gallery, as Fénéon was, or simply affiliated with a movement, so that it was impossible not to think that they were all more or less subject to influence.

People did not waste time influencing people who were powerless in a world where the economic factor became increasingly important, and the critics certainly wielded power. The standard advice to young artists was: "To become well known in the Heaven of the Arts (by God, the art dealer, and his saints, the art critics), address your prayers to the saints rather than to God."[19]

Kahnweiler was not surprised by these practices, as he had no illusions about the manner in which the French made their adjustments to deontology. For a long time he would keep in mind the humorous anecdotes on the incompetence of certain art critics which were making the rounds of the galleries, as told by Ambroise Vollard. Noteworthy was the one about the critic from *Événement* who, after looking at drawings by Manet, asked Vollard for the artist's address.

"Père-Lachaise, I believe," answered the dealer in all seriousness.

"What? He's dead?"

"Over two years ago."

"Oh, well, that explains why I didn't know the name. You know I've only been an art critic for three years."[20]

Even if the anecdote seems farfetched, it shows the contempt for critics certain dealers expressed among themselves. Kahnweiler, who did not have a higher opinion of them, was nonetheless careful to avoid making harsh statements about the profession in public. And in a man such as Fénéon, he genuinely respected the critic's reserve, discretion, economy with language, precision with which he spoke and wrote on artists and paintings, and the way in which he had devoted himself body and soul to one artist: Seurat. Not since Baudelaire and Delacroix had there been such a complete identification between critic and painter. Fénéon had taken up Seurat's challenge of reforming impressionism and made it his own cause. Kahnweiler admired the complete and absolute nature of this commitment and the way it challenged the reserve of other critics.

Kahnweiler was equally interested in another critic, but for different reasons. Louis Vauxcelles had unlimited influence in the art world. A staunch defender of the Republic and of Dreyfus, Louis Mayer had adopted the pseudonym of Louis Vauxcelles after his studies at the Ecoles du Louvre and the Sorbonne, when he launched his career in journalism. With his trenchant style, he quickly made a reputation for himself; his judgment was neither perceptive nor pertinent, nor even subversive. He seemed quite oblivious of contemporary art. But he was extraordinarily active, giving lectures, writing introductions to catalogues and articles for newspapers. He was the most widely published critic in Paris, with a true mania for writing, a blessing to all editors in need of copy. When he felt that he was spread too thin he began using other pseudonyms. He maintained his position of power, but his feverish writing, produced in an increasingly peremptory, superficial, and hurried style, would become a liability fifteen years later, when he was judged too prolix, too journalistic.

Kahnweiler had often read his articles, but on November 14, 1908, he had special reason to look for his name in the pages of *Gil Blas:* the Braque exhibit was reviewed, and at the bottom of the page the young dealer read: "He builds little metallic, deformed people which are terribly simplified. He disdains form, reduces everything—landscape, figures, and houses—into geometric schemes, into cubes. But let's not mock his efforts, since the work is in good faith. Let's wait."

Cubes—that was the first time the term was used to describe these paintings. Even if rumor had it that a member of the jury of the Salon d'Automne had said, "Braque makes little cubes," it was the first time the statement was printed. Good or bad, adequate or inappropriate, it was launched and could never be taken back. Cubism was baptized by someone who did not like it. The term was used meanspiritedly, to mock, in that narrow and precise way. Yet it would enter history.

Decidedly Vauxcelles seemed predisposed to this paradoxical role since it was he who, three years earlier, had tried to ridicule Matisse, Vlaminck, Derain, and Rouault, at that time exhibited in the Salon d'Automne. Among these paintings he had noticed a very "Italian" sculpture—the head of a child—and he had written, "The candor of this bust is surprising in the midst of the orgy of primary colors. It's Donatello among wild beasts [*les fauves*]."[21]

Thus fauvism, like cubism, would carry for posterity a name invented by a detractor. Yet it seemed quite in line, since the term impressionism also was invented in similar circumstances. Not quite knowing what to call a painting made from his window at Le Havre, Monet had simply said to the person in charge of editing the catalogue of a group exhibition, "Just write 'Impression.'" It became "Impression of Sunrise." The critic Louis Leroy, who wanted to be acidic and ironic, tried to turn it into ridicule (". . . since I was impressed, there must be some impression there.")[22] Thus he coined a name for a historically important group, and subsequently the word became universally known.

Kahnweiler drew a specific conclusion from the coincidence of having impressionism, fauvism, and cubism baptized by detractors: cubism might be the sign of a real and authentic movement. Yet he was also

cautious, warning people to beware of self-conscious and organized movements who selected a name for themselves, which betrayed the artificial
nature of the group or the domination of a leader.[23] Indeed, from the nabis
to the surrealists, by way of the futurists and constructivists, the next few
decades would not be without their self-proclaimed movements.

By the end of 1908 it was time to take stock and make certain
decisions. The circumstances of the Braque exhibition, its impact and the
public's reaction, made it appear as if the dealer had been correct. In
agreement with his artists, he decided not to give one-man shows at rue
Vignon, nor to enter paintings in the major Salons. Why show these
paintings to people who were not prepared to see them? Works would be
exhibited in the gallery as they arrived, and that would be the extent of it.
They would not be put on exhibit outside of the gallery, and he would do
nothing by way of publicity that would in any way be deleterious to the
works. This did not prevent Kahnweiler from continuing to circulate his
photos and his canvases abroad on request by collectors and art reviews.

Thus, at the time that cubism came into being in Paris, that city was
one of the least likely places to see the work, except for the artists' studios
and a small gallery on rue Vignon. In order to discover cubism in Paris in
1908, you had to search for it.

Still, the movement could only have occurred in Paris.[24] It was the
art center of the world, and an international spirit reigned there.[25] As an
indication of the times, the Italian futurist painters proclaimed the birth of
their movement and published the text of their manifesto not in Italy, but
in the Paris daily *Le Figaro*, on February 20, 1909:

> We want to set Italy free from the gangrene of professors, archaeologists,
> tourist guides, and antique dealers. We want to rid Italy of its numberless
> museums that cover it with innumerable cemeteries. Museums, ceme-
> teries! . . . the reciprocal ferocity of painters and sculptors killing each other
> with lines and colors in the same museum. Bring the flame to the shelves of
> the libraries. Dam up the flow of canals to flood the basement storerooms
> of the museums. Oh, may the current wash away those glorious canvases.
> Raise the picks and the hammers!

These artists assumed a stance of unbelievable bravado, and made
Kahnweiler smile. What was the sense of doing away with Rembrandts
and Caravaggios in order to impose a new style of painting? He thought it
was puerile. Taken individually, he did not necessarily dislike the work,
but the notion of a self-proclaimed historical movement seemed to him

truly astounding. You do not level the past in order to shape the future. For a young man educated in Stuttgart, it was beyond comprehension.

He watched the commotion and agitation from his observation post on rue Vignon. It was an important crossroad, as the gallery slowly developed a rhythm and pace. During these heroic years his daily work pattern almost never varied, as it was a routine that suited him so well.

It was the schedule of a free man. At 8:30 he took the streetcar from his home in Auteuil. Often in the carriage he would find Apollinaire or Marie Laurencin. By nine o'clock the metal shutters were raised on the Kahnweiler Gallery. The dealer's first task of the day was to devote himself to his correspondence. In this he was observing an absolute rule, which he followed during trips, long absences, wars, and revolutions: he answered letters on the same day, without delay. This seemed to him a sound commercial policy as well as an elementary courtesy. A person who was late in sending a reply, or who was haphazard or careless, or who did not answer his correspondence at all was not respectable. Some people could be judged by their handshake; Kahnweiler preferred judging people by the state of their correspondence. It was all the more important because he had not installed a telephone; even a minor appointment had to be confirmed in writing. By his own admission his handwriting was illegible, so he quickly learned to use a typewriter (he often asked his correspondent to excuse the formality of it), typing with equal ease in French, German, and English. He always made copies of his letters, which were immediately filed under the proper headings.

A part of his correspondence necessarily dealt with framers, insurance, the bank, the rent. Another portion was addressed to artists, who gladly went away for weeks or even months to work in the provinces or abroad. Kahnweiler's letters were a great help to them. These letters contained critiques, since he was the first to see the works and was able to compare them with what preceded them, and news about the little group in Paris. In 1909 Braque stayed in Normandy in La Roche-Guyon (Cézanne had preceded him there a quarter of a century earlier) while Picasso went to Spain. Kahnweiler's letters were all the more invaluable to them, because through him they could keep tabs on one another's progress from afar.

His correspondence revealed that his artists wanted to know the news from Paris and all about their friends. Without partiality, Kahnweiler functioned as a clearinghouse for errands and solving problems. He discussed the weather in such detail it appeared as if he truly believed that the climate affected his health. He gave his opinion of recent works and the latest exhibitions. Finally he discussed all sorts of practical problems: money, shipment of paints, and other details.

After having settled his correspondence, Kahnweiler would make studio visits to artists. If he had the time he would make the rounds of Montmartre. Vlaminck was a rare exception in not living there, staying instead in the neighborhood of St. Michel, in the fifth arrondissement. Kahnweiler's first stop would be the Bateau-Lavoir to meet with Picasso and other artists; next came rue Tourlaque (Derain) and then rue Caulaincourt (Braque). He visited Braque almost on a daily basis when the artist was in Paris.

At noon, if he could not return to rue Vignon, his assistant closed the gallery and Kahnweiler went home to lunch with Lucie. He never considered going to a restaurant, except for a hasty meal when the gallery remained open.

At 2:30 the gallery opened for the afternoon, with the dealer officiating. But by five o'clock the stray clients were virtually chased out by what poet Max Jacob would call "my friendly little circle on rue Vignon with its amiable president."[26] In good weather, almost every day his painters would descend from the Butte Montmartre in order to return Kahnweiler's morning visit. Braque and Picasso came to talk in the tiny office, while Derain and Vlaminck played chess. One day they all came into rue Vignon disguised as workmen. With their hats in hand they called out, "Boss, we've come for our pay."[27]

Of necessity the Kahnweiler Gallery became their meeting place, since they did not exhibit their paintings elsewhere or submit them to the Salons. The only place in Paris where their work could be seen was also the most pleasant gathering point. Many young artists who did not belong to this group would often drop in, before or after visiting Clovis Sagot.[28]

At the end of the day, when it came time to close, Kahnweiler would pull down the metal shutter and they would continue the conversation while strolling to his house. Often at home he would make hasty notes, writing sentences, words, impressions of Braque or Picasso or any of the others. These were simple notes to assist his memory, but would become notes for history.

When the artists went out as a group, they could head in two different directions: Montmartre to the north, or Montparnasse, with its large cafés, to the south. Each person had his favorite. The poets went with Paul Fort to the Closerie des Lilas; Max Jacob's friends to La Rotonde; the German artists to the Dôme; the Italians to the Petit Napolitain with Amedeo Modigliani, whose work had just appeared at the Indépendants. Often they would leave the cafés and continue farther on the boulevard

Raspail, to the offices of the review *Les Soirées de Paris*, where everybody from the avant-garde gathered, even Kahnweiler at times.

The most obtuse detractors of modern art would see this scene as the epitome of everything decadent. The right-wing critic Camille Mauclair found fodder to fuel his tirades of hatred. According to him it was a meeting of the cults of alcohol, cocaine, and the lively arts. It was a cesspool of the undesirables and the deranged who disgusted the whole of Paris and called out for a police roundup.[29] Adolphe Basler, who assiduously frequented these places, believed that if painting was the only universal language, then the Café du Dôme was a true Society of Nations, and for proof he mentioned the "expressionists from Smolensk, who came much later, followed by the dadaists from Moldo-Valachia [Rumania], the constructivists from Leningrad, the neo-romantics from Baluchistan, who were all there, and not just to drink vermouth-cassis."[30]

Still, in 1909, Montparnasse as yet took second place to Montmartre, and the dealer and his friends would usually go uphill to the Lapin Agile on rue des Saules, a cabaret that became their hangout. The low-ceilinged room was crammed with moldings of statues, paintings, and drawings, so the artists did not feel out of place. Everyone went there at night: Picasso and Pierre Mac Orlan, Paul Fort and Francis Carco, Max Jacob and André Salmon, the painter Poulbot and Jules Romains.

For a long time the place had been known as the Cabaret des Assassins, but when the caricaturist André Gill painted the sign for it (a rabbit jumping into a frying pan), the old customers renamed it Le Lapin à Gill (Gill's Rabbit), a pun on "Là peint A. Gill" (there painted A. Gill). It had been the favorite haunt of the painters Pissarro and Jean-Louis Forain, and playwright Georges Courteline. At the beginning of the century a new owner, Frédéric Gérard, gave it a second lease on life. Every artist and writer was asked to draw or write in the house's "guest book," a true "book of hours" of the cabaret. The owner, in picturesque garb, usually ended up looking like a peasant from the Abruzzi. He was reputed to be the first of the "Picasso idolizers" because on his wall there was a harlequin by Picasso whose costume of multicolored lozenges formed cubes. He often claimed it was the first major cubist work, adding, "I've turned down many offers for it by Americans."[31]

Late at night, leaving this whitewashed building with green shutters, high atop the Butte Montmartre, Kahnweiler and his friends strolled down the quiet empty streets, pausing for a moment of silence before the panorama. Paris was spread out at their feet, figuratively as well as literally, since they never had any doubts that they would triumph.

Often on Friday evenings Picasso took everyone to the Médrano

Circus, their favorite show. They ended the evenings backstage at a bar, gossiping with Grock and Antonet, the clowns who invented the costumes.[32] But whether at the Médrano Circus, or the Hermitage Café in Pigalle, the Lapin Agile or La Rotonde, on nights out in Montmartre or Montparnasse, Kahnweiler went along out of a sense of obligation. He loathed the noisy, smoke-filled nightclubs and cabarets, and trailed along only to please his friends and not to appear a stick-in-the-mud. Had it been up to him they would have attended more bourgeois entertainment; he would have taken them all to the theater or to concerts.

According to him, this world of cafés favored the development of two types of people: the very best and the very worst. The worst were the parasites who manufactured false reputations by linking their fates with the destinies of budding geniuses, and they used the creative energy of their friends to mask their own obvious lack of talent.

One whom Kahnweiler thought was archetypal of this sort was named Princet. In civilian life he was an insurance actuary, a specialist with numbers and statistics and probability as applied to insurance. Princet was to become famous for befriending the artists of the rue Vignon gallery, both as a mathematician and as an art lover. It was a small jump to his becoming "the mathematician of cubism." The rumor mill of Montmartre and Montparnasse credited this insurance man with a disproportionate influence on the so-called geometric minds of these artists, and for years articles and books would mention him as the mathematics professor of the cubists. When careless art historians repeated this falsehood, Kahnweiler would strongly denounce the charade, reminding them that men such as Juan Gris did not need math lessons, and that Princet was just a bistro acquaintance.[33]

The very best, for Kahnweiler, was a writer such as Alfred Jarry, who had passed away two years before. The creator of Père Ubu held an important place in what Kahnweiler used to call "our family folklore." He and Lucie quoted from Jarry's plays without even being aware of it.[34] Also among the best were poets of the stature of Max Jacob, whom Kahnweiler liked more than he admired. He felt great compassion for the misery in which Jacob lived and the total poverty which made the studios of the Bateau-Lavoir seem acceptable to him. When Jacob was in his element among poets and artists, he was a one-man celebration of ideas, witticisms, serious and humorous thought. Above all he wrote poetic satires, wearing a top hat, a dicky, and a frock coat. This was his uniform. Kahnweiler adored the man, but dreaded what he would say or write. Jacob's lack of psychological acumen was constantly leading him into trouble.

Kahnweiler wondered if there was a perverse streak in the poet that drove him to sow seeds of discord among his friends, so extreme was his need to provoke.[35]

Max Jacob was born in Brittany, of Jewish stock, and was a homosexual by inclination and defiance. He respected Kahnweiler for being one of the few individuals in the group to have both feet firmly planted on the ground and for being traditionally cultured but also continuing to evolve. He felt that Kahnweiler knew where he was going and what he was searching for in life. The dealer made a strong impression, one of confidence, harmony, serenity, and balance. Max Jacob had faith in him and knew that their friendship, though based on irony, was solid. One day in September he wrote, "Your being Jewish makes it appropriate for me to send you my wishes for the New Year (Autumn Solstice, my friend)."[36]

The year 1909 marked as important a turning point for Max Jacob as it did for Daniel-Henry Kahnweiler. One morning the art dealer paid the poet a visit to discuss ideas for a publishing venture and found him transfigured, unrecognizable. The day before, something had happened that in one stroke had wiped away his past life.

After a day of reading and research at the Bibliothèque Nationale, Max Jacob had returned home and put on his slippers, when suddenly . . . Kahnweiler listened openmouthed as his friend told him of the shock he had experienced:

> . . . I cried out. There before me made manifest was Christ on the wall. I fell on my knees and suddenly my eyes filled with tears. An overwhelming sense of well-being descended on me. I remained very still without understanding what was happening. In one minute I had lived for a century. It seemed that everything was revealed to me. At that instant I had the idea that I had only been an animal, and I was becoming a man. . . . Also instantly, when my eyes met the ineffable Being, I felt divested of my human flesh and only two words filled me: death, birth. The figure on my wall was a person of a grace beyond human conception. He stood still in a countryside . . . a landscape that I had drawn a month earlier, depicting the edge of a canal. From the sublime moment and after the sacred image had vanished, I heard in my ears a crowd of voices and sharp words, very clear, very meaningful, which held me awake the whole evening and the whole night without my feeling any other need than for solitude. . . . I remained kneeling in front of the large red curtain above my bed, on which the divine Image had appeared. I felt transported, I felt inside my head the unfurling of a sequence of uninterrupted forms, colors, and scenes which I did not understand and which much later were revealed to me as prophetic.[37]

Kahnweiler was shaken by the transformation in his friend, feeling even more the contradictions in his life as a man of the world of Montmartre who was also in flight from the world, a very poor man with upper-class habits. From now on the brilliant buffoon was also a mystic. This was not a passing incident, nor another string added to his bow, nor a means of renewing his poetic inspiration. Kahnweiler understood that he had sincerely undergone a great internal shock. This vision caused Jacob's conversion to Catholicism and later his retreat to the monastery of St. Benoît-sur-Loire.

Kahnweiler presented him with his current projects: "I would like to publish books illustrated by my artists. The first will be Apollinaire's *L'Enchanteur pourrissant* [The Decaying Wizard]. Have you got a book for me?"[38]

Established as an art dealer, he now ventured into publishing. The idea of bringing a poet and an artist together was not a new one. Since Mallarmé, this sort of joint effort had created a special genre.[39] Vollard had published a series of illustrated books, but Kahnweiler was different from his predecessors in that he only published new texts by unknown authors.[40] He eliminated the old notion of republishing the classics, so that he was in a sense a true literary editor who set out to discover the new rather than accept the known. This type of book, printed on the finest paper in a limited edition, became an art object in itself. Through his gallery Kahnweiler had at his disposal a whole range of artists, and he was familiar enough with poets of undeniable talent to be able to launch this venture.

The artists were there, the poets also—why shouldn't they meet over a book instead of at a bar? This way of thinking was typical of Kahnweiler. He believed that he was the best man to carry out such a project because of his professional involvement with art and his love of poetry. Once the project was under way, he asked each of his artists to illustrate a book. The publishing firm was located in the gallery and was called Editions Kahnweiler.

He was completely involved with each work, extremely careful about the choice of cover, format, paper, and especially the typography—not to mention the text and the illustrations. His preoccupation with technical details contrasted strangely with his easygoing indifference in matters of hanging and framing his paintings. The logo of the publishing company was invented by Apollinaire, but Derain made the actual drawing of the insignia—"HK," the two letters welded together. Kahnweiler would laughingly say, "These are the only two typographical flaws a well-printed book could bear."

The first title published by Editions Kahnweiler in 1909, *L'Enchant-eur pourrissant*, was also Guillaume Apollinaire's first published book. It was illustrated with thirty-two woodcuts by André Derain, the eighty-four pages were printed by Birault in an 8-by-11-inch format, and it was printed on Imperial Japan paper in an edition of 106 numbered copies.

The most striking aspect of the book was the sobriety and simplicity of design, which corresponded exactly with Kahnweiler's taste. The illustrations were not captioned, which did not make them easy to find. This was a deliberate choice so as not to introduce into the composition of the page an outside element that would be disruptive. The pages were also not numbered, which was an oversight. By the time Kahnweiler and Apollinaire noticed, it was too late; but this omission made the page of text balance the page of illustrations without captions, and it became the rule for future books.[41]

The book did not go unnoticed: the art journals all mentioned it, the magazines wrote about it, and it was even reviewed in some newspapers. In contrast to Kahnweiler's principles about the selling of paintings, as an editor he was eager and energetic about seeking publicity. He went about promoting the text and illustrations because his books were sold by subscription, and he considered it naive to think that he could sell out an edition by relying solely on word of mouth. But publishing did not slow down his other activities, for he was in the process of consolidating his working relationships with one particular artist and two Russian collectors.

Picasso had become less suspicious of him. It was not complete confidence, yet it was no longer outright distrust. They were in that intermediary stage when both parties were full of goodwill and ready to take the next step toward becoming friends and partners. Picasso always wanted to sell, but he wondered if Kahnweiler would always have the means to buy.

For Picasso to engage himself completely he had to be convinced that the dealer could offer certain financial support, as well as defend his work verbally and in print. Money was the key issue to be resolved.[42] For two years Picasso had been selling Kahnweiler a number of works, but he had also sold a great deal directly to collectors, such as the Steins. He remained wary, keeping in mind that Vollard and Weill had turned down his paintings long before *Les Demoiselles d'Avignon;* that Sagot was not a dealer of any scope; and that he had to sever relations with his very first dealer, a friend from Barcelona named Pedro Mañach, who was devoted and enthusiastic, with conviction and real business sense, but whose inefficiency and continuous presence in his studio were becoming oppressive.[43] Picasso did not want to rely on anyone, and Kahnweiler, who had keen psychological insight, did everything possible to respect his obsession with being independent while assuring him of complete moral and financial support. Kahnweiler knew that once he had him convinced, he would win.

They saw each other every day. Picasso was not very talkative, preferring to listen, but his reserve never meant acquiescence. He disliked comments and conjectures about or interpretations of his work. He left theories to critics, and to a painter who asked him about his work, he dryly replied, "Do not disturb the pilot."[44]

Kahnweiler was one of the few people with whom Picasso enjoyed conversing, having an exchange, not of confidences but of ideas. They did not agree in their appreciation of the masters, but they did agree about the art market. "In order for paintings to be sold at high prices, they must first have been sold very cheaply," Picasso asserted.[45]

Kahnweiler could only agree to this on condition that the artist always promptly received his share. He was always conscientious about payment in their relationship, remembering one of Max Jacob's anecdotes, which was humorous but more informative than it first appeared. Two or three years earlier the poet had brought a wealthy businessman to his studio on rue Ravignan to have him purchase a Picasso. The collector asked the painter the price of one of his drawings. "Fifty francs," was the reply. It was a reasonable price at a time when the artist could only afford to pay one franc for a complete meal. Glancing around the studio at all the drawings pinned to the walls or piled on the table, the collector made some rapid mental calculations and said, "But really, you are rich!"

This statement was far from true to the extent that Picasso sold very little for lack of collectors, but it was not entirely false either. From this apparent contradiction Kahnweiler drew a lesson in business.[46]

By the end of 1909 Picasso drew closer to Kahnweiler, while Matisse signed a three-year contract with the Bernheim-Jeune Gallery. During the same period two collectors began forsaking the impressionist and post-impressionist galleries to frequent rue Vignon.

They were both Russians, named Sergei Shchukin and Ivan Morozov, but they were not at all alike. They had different tastes, temperaments, and preferences. It was so unusual to have collectors from Russia in Paris that they rapidly became well known. Along with Hermann Rupf and Roger Dutilleul they would constitute the core of faithful collectors that would enable Kahnweiler, his gallery, and his artists to survive.

Sergei Ivanovich Shchukin was fifty-five, a wealthy broker who participated in the artistic and intellectual life of Moscow. The receptions and balls he gave were very popular, especially since they were held in his home, the Troubetskoi Palace. Worldly and refined, his wealth had not gone to his head, in contrast to his wife, who was extremely fond of luxury. He remained austere in his elegance, especially in comparison to the extravagant people surrounding him. His drawing rooms were open to the nobility as well as the bourgeoisie.[47]

His collection began with the purchase of Monet's *Les Lilas au soleil* from Durand-Ruel, the first impressionist painting to enter Russia.[48] Soon he owned numerous others by Pissarro and Gauguin, Cézanne and Sisley; and then came the nabis and the fauves. His Matisses (among the most important were *La Danse* and *La Musique*) conferred an unparalleled notoriety upon him in Moscow. Shchukin gladly showed his collection. He preferred special exhibits, but one day a week he allowed a public viewing of his collection. By the public he did not mean the man on the street, but friends of friends and relations. Nevertheless this included many young Russian artists who thus had direct access to the modern art of the West.

Between business and pleasure trips, Shchukin usually spent four months a year in western Europe. He never missed a chance to visit the galleries in Paris as well as the Egyptian department of the Louvre. Matisse knew him intimately. He had a particular way of choosing paintings. Stopping in front of a still life in Matisse's studio he would say, "I'll buy that one, but first I have to live with it for a few days and if I can still tolerate it and am still interested, then I'll keep it."[49] No doubt the work easily passed the test, since a little later he asked Matisse to decorate his palace in Moscow.

Starting in 1909 he bought Picassos and Derains from the gallery on rue Vignon, amassing an impressive collection even by French standards. Strangely enough, for him Picasso was cubism and would always remain so. He even purchased several at a time, averaging about ten a year. Braque, however, was an "imitator."[50] He owned only one of the five versions of *Chateau de La Roche-Guyon* (1909), and it was the single cubist painting by Braque in a Russian collection. Kahnweiler was never able to persuade him in this matter.

Ivan Alexandrovich Morozov was younger (thirty-eight in 1909), more corpulent, stronger, and more willful. But his selection was less daring. He was an industrialist whose cotton mills employed fifteen thousand people. His parents were eminent members of the Russian upper bourgeoisie, and they had decided to send him to the Polytechnic

Institute in Zurich. There his taste became westernized. In his travels he also began frequenting galleries, notably Vollard, Durand-Ruel, and Bernheim-Jeune, which had given him a direction. He began his collection with the impressionists. He was not influenced by Shchukin; rather, he wanted to continue the collection started by his brother Mikhail, who had died early in 1904. When he wanted his palace redecorated he did not turn to Matisse but to Bonnard and Vuillard.

Yet Shchukin and he were good friends. He was introduced to Matisse and Picasso by Shchukin. From Picasso he mainly bought paintings from the blue and rose periods. Matisse, who had observed these two collectors like an entomologist, believed that the differences between them could be defined by their ways of approaching Vollard. Both admired the works of Cézanne, but they did not buy them in the same manner.

"I want a good Cézanne," Shchukin would say.

Morozov wanted to choose for himself. "I want to see every Cézanne that you have for sale."[51]

With Kahnweiler, Shchukin and Morozov usually made their purchases by looking at a small black-and-white photograph. It was usually accompanied by a letter in which the dealer was careful not to persuade. He was not a chatty man but neither did he hide his opinion: "It's an important painting" or "a first-rate work" was how he expressed it; the price was usually stated with finality. But in fact he must have been flexible, since in the telegrams answering him both Shchukin and Morozov tried to bargain him down. Kahnweiler's telegrams closing the sale usually indicated that he made concessions without giving in completely. Even in his shorthand style he could not resist adding the phrase "just to please you" or "to make you happy."[52]

Naturally Shchukin and Morozov were not Kahnweiler's only faithful disciples from abroad. In 1910 a Czech named Vincenz Kramar became one of them.

Kramar quickly became a regular member of the group. He was an art historian specializing in the Gothic art of his country and unique in his devotion to modern art, which he discussed using the language of art history. Kahnweiler considered him the only art historian and true collector among the early devotees of cubism. The others were either merchants (Rupf), industrialists (Shchukin, Morozov), or writers (Uhde). Kramar enjoyed the prestige of having studied art history at the University of Vienna. Kahnweiler was impressed that his enthusiasm for modern art was as great as his research into the Gothic churches of Bohemia.

During his trips to Paris, which he made often between 1910 and 1914, he would bring photographs of contemporary works by Czech artists to show Kahnweiler.[53]

Every time a new painting by Picasso would come to the gallery, Kahnweiler would telegraph Prague and Kramar would hop on the first train to Paris. No sooner had the train pulled into the Gare de l'Est than he would visit rue Vignon—often arriving so early that he found the iron shutters still down. He would leave there only to visit artists' studios. Kramar, who would become the director of the National Galleries of Prague after World War I, kept a precious memento all his life: a dried-up apple, shriveled and blackened, wrapped in tissue, that Picasso had given him after using it as a model for a still life.[54]

Rupf, Uhde, Shchukin, Morozov, Kramar—these foreign collectors played an important role in the development of the new Kahnweiler Gallery. There were many others, of course, but they were primarily associated with the artistic and literary life of Paris. Gertrude Stein and her brother Leo were a famous pair. When they parted ways, the name "Gertrude" was alone enough for everyone to recognize who it was.

Stein was born in Pennsylvania, ten years before Kahnweiler. Her parents had settled in California, where her father headed the trolley company of San Francisco. They had sent her to Europe very early. After having completed medical school, she studied psychology and was initiated into automatic writing. In 1902 she and her brother decided to settle in Europe, and finally came to rest on rue de Fleurus when she was thirty years old.

After her meeting with Picasso in 1905 at the Bateau-Lavoir, she would begin to assemble an important collection of impressionist, fauve, and cubist works. 1907 was a milestone for her, since that was the year she met Alice B. Toklas, who would remain with her the rest of her life. Finding this new presence an unbearable intrusion, Leo Stein departed, taking everything with him except for the Picassos, which he disliked.

Gertrude was oddly dressed and solidly built, with a massive head, short hair, strong features, and no traces of femininity. This lesbian writer lived out her choices. She did not write, she worked at the process of writing the way a storyteller with a physical sense of speaking would. She wanted to renew the concept of literature. The art dealer, who got to know her as a familiar presence in Picasso's circle, was fascinated by her peremptory way of speaking, her lack of humor, and her dogmatism.[55]

He would soon become a regular at her receptions and dinners at rue de Fleurus, a famous nerve center for the international avant-garde in

Paris. Kahnweiler was one of the few to fully appreciate the qualities of Alice B. Toklas, despite her discreet self-effacing ways. She was overshadowed by the personality and talk of her companion, whose writings she would type out each day.[56]

Gertrude Stein was not only at the center of a storm of often contradictory and antagonistic forces, difficult individuals and temperaments; she was also the intellectual ambassador from the Bateau-Lavoir and rue Vignon to the New World. She did not have to cross the Atlantic; her home had become an obligatory stopover for Americans in Europe.

During the annual opening of the Salon des Indépendants in 1910, which Kahnweiler attended as a dealer, there was an enormous outcry against a large painting entitled *Nudes in the Forest* by Fernand Léger. Kahnweiler was immediately excited. But the critics had tried to dismiss it by giving it a pejorative name: "It is tubism!"

Again it was Louis Vauxcelles taking aim, and to join the attack he would create a neologism which would not catch on, much to his disappointment. For the ordinary person Léger was the artist who painted trees as if they were stovepipes and people as if they were cylinders with round heads. Vauxcelles's attack against him had the contrary effect.

"You understand," Picasso explained to Kahnweiler, "here's a guy who is showing something new since they had to invent a new name to differentiate him from us. It proves that he is doing something different."[57]

Not another word was needed for the dealer to visit Léger in his studio. There was no question of buying anything or even drawing up a contract; it was a simple visit. Kahnweiler was struck by the personality of the artist from Normandy. He was tall, freckled, and seemed the ideal of a northerner. Léger, only three years older than Kahnweiler, had studied architecture at Caen before coming to Paris, where he worked as a draftsman in an architect's office and then in a photographer's studio. He failed the admissions examinations to the Ecole des Beaux-Arts, and instead studied at different private academies. He remained under the influence of the impressionists until 1907 when he was overwhelmed by the great retrospective of Cézanne's work at the Salon d'Automne. (He had never seen *Les Demoiselles d'Avignon.*) A few years earlier he had been influenced by another exhibition of Cézanne's work in the same location. He felt that everything he did came from Cézanne: mass, form, outline, and composition. It had a salutary effect on the future of his work: he went home and destroyed the major portion of his old paintings. The *Nudes in the Forest,* whose syncopated rhythms and extreme originality had made such an impression on Kahnweiler, showed that he had eliminated the former impressionist influence. He claimed to be obsessed by one idea: the abstraction of the human body. Anyone who could speak in such terms and create such a painting was without a doubt a true artist.

Léger was not a member of Kahnweiler's circle, and it was too soon to introduce him. At that time he was experimenting with colors, as was Robert Delaunay, who had brought him along with Apollinaire and Max Jacob to the gallery on rue Vignon. Léger had the same reaction to cubism as Delaunay: "These guys paint on cobwebs."[58] Kahnweiler smiled, knowing the conversation had just started.

1910 was filled with promising new people. In addition to Léger, Kahnweiler had just met an amazing Spaniard, a friend of Picasso's. His name was Manuel Martinez Hugué, but everyone knew him as Manolo the sculptor. He was the son of a general whom he had not seen since his adolescence in Barcelona. Once in Paris, he seemed to reside permanently at the Café Vachette among the friends of Papadiamantópoulos, a symbolist poet better known under the pseudonym of Jean Moréas. Manolo led a poverty-stricken existence which he had a gift for transforming into a picaresque adventure through his use of language.[59] He was enthusiastic about bullfighting, spoke with a strong Catalan accent, and was an indefatigable conversationalist, a colorful and sympathetic storyteller who was to give his friend Kahnweiler food for thought in the years ahead.

The dealer had started buying a few pieces of Manolo's sculpture to assist him, but these transactions soon gave him a real insight into the psychological makeup of the artist. For a long time he fought for him, claiming that he had not received the recognition he deserved and which would be given him in the future. The difficulty arose from the fact that Manolo was better known than his sculpture. He was the colorful character who would order a sumptuous meal in the best restaurant and at the end of it would ask the maître d'hôtel for "the check and the police, please." This behavior obscured the artist in him. From the first, Kahnweiler had seen him as a sculptor of Mediterranean sensibility, with freshness and classical clarity which owed nothing in their development to his cubist friends. He was a vigorous artist, in touch with nature. Manolo was shrewd and intelligent behind the mask of a clown, but he was essentially a peasant. He had neither the detachment nor the perspective that would enable him to appreciate cubism without understanding it. Despite their numerous conversations and his patient explanations,

Kahnweiler could not overcome his skepticism. He knew that he had failed when Manolo questioned Picasso about the figures in his cubist canvases: "But how would you feel if your parents waited for you at the train station in Barcelona with faces like that?"[60]

Everyone burst out laughing and Picasso took it good-naturedly, but Kahnweiler was floored. He may have shrugged his shoulders at the man's naiveté, but he wondered how such a subtle artist, so close to his friends' work in many ways, could confuse the subject and the significance of the work. Henceforth he believed that in spite of the quality of his work, Manolo was incapable of making valid judgments on modern painting because he was intellectually too limited. Although this was a patronizing and elitist attitude, Kahnweiler did not fail to inform Manolo of this, despite their friendship, or rather for the sake of their friendship and the respect he had for him.[61]

Kahnweiler had trouble answering Manolo's comments because he had not reached the stage where he would formulate his own ideas about art. Decades later he could accept that in a literal interpretation certain women's heads by Picasso, in which one eye is seen in profile and the other frontally, could be said to appear monstrous. But everything changes when the essential is understood. The subject is not actual women, but that which is signified, a composition of elements that the artist uses to communicate everything he understands about and feels toward women.[62]

Kahnweiler's disappointment recalls that of Léger much later when he had installed *The Construction Workers* on the walls of the cafeteria of the Renault factory, and sitting down to a meal with the workers he overheard one of them comment, "Look at them, those guys could never do a lick of work with hands like that."[63]

Not exactly disappointments but surprises of another sort awaited Kahnweiler in his next publishing venture. The second volume was under way in the face of critical opposition that said he published good poets "illustrated by failures and artists who made pastiches that the Moreau firm then unloaded at the Salon d'Automne and the Salon des Indépendants."[64] His faith was as firm in painting as in poetry, and it was never shaken by the assault of mere scribblers. He reread Apollinaire's verses to him:

> *You, Henry, were the first to publish me;*
> *I must remember that in singing your praises.*

May you be celebrated in the paintings and verses
Of the triple étage *where dwell the witches three!*[65]

Everything was said in these lines by Apollinaire, who was a great poet, but perhaps not so great a friend, as later events would bear out.

The second book published by Editions Kahnweiler was a much-anticipated work by Max Jacob, who had written his first literary work, *Saint Matorel,* during the month of April. Kahnweiler had thought of Derain for the illustrations, which should not have posed any problems. But the artist refused in his fashion—politely, circumspectly, and with finality: "It's impossible for me to do anything for the manuscript. It's a wonderful work which leaves no room for me, and besides, much as I may admire it, my preoccupations which form the subject of my work are completely absent from this book (which accounts for its beauty in my estimation)."[66]

On reading Derain's long letter of explanation Max Jacob was disappointed but did not give up hope. If Derain was put off by reading a realistic part of the text, then let him illustrate the other parts. If he was afraid that such a good work would be read by only fifty people, let him be reassured to the contrary.[67] But the artist's refusal was final, and it took two months before Kahnweiler was inspired to ask Picasso, who had never illustrated a book before. At the height of summer at Cadaqués, Spain, he agreed to do four engravings. Max Jacob was surprised and overjoyed.

In Quimper, Brittany, poor Max dreamed grandiose dreams. Kahnweiler had asked him to write a brief introduction to solicit potential subscribers, as well as a brief biography. Max sent it to him, but it was not usable:

Born on Brittany's shore, M. Max Jacob was a sailor for five years, making voyages to Australia and the Far East. Later he lived the adventurous life of those who have an undeniable vocation for the arts. From Brittany and the ocean M. Jacob has acquired a sense of mystery and an unshakable faith in the supernatural and the divine. Life in Paris has given him a sense of irony while his sailor's heart remains fervent; and frequenting the highest society has refined the soul of this poet. Enlightened by the exquisitely civilized capital, this rare intellect . . .[68]

The sketch was delightful but unpublishable, as his readers might take it literally. Kahnweiler knew the reality of his life and would never forget his first visit to his quarters on rue Ravignan, seeing the bedsprings resting on four bricks, the torn wallpaper. He would retain this mental image as the epitome of the poverty and freedom of spirit of that dionysiac period.[69]

In September 1910 Kahnweiler, who often spent time in Picasso's studio, was asked by the painter to pose for him. After Ambroise Vollard and Wilhelm Uhde, whom he had painted five months earlier, Picasso decided it was time to take on his dealer, which did not displease Kahnweiler. Both vanity and tradition demanded that the dealer's portrait be painted by the artist he represented. It was the best illustration of their partnership for posterity. Vollard and Cézanne, Durand-Ruel and Renoir had understood this, and soon Léopold Zborowski and Modigliani, Alfred Flechtheim and Otto Dix would follow their lead. Besides, Kahnweiler was eager to compensate for the frightening portrait of him painted by van Dongen, all mustache and hair and narrow glance, a two-toned painting in jet black and brilliant red that he hung on the wall of his dining room.

Picasso made him pose twenty or thirty times. Kahnweiler's head dominated the canvas, which was painted without any preliminary sketches. The portrait was more difficult and complex to read than those of Vollard and Uhde, and could easily hold the key to the relationship between dealer and artist. Later people claimed it was inspired by *The Librarian* (1565) by Archimboldo.[70] The resemblance to life is less evident but there is a group of signs in the composition.[71] Reality pierces the space fragmented into geometric planes, as if inextricably molded: at the top there is a raised eyebrow, in the middle a fold of clothing, and at the bottom a resting hand, just a few barely discernible details that balance the painting. If it does not appear lifelike, it is probably a question of the period in which it was painted and its visual convention. A half century later Kahnweiler was stopped by a stranger in the Louvre who asked, "Excuse me, sir, did I see a portrait of you by Picasso? Could I be mistaken?"[72] Perhaps he was not referring to a pencil sketch executed in 1957, but to the famous cubist painting itself. Kahnweiler purchased the painting for his private collection. It was later confiscated as enemy goods during World War I and auctioned off when Kahnweiler did not have the means to buy it, then sold for the sum of two thousand francs by the Swedish painter Isaac Grunewald. It ended up in the American collection of Mrs. Charles Goodspeed, who willed it to the Art Institute of Chicago.[73]

* * *

By the end of 1910 Kahnweiler could see the direction his gallery would take, the artists he would represent, the collectors who were his clients. He could determine the prices that would cover his expenses at the gallery as well as allow him to pay the artists a fair share that would enable them to live modestly. He felt that it was the moment to act on his policy of increasing his presence abroad, which took priority over the French market. This was evident by the proportion of Swiss, German, American, and Slavic collectors among his clients.

The catalyst was the great exhibit organized by Roger Fry at the Grafton Galleries in London, under the heading "Manet and the Post-Impressionists." On request Kahnweiler sent eight paintings, three Derains and five Vlamincks. Fry's achievement was not only important for the way in which it influenced the subsequent evolution of English art, but also for the way it affected the taste and direction of the major collectors, such as Samuel Courtauld, an industrialist and art patron, who became aware of late-nineteenth-century French painting through this exhibit.

The paintings Kahnweiler first sent abroad were usually left on consignment. Unlike most of his colleagues, however, he refused to reciprocate in this matter, which soon became general knowledge. Later when he worked with the Brussels dealer van Hecke, Kahnweiler wrote a clear statement of policy:

> I make it an absolute principle to exhibit in the gallery only paintings that we own by artists we represent exclusively. I believe that today exhibitions carry little weight, have little effect in general, which is due to the fact that galleries do not have such a policy. . . . Regular galleries should only show their own artists. That is what I have always done.[74]

Alongside England, he primarily developed his dealings abroad in Germany and the United States. He would quickly find colleagues sympathetic to him across the Rhine. The reaction to modern art, that is to say French art of the Paris school, can be determined by the early articles of Paul Westheim and Herwarth Walden, who championed these works in newspapers and reviews.

Walden was a strong personality who had launched his periodical *Der Sturm* in 1910 and soon became an important associate. Located in the university section of Berlin, *Der Sturm* would become a permanent fixture of the European avant-garde. Walden was open to the incursions of every new movement, which meant that he was as eager to send German artists to shows abroad as he was to exhibit foreign artists in his own gallery. Kahnweiler reproached him not for his intellectual independence but for spreading himself too thin. Still, their intellectual affinity knew no limit until World War I and the resurgence of nationalism.

The United States, which had just opened as a new market, presented another problem altogether, not so much in the criteria for selecting artists as in the appreciation of art. Kahnweiler's problem was to educate the collectors' taste to accept cubism. The great private collections had values in common, which seemed almost immutable. They usually showed a concern for representational exactness, the illustrative and anecdotal. This sensibility was worlds apart even from the rules of baroque art, which was filled with mythological subjects and religious scenes. Portraits and landscapes were favored over nudes. The absence of a past in the New World could be seen in the attraction to the realistic depictions of historical events. These collections were formed according to social and didactic motives. The collector, in collaboration with the artists of his country, attempted to make a cultural statement by forming a foundation or a museum bearing the collector's name. The French, on the other hand, were more individualistic.[75]

Frequenting Gertrude Stein's salon was not enough to introduce American visitors to contemporary art. Only a handful among them was capable of understanding it. These were the most informed, the most intellectual, the most intuitive, who had an innate sense of the quality and the lasting aspect of art. If any of these—such as John Quinn and Chester Dale in New York, the Cone sisters of Baltimore, John Spaulding of Boston, Samuel A. Lewisohn and Albert C. Barnes—decided to open up his collection to include modern art, he might even influence museum curators to look at it. It was a possibility based on several factors: the lure of the new, the snobbish appeal of French art, and last but not least, the evolution of taste. The intellectual and artistic milieu that determined the value of an artist's work, even more so than the critic, had to be the mediator in this undertaking.

In 1910, from the American point of view, Paris was the place to be. That was where the fate of modern art was being determined, and that was where they wanted to buy. When the pendulum was finally given a push, the Paris art dealers, rejoicing in their success, never thought about the consequences—the equally strong return swing. When Americans became involved in the market for cubist paintings, prices quickly started rising in Europe, creating happy results but also causing a widespread confusion for which the dealers were unprepared.[76]

It was the fall of 1911 and the start of the new season on rue Vignon. The publication of *Saint Matorel* by Max Jacob had not produced the hoped-for commercial results, although it was widely reviewed in the press.

Kahnweiler had not expected anything from the Salon des Indépendants the previous April, nor was he disappointed. One visit there was sufficient to confirm his previous opinion of Léger. Not for a second did he regret the fact that the artists he represented were not exhibited there.

He had high hopes for the vacations of Picasso and Braque, who had the habit of going off to work together. So closely did they work that it was often impossible to ascribe new developments to one or the other—not paintings, of course, but ideas, concepts, and inventions. They would meet in Céret in the eastern Pyrénées, twenty miles outside of Perpignan. It was a strange fate for such a little town to suddenly find itself invaded by people carrying palettes and brushes. After these denizens of Montmartre, other painters would spend summers there. One day a collector would buy a summer house there, and inevitably Céret would have its own small museum of modern art. Unwittingly, Céret would become known internationally as the subject of countless paintings shown all over the world.

Picasso and Braque worked together every day, and the discoveries of the one benefited the other. That was the reason Kahnweiler always refused to ascribe to one or the other the first introduction of a new element in the work. "It proves nothing," he would repeat.[77] By contrast he was very formal in affirming the fact that, at the height of their work in 1911, both were conscious of the classic elements in their painting: strong draftsmanship, economy in their use of colors, and the composition dominating all other aspects of the canvas.[78] Their paintings increased in complexity, both in the details and in the composition of the whole.

Braque always recalled this period with nostalgia, feeling strongly that those days and nights at Céret were a rare experience. He and Picasso told each other things that no one else would ever speak of and that no one else would ever understand. That was how he had experienced the time spent in the mountains.[79] In Céret they were on another planet, in their own world. Kahnweiler, who received their letters in Paris, was the only person who knew from day to day the exact nature of the transformation of their work.

During this period, cubism was still under attack in Paris. The controversy was fueled by preparations for the Salon d'Automne. Kahnweiler's artists would not exhibit their works in it, but there were paintings by Albert Gleizes, Jean Metzinger, Léger, and Henri Le Fauconnier which bore the brunt of it for everyone else. Régis Gignoux's article, from the September 24 issue of *Le Figaro*, is typical of the critics' reaction:

> We tried to take it seriously because someday a great artist could come along and use their method without being enslaved by it. But the cubists have to explain their pretensions more clearly, otherwise we will assume that spatial geometry is better suited for their speculations, or that their mathematical distribution of colors is more useful and better suited to industry.

But worse was to follow—more vindictive, outraged, and blatantly meaner in tone. The critic for *Paris-Midi* immediately came to the point:

> The cubists are a bunch of jokers, followers of Picasso, who was a talented colorist and now an equally talented imposter. He composes nudes geometrically, pyramidally, rhomboidically. It's frighteningly ugly and of a ridiculous pretentiousness. The cubists reduce the human figure to a mass, a parallelepiped cube. They claim to be reacting against Matisse's orgy of colors. The innovators are Le Fauconnier, Metzinger, Gleizes, and Léger. The latter replaced the cube with tubes and he is a tubist. His model is the iron pipe, so that it's not painting, it's plumbing. They rightly belong in the Salon d'Automne; laughter is healthy.

Apollinaire's defense was of little use against these attacks. Landscapes? "They look like games of solitaire." Still lifes? "You could take them for a pile of stones." Portraits? "Rhomboidical."[80] This word again, when so few readers of the daily papers knew what it meant. When critics used the term, they felt they had said it all. The word took on a life of its own, as a convenient mocking designation of everything indefinable about cubism.

The last word on the subject was given by Gabriel Mourey, who reviewed the Salon in *Le Journal* of September 30:

> I must admit, I do not believe that cubism has a future . . . and even if it did it would not prevent Raphael, Titian, Holbein, Velázquez, Watteau and Ingres, Delacroix and Puvis de Chavannes from being great masters. I am tempted to say that cubism has had its moment, it's the swan song of impotent pretensions and self-satisfied ignorance.

Kahnweiler read these diatribes and merely shrugged his shoulders. It did not matter that cubist paintings were compared to children's building blocks or their parents' jigsaw puzzles. With the exception of Léger, he did not like the artists under attack at the Salon d'Automne. He considered them imitators, without a spark of originality. He was appalled that these were the artists thought to be representative of cubism, as he did not know them. It was the risk he had run when he had decided that the artists of rue Vignon would not submit any work for exhibition in the Salons. This bad publicity, indirectly aimed at them, was the price they paid for being absent.

Still, Kahnweiler's album of press clippings about the gallery and its artists had increased in volume. The notices had become longer, better informed, and international: the *Volkstimme* of Frankfurt, the *Berliner Morgenpost*, *La Gazetta del Popola* in Turin, *Le Journal* of Brussels. This recognition abroad was encouraging to him, since it had always been his goal, even if *The Sunday Times* of London warned those who planned to visit the Kahnweiler Gallery: "It is virtually impossible to give the British reader a description of the paintings done by the radical artists of Paris."[81] At least this was to the point.

If it was necessary to be thick-skinned in order to represent the cubists in this ignorant world, Kahnweiler was well-equipped to meet these attacks on his artists. His capacity to withstand the turmoil was due not to his indifference but to his detachment. They were speaking in terms of an overnight phenomenon whereas he was prepared for the long haul. Only in his letters to Rupf did he express his feelings, denouncing the crassness and the intellectual mediocrity of these critics who obscured everything.

Max Jacob had just published a second edition of poems—*The Burlesk and Mystical Worlds of the Late Brother Matorel, Who Died in a Monastery*—illustrated with seventy plates by Derain. Jacob encountered problems in his native Quimper, where the local papers called him the "cubist druid" as an insult. Street urchins mocked him. People stopped him to ask what a druid was and why he was called a cubist. He had a good laugh at all this,[82] but it did not help the sales of his books.

Cubists and fauves had become meat for satirical journals. The swell of attacks began with the preparations for the Salon des Indépendants. Louis Vauxcelles was ready and took aim: "The cubists and futurists are only important to one another. They are mere children sucking on their thumbs."[83] And later: "Picasso is the leader of these cubist gentlemen, somewhat in the style of Père Ubu-Kub."[84] At the same intellectual level, the journal *Assiette au Beurre* said: "The Kahnweiler establishment offers its visitors a series of riddles whose authors are Messrs. Pablo Picasso and Braque."[85]

These attacks were of little consequence to the dealer. What did matter was the confidence displayed by Gertrude Stein, who purchased Picasso's *The Architect's Drafting Table* for twelve hundred francs. Or that Juan Gris's *Homage to Picasso* caused a critical storm at the Indépendants. Or that in Munich Picasso was held up as another Cézanne by a new art journal entitled *Der Blaue Reiter*, published by two artists, Franz Marc and Wassily Kandinsky. A writer for *l'Intransigeant* was so impressed by the importance accorded to French art abroad that he sounded an alarm about this new art: "It could have serious repercussions on diplomatic relations."[86] But that was still in the future.

The brouhaha raised by the cubists at the Salon in April 1912 had the happy result that for the first time ever a popular newspaper sent a reporter to investigate the notorious gallery on rue Vignon where such strange experiments were being conducted. Jacques de Gachons, a novelist and art critic writing for *Je Sais Tout*, entitled his article "Painting from Beyond Tomorrow." According to his report,[87] he had barely stepped inside the gallery when he felt that he had made a mistake: "Sir, I was told that you show the best of the cubists."

Kahnweiler seemed quite offended, becoming defensive, raising his eyebrows and narrowing his eyes. The journalist, struck by the sobriety of the place, caught sight of the paintings on the walls and realized that he had not made a mistake.

"Sir," came Kahnweiler's reply, "I know there are people who call themselves cubists for the sake of publicity, but my artists are not that sort of cubist."

The assertiveness of his reply revealed his confident state of mind. The journalist explained that he was assigned by *Je Sais Tout* and found himself even deeper in trouble.

"Then, sir," continued the dealer, "don't persist, please. I would prefer that your magazine did not write about my artists. I don't want anything trying to ridicule them. These artists are also my friends, they are sincere, they are innovators of great integrity—in a word, they are artists. They are not entertainers who spend their time amusing the crowd."

The journalist protested that his intentions were good and the real purpose of his visit was to inform his readers about the avant-garde of the day. Kahnweiler had appeared irascible, but was now somewhat mollified by this information. The dealer agreed to cooperate and gave an interview. He showed the visitor his photograph albums containing works by Picasso, Braque, Derain, and Vlaminck, in chronological order. The critic became interested in seeing development and influences. Realizing that these works represented the world in a way he could not grasp, he asked for explanations in all good faith. Kahnweiler did not need to be asked twice.

"I understand that deciphering the most recent works of Picasso and Braque is difficult. I have been initiated since I witnessed the evolution of these paintings. I know the artists' intention. For example, this is a painting of 'the Poet.' "

The polite young journalist tried to hide his surprise. He was not hostile, just amazed. He thought he had been looking at a landscape and it turned out to be a poet.

"Yes, he is seated," Kahnweiler said. "This is his brow, here the arm, this a leg."

"What about this line here, slanting down?"

"It doesn't correspond to anything concrete, but notice how expressive it is since it immediately caught your attention. His hands . . ."

"Where are the poet's hands, please?" asked the critic, caught up in the game.

"Here's one hand."

"How strange."

"Isn't it?"

The young visitor continued, leafing through the album. "What about this?"

"This still life is one of the most perfect paintings by Picasso; there's the violin, the open fan, the glasses, a manuscript of loose pages, and the pipe there . . ."

The journalist responded to the strength of Kahnweiler's convictions. He compared the young art dealer to a great couturier or a rosarian who could speak easily about his latest creation. Because he had not met the artists themselves, he wanted further information to conclude the interview.

"Mr. Picasso is Spanish, no doubt."

"Yes, he was born in Málaga."

"Is he young?"

"Approximately thirty years old."

"And Georges Braque?"

"Thirty."

"French?"

"Yes, he was born in Argenteuil."

"Maurice de Vlaminck is Belgian, no doubt."

"He was born in Rueil. And Derain was born in Chatou."

"All from the suburbs. That's a strange coincidence. Do they know one another?"

"They are now inseparable."

The journalist concluded the interview with a promise to be impartial, to publish reproductions of the major works of the artists in order that the public might form its own opinion. He was a man of his word. Heading the page were two still lifes by Braque and Picasso. The photographs were black and white but he conscientiously described the muted and sharp colors in the caption. In writing up the gallery he did not produce a panegyric of Kahnweiler, admitting that his taste ran toward Chardin, Fantin-Latour, "and even Ingres." Yet this first article was enormously important to the history of the gallery, its artists, and the promotion of their works.

André Masson was only sixteen years old at the time. He had had his first aesthetic experience at the age of eight on seeing a painting by James Ensor in Brussels and now the reading of the article in *Je Sais Tout* threw him into a second state of shock. It informed him of the existence of Kahnweiler, who would become his dealer ten years later, and he was disconcerted by the reproductions, since he idolized the works of Cézanne and van Gogh. Cubism was a revelation that would take years for him to integrate.[88]

During the month of April a carefully dressed person, whom Kahnweiler had never seen before, entered the gallery. Without saying a word, he scrutinized the Picassos and Braques.[89] Kahnweiler, true to his principles, would never have said a word lest he interrupt his contemplation. And yet, here was a person with whom he would have found much in common: a thirty-three-year-old painter, half German, half Swiss, associated with the founders of *Der Blaue Reiter* in Munich, very influenced by Cézanne. In addition, he was an excellent musician—exactly the sort of person Kahnweiler would have wanted as a friend. The artist would have won Kahnweiler over instantly—or at least fascinated him. But neither spoke to the other and they would only meet again twenty years later, when Paul Klee became a friend as well as a gallery artist.

Picasso teamed up with Braque during the summer of 1912 to work, first at Céret and later at Sorgues in the Vaucluse. They could paint in peace knowing that in Paris Kahnweiler was looking after everything. He had gained Picasso's confidence. The artist relied on him to settle troublesome financial problems. While he was away Kahnweiler needed more paintings for the gallery. Picasso sent him a letter to give the concierge: "Permit Mr. Kahnweiler (with my authorization) to remove paintings from my studio. With my best regards, Madame."[90] The dealer used the note to remove twenty-five paintings.

Whenever the artists needed anything Kahnweiler hastened to satisfy them. Picasso complained about not having his possessions around him—unless he was reduced to only using white, he wanted to have at hand all of his paints, from Veronese Green to Cadmium Yellow. He missed his easel as well. The dealer set about remedying the situation. He found it easier than settling Picasso's emotional difficulties, which were numerous and complicated. Kahnweiler needed all his tact to keep Picasso's girlfriend at a distance without misleading her. The beautiful Fernande Olivier had been replaced in Céret by a new girlfriend, Eva (Marcelle Humbert). The art dealer had not as yet perceived the extent to which the women in Picasso's life would influence his work.

Fernande Olivier was used to seeing Kahnweiler in the Bateau-Lavoir studio and had studied him. She saw him as a clever and able man who always knew what was happening, and described him as "very young and German in style, intelligent, tenacious, shrewd, but not as much as Vollard. . . . He was a real Jewish businessman, knowing how to take risks to win, a man of action who bargained for hours until he tired out the artist, who, finally exhausted, would agree to the reduction in price he wanted. He knew very well what he had to gain by exhausting Picasso."[91]

Kahnweiler took exception to everything she said and categorically denied it. He had felt from the very beginning that she was dangerous, and he was not wrong. While Picasso was in Céret, Kahnweiler's function was to shield him and prevent her from reaching him in any way possible. It was a thankless task. One morning he received a note saying, "It is your duty to forward this letter to Pablo. . . . You will prevent irreparable damage by sending this letter by registered mail."[92]

She took possession of the artist's studio on rue Ravignan and requested that the dealer return the keys to her without removing anything from the premises. Otherwise she would have him charged with illegal entry! This was an unsuspected side of being an art dealer.

This was the most colorful of Kahnweiler's services to Picasso. Through letters he kept him up to date about business: what of his had been sold at the Hôtel Drouot auction house; the going prices of paintings; current exhibitions; the publication of a book on cubism by Gleizes and Metzinger.[93] In exchange Picasso wrote about the details of his daily life, the weather, and the painting he was working on. When pressed by his correspondent, who was eager for news about his progress and the state of his canvases, Picasso would sometimes comment on his own work: "I think my work has become more robust and has gained in clarity. Well, we shall see, and you shall see. It is not nearly finished, and yet I feel more certain."

Five days later he sent the following note: "You inform me that Uhde does not like my last paintings in which I used enamel paint and flags. Perhaps I shall end up by disgusting everyone, and I have not yet said everything."[94]

Kahnweiler kept him up to date about the problems of moving his studio from rue Ravignan to boulevard de Clichy, and the search for new living quarters. He was the indispensable agent who sent the artist his palette, paints, easel, pillows, and yellow-flowered kimono so he would feel at home even away from Paris. He was the friend who would not hide anything about a collector's reservations or disappointment in a given painting. Even during the month of July, when he went on vacation to Switzerland, Kahnweiler kept up this epistolary exchange. He did not want to upset the artist by interrupting the routine. Sparing him any irritation was vital to Kahnweiler, as he believed that guarding the artist's peace of mind while he accomplished his work was the primary function of an art dealer and justified his own role.

When Braque joined Picasso at Sorgues, they quickly fell back into their routine: "Nothing new to report except that I part my hair in the middle now. I did buy the toothbrushes I mentioned earlier and urged on you. If you smoke I advise you to also buy pipes from Marseilles."[95] As they had done earlier, the two men painted together, side by side, and it came through in the paintings. Kahnweiler had to correspond separately with each of them to maintain his friendship and business dealings with them.

While his correspondence with Picasso was even-tempered and smooth, Kahnweiler's exchange with Braque had highs and lows, revealing the tensions and differences between them which were as much aesthetic as financial. The postcards sent by Braque were always surprising in tone, ranging from a simple "Bonjour!" in block letters to the ambiguous informative style of "Georges Braque, born on the thirteenth of May in Argenteuil, Seine-et-Oise, sends you his friendly regards."[96] He kept his dealer abreast of the direction of his work, his new discoveries, without forgetting the local color: "I read in the papers that cubism has stirred up more of a commotion than the shindig of Saint-Polycarpe. News of it has even reached Sorgues, but we haven't been discovered up until now."[97] In September Kahnweiler sent paintings for a show at the Moderne Kunst Kring in Amsterdam, including works by Braque, Derain, Vlaminck, and Picasso. Braque and Kahnweiler suddenly had an angry altercation over the choice of one of the paintings, but the artist had the last word.

Kahnweiler did not admit defeat and refused to pay the price asked for one of his paintings. The position taken by each individual is clearly revealed in the language of Braque's answer. "Your surprised reaction seems exaggerated to me. I was equally amazed to read that you thought a hundred francs was an awfully large amount. Yet you have requested I not make any sales except through you, which eliminates any chance I might have had to compensate for the extremely modest prices you pay for my work. Really, you confuse me with your demands. I hope that in the future you will be more flexible and generous since I am conceding to your wishes so that everything between us is clear, and we shall get along better in the future."[98]

Both parties showed goodwill. Kahnweiler did not want to press his point when his artist's work was undergoing such a transformation. Now in some of his canvases he had placed black letters. While Picasso was briefly absent on a run to Paris in order to move his belongings into the apartment Kahnweiler had found for him in Montparnasse, Braque had invented the collage—works composed of glued paper.

On returning to Sorgues, Picasso also took up this discovery, and in turn introduced the technique into his work by pasting a real stamp on a still life, or a piece of oilcloth with the pattern of caning on the seat of a chair. The technique was used not to create the illusion of a trompe l'oeil, but to affirm concrete reality as part of the plasticity of the composition. Nails, newspaper, cards, oilcloth, wrappings and stuffing materials . . . instead of inventing or depicting them, it was more direct to integrate a fragment of the real and thus to transform it. Picasso, discussing these pieces with Braque, defined them as his "process of using recent dirty waste paper."[99]

It was not that Braque conceived of the "idea" of gluing paper, but rather that the way he used it was a revelation. The process was "anti-scientific," according to him, as science proceeds by a logical sequence of acquired knowledge through repetition. "The 'revelation' is the only thing they cannot take away from you," he would say.[100]

The first painting created by this revelation was *Compotier et Verre* (Fruit Dish with Glass), a charcoal sketch measuring eighteen by twenty-four inches incorporating paper that imitated oak paneling, which Braque had bought while shopping in Avignon.

These were works which Kahnweiler could not wait to have in his hands. He had defined his artists as "innovators," and to his great pleasure he saw this confirmed when he received the article in *Je Sais Tout*. Certainly Braque and Picasso were conducting extraordinary experiments in their studios in the Vaucluse. Kahnweiler never forgot the adage: "When an intuition becomes a revelation, it originates from a genius."

In October and November, Kahnweiler was filled with enthusiasm for this innovation. It made him forget everything, including the existence of exhibitions that everyone was discussing: the futurist exhibit at the Bernheim-Jeune Gallery, and the Douanier Rousseau retrospective in the same place. There was a disturbing incident at the Salon d'Automne at the Grand Palais, when Louis Vauxcelles was confronted by certain cubist painters and loudly insulted in choice language. The injured party wanted to settle the dispute on the field at dawn, but the artists declined. The critic was prompt to point this out: "The principles of cubist morality forbid them to fight duels."[101]

Inflamed by this incident, Vauxcelles a few days later took an extreme stance that foreshadowed a certain moral bankruptcy among critics. "There is something too German, too Spanish in this fauve and cubist business. Matisse might as well become a naturalized Berliner, and Braque only swear by Sudanese art. The fact that art dealer Kahnweiler is not actually a compatriot of old man Tanguy, or that lewd van Dongen is a native of Amsterdam and Pablo Picasso of Barcelona, is of no importance in itself."[102]

It mattered enough to become the subject of an article, and even more worrisome was the fact that it was published by a leftist newspaper and signed and written by Vauxcelles, whose real name was Mayer. Kahnweiler read it and noticed the attacks, but he did not want to be distracted from more essential issues.

By the end of 1912 Kahnweiler's artists had been represented in exhibitions held in Cologne, Düsseldorf, Frankfurt, and Munich. But for Kahnweiler, the basic issue was how to handle a situation that could be detrimental to his artists: the increasingly important place granted by the art world to those artists Kahnweiler would call "the false cubists," the imitators he so thoroughly disliked. They caused quite a stir in October when they staged a group exhibition as the Salon de la Section d'Or (the Golden Section), mounted in a gallery on rue La Boétie. Not all the artists in the show aroused Kahnweiler's enmity—Léger and Gris he simply thought out of place there—but many others such as Roger de la Fresnaye ("a charming minor painter"),[103] Frank Kupka, Marcel Duchamp, and Raymond Duchamp-Villon were what he called *ersatz Kubisten,* mere by-products. The worst were Gleizes and Metzinger, who earned his contempt by publishing a book called *On Cubism.*

His objection to them, their paintings, and their writings was that he considered them doctrinaire, theoretical, and academic. They wanted cubism to be a formula, whereas this mode of painting was a liberation which owed its accomplishments to feeling and intuition. They wanted to systematize something intuitive. But reality should not be reduced to geometry, emotions not constricted to a procedure. They took it on themselves to become spokesmen for a whole movement when they only represented themselves.

It was a dreadful misrepresentation by these people, who usurped everything that Kahnweiler had patiently built up. What had been shared discoveries they wanted to make into a platform, sanctified by a name on the cover of their newly published manifesto, a name conferred by a hostile critic. Kahnweiler thought the term "pitiful,"[104] even if he had to use it. Even the name Section d'Or set his teeth on edge.

It was a term discovered by Jacques Villon, the only painter among them Kahnweiler believed in, despite everything, because of his sincere effort to reconcile impressionism and cubism. Most of the artists in this group worked out their ideas in Villon's studio in the Paris suburb of Puteaux. They were referred to as the Puteaux Group, until they mounted the exhibition on rue La Boétie. They chose the name of La Section d'Or to represent a whole set of values and their antecedents. (The term was inspired by Leonardo da Vinci's work and that of other artists on the "divine proportion" of geometry, "the ideal proportion between two different volumes.")

Kahnweiler believed that the artists of the Puteaux Group had only retained the geometric fractioning of the works of Braque and Picasso. Even Delaunay, whom he held to be a gifted artist, seemed to him a deviator, not someone who continued the exploration of analytical cubism. He had introduced color in the most abstract way.[105] The dealer renewed his efforts in explaining to collectors that the geometric impression was not the most important aspect. It was a spectacular effect and leapt out of the canvas but the viewer should not fix on it. It disappeared as one became accustomed to it.

The "cube" was not an end in itself but a means of becoming conscious of the three dimensions of bodies in general. The shapes, whether cube, sphere, or cylinder should never be given too much importance in themselves.[106] The real problems confronting the cubist painter were straightforward enough: composition, color, light as a means. The dangers they risked were equally apparent: the trap of being ornamental, and even more pernicious, the temptation of resorting to a reductive geometry. Within the dimensions of a canvas, the surface plane can be free of objects, or the artist can place the world there; it can hold what the artist knows of the universe—if he has other things in mind than "the golden section" or mathematical solutions.

Kahnweiler went so far as to say that the Section d'Or painters imitated not nature but other paintings.[107] The lesson of Cézanne, the master of them all (both true and false cubists), clearly showed another path of exploration: to represent, on a two-dimensional canvas, three-dimensional solids.[108] Kahnweiler believed that Cézanne had revived the concept of structure, that he made people understand that paintings did not just show a piece of nature. Gleizes, Le Fauconnier, and their circle saw only the cubist style and had not made a personal investigation of the external world. They had not questioned what they knew about the subject and limited themselves to its superficial appearance. With such an approach they could only produce decorative works.

Kahnweiler considered Derain and Vlaminck closer to the cubists than their disciples of the Section d'Or. According to him, there was an inherent naive cubism which remained representational; Derain resembled Picasso and Braque in the way he composed his paintings, even while maintaining the imitation of reality. This is what he meant when he told Kahnweiler, "What I attempt to do is hide the scaffolding."[109]

The two creators of cubism shared Kahnweiler's disdain for the artists who exhibited in the Section d'Or. Many years later, after Picasso's studio had been robbed, he was visiting a gallery showing these poor imitators. "You've been robbed, I heard," the dealer inquired with sympathy.

Picasso, eyeing the canvases on the wall, said, "I've been plundered."[110]

Braque reproached the Puteaux Group for systematizing what had been spontaneous. Neither he nor Picasso had deliberately set out to become cubists, adopt a label, or launch a movement in art, nor even a new way of representing the world. They were reacting to the great masters and their contemporaries. Their reaction took form when they saw that they shared the same state of mind. One could not become a cubist any more than one could sit down and invent cubism. Gleizes and Metzinger's book, On Cubism, and the group show of the Section d'Or would irritate Braque. "The moment people started defining cubism and setting limits and principles for it—I must say I had to get the hell out of there."[111]

The positive effect of the disturbance was that it forced Kahnweiler to step out of his hutch on rue Vignon and go into the world to defend his artists. It was not a question of throwing down a challenge, nor sending fiery replies to publications. He had to know the nature of the situation. The previous year at the opening of the Salon d'Automne he read in the papers: "Do you know what they call M. Metzinger and M. Picasso, the leaders of the new school of painting?"

"What?"

"The Cubic Masters."*[112]

He did not take the insult as intended. He did not care that stupid people derided what they could not understand. What offended him was the association of Picasso with Metzinger, as well as the description used by Apollinaire to defend these artists against attackers: "The violence, the attacks prove the vitality of the new painting, and the works produced will be the admiration of future generations while these wretched detractors of French art will be quickly forgotten. Remember that they attacked Victor Hugo, which did not diminish his glory. On the contrary."[113]

Only Apollinaire would dare to place Gleizes on the same level as Hugo in conversation and to grant these canvases a future existence. The only thing accomplished by Gleizes and Metzinger's book and by the Section d'Or exhibition was that they formed a shield. It allowed Kahnweiler's artists to work in relative peace, but it was a heavy price to pay to have this protection; the price was silently condoning an imposture.

This controversy forced Kahnweiler to reveal himself, ready or not, as the defender of cubism. There was never a doubt about the sincerity of his aesthetic judgment. He had made it clear to everyone that the only real cubists were his artists, and that his was the gallery of cubism. He was convinced that this liberating movement in art, which he had carried to the baptismal font only a couple of years earlier, would never grow or develop outside of his control and management. At the end of 1912 Kahnweiler was ready to ask all his artists to sign contracts. He was procedural by nature and extremely legalistic, and this step would define his relations with artists on the threshold of a turbulent period.

There were no standard contracts for most galleries at that time.

* Untranslatable pun: the French "maîtres-cubes" is homophonic with "mètres cubes," or cubic meters (trans. note).

They varied with each dealer, ranging from a mere handshake to as many as twelve detailed clauses drawn up by lawyers. Even in this aspect of the profession Kahnweiler would leave his mark.

Starting in the fifteenth century painting had become the product of a social exchange. The patron was a client who ordered work with all the stipulations implied by such an action. The most important specifications concerned the content of the painting according to a preliminary sketch (figures, landscape), the dates of delivery of the painting (with fines for lateness), the payment to the artist (means and schedule of payment being specified), and finally the nature and quality of the colors used. Even the concept of painterly skills, so dear to the Renaissance, was taken into account by the contract in far greater detail than one would imagine. The price of the work varied according to the amount of surface to be covered, the time that would be required, and the additional expenses incurred by the specification and quality of certain colors, such as gold and ultra-marine. Ultramarine was expensive and delicate, being made of ground lapis lazuli from the Orient. The requirement of these colors in the contract could be interpreted as a desire to place an external sign of wealth on the painting. The last consideration that determined the price of the work under commission was whether it was a painting or a fresco and what proportion of the painting was executed by the master himself as opposed to his apprentices and students in his workshop.[114]

The disappearance of the patronage system in favor of a new type of collector that included both the bourgeoisie (of average means) and the high bourgeoisie (of great wealth) would completely alter this situation. The artist was no longer restricted to working according to the specifica-tions of his patrons. Van Gogh summed up the essentials of the problem in a letter to his brother: "The knot of the problem, you see, is that my possibilities for working depend on the sales of my work. . . . To have no sales and have no other resources renders it impossible to make any progress, while everything would go smoothly if the situation were the reverse."[115]

That said it all. In 1905, two years before Kahnweiler opened his gallery, artists' rights were the subject of public debate. In the new socialist daily newspaper l'Humanité, Jean Ajalbert started an investiga-tion of the problem. He presented the painter as a wretched, exploited individual who was refused the royalties which were granted composers and writers. He pointed out that the art dealers, who worked hand in hand with speculators and art patrons, comprised the most disgraceful category, since they were rewarded for their hypocrisy. Ajalbert was fighting for residual rights so that the artist would not be completely excluded from all future commercial transactions concerning his work.

The journalist's investigation gained momentum when it elicited the participation and suggestions of such artists as Henri-Gabriel Ibels, Paul Besnard, Eugène Carrière, and Claude Monet; the Friends of the Luxembourg Museum; lawyer José Théry; and former minister Raymond Poincaré. The last and most unbelievable was Léon Blum, the most distinguished critic of the avant-garde for *La Revue Blanche,* who terrified everyone with his suggested projects.

Léon Blum wanted to remove the necessity for the artist to earn money by relieving him of all material needs. "Art is not and should not be a profession," he wrote. "The artist must live, but he should not make a living from his art, painting being an activity of leisure. The artist should find another means to support himself so that he can bring to his painting a sense of the community. The state is above the artist and art, so art must be socialized. This may seem difficult, but it is feasible"—if one can mentally put oneself in a socialist state. Blum's suggestions were not accepted.[116]

This was far removed from the cynicism of Vollard, who clearly defined his financial dealings with the artist. Edmond Jaloux had written in his column in *l'Excelsior* that the sculptor Maillol had been able to live for years due to the generosity and intelligence of his dealer. Vollard replied that he admitted to intelligence and he felt flattered but that to call an art dealer generous was not a compliment. "I am embarrassed at getting this public recognition of generosity in the relationship between a dealer and an artist. It is as if a prospector who purchased some land where he hoped to discover gold showed generosity toward the person who sold him the land."[117]

It was not at all in this cynical spirit that Kahnweiler offered contracts to his artists, but neither was he philanthropic. If he had been motivated solely by the prospect of making a profit, the gold mines of Johannesburg would have satisfied him better and more rapidly. On the other hand, simple love of art was inappropriate because of its connotation of gratuitousness and total lack of interest in money, which was obviously not the case. What were his motives for introducing this aspect of contractual rights between him and his artists?

Kahnweiler believed that contracts between a dealer and his artists should be the exception and not the rule. They were only justified when both parties, in mutual confidence, joined forces to face a hostile public. If that was not the situation, the artist did not need an intermediary person to defend his work.[118] He felt the bond was rooted in good faith: one cannot work for long with a person one does not understand or respect, or in whom one has no confidence. The working relationship was agreed to before, in friendly conversations, without misunderstandings, compromises, or concessions, and without the need for legal advice. The law was only applicable "postmortem," in the settling of an estate or the discussion of inheritance.

All his life Kahnweiler was convinced that the contract served to reassure. What mattered to him was respecting his word once given, and never failing his commitment. He never passed judgment on other galleries except on one point, the only one that caused him to break his reserve: this was the clause certain dealers forced on their artists, specifying the number of canvases the artist had to deliver, an attitude Kahnweiler considered criminal. "They are criminals who should be shot!"[119] The goal of a contractual relation between the dealer and the artist was to give the artist the freedom to work in peace and not to impose on him a hellish production schedule.

A number of artists had first refused contracts with galleries. The art dealer enjoyed the privilege of making his choice before anyone else as soon as the paintings were completed. This practice was fairly common, but there was no question of such a clause for Kahnweiler. He could not even conceive of it for himself, due to a fundamental trait of character: loyalty. That was his driving motivation in coming to terms with his artists.

The exclusive rights to the artist's production would become his obsession; it was in keeping with his possessive and imperious nature as well as his commercial logic. He would bear the success and the failures of the artists he liked and supported. In ethical terms, it was known as reciprocal loyalty; in commercial terms, it would be called a monopoly. In a letter to the sculptor Manolo he spelled out his position unequivocally: "All of your work must pass through my hands, and I will not tolerate any exception to this. For so many years I have been a faithful supporter of your work, and I believe that I have the right to also demand your loyalty. On this point I will never make any concession."[120]

In exchange for exclusive representation he offered security. He would pay a monthly stipend that would enable the artist to live and work without any concern for the sales and dissemination of his work. The stipend, which was guaranteed even if there were no sales, was not legally considered a salary, a fee for contracted work, or a dividend. Rather, it was an advance against income which would be produced from future sales.[121]

Georges Braque was the first artist to whom he sent a simple letter-contract, on November 30, 1912. One party was bound to sell everything, the other to buy it, for a period of a year. The prices would range from sixty francs to four hundred francs according to the size and format of a canvas. The artist would be paid between forty and seventy-five francs per drawing. There was a special clause for "collages" of glued paper, "paper and wood, marble or any accessory," which would not be considered as simple drawings embellished with different materials. Like the paintings, the collages would be systematically photographed.

A few days later, on December 6, Kahnweiler repeated the same terms to Derain, only the prices were slightly higher. He would have been paid 275 francs, for example, while Braque would have received only 200 francs for the same sized canvas.

On December 18, when Kahnweiler mailed a letter contract to Picasso, things became slightly complicated. The artist answered him the same day:

My dear friend,

I want to confirm our conversation as follows. We agreed to a period of three years beginning on the second of December, 1912.

During this period I commit myself to not selling anything to anyone other than you. The only exceptions are the old paintings and drawings which belong to me. I will have the right to accept orders for portraits and large-scale decorations for specified places. It is understood that the right to reproduce all the paintings you have sold belongs to you. I commit myself to sell to you at fixed prices my entire output of paintings and scultures [sic] and drawings and engravings, reserving for myself a maximum of five paintings a year. I will have the right to keep as many drawings as I will deem necessary for my work. You will leave it to me to judge when a painting is finished. It is assumed that during these three years I will not have the right to sell the paintings and drawings I retain for myself. On your side, you are committed for three years to buy at fixed prices everything I will produce in paintings, gouaches, and at least twenty drawings a year.

The prices were carefully listed: 100 francs for drawings; 200 francs for gouaches; paintings ranging from 250 to 3,000 francs, depending on size; with "prices of scultures [sic] and engravings to be negotiated."[122]

Kahnweiler understood quickly that with Picasso he could never have the same relationship as with other artists. Picasso knew exactly what he wanted; he drew his determination from some former experience that had left him bitter and distrustful. His letter clearly tried to cover the essentials. It was as detailed as that of Juan Gris would be pithy: "I declare receiving your letter confirming our discussion yesterday. I subscribe completely to the terms we agreed upon that are contained therein. Accept my sincere expression of friendship."[123]

The essential difference between these relationships is defined by these exchanges. On one side was Picasso, the artist conscious of his worth, who considered each of the dealer's proposals and refused to give in to him completely, thus retaining a portion of his own territory. On the other was Juan Gris, who was modest and self-effacing and agreed without any reservations. If for Kahnweiler Picasso was *the* artist who dominated his century, Gris was an extraordinary man and very dear friend.

When speaking about Gris, Kahnweiler always ran short of superlatives. They had first met in 1908 at the Bateau-Lavoir. Every time Kahnweiler visited Picasso, he saw Gris working obstinately in his corner. It was said that when Gris petted a dog he did it with his left hand so in case he got bitten he could continue to draw with his right hand—or at least Max Jacob said so.

From time to time Kahnweiler would speak to the young man from Madrid. He was not yet called Gris, but since José González was too common he decided to invent another name with the same initials that was more appropriate for an artist. The choice of name (Gris is French for "gray") reveals an aspect of the man, his discretion. He had lived on rue Ravignan since 1906, but there was never any talk about him. While Picasso was painting *Les Demoiselles d'Avignon*, Gris was sending satiric drawings to comic publications in France, earning his living with them. Later, either because of necessity or because Kahnweiler did not have control over it, this aspect of his work would be ignored, dismissed, or even despised. But the fact is that Gris was one of the most important magazine illustrators at the beginning of the century, as can be judged by his production: five hundred drawings and a hundred vignettes in seventeen different periodicals.[124] He was a keen observer of politics, cultural and social affairs. He even wrote captions, and to change media he drew publicity posters for Byrrh apéritif. This could well have become his career but fate, circumstance, and his own genius dictated otherwise.

The major comic papers were in financial difficulty in 1912, and Gris had to look for something else. He separated from his girlfriend, sent his young son back to his sister in Spain, and gave up drawing (as not being well-enough paid) in favor of painting, which was not better paid but which took him over completely.

In 1910 he did his first watercolors, and a year later was selling oil paintings to Clovis Sagot. Kahnweiler rekindled their acquaintance and got to know him better during the period when Gris was changing his own direction, and from the very beginning probably what pleased Kahnweiler enormously was the fact that Gris had a serious side.[125] Modest yet determined, his faith in his art was unshakable in spite of periods of discouragement on seeing the notoriety, prestige, and financial success of Picasso. (At such times Kahnweiler always attempted to be supportive.) He preferred his own library to café life, and he collected books on scientific and parascientific works, biography, the occult, and the cabbala.[126]

His asceticism in front of the easel contrasted sharply with his joie de vivre. He disliked anything equivocal and used words sparingly. Kahnweiler reproached him for undervaluing his talent. He was known to be an extremely scrupulous person. By choice he was French, with a great love for the language and civilization of his host country. He loathed Spain and could hardly wait to be naturalized. Kahnweiler dwelt on his character when writing of his work[127] because his canvases reflected it exactly: in them everything was ordered, clear, and pure. His greatness lay in his classicism. This man had a high moral sense, with an undeniably elevated intellect, and as a painter was full of humanity. Gris gave a great deal of thought to his painting without making it cerebral.

At the end of 1912 and beginning of 1913, when Kahnweiler went to Gris as both a friend and an art dealer, with the intention of placing him under contract, he still remembered the illustrator that Gris had been. He spoke of the appearance of his first paintings, which he found magnificent.[128] The artist progressed rapidly from analytical cubism to synthetic cubism, to use the definitions Kahnweiler would establish later. In other words, he no longer painted multiple views of the same object but a sequence of signs designating the object without depicting it. He wanted the painting to be more faithful, more precise, more exact than a photographic reproduction. Kahnweiler purchased his first Gris at the end of February 1913, the day after signing their contract.

Picasso was not happy about this relationship, to put it mildly. He was offended to see "their" dealer's affection and admiration expressed so openly. In such a small gallery two Spaniards were one too many. Picasso was merciless. Up to the day that Gris died, this rivalry that dared not utter its name was at the expense of Juan Gris.

In their relationship Kahnweiler had the upper hand, and yet the painter remained loyal to him against all odds. He heeded his advice and turned to him when he needed a counselor. Kahnweiler was not only indebted to Gris for helping him understand other artists, but for becoming a lifelong friend. He had found the best representative of his aesthetic ideas, and he had initiated the career of a major artist.

Hermann Rupf, Gertrude Stein, and dealer Léonce Rosenberg were among the first collectors to buy Gris. But to his never-ending disappointment Kahnweiler was unable to place a Gris with Roger Dutilleul or Wilhelm Uhde. Gris's style was too puritanical, too grammatical, not romantic enough for the French collector. The German collector conceded the good points about the work, but reproached Gris for having fallen into a mannerism, anti-Picasso in spirit. He would spell it out in terms that horrified Kahnweiler: "What [Picasso] forged in precious metal, with Gris it's only cardboard made to resemble metal. . . . His Pierrots are napkins cleverly folded into cubist shapes, and you can see right through him."[129] "The Picasso business," as Kahnweiler called it,[130] rested entirely on the support of four or five individuals, a handful of serious collectors who were loyal and regular clients. He needed to build the same support system for Gris, who would then gain a certain renown.

1913 was full of promise. To the four artists under contract (Braque, Derain, Picasso, and Gris) he added Vlaminck on July 2 and Léger on October 20. It was inevitable that Vlaminck would follow in the footsteps of his friend Derain, and in fact Kahnweiler had been buying a great deal from him in the several years since he had inaugurated the gallery with his paintings. The contract only made official what was already a fact. Actually a handwritten letter, it offered the same terms as the others had, specifying the duration of the commitment (two years), and stating that at the end of one year prices would be revised upward.

Aside from these legal questions Kahnweiler and Vlaminck had much else to discuss. They jointly owned a sailboat and a motor-powered canoe that they used on the Seine. These were respectively baptized, in honor of the first books by Max Jacob and Apollinaire, *Saint Matorel* and *L'Enchanteur pourrissant*, which did not fail to startle other boat owners. When not discussing matters of navigation, they had another subject to disagree on: the war. This was war with Germany, of course, which the artist believed imminent and the dealer thought impossible, bringing forward intellectual arguments to defend his position.[131]

His relationship with Léger was completely different. When Kahnweiler offered him a contract, Léger was an artist between two lives. He was in a creative fervor, freeing himself little by little from the influence of Cézanne. He had shown his work at the Salon de la Section d'Or without belonging to the Puteaux Group. He felt isolated, rejected by his milieu. He needed a show of confidence, frustrated as he was at trying to break into a closed circle. [132]

The contract that Kahnweiler offered him was an anchor. The moment he received the offer he took it to his mother, a peasant from Normandy who was terribly skeptical about his future: "You cannot earn a living by painting pictures." When she read the letter-contract, she started to half believe, without completely relinquishing her doubts. She took it to the village lawyer to have it certified, just in case. Once this was done, she took the train to Paris to look at her son's paintings. She never thanked Kahnweiler in his gallery, but rather God in the Church of the Madeleine: "Fernand is going to earn his living."[133]

Léger would always recognize that he was indebted to Kahnweiler, who showed confidence in him and supported his efforts. For the first time, he could support himself by painting. The exclusive contract was for three years, with prices ranging from fifteen francs (for a line drawing) and seventy-five francs (a drawing of number 25) to five hundred francs (for any painting over number 120). Of the six contracts Kahnweiler signed, this was the only one in proper form. The lawyer whom Léger's mother consulted not only made sure it was legally sound, but he also placed a notary seal on it.

In all of its six years of existence, the Kahnweiler Gallery had never been so open to foreign markets as in February and March of 1913. While everyone in the art world kept repeating, "Paris is the center of everything that is happening," Kahnweiler was exhibiting everywhere except in Paris. France was not ready for an exhibition, and in any case his gallery was open to everyone with his artists' most recent paintings hanging on the walls. The fact that two out of three collectors were not French could not be explained by money alone because there were many solid commercial and industrial fortunes in France. However, they were less daring than those beyond the Rhine and across the Atlantic.

Cologne, Moscow, Munich, Prague, Berlin, Edinburgh, Düsseldorf, Dresden, Frankfurt . . . There was a huge turnover in the paintings by Picasso, Vlaminck, Derain, Gris, van Dongen, and Braque as well as the sculptures by Manolo. It made Kahnweiler expand his field of activity to such cities as Liverpool, St. Petersburg, Budapest, Bremen, Stockholm, and Zurich.

In New York on February 17, in the 69th Regiment Armory on Twenty-fifth Street, an exhibition opened that would mark a date in the history of modern art in the United States. The Armory Show, as it became known, was both an event and a revelation. With sixteen hundred works, it was enough to inspire the avocation of many collectors (which occurred on the spot) and show a different aesthetic to American artists (which would take time to be assimilated). Behind the scandal it provoked and the great success that followed, there was one man, John Quinn, a New York business lawyer who moved heaven and earth to amend the Payne-Aldrich customs tariff to abolish taxes on the import of contemporary art.* That year he won his case. His initiative stimulated his contemporaries, wealthy collectors who were not in a league to collect the old masters.

Quinn had only recently started buying in Europe. He used scouts—people who went searching out works for him—whom Kahnweiler learned to recognize. Among them was a Frenchman, an astonishing character named Henri-Pierre Roché, who spent fifteen years buying paintings for the Quinn collection.

Roché would become known for something other than his private art collection during the fifties when he published two novels, *Jules and Jim* and *Two English Girls and the Continent*. He commuted between Paris and New York, and in both places he knew everybody. At the Bateau-Lavoir he conversed with Picasso; in Montparnasse he boxed with Braque, using his English defense. In New York he frequented black jazz clubs, avant-garde galleries, and the theater. Later, when publisher Gaston Gallimard and actor Charles Dullin were on tour with the Vieux-Colombier Troupe, Roché would serve as their guide to nightlife in New York.

Roché had a knack for witty remarks, and his sayings could form an anthology of maxims for collectors. "Possessions will someday become burdens"; "Standing before my paintings I already prefer them in memory than as themselves"; "The drunkard wants to empty his wine cellars before he dies; I, my walls."[134] He and Kahnweiler got along well since they started out at the same time in the same field. But though they were both people who searched out and sold art, their goals were very different. Roché would never forget his first visit to rue Vignon: "In the beginning of cubism, Kahnweiler in his small shop introduced me to cubist Picassos and Braques without saying a word. He *introduced me*, and his manner said it all. He had the simple authority of someone who announces. For him, cubism, newly created, was already a classic. There was a Braque I really liked, but put off making a decision. By the next day

---

* Established in 1909, the Payne-Aldrich customs tax had, until this point, allowed the duty-free import to the United States only of paintings one hundred years old or more.

the painting had been sold. I had to wait twenty years in order to buy it. It had come to me as a revelation, but only after the fact when I remembered how Kahnweiler had shown it to me."[135]

When Kahnweiler moved from rue Théophile-Gautier to a place on rue George-Sand, also in the sixteenth arrondissement, he suddenly realized that he was also a collector. What surprised visitors to his home was not the presence of paintings by his artists on the walls, but the striking contrast between them and the very traditional furniture, which was the antithesis of avant-garde. It was as if in this secret garden he lived only in relation to what was on the walls, unaware of the rest which was relegated to the realm of decoration. Unlike some of his colleagues, he was never sorry to sell a painting he loved, and he did not find it painful to see it leave. After all, paintings were made to be sold, and his vocation was not to keep them but to move them out into the world. "I am not a fisher of paintings, I am a fisher of men," he would often paraphrase Saint Paul. [136]

In 1913 Kahnweiler and his wife, Lucie, spent their August vacation in Italy visiting museums and galleries. In the triangle of the Duomo, the Uffizi Gallery, and the church of San Lorenzo, the surfeit of artistic beauty did not overpower him; he was too level-headed for that.

His artists, meanwhile, were scattered in the countryside, painting. He received a letter from Picasso in Céret, asking him to remit money to Max Jacob so he could join him: "Put it on my account."[137] Gris wrote in a modest style but addressed him warmly as "Dear Boss" and asked him to pay his rent if he wanted him still to have an apartment on his return. [138] Kahnweiler smiled at all this, from a heightened sense of duty. Braque wrote from Sorgues, "Your opinion of my paintings gave me great pleasure, all the more so since it's the only reaction that I have had here, where my isolation has made me lose all critical sense. This is the advantage of being in the country."[139] These were the moments that moved Kahnweiler, when he felt a strong sense of who he was.

In *Gil Blas* he read an article on the Salon d'Automne by the ubiquitous Louis Vauxcelles.

Cubism has to be fought! The snobs of overrated paintings have all cried, "Marvelous!" at the sight of them. A few sluggards from the press and some sloppy versifiers joined the chorus. Even we contributed to this when we attacked this monstrous school, and in addition we made the mistake of feeding their insatiable appetite for publicity. The beast enjoyed every minute of it. In fifteen years when we look back on cubist paintings of 1910–1913 (if their creators haven't destroyed them by then), they will appear as a fleeting phenomenon without any relation to artistic movements. . . . Every room of the exhibit at the Grand Palais has its cubist the way every hospital ward has a dangerous psychopath.[140]

Kahnweiler did not even bother to laugh.

For Kahnweiler 1913 remained associated with two men (aside from his artists) who left their mark on this period in widely different ways: Alfred Flechtheim and Guillaume Apollinaire. With the first he developed a strong friendship, but he strained his relationship with the latter to the breaking point.

He had known Flechtheim for four years as a grain merchant when, in December of that year, he decided to become an art dealer. The cause of this transformation from comfortable businessman to collector of modern art was the enormous success of the Sonderbund exhibit that he organized in 1912 at Cologne in collaboration with the curators of the museums of the Rhine district. The man who opened his first gallery in Düsseldorf (there would be others in Berlin, Frankfurt, and Cologne) was the exact opposite of Kahnweiler in character.

He was startlingly colorful and won everyone over by his sense of humor, his jokes, and his derisive wit. Kahnweiler had always been impressed by his vitality and daring.[141] He said of this man who would quickly become one of the greatest art dealers in Germany: "He is a salesman of the first order. If he cannot get better results, it is because the maximum that can be done has been done."[142]

The expressionist painter Otto Dix left a portrait of Flechtheim that captured him to the core. He is shown in full action, the dealer surrounded with canvases by Picasso, Braque, and Gris, details of which can be recognized, and the expression of his eyes and his smile are eloquent. He was the dynamic businessman, permanently chewing on a huge cigar, both cunning and effusive, and revealing above all his great passion for modern art.[143] In the period between the two world wars Christian Zervos, who was the most cultivated of art critics, as cosmopolitan and polyglot as Kahnweiler (a rarity in art circles in France), visited Flechtheim in his Berlin gallery for an interview to be published in Les Cahiers d'Art. He was struck by the personality of this unusual dealer and wrote a profile that captured his character both as a young man and throughout his life: nervous, agitated, lively, shrewd, joyful, despairing, sensual, unfair, enthusiastic, chatty, theatrical . . . that was the word, theatrical, in everything and with everyone.[144]

Originally from Westphalia, Flechtheim should have been a grain merchant like his father and grandfather and great-grandfather, and perhaps even his forebears before that. But one day an errand took him to rue Laffitte, and instead of going into the bank that was his destination, he went down a side street into the shop of Clovis Sagot, leaving with two etchings by Picasso. The very sympathetic dealer introduced him to the artist, who made a great impression on the young merchant. Shortly afterward, at the Bernheim-Jeune Gallery, he was charmed by the personality of Félix Fénéon, who sold him watercolors by Rodin, potatoes by van Gogh. Then he made a fateful encounter: "For me the decisive meeting was with Kahnweiler, who influenced me to become who I am now, a spreader of propaganda for contemporary French art in Germany, what Paul Cassirer was for the impressionists."[145]

If Kahnweiler influenced Flechtheim's decision to lead a new life, it was not by direct admonition, since Kahnweiler did not want disciples. He simply encouraged Flechtheim to make the change when he understood that this talented businessman had a sincere passion for art and would be infinitely more useful to their common cause if he abandoned grain transactions for the sake of modern art.

In December 1913 Alfred Flechtheim inaugurated his first gallery in Düsseldorf by hanging the works of German artists from the Rhine area who were known at the Café du Dôme—Rudolf Lévy, Purmann, Ernesto de Fiori—alongside those sent by Kahnweiler or by Uhde, such as the Douanier Rousseau. But even in this new incarnation he kept his biting wit. When Christian Zervos asked what artist had had the greatest impact on Germany since the beginning of the century, Flechtheim answered without skipping a beat: "Schmeling, the boxer."[146]

The art dealer was the honorary president of the Boxing Club of the Jewish Maccabee Sports Association and of the Police Constabulary of Berlin. It is understandable that Kahnweiler found a personality so different from his to be seductive, and they formed a solid friendship. He became closer to this type of man as he became more estranged from his old friend Apollinaire.

At this time Kahnweiler formed three opinions about Apollinaire that remained unchanged: he was a great poet; he was the finest of men; but he was an inconsequential, not to say worthless, art critic. The literary praise was not given merely to counterbalance his attack on the art critic; he would always cut off any protest with, "I know what I'm talking about, I was his first editor!"

Never would he have published Apollinaire's writings on art. Kahnweiler believed that Apollinaire knew nothing about art, and his information could not be trusted because it would be erroneous. He even believed that he deliberately distorted the truth out of some inner compulsion. He accused him of writing journalism, which, coming from him, was not meant as a compliment. When in 1912 Apollinaire praised "the cubists of the Salon," those hanging on the walls of the Indépendants, the dealer felt that this was too much and even threatened to bar his entry into the gallery.[147]

The crisis in their relationship came as a direct result of Apollinaire's having published his book *The Cubist Painters, an Aesthetic Meditation* (with the same Eugène Figuière who had brought out the Gleizes and Metzinger book in 1912). When the art dealer read it he found it fine on a poetic level but pernicious in content. "Wonderful lyrical passages, but they are only vague mutterings, and as for the rest . . ." he would later write.[148]

In his indignation he believed that Apollinaire had discredited himself. He would write almost anything on a subject about which he knew very little. Instead of making an analysis of cubism and writing an essay, as would be proper for any self-respecting critic, he let the artists speak, recounted anecdotes without direct bearing on the subject, and tried to gloss over disparate and contradictory aspects in his effort to please his friends from Montmartre and Montparnasse. Perhaps the poet would have been better advised to write in the defense and portrayal of one artist, instead of making himself the herald of a so-called school, which was no such thing.

Apollinaire had introduced Picasso to Braque, and according to Kahnweiler, if his contribution to art history stopped at that, it would have been quite an accomplishment. But he wanted to speak for the cubist painters. It was a worthy ambition, but the level of aesthetic consideration was on a par with café conversation and should never have left the barroom. For Kahnweiler the only true merit of Apollinaire's work was as a document about the milieu, the period, and the way artists wanted to be understood.[149]

Kahnweiler was merciless, especially toward friends, when "his" art was at stake. But he was not alone. In Montmartre and Montparnasse Apollinaire was condemned for his poor judgment and biases. Braque and Picasso liked him as a friend and poet but, like Kahnweiler, they refused to take his art criticism seriously and especially denied that he had exerted any influence on artists. They even began saying that it was the other way around: "I don't think that he understood anything about painting," Braque always said. "He could not tell a Rubens from a Rembrandt."[150]

His book did seem light. How could he command respect with such statements as, "Looking at a painting by Léger makes me happy"?[151] There had to be other ways of explaining the work. Similarly, Apollinaire thought he could deal with perspective by dismissing it as a miserable device, the reverse of a fourth dimension. When Kahnweiler heard about the publication of the book, he feared the worst, having gotten a foretaste from Apollinaire's articles in *l'Intransigeant*. Reading the book, one had to wonder whether the author had really considered the artistic problems confronting the painters. Take, for example, the following selections:

Metzinger: "His art is never petty. This little boy is entitled to the attention he has received." Rouault: "These frightening caricatures of the works of Gustave Moreau are truly painful to behold. It makes the viewer wonder what inhuman impulses the artist was following when he conceived of them." Van Dongen: "[His] paintings express what a bourgeois suffering from enteritis would call daring. As for me, I do see the talents of the painter, but also a vulgarity the artist tries to turn into brutality." Pierre Chapuis: "[He] seems to be a van Gogh painting with melting candy. But he is a painter, without question; his *Fleurs,* his *Cagneux* and especially his *La halte* are lovely." Dunoyer de Segonzac: "He uses up unnecessarily huge amounts of canvas and paint."[152]

The misunderstanding could come from Apollinaire's insisting that he wrote as an art critic, whereas Kahnweiler thought that he was a writer on art. He deplored that so much of art criticism was focused on the biography of the artist, his assumed reactions and intentions, and all the details of his life, instead of looking only at the work. Kahnweiler refused to accept these methods as valid. He was concerned only with a historical point of view that would place the painting in perspective.

All of his life he debunked the criticism of Apollinaire, not without praising his real qualities. By diminishing him, Kahnweiler sought to boost other critics whom he felt were underappreciated, such as Max Jacob, whose clownish mask and pirouettes hid the serious nature of a truly thinking man; or Pierre Reverdy, who placed the logic of a work of art in its composition and held a theory of cubism that was similar to Kahnweiler's.[153] These names are mentioned in relation to Apollinaire because they are poets from the same sphere of influence.

At the same time, two works were published in Germany which Kahnweiler found more serious. Fritz Burger, in *Cézanne and Hoeller,* acknowledged the importance of cubism and Picasso's position. It was overwhelming for Kahnweiler, as the critic seemed to have understood the essentials: "The fact that Picasso represents objects seen from different sides is not essential to his art, even if the younger generation of artists in Paris believe it. What is being questioned is not the changing aspects of the object, but the different relationships that are established between its various aspects and the environment while its individual, concrete existence is being negated." The second book was written by Max Raphael, who, along with Kramar from Prague, was one of the rare art historians who had followed cubism since its origins. His *From Monet to Picasso* was the first German book specifically about cubism, and the first time Picasso's name appeared on the cover of a book. The artist was only thirty-two years old.

Kahnweiler tried to settle his differences with Apollinaire by correspondence, which only resulted in cooling relations further. Using as a pretext the publication of his first major volume of poetry, *Alcools*, Apollinaire wrote a letter that barely contained his feelings:

> I have learned that you find what I have to say about painting totally uninteresting, which seems curious to me coming from you. I alone defended as a writer those painters you then discovered through me. Do you think that it is fair to try to destroy the only person who can lay the foundation for future understanding of art? In these matters he who tries to destroy will himself be destroyed because the movement I uphold has not come to an end, nor will it be stopped even if everything that is done against me were to rebound against the whole movement. This is the plain warning of a poet who knows what must be said, where he stands, and who others are in matters of art.
>
> With cordial regards[154]

Kahnweiler was floored by the letter, revolted by the hateful tone. Apollinaire had gotten what he deserved. So much bravado and pretension and such twisted truths! What nerve to write about painters "discovered through me," when Kahnweiler had introduced the poet to Braque. With those menacing words—"destroy," "warning"—he had gone beyond the acceptable. Kahnweiler hesitated about how to answer him and in the end chose to be precise, dry, and derisive: "I received your strange letter. In reading it I didn't know whether I should be angry. I decided to laugh."[155]

It was hollow laughter. He had been hurt, and he would never forgive. Their relationship came to an end, but nothing ever prevented Kahnweiler from continuing to speak of Apollinaire as a great poet and a bad art critic.

* * *

In 1914 Kahnweiler was still persuaded that war was impossible, and at every opportunity he argued against Vlaminck's fears. War was simply inconceivable to a francophile German who had spent twenty years in Germany and nine in Paris, and who could thus analyze the mood of both sides.

The gallery was doing well. It was not overwhelmingly prosperous, but business was gradually improving. His handling of Picasso was bringing good results. In the last year Kahnweiler had purchased 27,250 francs' worth of paintings and drawings payable in three months.[156] Then, from Gertrude Stein, he purchased three Picasso paintings for 20,000 francs and *The Man with the Guitar*. He resold *The Acrobat with Ball*, a big canvas from 1905, to Morozov for 16,000 francs in gold, which set a record for the period.[157]

This enabled him to review Gris's contract with readjusted prices of 20 francs for a drawing and 240 francs for a 25-by-36-inch canvas.[158] Kahnweiler wanted to be fair, as with the monthly stipend for Manolo. The artists could hardly complain, since of all the artists in Europe the French, with their exclusive contracts, enjoyed the greatest financial security. In Italy and Germany this system would be almost unheard-of: avant-garde artists could not hope to obtain financial security before the age of forty or sixty.[159]

Of all the collectors of Picassos, the two Russians seemed the most enthusiastic and prompt to respond, despite the great distance. In February 1914 the art dealer sent numerous photographs and letters, and Shchukin and Morozov cabled in return. The same day that Kahnweiler purchased *Young Man on a Horse* from Leo Stein for 10,000 francs (which he would pay a little later), he offered it to Morozov by sending a photograph. The price was double what it cost him. The collector from Moscow already owned *Young Girl with Ball*, and now could be the owner of the most beautiful "early" Picasso works. The argument seems to have made its point, since he then proposed *Woman in Front of a Coffee Table* for 8,000 francs and *Crouching Woman* for 9,000 francs.[160]

With Shchukin, Kahnweiler pushed Derain. At the beginning of the month he sold him two paintings for 4,500 francs, then offered him *The Luncheon* for 12,000 francs. This painting, which had taken two years of work and which Kahnweiler considered Derain's most important opus to date, was not yet dry because of the heat and humidity. Still in the studio, barely finished, it was already sold.[161] It was an accomplishment he would not soon forget.

In the meantime the young dealer was living in a state of euphoria. On February 1 he signed his first important foreign contract with Mr.

Brenner and Mr. Coady, the owners of the Washington Square Gallery in New York. The contract would last one year, in which Kahnweiler committed himself to place in their charge for October an exhibition of ten paintings by Juan Gris, followed in December by ten paintings by Picasso. Accounts would be settled three times a year, and they had exclusive representation in the United States for the sale of Braque, Gris, Léger, and Picasso. In return the gallery was bound to buy 2,500 francs' worth of works, and they were responsible for the cost of transportation and insurance the moment the works left the rue Vignon gallery. Hardly a month and a half after signing this contract Brenner and Kahnweiler agreed to extend it to May 1, 1916, under the same terms but raising to 5,000 francs the amount they were bound to purchase. On April 22, 1914, a codicil was added to extend the contract to all gallery artists, and their commitment to buy was raised to 6,000 francs.[162]

Thus Kahnweiler's gallery had opened a promising market at the same time as he was assured of bringing in supplemental regular income. He found this very reassuring, and in turn he could reassure his artists. The dealer could make his morning rounds of studio visits without fear of being asked about specific things he could not answer. He began with Léger on rue Notre-Dame-des-Champs, Picasso on rue Schoelcher, and Gris at the Bateau-Lavoir. Then he would head up the Butte Montmartre, passing women in housecoats fetching hot water, to reach Braque's studio in the Hôtel Roma on rue Caulaincourt. The studio was a glass cage, which reminded him of a lighthouse. From this balcony overlooking the capital, Braque could see through his binoculars all the way to the suburb of Argenteuil. Kahnweiler always found him working, humming and whistling like a house painter. Next was Derain on rue Bonaparte in the center of town, where his studio was in a bourgeois apartment house two steps from the Ecole des Beaux-Arts. The studio had north light, and there were many canvases without frames among his tools, musical instruments, and scattered objects. His dog would be asleep on the couch.[163]

Then came the hour of truth. For the first time, the paintings so dear to Kahnweiler had to face the ultimate test, the public auction block. It might be a test from which they would not recover for a long time. It was a risk and a gamble. Some people were already rubbing their hands in anticipation of the downfall of cubism.

The auction took place at Hôtel Drouot on Monday, March 2, 1914, in rooms number seven and eight, under the supervision of Henri Baudoin and the expert appraising eyes of Bernheim-Jeune and Druet. The gavel would signal the opening of an auction of international scope, the sale of the Peau d'Ours collection, which by now had passed its ten-year limit. In accordance with the bylaws, everything had to be auctioned off.

By two o'clock the salesroom had filled with art dealers, collectors, artists, and journalists. There was Countess Antoine de La Rochefoucauld, Prince Bibesco, Gustave Coguiot; critics André Warnod, André Salmon, and Max Jacob; fashion designer Paul Poiret; theater director Jacques Hébertot; and from official ranks there was Paul Jamot from the Louvre,[164] who was not there to buy—it would be a long time before cubist paintings would hang in the national museums. Rather, it was the attendance of dealers that was most interesting, and Kahnweiler was there to take it all in.

Ten days earlier he had written to Shchukin and Morozov, offering to send them the auction catalogue and to bid for them without charging any commission. For the Russian collectors it had been pointed out that the most interesting painting in the auction was *Les Bateleurs* (Family of Acrobats) by Picasso and the success or failure of the auction rested on its sale.[165] Seated not far from Kahnweiler was the massive presence of Ambroise Vollard. Most of the other dealers came from abroad: Flechtheim from Düsseldorf, Gaspari from Munich, Gutbier from Dresden, and Thannhauser from every part of Germany.

The rest of the public was made up of curiosity seekers, such as a white-bearded man, greatly decorated, who stirred up much laughter with his booming protest of indignation: someone had dared to compare Rembrandt and Picasso right in front of him. In one corner of the room Marcel Sembat, a socialist deputy from the eighteenth arrondissement who was a collector of modern art, could not suppress a smile on recognizing other deputies.[166]

The sale started with the canvases of Emile Bernard, Pierre Girieud, Jean-Louis Forain, and Henri Edmond Cross. But people had not come for those works. The cubists would come after the fauves and others. Van Gogh's *Flowers in a Glass* went for 4,000 francs, *Feuillage au bord de l'eau* (Plants at the Water's Edge) for 2,000 francs, and Matisse's *Les Oeufs* (Eggs) for 2,400 francs. Paintings by Derain brought between 210 and 420 francs according to size. Vlaminck's *L'Ecluse à Bouginald* (The Lock at Bouginald) sold for 170 francs. Picasso averaged 1,500 francs.

At last the prize piece of the auction was up on the block—*Les Bateleurs*, also known as *La Famille de Saltimbanques,* an oil painting 90 by 84 inches in size. The bidding would start at 8,000 francs, it was timidly announced. Among those in attendance it was generally known that André Level, director of the Peau d'Ours collection, had acquired it for 1,000 francs. It had remained rolled up for several years because no member had an apartment big enough to hang it. The bidding rose steadily, to finally hit 11,500 francs. Heinrich Thannhauser carried off the prize. No one else could compete at that level. But the gavel had hardly fallen when the rumor began that the dealer would have paid twice that amount to own the painting.[167]

Kahnweiler quickly made his way to the exit in order to be the first to bring the news to Picasso: the total of the sale was 106,250 francs for the Peau d'Ours collection. The final sales far exceeded the initial subscription. According to the original agreement, each subscriber would have his investment returned with a 3.5 percent rate of interest. Twenty percent of the proceeds of the sale was put back into the hands of André Level in payment for his services. Each of the artists would have a share of 20 percent of the profit, so that they would divide 12,000 francs among themselves.[168]

Here was the proof—there was a market for contemporary art. The reactions to the sale varied. Inevitably, there were people who recalled a drawing by Picasso which could be had for less than 20 francs ten years ago now auctioned at 2,600 francs at Hôtel Drouot, and that when *Les Bateleurs* was first placed in the window of a gallery, it drew crowds of idlers and passersby burst out laughing.[169] The daily *Paris-Midi*, started two years earlier as a popular conservative newspaper, saw in the success of the Peau d'Ours collection the proof of German interference in French art. The Germans were accused of using painting as a Trojan horse to confuse, subvert, and conquer France. Why would a man such as Thannhauser invest such a large sum of money in the daubings of a Picasso if it were not for the purpose of sowing discord and doubt into the French art market? What other reason would such a large number of German dealers have for coming to the auction? The worst of this was that such arguments always fell on fertile ground.

High prices were paid by undesirable foreigners for grotesque and misshapen works, and it is the Germans, as we have always warned, with reason, who in two weeks paid and raised these prices. They have a clear strategy: naive young painters will be caught in the trap. They will start imitating the imitator Picasso, who made a pastiche of everything and, running out of material to imitate, sank to the cubist bluff. Thus the qualities of balance and order which are characteristic of our national art will gradually disappear, much to the great joy of M. Thannhauser and his fellow countrymen, who will one day suddenly stop buying Picassos and by then will move everything from the Louvre *gratis*, without any protest, because our blind snobs and intellectual anarchists are their unwitting accomplices. The money they spent yesterday was well invested.[170]

But of all the reactions to the historic sale the pinnacle of absurdity was reached not by an art critic but by a doctor, a self-proclaimed art lover, who claimed to have found a scientific explanation for cubism: a pathology. One need only look at a Braque or Picasso with eyes half closed to observe a scotoma, a common symptom of opthalmic migraines. All these distortions, these shapes in flux, these broken lines, were, he said, an effort to systematize a transient phenomenon of visual pathology.[171] In other words, cubism could be cured. Kahnweiler should have felt reassured— his condition was serious but not irremediable.

On the morning of June 12, 1914, at the Parc des Princes, there was a large gathering of journalists and celebrities from the art world, who were waiting for a duel to begin. On one side was Gottlieb, an expressionist familiar to the Salon des Indépendants and the Salon d'Automne; on the other was Moïse Kisling, a character from Montparnasse. They were both dressed in dark slacks and white shirts. In the first round the men fired at each other from a distance of twenty-five yards. Then they returned to the racetrack where they continued to fight, using Italian sabers. They wore metal guards around their necks as a protection from . . . decapitation?

"Allez, messieurs!" cried the director of the duel, M. Dubois, a master of arms.

One blow was parried. A duelist lost his hair, with an awful three-inch slash in his scalp, and he began bleeding profusely. Then the stronger of the two struck again. After the scalp it was the nose; but once a dressing was applied they started up even more ferociously, and one duelist lost a bit of chin. It was a slaughter. The master of arms ordered the duel to be stopped, but the combatants insisted on continuing in this way for six more rounds. Dubois himself was almost wounded, but he succeeded in grabbing hold of one of the fighters and ordering a stop to the massacre. On the benches both bohemian and fashionable observers heaved a sigh of relief. The reporter for *l'Intransigeant*, who covered the event and had attended many duels, was astounded by this one. "They fought with a fierceness that was foreign to our customary ways," he noted.[172] It was true they were both from Poland.

By the end of the duel, people had to pick up the pieces. Everyone asked why there had been such vehemence. The special reporter from the *Miroir* knew the underlying motives. "It was a matter of honor. They did not think about art in the same way."[173]

Two weeks later came the assassination at Sarajevo. Then it was the real war.

War was a vicious rumor by alarmists; it was important not to panic. At the end of July 1914, after President Poincaré and Premier René Viviani's trip to Russia, after Austria's ultimatum to Serbia, after the union demonstrations against war, Kahnweiler was making plans for his vacation as if nothing had happened.

Planning to leave for a month, he would return in five years.

Vlaminck was in despair on seeing people blithely going on holiday— they were so unaware. For a long time he knew that a German invasion of Paris was imminent. Without even consulting Kahnweiler, his co-owner, he had sold the two boats for three hundred francs and sent him his share.

What if Vlaminck had been right all along? Kahnweiler thought of Picasso's advice to take out naturalization papers. "In case there is a war it will get you out of hot water." Kahnweiler always said he fully intended to do it once he had passed the age for military service—it was impossible for him to carry arms under another flag.[174]

He had remained profoundly German despite circumstances. Even when he moved to Paris, he refused to recast his name in French. He did not want to follow the example of the Polish painter Ludwig Markus who, at the urging of his friend Apollinaire (formerly known as Guillaume de Kostrowitzky), had become Louis Marcoussis, from a local name in the countryside. Or of the Russian painter Leopold Stzurvage, who decided to lighten his name by eliminating the consonants *t* and *z*, making it Survage. Kahnweiler wanted his name, his identity in every sense of the word.

Kahnweiler and his wife had planned to spend their vacation in Italy, and at the end of July they were in upper Bavaria, where they went into the mountains. On July 30, the evening after Austria-Hungary declared war on Serbia and Russia started full mobilization, and a few hours before Germany delivered an ultimatum to France, the Kahnweilers succeeded in crossing the Swiss border in the middle of the night.

On August 1 they were on a train taking them toward Italy. During the long voyage, every time the train crossed a bridge Kahnweiler hoped it would collapse and everything would be over.[175]

He finally understood that war had arrived. Everything was coming to an end, everything was lost. As he sat and sorted out his thoughts, words, bits of conversations, and faces came to mind as if the people in his memory were sitting in the compartment. He thought of all his conversations with Vlaminck, who had been right all along. Only last month he had received a worried letter from Derain: "The political situation seems very strange to me . . ."[176] He had understood that in far-off Avignon; whereas Kahnweiler, who had been in Paris, had refused to see anything. When the train crossed the frontier into Italy, he thought of the last seven years that had elapsed since the creation of his gallery. They had been "Dionysiac years,"[177] filled with joy, and so carefree that he could work with artists in total disregard of critics and the general public. Perhaps that would never again be possible.

In the dark hours between the last day of July and that first day of August, Kahnweiler was totally conscious that the fate of Europe hung in the balance. A world was disappearing, or rather, a certain concept of European civilization. He who had ignored the reality of danger now had presentiments about the course of history. He was a man of good faith and so could admit that this war was precisely the one possibility he had never foreseen. His whole life had been based on the belief that it could never happen. He sighed, "I never wanted to believe it, right up to the last minute. Without the machinations of the Austro-Germanic military clique, it would have been avoided again this time."[178]

Rome was the next stop, and he had to decide on a course of action. Enlisting was out of the question since he was a pacifist; unbending and firm in his principles, he would never carry arms. Even admitting that, the crisis made him waver: if he were given a rifle, against whom would he take aim?

As a German subject he ought to enlist in the kaiser's army, but that was unthinkable as it would bring him face-to-face with his French friends. If he enlisted in the French army it would be the same situation, only this time he would be forced to confront his childhood friends. Not only would he be a deserter, but a traitor as well. He visualized other alternatives, such as volunteering with the French army as a stretcher bearer. As a man without a country, he could enlist in the Foreign Legion, as had the dueling painter Kisling. None of these choices seemed plausible. The idea of killing was repugnant to him. Heavy helmet, pointed helmet, or white képi—he came to the decision that he would not participate in this war.

It was August 2. Picasso had worked in Avignon during the summer, not far from Braque in Sorgues and Derain in Montfavet, and they had seen a lot of each other. That was over now; socialist leader Jean Jaurès had just been assassinated and a general mobilization was announced. Belgium had been invaded. The two French artists had to report back to their military board, leaving their Spanish friend behind to continue work. Picasso accompanied them to the train station. He later told Kahnweiler, "I never saw them again."

It was a manner of speaking; of course he saw them again; but they were not the same. The war changed those who went away and those who stayed behind. War changed everything. For the artists of rue Vignon, the ivory tower was gone, and the days when they could work as a team were over. They would continue to work, obviously, but on other things and in different ways. Just as the war of 1870 had put off the project of some future impressionists (that of creating a cooperative to sponsor free exhibitions rather than the competition in the official Salons), the war of 1914 marked the breakup of the pioneering circle of cubist painters.[179]

On August 2, in Rome, the Kahnweilers checked into the Hotel Eden, as was their habit. "Heini" could not hold still; he ran out of his room periodically to the streets for the special editions that succeeded each other at a disconcerting rate throughout the day. Then the next day came the dreaded news: Germany had declared war on France. Kahnweiler experienced a personal collapse while awaiting that of the nation.

He felt destroyed in several ways—as a rebel and as an enemy, German by birth and French by choice. If he were forced to enlist, it would be with France.[180] At the moment he could not see what sort of service he could render. He had to continue traveling.

He had wanted to go to Siena, a place he knew well and whose beauty he appreciated. They decided to go there despite the war; the round-trip tickets had been purchased. When he was installed in his new hotel room, he returned to his favorite activity, letter writing. Hermann Rupf, his most steady correspondent, advised him against returning to Paris; since he did not want to return to his native land, Rupf suggested that the Kahnweilers go to Switzerland.

Gris also wrote him often, never more so than now. Kahnweiler suddenly became conscious that his artists needed him in order to live and for basic necessities. Gris, who was describing the misery of the situation, was beginning to panic and could not hide it. He needed three hundred francs.[181] The letter, though dated August 1, had been delayed, and it was quite an accomplishment to track him down. As it took a great deal for the artist to bring himself to even ask for money, Kahnweiler rushed to send him a money order and would continue to do so for several months.

He was worried both about his artists and the fate of his paintings, and what would become of his stock and of his gallery. His friend Eugène

Reignier kept him up to date in his letters. It was rumored in Paris that Fénéon had had all the paintings of the Bernheim-Jeune Gallery transported to Bordeaux, where he entrusted them to a collector thrilled at this undreamed-of windfall of fifty-four crates. Kahnweiler refused to move his paintings. Brenner, his business colleague from the United States, had pleaded with him, "Let me take them to New York."

"No, no, we mustn't do that, we must leave them where they are. Anyway, nothing will happen to them!"

With this obstinate refusal Kahnweiler had sealed his fate without realizing it. The gallery remained closed, but he continued to pay the rent on it so as not to despair of the postwar period. His enforced Italian vacation was lasting four months, far too long. He could no longer stand it; he had to make up his mind. Everyone was on the move except for the Kahnweilers. Even if his choice was more difficult than that of his friends, he must move forward. Rupf convinced him, having promised to help, and he and Lucie decided to go to Switzerland.

In the final analysis, the true break in the life of all these men was not the beginning of the twentieth century, but the first shots fired by the cannons of World War I. Until now Kahnweiler had been a man of the nineteenth century; henceforth he was a man from the days before the Great War.

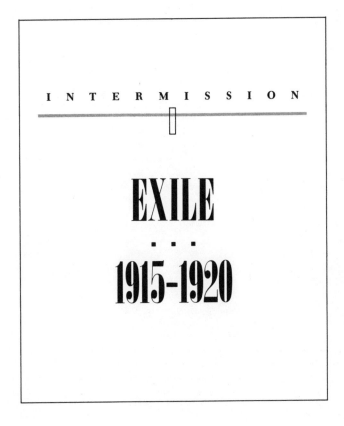

INTERMISSION

EXILE
· · ·
1915-1920

▭ The Swiss have a saying that can apply to different circumstances: "neutral but not cowardly." They are fond of saying, "Here we do not return refugees to their country of origin. The number of diplomats assigned here has increased so rapidly that we have become the turnstile of Europe. Here people still take the time to enjoy life despite the catastrophe." That was Bern at the beginning of 1915.

Kahnweiler and his wife arrived to stay with Rupf; by making this decision, he committed himself for the next five years, which would be years of curtailed business activities and intense reflection. Making the best of his position as a neutral intellectual, he would turn toward the past; he wanted to record his experiences in the realm of painting and piece together all the disparate, often contradictory elements about a period he knew had been heroic, but which now had come to an end. Kahnweiler was a man with a sense of perspective and proportion. This enforced exile was the opportunity to take the measure of things.

For the duration of the war he would devote himself to writing. When he was not writing, he attended courses in philosophy at the university and would spend long hours reading and trying to fill in the gaps of his education, especially in the history of art and aesthetics. When not pursuing his studies, he would try once again to become the art dealer he always felt himself to be.

* * *

As soon as they had settled down, Rupf lent them the amount they needed for living expenses and would continue to do so. Needless to say it was tacitly understood between the friends that the loan would be repaid as soon as Kahnweiler was back in business—something Kahnweiler tried to do while still in Switzerland. It was as much a question of principle as of pride.[1]

Kahnweiler immediately took up where he had left off, but without a gallery. He increased his letters to artists, asking for paintings. In Switzerland he could still sell, but on a very limited scale. Rupf was the most avid collector; he wanted more Braques, Manolos, and others. All this was nothing compared to the volume of business at rue Vignon a year previously: Kahnweiler would need several Rupfs to earn enough to be materially independent. But in Bern it was difficult, because the town and canton were traditional, conservative, and closed to the outside world. Other than Rupf, there would be only one other true collector of modern art, Walter Hadorn, and these two did not constitute a market.

Kahnweiler tried farther afield, throughout Switzerland, but he prospected in vain and was quickly discouraged. Rupf was unique in the area. Kahnweiler thought of him as the model of the true collector, who loved what he purchased. The idea of appreciation in value never even dawned on him, and he only rarely let go of paintings. He resold only when he found that a work on his wall had become unbearable. He also gave much thought to his acquisitions, and his library, containing the whole of the history of art and philosophy, bore witness to that fact.[2]

Rupf was initiated into contemporary art by Kahnweiler, but he in turn influenced Kahnweiler politically. The young art dealer was and always would be a socialist, but he was never militant. He used his powers of persuasion in the service of art only. He agreed with Rupf politically that this was the last dynastic war, and fighting to gain territory was not a cause everyone supported.[3]

Most of the emigrés who passed through Rupf's drawing room needing help or a reference were sent by the Socialist Party. There Kahnweiler quickly became acquainted with an exceptional political personality. Robert Grimm, three years older, had already become a national representative and was about to be made president of the executive committee of Bern's Socialist Party. He was an efficient politician, a convincing speaker, a shrewd strategist, and a doctrinaire whose personality dominated his party.[4]

Grimm had persuaded Rupf to join his newspaper, the *Berner Tagwacht*, as an art critic. Rupf started by writing reviews of exhibitions, then long articles on the function of the critic as a mediator, the social position of artists in a capitalist society, the democratization of painting, and the substitution of the art dealer for the patron of the arts.[5]

Kahnweiler was impressed by the socialist leader, but he realized that it was not his world. Although he would agree to lecture on modern art at a workers' university under the aegis of the Socialist Party, he remained true to his reserved nature and never became further involved.

Later he realized that had he frequented Grimm more often, he would have met Karl Radek and the other Bolshevik leaders. At the university library he often worked next to a young Russian even more retiring than he, of the same age, who was similarly lost in his books. They saw each other but never spoke, remaining absorbed in their work. Finally, Kahnweiler attended a lecture, and there on the podium he saw his fellow student: Grigory Zinoviev, who had organized the Kronstadt revolt of 1906, and who would soon become the president of the Comintern.

At first Kahnweiler's life in Bern was more political than artistic, reflecting the situation at large in Europe. He soon grew bored with it, and the moment the postal system functioned again his only thought was to obtain news of his artists, his family, and his friends. What had become of them? What if they had been killed during the first day at the front like Charles Péguy, a lieutenant in the infantry, one of the first struck when the fighting started, and the first French writer killed in the war? During his five years in exile Kahnweiler's correspondence with France was the chronicle of artists in torment.

He had stopped worrying about Max Jacob when he received this letter: "I spent the month of August [1914] at Enghien as a civilian ambulance driver but in reality revising my manuscripts in a garden full of vegetables and weeping young mothers."[6] Max Jacob would never change. He went so far as to send a congratulatory letter to Maurice Raynal for having been wounded: "It's good for the honor of the whole corporation!"[7]

Marcoussis, meanwhile, was an artilleryman who showed his officer's braid to Gris and was infuriated at being called "corporal." He had taken to cursing furiously and studied ballistics manuals in order to be promoted to second lieutenant.[8] Metzinger was a medic in Sainte-Menehould, Max Jacob had found an office at the Sacré-Coeur, and Léonce Rosenberg, the art dealer, joined the English, where he was a translator for the Royal Flying Corps. Apollinaire had been a sergeant in the artillery and during a leave from the front was transferred to the infantry as a second lieutenant.

There was also the bad news that Braque had been wounded in the head and had undergone a trepanning operation. It would be a year before he was strong enough to paint again. Vlaminck, who had become an industrial draftsman, first worked in a munitions factory in the Paris region, then in the aviation center at Le Bourget. It was rumored that Derain, a foot soldier, then artilleryman, was making masks out of the shell casings.[9] At the front he drove a heavy tractor pulling artillery. And there was a story about Léger, that the commander of his brigade and the captain of engineers had lined the walls of a shelter with his paintings and drawings. But try to confirm this.

Léger had been mobilized at the beginning of the war, and his pencil sketches bore witness to the hardships the ordinary soldier endured. He drew the men in the trenches, their world of mud, iron, and blood. This genius, drawing in notebooks, said that his world had been renewed by contact with the people: "It was at the front that my feet touched the ground. . . . I experienced war. . . . That's how I was formed."[10] A stretcher bearer at Verdun, he was running to the place where a shell had exploded to help a wounded man. A soldier called out to him, "Don't rush. We can pick him up with a sponge." The man was all pulp. Later in the war, Léger would be gassed.[11] He would speak for a long time about this war and could not forget Verdun, saying that he could never again be a "cubist, who reduced men to pieces." When Kahnweiler returned he would become severe with him, trying to put a limit to all his talk about how the war had renewed his art. "He had been impressed by the 75-mm shells, but he could just as easily have watched them in a practice maneuver."[12] For the painter, the state of war was nothing more than life at an accelerated pace, whereas for the art dealer it was the exact opposite. At the end of the war there were only two categories of men, those who did not go to the front, and those who had returned.

It is inconceivable that Kahnweiler did not understand that such an experience could change a life. Even a pacifist could conceive that, and there were many examples on both sides. Oskar Kokoschka, who had enlisted in the dragoons, received a bullet wound in the head and was bayoneted in the lungs during an attack in Galicia. After he recovered, he would return to the front as an officer in charge of war painters and journalists. How could he help being marked by the war?[13] Max Beckmann, who was the same age as Kahnweiler, had exhibited his paintings at Cassirer's with great success in 1913. The war broke his momentum and transformed his painting. As an enlisted man he was assigned to the medical corps, but he had to resign a year later due to a nervous breakdown. His paintings from this period are filled with his painful experience. He would become a great expressionist painter, but he was not alone since his fellow countryman Ernst Ludwig Kirchner also suffered a nervous breakdown after being mobilized. The daily routine of military life and the horrors of war destroyed him, as can be seen in his self-portraits of 1915. Even Kahnweiler's brother Gustave was permanently marked by having fought in a regiment of mounted cavalry. The few artists left in Paris to continue working were the Spaniards—Picasso, Gris, and Manolo—but they were alone.

On January 4, 1915, Kahnweiler registered as a businessman on the city rolls of Bern. When he applied to the authorities of the canton for temporary residence, asking for papers that would allow him to remain until the end of the hostilities, the police investigated his past. Naturally there was nothing to be found, as his life had been more peaceful than most of the refugees requesting asylum from the Swiss state.

The authorities were open to his plea that he was over thirty years old and thus could not enlist in the reserves. Also because of the war and his German citizenship, France had sequestered all his worldly goods until such time as hostilities ceased. The investigation showed that it was unlikely he would ever be a charge of the state. His father was an upstanding businessman of Frankfurt who was in a position to support him should the need arise, but even more important, the honorable Hermann Rupf, so well known in Bern, would guarantee Kahnweiler and his family and was prepared to post a bond. Kahnweiler's papers were stamped and sealed, and he, along with his wife and sister, was granted asylum by the Swiss.[14]

During the next five years they would have three homes. Twice they moved in with Rupf, for the first three months and the last seven months of their stay. They would also avail themselves of the hospitality of their friend Bernard Glaser, a bibliophile bookseller who was one of the first subscribers to the Kahnweiler editions, and their third home was the Pension Boisfleury.

Once these material and legal matters were settled, Kahnweiler started to work, writing and maintaining his correspondence. He was as concerned about the predicament of artists in Paris as of art dealers there. Not that he was overly curious or jealous or competitive, but he understood that his artists were in a vulnerable state since they were deprived of their income. He felt helpless as he knew others would take advantage of the situation; that was plain commercial logic.

Everyone in the Paris art world knew that his stock had been sequestered as enemy holdings: he was German, and it was wartime. At first his paintings had been stored in a damp warehouse in rue de Rome. Luckily the administrator, with whom he was on friendly terms, succumbed to his entreaties and moved them to a better location. Strangely, it was the younger, less-established dealers who first made inquiries. Paul Guillaume asked Apollinaire how he could obtain and sell the cubists, and received this letter in reply from Military Sector 138:

"I'm afraid that Kahnweiler's artists are all taken, especially Picasso, but give it a try. For Picasso you would have to guarantee fifty thousand francs a year. The others need less, but Braque was wounded, a convalescing lieutenant at the Hôtel Meurice . . ."[15]

Others asked, but the most determined and efficient was Léonce Rosenberg, thirty-eight years old, owner of the Galerie L'Effort Moderne, who had bought Gris and Picasso works from Kahnweiler before the war. He understood immediately from Gris's letters what was happening. The artist could no longer make do with the meager income from his two most fervent admirers, Brenner and Gertrude Stein, and Kahnweiler on his side had had to stop sending his stipend for lack of funds.

Gris was the personification of the gentleman, but he was in a desperate state when Léonce Rosenberg visited him with the avowed intention of buying his paintings. Rosenberg had made discreet inquiries and had backed off when the artist had mentioned his contract with Kahnweiler. When others asked the same question, but with less tact, he could insist the painting they wanted was unfinished, or that he did not need the money. But it was impossible for him to continue this, try as he might to resist. He was beginning to feel his work had progressed. If it had not been for the war, Kahnweiler might have been reaping the fruits of his patience: "My canvases are starting to have a unity they did not have before. It was that inventory of objects that I found discouraging. I still have to make a great effort to attain on the canvas what I can visualize. I feel that although my ideas are developed, their plastic expression is not. I lack the aesthetics that only experience can give me. I am so engrossed in my work that I never go out and never see anyone."[16]

He was working well, and it would have been criminal to slow down his creative drive because of a question of money. Kahnweiler made a decision that violated all his principles; he released him from his contract. Rosenberg immediately bought eleven paintings. He had been waiting for the opportunity. The correspondence between Kahnweiler and Gris would become less frequent, and by the end of 1915 it would cease altogether for the duration of the war. Each man worked at the task at hand, the artist at painting, the dealer at writing. They knew that their friendship would survive intact. On his table Kahnweiler kept Gris's last letter, of December 4, which he often reread: "Sometimes everything that I'm doing in painting feels so stupid. The sensitive and sensuous side must still exist but there's no room for it now in my paintings. Perhaps I am making the mistake of wanting to find, in a new art, the pictorial qualities of classical art. All the same I feel my paintings are excessively cold. Yet Ingres is cold and Seurat also. Seurat has that meticulous quality I dislike intensely in my own work. I would so much like my painting to have the ease and coquettish quality of unfinished work. Too bad! But after all, I make paintings that are as I am!"[17]

Would Léonce Rosenberg understand such an artist and would he have the sensitivity to know how to be supportive? Kahnweiler had his doubts, as he believed his rival and peer was a "well-intentioned man" with a limited artistic and commercial sense.[18] He reproached him for indiscriminately mixing on his walls the master cubists and their imitators.

The man had his flaws. He was frantic, irascible, and vain, but he guaranteed the artists' livelihood during the absence of their mentor. He approached the cubists as "a novice to an unknown religion"[19] and purchased works by Gris (placed under contract November 1917), Picasso, Braque, and Léger. He played a role that Kahnweiler believed was "absolutely praiseworthy."[20] He had understood what their situation would have been if Rosenberg had not been there.

Kahnweiler's task was made more difficult because France was in a state of war, with all the consequent upheavals of daily life in organized society. It was not a propitious time for selling paintings. Gris had told Kahnweiler that he no longer took his meals in the watering holes of Montmartre and Montparnasse because he did not want to hear the rude remarks about the artists of rue Vignon and their "manager."[21]

Obviously, this was not a good time to be a German and Jewish dealer in France. So many grudges and bitter feelings exacerbated by the war were expressed openly. Some were baldly contradictory. Nathan Wildenstein received the following note: "Sir, I am the widow of Edouard Drumont, the fierce anti-Semite. I hope that this will not make you less impartial in your dealings. I have paintings to sell and hope that you will come to see them."[22]

More serious and significant was a lecture by Tony Tollet at a meeting of the Academy of Sciences, Literature, and Arts in Lyons under the following title: "On the Influence of the Jewish-German Corporation of Paris Art Dealers on French Art."[23] According to the speaker, things first went wrong in French art with the impressionists, a school that was launched by and owed its fame to those dealers who knew how to profit from it. These dealers quickly prospered by cultivating wealthy collectors, by buying all of the works of an artist in order to speculate with full control over the stock, and by falsely inflating the prices. He blamed them for having influenced and bribed critics and having started art magazines in order to better control the market: "These are standard business practices, and Jewish art dealers are only doing their work, we might say. If in addition to all this they happen to be German, then it becomes apparent that they are methodically undermining French culture and exerting an influence on French taste."

It came as no surprise that this academy condemned snobbery and decadence, and they earnestly called for a return to a true French art. The speaker did not cite a single name in the course of this exposé, knowing that for every Kahnweiler or Rosenberg, Wildenstein or Weill, there were several Durand-Ruels, Vollards, Sagots, Tanguys, or Guillaumes.

In 1916 it was said in Bern that the Swiss army was a past master of not waging war. It was a saying that a man such as Kahnweiler would gladly take up as his motto.

The throngs of refugees did not stop growing. The right of asylum was a tradition and the duty of every Swiss citizen. A large portion would certainly have preferred Paris or London; but this neutral country was the best place in troubled times, and due to the force of circumstances it became an intellectual and artistic center for Europe and the scene of many intrigues and plots. In 1913 the diplomatic community in Bern numbered seventy-one; five years later it had increased to two hundred twenty-four.[24]

There was a wide diversity of people there: Russians such as Lenin, Zinoviev, Sokolovsky. The day he arrived, Lenin paid a visit to Grimm at home but the socialist leader refused to publish Lenin's articles in his newspaper, persuaded as he was that they would be understood as a call to civil war in Switzerland.[25] The Russians, who went from Bern to Zurich, were the most agitated of the exiles from central and eastern Europe. They were not all involved in revolutionary activities, however. Igor Stravinsky, at the age of thirty-four, was already known as the composer of *The Firebird, Petrushka, The Rite of Spring,* and *Rossignol.* He fled to Switzerland from France, leaving Sergei Diaghilev's Ballets Russes behind, and it was to Paris that he dreamed of returning after the war.

There were also German exiles whose pacifism was their common link. Kirchner, the painter and engraver, withdrew to Davos to forget his traumatic military experience. Paul Cassirer, the art dealer of the impressionists and the post-impressionists in Berlin since the beginning of the century, spent his time in exile publishing the art review, *Kunstlerflugblatter*, with drawings and caricatures appropriate to these times of war. Ludwig Rubiner, editor in chief of *Zeit-Echo*, and René Schickele, who directed the magazine *Die Weissen Blatter* in Zurich, tried to continue their work as before.[26]

The country was a crossroads and a tower of Babel. The poet Ivan Goll was in Lausanne; James Joyce was writing *Ulysses*, his "prose cathedral," in Zurich; and Georges Pitoëff, who was not sorry to have chosen Switzerland for his honeymoon, had settled in Geneva with a troupe of actors. Of the French, novelist Romain Rolland was the best known, and his articles in the *Journal de Genève*, collected and published as *Au-dessus de la mêlée*, would have such an enormous impact that he would receive the Nobel Prize. "To each his duty: to the army to defend the soil of the Fatherland; to thinking men the defense of their sanity." Kahnweiler felt close to a thinker such as Rolland, who was an advocate of Franco-German reconciliation and criticized Prussian militarism and the Wagnerians, but he made no effort to seek him out.

Paul Klee felt that he had made great progress in his own work every time he visited the collection of his friend Rupf. Kahnweiler was meeting a variety of artists. Hans Arp was an early acquaintance with whom he started corresponding in November 1915. The sculptor, poet, and painter from Alsace was half-French, half-German and was sometimes called Hans and sometimes Jean. His conflicting double culture was very attractive to Kahnweiler. At the beginning of their friendship the art dealer impressed Arp by knowing his reputation from having visited, as Klee had, Rupf's private collection.

It was due to Arp that on a trip to Zurich Kahnweiler made the acquaintance of a young Rumanian poet, Tristan Tzara, an excitable personality. Kahnweiler was captivated. As an editor he especially enjoyed Tzara's volume of poetry with a title that he wished could have appeared on his own list between Apollinaire and Max Jacob: *La première aventure céleste de M. Antipyrine* (The First Celestial Adventure of Mr. Antipyrine). In Zurich on February 5, 1916, at 1 Spiegelgasse, the inauguration of the "Cabaret Voltaire" took place in an old brasserie. The event would have remained inconsequential if Tzara, Arp, and their friends had not selected the hybrid place—a café, theater, and gallery—to launch a movement they called "Dada." Kahnweiler was surprised, amused, and interested, although cautious at first. He was afraid that in its general and systematic questioning of everything it would attack cubism, which was so dear to him. He had cause to worry. If for Tzara and his friends cubism was "everything marvelous and extraordinary," they also wanted to surpass it, considering Picasso, Braque, and the others as old classics already.[27]

Kahnweiler looked upon them with a cold eye: they were good people who wanted attention and gesticulated with hands and feet to amaze the good Swiss. He believed that the movement was artificial, and like so many "schools" would come to naught,[28] but he enjoyed their nihilism. This way of expressing despair, this taste for tearing everything down was suited to the mood of the times.[29] He maintained his distance from the Cabaret Voltaire, feeling skeptical about movements that claimed to be self-created, when in fact they were engendered by circumstances—the war, in this case. But he stayed informed about its evolution and its potential impact on art, and he awaited the first dadaist publications. Hans Arp's exhibit of collages impressed him even though he felt that the work was immature.

Arp helped Kahnweiler by introducing him to René Schickele, also from Alsace, because Kahnweiler had finished writing an essay entitled "On Cubism" and wanted to place it in a review of some standing. It was not his only writing since settling in Switzerland, but it was the first he wanted published. It was accepted by *Die Weissen Blatter*, but Kahnweiler had a rude shock on reading it when he noticed that the editor had made numerous cuts without telling him.

Disappointed and furious, Kahnweiler would look for an editor who would respect the integrity of his essay. Four years later he would have the satisfaction of giving his revised and augmented text to Delphin Verlag, which would publish it under the title *Der weg zum Kubismus*.[30] The work is basic to the history of cubism and to the life of Kahnweiler. The text (some fifty pages long) has been translated as *The Rise of Cubism*. Originally it had been conceived as part of a larger treatise he would never write, to be called *The Object of Aesthetics*.

In 1915–1916 Kahnweiler was one of the few people in Europe who could write a history of cubism from firsthand experience. He had been a participant and a witness, having watched the development of the paintings to their full term, so to speak, and was not someone to obscure the subject, or make vague conjectures about what the artist wanted to express. He believed he understood the work because he was there. He knew the painters' surroundings, their states of mind, their personal problems, their doubts, their hopes. He was always the first person they informed about their inner lives as well as their daily circumstances, even when they were far from Paris.

He was "the true witness of the heroic years of cubism." His book is a document of the period, a text filled with ideas, theories, and concepts based on the clinical observations of his artistic experience. Furthermore, he was perhaps the only person in Europe with a photographic collection of every stage of these paintings, as well as a full record of press clippings of articles on cubism between 1907 and 1914. His memory was strong and precise, but he was frustrated by his exile and by not having access to this invaluable historical iconographic record. The materials had been gathered, classified, organized, and labeled, but it was sequestered with everything else in his gallery.

There was yet another factor which made him the best person to write the history of cubism: he was no longer working in the midst of it. Had he still been a dealer at his desk in Paris, he would never have decided to write down his experiences. The demands of business and lack of time were not as conducive to the task as was his exile in Bern. He felt that when an art dealer wrote the "history" of the painting he loved and represented, he was also writing a promotional work, and Kahnweiler would never have permitted himself to do that.

His extensive wartime reading and education naturally altered his thinking and influenced his writing. Switzerland was the ideal place to obtain the books he needed for his work. He had the long-awaited volume by his friend Carl Einstein, *Negerplastik*, published in Leipzig in 1915. Kahnweiler had read it through several times and considered it *the* reference book on African art and sculpture, but also indispensable to an understanding of cubism. He would think about fragments of conversations he had had with Einstein before he left France: "All the same, cubism would not have impassioned us as it did had it only been an optical phenomenon."[31] This statement, which he considered from every angle, caused him to think about his own recent experiences. He consulted other respected sources, such as the writings of Alois Riegl,[32] from whom he drew the idea that all art is the perfect expression of its cultural milieu. It is from a lack of ability to imitate nature, or to continue producing traditional concepts, that a society decides to produce different forms. For Kahnweiler the artists produced not *objects*, but *concepts*.

It was not coincidental that the first word of *The Rise of Cubism* was "impressionism." This was the starting point, and Kahnweiler praised its qualities—"It transformed the palette and destroyed ancient laws, useless precepts"—in order to better denounce the mediocre goals impressionism set for itself. From the group he isolated Cézanne and Seurat to make them the precursors who showed both the way back to the composition of the canvas and the use of light as a means of showing objects as three-dimensional. In fact, according to his point of view, Cézanne more than the impressionist school should be credited as the originator of modern painting. After this vital preliminary statement Kahnweiler proceeded to the heart of the matter: how Braque and Picasso confronted the problems of form and color.

The book comprises various pieces, written at different periods of reflection and arranged chronologically. He was far removed from the critic Maurice Raynal, who said, "Attributing dates to a work of art, like giving its market value, is for the purpose of exalting it or diminishing it."[33] Kahnweiler insisted on giving dates to show the lines of development and influence, as well as the interruptions.

In 1907—the year of *Les Demoiselles d'Avignon*—came the end of optical representation in painting. Kahnweiler called it a "demarcation point in the history of art";[34] it marked a transformation in the concept of representation of space which had not altered since the Renaissance.[35] Despite his lack of perspective, Kahnweiler also named 1914 as the end of an era. He seems to have understood that after the war the cubists of the heroic period would no longer act in concert like a team of mountain climbers attached to the same safety rope; that they would turn their backs on the collective quest to isolate themselves in an individualism heightened by success, which is exactly what did happen.

The separation, the psychological trauma, the disorientation, and the return to a postwar life would have delivered a brutal blow to the momentum of the cubist movement in any case. Kahnweiler was convinced that no new style could have come of it. The natural growing apart of the cubist group was accelerated by the war.[36] He believed that the cubist period had come to an end, although it would continue individually as long as a cubist painter survived. It would be recorded in history as a period of transition with as great an influence as that of Giotto on his followers.[37]

One aspect of his position, which he developed in his text, became increasingly important: his rejection of painting that he found objectionable due to its ornamentation or decoration. These two words he would use to designate paintings he judged beyond redemption, such as when he began to reject Matisse, and especially when he dismissed out-of-hand abstract painting. The following passage expresses his uncompromising artistic position:

It is appropriate to bring up a trend that has set for itself the goal of painting without a subject, in order to compose harmonies of colors on the canvas without making any reference to an object in nature.

My attitude toward this trend cannot be left in doubt. They can certainly create pleasing works, but they are not "paintings." The problem of painting, the concentration on the multiplicity of forms in the world within the unity of a work of art, is a problem unknown to this school. It has cast aside the problems with which lyrical painting has wrestled for years. The works are decorative and will ornament walls, but that's all. It's not artistic vision that is the genesis of the work, it's the sense of decoration. That is all that these paintings ever will be, decorations.[38]

In time, this judgment would grow so intransigent as to brook no discussion. Conversely, when he exalted the work of a favorite artist as the highest attainment of painting, notably Masaccio in the Carmine Church in Florence, he would exclaim, "There is not a bit of concern for ornamental decoration: it is reality, absolute truth."[39]

For his part, Kahnweiler wished that decorative painters would leave off painting to take up ceramics, weaving, or glassblowing. The most nefarious of their activities, he felt, was their distortion of collage techniques for decorative ends. It was opposed to the nature of true painting: "The aim of painting is simple, objective, and realistic," he would say, identifying with the cubist struggle, as if he had collaborated on creating the actual works. It was an expression of pride, as well as humility, from a refugee in Bern who posed as the repository of the truth about cubism. He was the guardian of the temple and the watchdog of orthodoxy at the age of thirty-two. He was an art dealer without portfolio.

By 1917 Kahnweiler was becoming very impatient; he was finding time heavy on his hands and Switzerland too small. He had never felt more "removed from the world"; he hardly ever left Bern. He felt less in sympathy with Romain Rolland than with Stefan Zweig, who wrote, "It is strange that what is considered liberty in Switzerland from afar has a different appearance when one is actually there. They [the Swiss] are perched on a steeple, isolated, detached, and in a way, lost. This little parcel of land is also a prison. It's a Robinson Crusoe existence when it comes to intellectual life."[40]

Kahnweiler no longer made the journey to Zurich to attend Tristan Tzara's lectures or the dadaist exhibitions. He was satisfied to read about them in the review *Dada*, "the only one striving for new ideas," according to him.[41] It was regularly sent to him by the young rebels of the Cabaret Voltaire.

The worst part of this enforced idleness was the feeling of isolation and powerlessness. Elsewhere the world was changing drastically. It made Kahnweiler ill to think of it; he had lost thirty-five pounds. His correspondence with France had slowed to a trickle, and the papers and magazines reminded him cruelly of his absence from the scene.

In Russia the revolutionaries had forced the abdication of the tsar. In April Lenin had left Zurich to return to his country in a lead-lined railroad car. The German High Command had favored his passage through the territory they occupied as part of the effort to undermine the enemy. Vicious rumors had it that revolutionary soldiers were cutting up the Rembrandts in the Hermitage to line their boots. There was also the news that Marc Chagall had been made a commissar of art by the government in Vitebsk. Kandinsky, who had suffered so much from the war and had not been able to paint for the past two years, had returned to Russia and shortly afterward was nominated to a membership in the artistic section of the "People's Commissariat for Public Education," as well as to a professorship of the Moscow Academy of Fine Arts.

Kahnweiler was less affected by these developments than by events in the Paris art world that marked the transition between the prewar years and the twenties. A new periodical was launched, *Nord-Sud,* and in its very first issues published Pierre Reverdy's study of cubism. While Kahnweiler respected the poet and the subject enthralled him, it made him realize that he was no longer part of that movement. Kahnweiler, who wanted a monopoly on any commentaries on cubism, saw himself dispossessed by reason of his extended absence. It was not enough to write for the German press; he needed to be in Paris and publishing in French.

He consoled himself by reading, in the next issue of *Nord-Sud,* Georges Braque's essay, "Pensées et refléxions sur la peinture" (Thoughts and Reflections on Painting). He admired it so much that he translated it into German and sent it to *Kunstblatt,* which he considered the best art periodical in the German language. He felt as if his friend, his artist, had written it as a personal communication, discreetly veiled by his maxims, which divulged nothing but sounded so right. Reading it, Kahnweiler kept in mind Braque's paintings, tone of voice, smile, and glance:

> To paint is not to depict. . . . Writing is not describing. . . . I love the rules that adjust feelings. . . . The vase gives a form to the void, music to silence. . . . To make progress in art is not to extend one's ground but to become more familiar with one's limits. . . . Painting is not the art of doing everything.

This is the way Kahnweiler would always remember these formulations.[42]

In May 1917 Paris was still the capital of a nation at war, whose armies experienced the first mutinies at the front and whose government faced general strikes, more than it was the city of Picasso and Diaghilev. Rioting broke out at the premiere of Jean Cocteau's ballet *Parade* at the Théâtre du Châtelet. From the audience there were cries of "dirty Boches," which must have amused Picasso and Diaghilev. The audience hated the stage design by Picasso and the music by Erik Satie, a composer of genius who was part of Kahnweiler's circle of friends. He was a little older and was affectionately greeted as "our dear master." Who else would have introduced a typewriter into a symphony orchestra!

As the news reached Bern, the scandal created by *Parade* secured the reputation of Diaghilev as the impresario who would coordinate artists with temperaments as diverse as Cocteau, Picasso, Satie, and the choreographer Léonide Massine. By presenting *Parade* as a synthesis of all the arts, the Ballets Russes stopped being a Russian phenomenon and came to represent the international avant-garde. The controversy over *Parade* enlarged their scope and reputation. Reading about it, Kahnweiler felt that he belonged at the premiere of *Parade* rather than in his study, where he felt that he was going around in circles, or in the museum at Bern, where the Hodlers held no secrets for him.

He was even more impatient when he learned that the art market had started up again in Paris. Fénéon had recovered the stock of the Bernheim-Jeune Gallery, which he had stored at the start of the war with a collector in Bordeaux. That was a sure sign. Fénéon was so full of surprises: his friends recounted how at the beginning of the Russian Revolution when the Bolsheviks seized power, he made out a will leaving his personal collection—including one of the most complete collections of the works of Seurat—to the Russian people. He tore up his will when, in the course of a bloody reprisal in Russia, his anarchist friends were all killed.[43]

The art dealer whom Kahnweiler watched with the greatest interest was the shrewd, efficient Léonce Rosenberg. That year he would place Braque, Gris, and Léger under exclusive contracts. "It was to his credit," Kahnweiler always said, but it was a bitter cup to swallow, especially as these artists were dear to him and the market had suddenly come back to life.

With the increase in activity writers were publishing thoughts on aesthetics, new periodicals were being started, and exhibitions were opening one after the other. Art auctions of substantial quality were taking place at regular intervals. Hôtel Drouot was never empty, it was said, despite the offensive at the front. The industrialists and manufacturers who were profiting from the war purchased whole collections, without inventories. The American market raised the prices so that a painting by Monet priced at 37,000 francs a year before had recently been sold for 79,500 francs in New York. It was a new market, with a new clientele, and now there were international prices. Another indicator was reassuring: the price of a canvas stretched on a frame had gone up 150 percent, and the price of brushes by 40 percent.[44]

All this promise came to term in 1918, when everything seemed intensified in spite of "events," as people modestly called the war, even in Switzerland. Without leaving the country Kahnweiler attended several important exhibitions: young Swiss painting in Zurich, the Rodin and Dada exhibits in Geneva, and, at the Théâtre de Lausanne, the Pitoëff production of *L'Histoire du Soldat* by Ramuz and Stravinsky, without neglecting to mention the momentous occasion of the opening of the Kunsthalle as a center for contemporary art. In November people really feared the country could fall into anarchy during a general strike lasting twenty-four hours. The mobilizing of four infantry divisions and four cavalry brigades to maintain order in Zurich brought home to even the most peaceful refugee just how precarious the policy of neutrality was.[45]

The great breakthrough came in November, after the concerted offensive of the Allies and the crumbling of Austria-Hungary. Even before the armistice was signed in Rethondes, Kahnweiler for once felt that it was over for those who were fighting and for those who were not in the fight but could stand it no longer. He admitted that during all these years he had lived in a state of stupor and confusion.[46]

Now he was even more avid for information about what had happened to his friends. The questions jumped from his letters and his conversations as the process for peace gradually got under way. It almost seemed as if he thought he was soon to see them all again. He learned that Carl Einstein, that impassioned critic, was one of the leaders of the worker-soldiers' rebellion in Brussels. He heard that his German colleagues were once again in full pursuit of their share of the market, as they had been before the war, and Kahnweiler could not claim all the paintings placed with them on commission.[47] He learned that in Russia the great collections of Sergei Shchukin and Ivan Morozov, like their factories, had been nationalized by the state and would form the nucleus of the Museum of Western Art in Moscow. But what of Apollinaire and Picasso and the others?

Those who were there would never forget the scene as Apollinaire lay dying in Paris. The crowds were screaming below his windows: "Down with Guillaume! Down with Guillaume!" In his delirious state, drifting in and out of a coma, he believed they were screaming against him when it was the kaiser they meant. "Our poor Apollinaire," as Kahnweiler would always say, never recovered from his wounds.[48] During the last two years of his life, after he had been wounded in the temple by a bursting shell and had been trepanned, he published numerous articles in the newspapers, as well as *The Poet Assassinated* and *Strollers Along Both Banks* and staged his play *Les Mamelles de Tiresias* (Tiresias's Breasts), working as if he were in a hurry. Painters immortalized him in portraits as a soldier-poet with his head bandaged. Reverdy expressed it well: "The war, symbolically, wounded him in the head."[49] Kahnweiler had not seen him for the last four years, but he still wrote his obituary for *Nord-Sud*.

Picasso had continued to work and was dazzled by his new friends. He exhibited with Paul Guillaume, in the company of Matisse, and was meeting more dealers, including Paul Rosenberg, who had obtained the right of first refusal.

Kahnweiler's first friend in Paris, Eugène Reignier, the person to whom he owed so much and who had been his mentor and the most intelligent employee in Tardieu's office, was now dead. He had been struck down by the Spanish flu, which was as devastating and took as severe a toll as the Battle of Verdun.

Wilhelm Uhde was ill and had withdrawn to Wiesbaden. The chief "dômier" of Montparnasse suffered from being exiled to his own country. In compensation he had re-created a studio atmosphere around his desk, where he started writing *Picasso and the French Tradition.* He felt forgotten by the world when he read in the newspapers about a sale of French paintings in Germany. He was disillusioned that he, who had done so much to promote the works of these artists, was never notified, as if he were a run-of-the-mill art collector. What bitterness to swallow! "With my faithfulness to friends I sometimes feel crazy," he wrote Kahnweiler after four years of silence.[50] Kahnweiler thought about how sad it was that these two Germans who were crazy about France were forbidden access to it.

Remaining in Switzerland was not a real option, because the country was so small. "I prefer to fight," wrote Kahnweiler when he was feeling in top form.[51] "I feel so old in Bern," he would say when he was discouraged.[52] He experienced every shade of feeling between the two in anticipation of returning to his adopted city. He was beside himself when certain rumors were spread out of sheer malice by people in the Madeleine district, who claimed that the cubists' dealer wanted to remain in Switzerland.[53] There was no way to contradict this except by appearing in person at the gallery on rue Vignon, open for business. He was determined to continue his business in Paris and nowhere else. From there he wanted to expand further into foreign markets.[54]

He could not return until after the ratification of the Treaty of Versailles. As negotiations drew out for months on end he would mutter, "damned ratification," his favorite expression. The day it was passed he was the first in line at dawn in front of the French consulate to obtain his entry visa.

With canvases by Vlaminck and van Dongen he had been able to conduct some business. He still received letters addressed to "Galerie Kahnweiler, Viktoriarain 15, Bern," which was the address of his friend Glaser. His correspondents assumed that he would continue his business as before, ignoring the difficult period he had been through. In order to stay abreast of developments in the art market he corresponded with two art reviews, *Der Cicerone* in Hanover and *Das Kunstblatt* in Berlin; and with the dealers he knew well: Caspari (Munich), Heinrich Thannhauser, Paul Cassirer (Berlin), Alfred Flechtheim (Düsseldorf), Goldschmidt (Frankfurt), and Bernheim-Jeune (Zurich). He wanted to be well informed because he had to regain his market and his artists as well. Between August and December 1919 he conducted a campaign by mail to win the support of his artists in the struggle to regain his stock, which had been sequestered by the government during the war.

Juan Gris was the first person he contacted after four years of silence. Gris had exhibited his work in April at Léonce Rosenberg's Galerie L'Effort Moderne. Even Gris admitted that it had been a success. The extraordinary aspect was that, next to Francis Picabia and other dadaists, he appeared classically sober. It was as if it were still the year 1910, the contrast was so striking. It created a feeling that history had accelerated, which was not unpleasant. Gris had matured, gained confidence and mastery in his art:

> I want to continue the tradition of painting by plastic means and bring to it a new aesthetic based on intellect. I believe that you can borrow the means of a Chardin without accepting either his style or his notion of reality. Those who advocate abstract painting bring to mind weavers who would make cloth by stretching their threads all in one direction, without those that would hold them together. Without some idea of plasticity, how do you set limits for representational freedom? Without concern for representational realism, how do you set limits for freedom of plasticity?[55]

Kahnweiler was surprised to discover that he was not the only person who had studied aesthetics during the war years. He felt even more in communion with Gris about his repudiation of abstract painting and ornamentation than he had before the war. Instead of entering into a commentary Gris went straight to the heart of the subject. His opinion of young artists in Paris, of the dadaists, or of the sculptor Henri Laurens was of interest to Kahnweiler, but not as much as Gris's own work.

"What you have told me about your paintings has made me want even more to see them, and to handle them again. I ask you to please send some to me. I hasten to add that legally you have the right to send and to sell paintings to me. Please tell me how much you want for them. We will easily come to an agreement about it."[56]

Kahnweiler also requested drawings. He wanted to have everything, from the most recent works to the intermediary period, with everything clearly dated. He felt that it was the only way to catch up with the last five years and make up for lost time. The artist could roll up his canvases and drawings and send them by regular mail.

It was all very simple for Kahnweiler but not so for the scrupulous Gris. It was a question of principle and professional ethics. He had been under exclusive contract with Léonce Rosenberg for the last two years and he would not break his word even for a friend. Everything that he painted went straight to the Galerie L'Effort Moderne. He appreciated Kahnweiler's continuing interest in his work, but he squelched his enthusiasm, knowing his own means and limits. He felt that he was far from attaining the mastery of a Braque, whom he continued to praise even if Braque spoke badly about Gris's work and refused to have his own paintings hung in the same room. In response to Kahnweiler, Gris described artistic life in Paris with great perspicacity.

Picasso is making beautiful work when he finds the time between the Ballets Russes and a society portrait. The others are not that wonderful. Léger still has great qualities but more and more he is tending towards dadaist excesses. There's a new recruit, [Gino] Severini, who dropped futurism two or three years ago. [Henri] Laurens, the sculptor, is a friend of Braque, and maybe a bit his student. Among young sculptors [Jacques] Lipchitz is perhaps the most talented and the most serious. He has a great future in my opinion because he works well and has made great strides in a short time. The most surprising thing is the sudden flowering of poetry. Reverdy is one of the best and the first who has influenced many young poets. There are extraordinary ones like [Raymond] Radiguet, who is barely seventeen years old and who writes with great charm. It's the followers of Reverdy who are connected with our painting and increasingly distancing themselves from [Blaise] Cendrars and Tzara. There are also young musicians but I know nothing about music. There's [Georges] Auric who is only twenty and people say he's wonderful![57]

Kahnweiler found this informative and interesting but he would not let up. The contract between Gris and Rosenberg was an obstacle he was trying to get around. It had started in 1917 and was not retroactive. The dealer had not bought out the whole studio on rue Ravignan; therefore Gris could send Kahnweiler the paintings completed between the declaration of war and 1917. Kahnweiler won partial rights to the works completed in 1914. Rosenberg had the foresight to make Gris sign a separate commitment for his other works. Kahnweiler insisted on those from 1915, which made his attempt to regain his territory painful and difficult. The artist did not want to offend the art dealer he sincerely admired and to whom he was grateful, and the art dealer did not want to ask for charity either, so that from letter to letter he always asked for more and then he admitted to his friend: "I must tell you that for the duration of the war I have lived on funds borrowed from a friend and now it is necessary for me to carry on my business."[58]

Kahnweiler's pride made this a difficult thing to admit, even to a friend. Gris conceded because he did not relish refusing his friend. But from concession to concession, trying to steer between Rosenberg and Kahnweiler and protect what was right and what was loyal, he would have nothing left except for collages from 1913 that he did not think much of, an assessment with which Kahnweiler agreed.

For a dozen works Kahnweiler sent Gris only the sum of 750 francs, which expressed his disappointment very clearly. There was nothing more that could be done, and he had to give it up. They agreed to remain friends even though they could not work together. Kahnweiler admitted to losing the contest but did not believe for a second that Rosenberg was a better art dealer. It was both a commercial and ethical concept: "I have always given as much thought to my painters as to myself when drawing up a contract and it was always for a brief period so the artist could always reap the benefits of the growing success of his paintings as shown in the prices of the contract. I would never have had such a dastardly notion as a forty-sixty contract that was only binding on the artist. No doubt he was easy prey."[59]

After Gris, his next campaign was Braque. Kahnweiler immediately said that he wanted to work with him in the future and spoke to him openly as a friend. All that he had patiently built up over seven years had been shattered, and he had to start over again. He knew that Braque had an exhibit at Rosenberg's in March. The artist sent him a few drawings just to show him,[60] which he bought immediately. The painter wanted to protect his independence, but his contract with Rosenberg lasted until 1920. Kahnweiler would handle this situation, but he continued to wonder about the two dealers who had divided up his territory, Léonce Rosenberg and Paul Guillaume.

While asking straightforward questions, he also expressed his doubts about their financial and intellectual abilities. But along with all the arguments, Kahnweiler told Braque what he had in mind. Switzerland was a wonderful country, but to be truthful he could stand it no longer. Braque was in a position to help him out of this state of affairs.

The means were simple: Braque had only to send him some recent paintings, which Kahnweiler would sell in Switzerland. He had to be discreet so as not to alarm Paris art dealers about this transaction or about his determination to reopen the rue Vignon gallery with the backing of a friend from the financial world. He did not want this project made public because he was obsessed about his competitors. This arose from his most basic preoccupation: the exclusive possession of all an artist's works.

From Bern he started gathering information. In his opinion Paul Rosenberg was only a second-rate dealer, because he actually took out an advertisement in the November issue of *La Nouvelle Revue Française* that included his name and address in it and announced that he bought paintings by van Gogh.[61] This was worthy of an interior decorator, not an art dealer. Kahnweiler warned artists to be careful of Léonce Rosenberg because he could never hang on to his money, and when he had dealt with him every transaction had required endless maneuvers. Rosenberg still owed him a tidy sum after all these years.[62]

Kahnweiler resented Rosenberg and he wanted to hit hard so that Braque would pay attention. Braque complained about Gris and was also critical about the evolution of another artist about whom Kahnweiler wanted to hear:

> . . . As for Picasso, he wants to create another style, the Ingres style. You want to know what I think of his development. I think that it is natural to him, it remains true to his artistic temperament. Aside from this Picasso remains what he has always been for me, a talented virtuoso. Luckily France is not a country full of virtuosos.[63]

As he had when he had approached Gris, Kahnweiler prepared everything carefully. He praised Braque's *Pensées et Maximes*, which he had translated into German, and he especially appreciated his ideas on light. Kahnweiler asked him about money. Braque wanted to sell, but Kahnweiler found the prices he asked unjustifiably high. He wanted a bulk-order reduction and insisted that Braque not sell more cheaply to anyone else, and never at less than two hundred francs apiece to Japanese collectors. It was in Braque's own interest. "The minimum that an art dealer should earn on a sale is 100 percent if you consider the cost of the frame that is provided and the cost of shipping, all of which is exorbitantly high these days."[64]

A month later Kahnweiler nailed down his subject. He could not commit himself to paying set prices, but to compensate for that he would happily make an adjustment and strive to pay the price that Braque asked for his work. If Braque maintained his prices Kahnweiler would give him a lesson in commercial tactics after first describing the winters in Bern, the stifling boredom, and the famous cloud cover that settled between the Alps and the Jura mountains.

> . . . An art dealer, including myself, cannot in any way pay more for a painting than half the price paid by a collector. But more than that, questions of price can't be explained in a word or with numbers only. It was fine when we drew up our contracts, but nowadays! I must tell you about other factors that exert an influence on the price. Thus, a dealer can pay more for a painting if he is the first person to see it. (That is why so many dealers give contracts for the right of first refusal.) These paintings will lose in value if another dealer or if collectors have already seen it. You will easily understand why. Obviously the intrinsic value of the painting will not have diminished. But a dealer does not have unlimited funds; he has to work with a specific capital. Therefore he must immediately sell a portion of the paintings he has bought or else he would use up his capital. Well, his chances of making an immediate sale are greatly reduced if collectors or other dealers have already passed by the painting in question.[65]

Braque was not totally convinced. He had become more ambitious, more aware of his value, as opposed to Juan Gris, who was inclined to minimize his own worth. Kahnweiler's letter, written the day the armistice was signed at Rethondes, marked the beginning of financial hostility between him and Braque. It would continue this way for decades and would be the subject of their disagreements, and yet it did not spoil their friendship. Until the end of his stay in Switzerland, Kahnweiler was asking Braque for recent paintings and drawings.[66]

After Gris and Braque it was Derain's turn. Kahnweiler approached him with the same questions: Are Paul Guillaume and Léonce Rosenberg committed to your career? What are you working on now? Can you send me paintings and drawings? He let Derain know that he valued his judgment, and that his future course of action depended on his and Braque's response.[67]

Derain was extremely clear about his situation: "Since the war I have had more success. No doubt it's due to the fact that I paint less. This world is incomprehensible."[68]

Kahnweiler was not satisfied with this. Time was wasting. He needed paintings he could buy at the right price so he could earn money. He applied pressure on Derain, urging him to climb the stairs of his studio on rue Bonaparte and get to work. In an attempt to force a decision, he pleaded his cause: "It seems to me that I haven't been an ordinary art dealer."[69]

Derain agreed, but urged him to be patient. To act hastily would be awkward. The artist had made disastrous commitments during the war, and he was not yet free of them. This was not the time for him to break contracts. "It would make the atmosphere around me too oppressive. At this time in Paris the sale of paintings is carried out with a cynicism and vulgarity that was unknown to us until now, and it is harmful for everyone."[70] Thus Kahnweiler should remain patient.

After Derain, Kahnweiler hurried to approach Vlaminck. He wanted to reach him at all costs, having learned that the painter was about to sign a contract with a Swedish art dealer named Halvorsen, who already owned some of his work. Kahnweiler understood that he was no longer in a position to demand exclusive rights, and he implored Vlaminck not to limit himself to one dealer, no matter who it might be, but rather to sell to everyone. He said he was prepared to buy immediately, at the new prices, any canvas Vlaminck selected. He pleaded friendship, as Vlaminck had been the first artist the Kahnweiler Gallery had placed on its walls. This was reason enough for Vlaminck not to do him the wrong of signing a contract with another dealer. He was not asking for a demonstration of gratitude, he wanted simply not to be cut off now when he was finding it so difficult to reestablish himself.

Shortly after Kahnweiler had made his point, Vlaminck agreed to send him rolled-up canvases, insisting that Kahnweiler buy them at his prices. Kahnweiler was not successful in making his artists heed his warnings. As with Braque, he felt that a few cynical lessons in business strategy were in order:

. . . Take advantage of the situation to up the ante for every purchase by Halvorsen and other dealers from Scandinavia who are now circling around you. These people are buying from you at this time because in their countries the French franc is only worth half of its former value. They will throw you away like a squeezed-out lemon the day they find it more advantageous to do so. Thus you must make them pay the retail price in Swedish kronor or English pounds, and it would still not be expensive for them. "The dealer's price" means nothing. There has to be another price for a dealer—whether from Paris or elsewhere—who takes a picture now and then as opposed to a dealer who is a *reliable supporter* who can *always* be counted on. At this time, in all countries, people are wildly buying jewels, works of art, antiques, everything. That's how people place their money to avoid taxes. All this will come to an end soon. Taxes will take away people's money, and there will be an economic depression. That's when you will see who are your real art dealers. If you really thought about it, you could already tell by now![71]

It was exhausting, this struggle to win them back, hammering in the same arguments, pleading, laying himself bare. If he overdid the act, it could turn against him and his most hardened artists might take advantage of the fact that "Dear Kahn" really needed them now. There was a thin dividing line between a man who wanted to be acknowledged for what he had accomplished and a man who was financially desperate. Kahnweiler tried to do his best.

After Vlaminck, he went on to Manolo, the Spanish sculptor, who presented a delicate problem. He used to live on the monthly stipend provided by the dealer, and though always in straitened circumstances he managed to squeeze by. Kahnweiler could not resume that relationship because he had no guaranteed source of income. The problem was complicated by the fact that Manolo's work was difficult to sell; he had few collectors, not enough to form the core of a market. An artist such as Manolo, before the war, had been one of the gallery's obligations and luxuries. This was no longer possible, and the problem was how to explain it without being brutal. Kahnweiler looked forward to the day when he could reopen his gallery in Paris and thus could once again guarantee Manolo a regular stipend. In the meantime he could only send him small sums of money in exchange for drawings that were easy to send by regular mail and easy to sell while waiting for works in terra-cotta. Manolo also seemed to have been living in a precarious situation: "Do what you can, but do it quickly," he begged, leaving the price up to the dealer.[72]

Manolo had not changed at all; he was totally unrealistic. From Céret, where he was working, he shipped some terra-cotta sculptures to Bern by train. But they never got through, having been turned back by customs at regular intervals either because they were wrapped in news-papers inside the case, or because he had not tied the package or filled out the customs forms correctly. Out of desperation he sent them through the mail. Every time Kahnweiler received a package he expected to find only broken pieces inside.

Manolo had no understanding of business, but sometimes Kahn-weiler wondered if this was not all an act. From Manolo's habit of speaking to Kahnweiler as a friend, he forgot that he was his art dealer. Since Kahnweiler never forgot this fact, he sometimes wanted to tear out his hair in frustration: "To clear up business questions, my dear Manolo, you are wonderfully naive. You ask me if you should sell to Madame Druet. But I am your art dealer, and Druet is my competition. And what you sell to collectors is that much business that I lose. I buy everything that you make and you only sell to me. . . . I am against your selling anything to anyone else but to me."[73] He could hardly have been clearer, but that was not the end of it.

Léger and Picasso were next on his agenda, but as soon as Léger returned to Paris he got in touch with Kahnweiler. By legal contract the major portion of his work went to (yet again) Léonce Rosenberg. Excluded from the agreement, however, were drawings and watercolors, which he would send to Kahnweiler in Bern for the time being. But what touched Kahnweiler profoundly was this unsolicited word of appreciation: "You were the first person who *dared*, and we know that your name will always be fixed in the annals of modern art."[74]

Ten years earlier Kahnweiler had brought Léger out of his isolation and solitude and had proved his devotion. Now the artist returned the sentiment even if he was not free to act on it. But the encouragement given Kahnweiler was priceless.

Picasso was the mystery. Not one word did he send to renew their relations. They had corresponded during the war but it had stopped a year before, and there had been nothing since. Picasso had exhibited with Paul Rosenberg in October, and of all the artists of Kahnweiler's gallery, Picasso was the only one who could really do without him. He had the means now. After obtaining more information Kahnweiler grew to understand that the problem was more complex. The gap between them also existed between Picasso and the other artists.

They had been fighting at the front while he had been able to continue his work, and he had evolved in a direction that made them skeptical. Kahnweiler finally had to admit that he understood neither "his evolution nor his politics. It was obviously out of political consideration that he never showed any cubist drawings."[75] It seemed that Picasso had changed; he continued his development toward the classicism that had appeared just before the war. It worried Kahnweiler because he never knew how far the artist would go. He felt apprehensive, and it disturbed him more than the pack of rivals who were courting Picasso. From afar, and despite being removed from the works, he could understand that this evolution, placed in its context, was understandable. Since the end of the war there had been a return to order in every aspect of life. In art it was a neoclassicism that could be seen in the poetry of Pierre Reverdy, the musical compositions of Erik Satie, and in paintings by . . . Picasso. This trend might express a social need rather than the temper of the times; such phenomena were never isolated.

Braque and Gris had warned him that Picasso had entered his "Ingres" phase. Kahnweiler found it somewhat cold, but on consideration he recalled having seen early versions of this stage in drawings of a seated man, done in one session and with great clarity, which Picasso had shown him in 1914 with the comment, "Isn't this better than my earlier work?[76] It is the best I have ever done."[77]

If Picasso needed to prove to others or to himself that he could confront the classical tradition and express himself through traditional means, his effort was "successful." Kahnweiler only hoped that this direction was not taken at the expense of the cubism still in him.

Kahnweiler was still stuck in Bern until the formalities of the ratification were settled. As the end of his waiting drew nearer he switched gears. After asking his artists to join his gallery again, now he had to ask them to support his effort to regain his stock, which had been sequestered as German possessions. This was the second phase of his planned return. Léger, Braque, Derain, and Vlaminck all did their share, and they had two advantages over everybody else: they were French and had been honorably discharged from the army. In France in 1919, being a young veteran was a decided advantage.

Kahnweiler explained the situation to each of them in the same terms: he had to do everything possible to prevent his unfortunate predicament from becoming a disaster. If his stock continued to be sequestered, the huge number of paintings would all be sold off as enemy property, flooding the market and proving equally harmful to the art dealer and artists involved. It was a matter of saving his business, and their earlier works, as well as the value of their future production. These were all aspects of one problem, and to separate them would be foolish.

All four artists were sympathetic and prepared to act. Braque and Vlaminck were fighters by temperament. Derain had his doubts about what could be done. Kahnweiler had to insist and sent him a letter with a copy of the sequestration decree in the *Journal Officiel:*

> I have not been just an ordinary dealer . . . do this for me. I am counting on the four of you. . . . If the four of you petition for the return of my stock, so that I can be permitted to resume my business, they will do it. . . . I can't tell you how distasteful I find all this. It's so ugly. To have worked so hard, in good faith, for a worthy cause, and still have to fight every day for one's wretched possessions. It was hardly worth it, by God, to have been upstanding and honest to the very end and then in time of peace to be forced to fight like a madman for the return of what had been acquired not only with my money, which doesn't merit consideration, but with the commitment of my whole existence, which deserves great consideration.[78]

Finally it was Léger who manned the battlements. He received an appointment to meet with M. Nicolle, the administrator of sequestered goods, who confirmed to him that the liquidation of all German goods would be made to reduce the war debt. As for the Kahnweiler problem, he would do everything possible to resolve the situation in a way that would not be detrimental to French artists.[79] That was far from reassuring, but it was a first step. Kahnweiler foresaw a hard road full of pitfalls, but now he determined to carry the fight wherever necessary—he who used to be a pacifist on every front.

He was still in Switzerland in 1920. His bags had been packed for weeks, and for the last months Kahnweiler was in a frenzy of epistolary and critical writing. Once he returned to being an art dealer he would not write for publication, so he now published, in the German language reviews (*Das Kunstblatt, Der Cicerone, Monatshefte fur Kunstwissenschaft, Feuer, Die Weissen Blatter*), articles entitled "The Boundaries of Art History," "The Essence of Sculpture," "Form and Vision," studies on Derain and Vlaminck, and works on a text that he kept for himself, "Genesis of a Work of Art."

For some articles he used his pseudonym of Daniel Henry, but everyone in France knew his identity. He attempted to set himself up as the historian of his art. He strove to be the first to have conceptualized cubism, despite other, parallel attempts that remained incomplete and fragmentary. He was more than an important witness: what he wrote and said about cubism would be used as a reference for decades to come.

For him, painting (like all the plastic arts) is a system of writing. It cannot be a reflection of nature. As with any form of writing, it appears as a system of signs inviting the viewer to read it. These signs, which represent the external world, enable the artist to communicate visual experiences to the spectator without having recourse to the "illusion of imitation." In "Genesis of a Work of Art,"[80] Kahnweiler complains of the use of the word "beauty," which should be applied exclusively to a work of art. From being improperly used the term "beauty" had taken on the meaning of giving pleasure in response to an awareness of it. That was too subjective. To make it the exclusive property of a work of art, this awareness would have to be externalized and made universal. Thus, beauty would be reserved for the ultimate creation of the human intellect. Kahnweiler realized that this would take time.

Cubism depicted another representation of the world. In 1919–1920, being familiar with cubism meant shedding the five-hundred-year tradition of perspective and illusion. It not only changed how we saw painting but how we understood it, and thus how we understood the world. That could hardly be accomplished in seven years. Contrary to what the visual distortions made people assume, the cubists wanted to present a more accurate representation of things. To achieve this, the cubist painter would retain only the permanent aspects of his mental images, whereas the impressionist painter would devote himself to capturing the ephemeral.

Looking at the same bottle of wine, one would paint what he knew about it, the other what he actually saw. The visual creation of the cubist painter is the sum of all the images fixed in his memory. It is not enough to know that a cube has six sides. The artist has to avoid showing them in a fixed structure in order to distinguish them in a moving perspective. The painter who does not understand this—it can be seen in all the minor followers of the cubists—inevitably fall into a play of geometry, a reductive process, which is merely decorative. By showing us a bottle from only one angle a traditional painter depicts what he perceives, while a cubist, showing it frontally, in profile, from above and even from below, tries to convey a sum of information.

People have to learn to "read" a painting, even to "decipher" it. Like any foreign language, a painting has an unfamiliar alphabet. Kahnweiler never let up on this idea for a moment, and in his professorial explanations sometimes forgot that he had ten years' advantage over his listeners. He had known these paintings from their inception. He had seen the original sketches and their evolution, and he was intimately acquainted with each artist. No one could be better informed about the history of each painting. He was not making assumptions: he knew!

Considering the disparity between himself and the ordinary viewer, Kahnweiler was extremely patient, an indispensable trait if you take his readership into account. From his point of view a painting does not exist in a void. It is born out of a collaboration between the artist and the spectator. A still life by Gris has no existence as long as the viewer can only see a confusion of lines and disparate distorted objects. It comes to life when the viewer becomes aware of the artist's intention: here is the uncorked neck of the bottle, there the label, there the outline. Each of these signs takes on meaning in relation to one another and preserves the unity of the painting. The composition of the whole is predominant over the details and determines the appearance of the work. It gives it its truth. Gris said it in a few words: "The objects that I paint, if you move them to a world which is not theirs, will die. They would die even if you wanted to move them from one table to another."[81]

Kahnweiler did not care about the question "what does it mean?" Even in jest he would never give the answer that Louis Carré did to such a question: "Between seven and eight thousand francs."[82] Even if Kahnweiler's elitism were indifferent to the public, he would not mock the spectator's ignorance. What was important to him was the universal meaning of the painting's reality, not the way in which it captured such and such a detail. Those who persisted in asking "What is it supposed to be?" were trapped by a useless logic that evaluated a work in terms of the quality of its imitation. It was a question of informing the eye and educating the sensibility, not of intelligence.

At the same time he was careful to prevent interpretations of the opposite extreme. It was important to him that cubism not be made into nonfigurative art. It was a notion, often thrown out glibly, that immediately irritated him. He was always careful to explain that cubism attempted a more truthful, more concrete, more structured representation than had ever been attempted before. The cubist painters tried to solve two problems: a figurative image more true than illusionist representations; and the composition through which they confronted the conflict between their perceptions and experience, and the medium in which it is depicted. To resolve this conflict they started inventing new signs, and thus arrived at a new method of inscription. Every aspect of this struggle can be seen in the development of Picasso's paintings in particular and, in different ways, in those of Braque, Léger, or Gris. Kahnweiler was the first critic to distinguish between two different periods of cubism: analytic cubism, in which the artist accumulates information about an object; and synthetic cubism, in which all the knowledge about an object is condensed into one shape.

Kahnweiler never even ventured a definition of the spirit of cubism. He understood that the four great cubist painters were of completely different temperaments. Still, they had things in common apart from their gallery and dealer. There was a continual sharing of ideas and feelings, as no one thought of keeping his discoveries to himself. And there was a certain affinity among them, due to the proximity of their studios and their shared summers in Sorgues, l'Estaque, Céret, or elsewhere. In this sense the spirit of cubism went beyond this group of four pioneers to include, for different periods, artists such as Derain and Vlaminck.

At the same time, Kahnweiler found that if he thought of Léger and Gris as classical, then Picasso seemed to be baroque, and Braque fell into neither of these categories. Rather than mislead by creating artificial relationships, Kahnweiler preferred to take the definition of cubism beyond such things to those aspects either articulated or observed. In other words, he defined cubism as an attitude, as a way of life. For a long time he subscribed to André Masson's definition: "Great painting appears at intervals as works charged with all the energy of the people who make them."

Fernand Léger, the subject of an article Kahnweiler would write in 1919, seemed to him so completely different that he remained apart even in the medium he used. Léger wanted to stress the integrity of forms by making them crude cylindrical shapes. He did not balk at distortion, or playing with size and proportions of the object, or using light and color to define the form. Léger was seeking the extraordinary energy of three-dimensional forms and their strident bursts of color. He felt challenged by the energy of the painting, the way it imposed itself triumphantly. There was an immense power in his work.[83]

Kahnweiler gives us the key to all of his thoughts during these years, as far as method is concerned, in his essay "The Limits of Art History," his last publication from this period. It was devoted to the aesthetic pleasure derived from representational art and the hedonism in the way the work is perceived. If the work of art is created from the conflict between man and his environment, then the great artists are those who create a new style by rebelling against the traditional world. "The great masterpieces," he wrote, "are those which alone will remain to illustrate the whole of art history as succinctly as possible, in its strictest continuity. Those works considered indispensable to form the continuity, those will be the great works of the art of humanity."[84]

Kahnweiler was opposed to anecdotal or biographical narratives on art, finding them trivial and false. He was convinced that in order to integrate art with the history of humanity, the economic, social, political, even cultural conditions for the production of art should be studied with greater perspective and in context. There was no alternative if art history was not going to degenerate into "sterile professional ratiocinations."[85]

Kahnweiler could not repress his feelings of bitterness when he attended an exhibit of certain cubist artists at the Galerie Moos in Geneva, where he saw hanging works by *his* artists. This was what had happened to cubism during his absence, he thought, gathering information without looking, like an investigator. He was amazed by the development of Gris's work. There were a few surprises, much confirmation, and one discovery.

He found a painted bas-relief by the sculptor Henri Laurens truly admirable. Laurens seemed to have resolved the old problem of cubism: shading was not an issue in his work, since there was physical depth. The conflict between color and light had vanished now that color was applied to forms in high relief. Kahnweiler had heard little of Laurens, though he knew he was a close friend of Braque's. On the whole, he believed the sculpture partook of cubist aesthetics and was a completely realized work.[86] Now he wanted to meet the artist.

In February 1920 Clemenceau was defeated at the polls and Paul Deschanel was elected President of the Republic. Alexandre Millerand attempted to form a government. The railwaymen of the C.G.T. (the French national labor union) and the miners of the north were preparing for a general strike. The Socialist Party had inaugurated a national convention, which voted down the Second International. Picasso refused to participate in the exhibition of major and minor cubists in the Salon des Indépendants. That was also a sign of the times. Modigliani died that month at the Hôpital de la Charité.

Whether he was superstitious or not, Kahnweiler left Switzerland for France on February 22; he could not help thinking that twelve years earlier he had left England for France on the same date. He felt that a new cycle had begun. He knew that it would be a struggle and that he would have to start all over again.

On the train taking him and his wife back to Paris, he wanted to be optimistic, after a month's vacation followed by five years of enforced idleness. He reread a postcard, dated January 3, 1920, that he kept in the pocket of his jacket: "Dear friend, we send you our greetings. We have just been taking care of your business." It was signed by Vlaminck, Derain, Braque, and Léger. It was only a postcard, but invaluable to him.

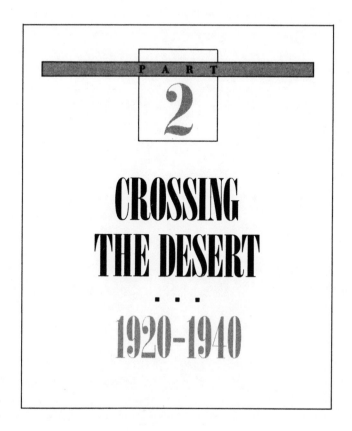

CROSSING THE DESERT

. . .

1920–1940

⫿

FORGETTING DROUOT

Kahnweiler's most urgent problem at this point was finding an apartment for himself and his wife. Eight days after they arrived in Paris they moved into a place on rue Poussin, not far from their former address; then he began to put into effect the campaign he had been planning during the last months of his exile. With his usual methodicalness he divided it into three stages: winning back his artists, reopening his gallery, and recovering his market. Always at the forefront of his mind was the recovery of his confiscated stock.

The specter of total loss had become an obsession. The fact that he was not alone in this predicament—that Uhde's collection, for example, was equally threatened—was no more consolation to him than citings of historical precedent. He knew that the collector Rouart had saved old Tanguy from deportation, but nothing seemed to change his own position. He counted on the influence of two collectors in political circles: Marcel Sembat and Olivier Sainsère. Sembat had been a socialist deputy and former minister but he died (in 1922) before his actions could take effect; and Saincère, the secretary-general of the president of the Republic, seemed to be struggling in vain. He was going against the nation's anti-German, nationalistic mood. At every opportunity Kahnweiler would tell the authorities: "What you are doing is idiotic. These auctions will lower the prices of valuable paintings. The first one will fetch one thousand francs, the second five hundred, and so on."[1]

The auctioning off of property seized by the state seemed to be the inevitable fate of his paintings. His only hope lay in direct, hard negotiation. On April 24 he had an appointment at the concierge's office of his former apartment building. Much to Kahnweiler's bitter disappointment, it turned out that M. Zapp, the administrator of sequestered property, had summoned him there only to return personal articles.

Without his paintings, all he had were painters. He started making the rounds of artists' studios again. Derain was completely behind his effort and signed a new contract that would go into effect on April 2. Once these sordid details had been settled they could turn their attention to the all-important interest they shared: painting. They conversed at great length, and on leaving the studio, Kahnweiler hastily jotted down: "Derain said that what he had to acquire in addition to drawing was the substance, the projection of the painter's soul onto the canvas. Neither harmony nor anything of the sort, only the substance. The substance should be neither too fluid so that the eye passed right through it, nor too opaque so that it stopped the eye. That was the quality of Cézanne as opposed to Sisley, who was infinitely more harmonious."[2]

Vlaminck also agreed with his plans, and Kahnweiler left his studio with four paintings under his arm for which he paid the sum of 2,950 francs. He had not asked anything of van Dongen, as they had stopped business dealings, but van Dongen invited him to his studio in the Villa Saïd on avenue Foch.[3] Manolo became the first to whom Kahnweiler paid a regular stipend. He knew how precarious the artist's situation was. They signed a five-year contract, stating that the dealer would pay him a thousand francs a month, with increases adjusted to the sales of his works. Kahnweiler purchased twenty-three sculptures, one terra-cotta, a bas-relief, and drawings for the sum of seven thousand francs, which Manolo only received two weeks after the transaction. It came just in time, as he could no longer even afford a bag of plaster. But he never lost his sense of humor in such circumstances:

> Convinced as I am about your loyalty to me as well as your flair for business, I accept your terms, I who understand nothing about business. I can only offer you one guarantee, that my work will be the best that I am capable of, and that I will often beat my own record, that is to say, when I make a good piece of sculpture, a few months later I will make an even better one.[4]

It was more difficult with Picasso, much, much harder, which Kahnweiler had expected. Even with Paul Rosenberg's contract for the right of first refusal, the artist still sold to everyone at his own prices. Kahnweiler knew that relations between them had cooled, even if Juan Gris, returning from a visit to Picasso's studio, told him that the artist bore him no ill will. But Gris did not know the whole story, because Picasso would never have told him that he was angry with Kahnweiler about twenty thousand francs which had remained unpaid since 1914. Picasso was unyielding on the subject. Ten days before he left Bern Kahnweiler had written him in an effort to clear up the misunderstanding between them:

> I never had any money at that time for a very simple reason. I enjoyed a line of credit with the bank and I worked with the credit. Let me explain what that meant. The bank would authorize up to a certain sum of money for me. When war broke out with the moratorium, the first action taken by the bank was to suspend my credit. Secondly, those who owed me money, whose payment would have enabled me to pay your twenty thousand francs, now refused to pay. I give Shchukin, who owed me an enormous amount, as an example, and Rosenberg, who owed me twelve thousand francs.[5]

Picasso would not listen. To reinforce his point Kahnweiler promised not only to send him a copy of his forthcoming book on the genesis of cubism, but also to write a monograph on Picasso, which was already scheduled for publication by the end of the year. But there would never be a book on Picasso by Kahnweiler. They would eventually settle their differences over the years, but the dealer could not count on Picasso's help during this crucial period. The loss was all the more difficult to bear as Picasso, of all the artists in Kahnweiler's gallery, could command the highest prices, and his paintings constantly brought in new collectors.

Kahnweiler was not disappointed; he had half-expected Picasso's reaction, just as he knew he had Gris's unswerving loyalty. He had left Gris as a young painter whose work he loved, and now he returned to find a master.[6] Gris was bound to Léonce Rosenberg until the end of the year. It was understood that on termination of the contract he would return to Kahnweiler. They managed for the time being, but the artist longed to return to his friend and manager with an urgency rare in this milieu.

Braque was not a disappointment either. His was one of the first studios Kahnweiler visited as soon as he returned to Paris. They had much to discuss; as was his habit, Kahnweiler jotted down the following as soon as he was home, so as not to forget it:

> The painter thinks in form and color. The opposite would be to think in terms of objects (Gris composes his still lifes like a maître d') or to think in terms of

paintings (Léger). To break down form and color is the most important according to him.[7]

Braque could be a hard man, but Kahnweiler was in a position to attenuate his criticism. At the same time Gris had written to him: "I have just seen recent paintings by Braque and I find them flabby and diffuse. He's turning back to impressionism. I was glad to feel that I did not like them because I had shed a great burden. His earlier paintings pleased me so much that they crushed me."[8]

His reaction was understandable in the context of Braque's refusal to have his work in the same room as Gris's work at the Salon des Indépendants earlier that year. Kahnweiler had been prepared for this discord and he no longer held any illusions on the subject. The cubist group, if it ever existed, had been shattered. The events during the war had exposed differences and hidden grudges.

Braque wanted to join him, and he was prepared to defend the Kahnweiler Gallery in every possible way against the threats of the government. He agreed to the terms of a contract that would take effect in May. He was committed to selling all of his works to Kahnweiler, with the exception of five canvases. Kahnweiler would pay 130 francs apiece for canvases sizes 1 to 60, and beyond that they would agree to a price according to the importance of the individual work. For the five paintings Braque reserved for himself, he could not part with them for under four hundred francs apiece to a collector, and three hundred francs to a dealer.[9] Six months after signing the contract Braque was already asking Kahnweiler to send him five thousand francs.[10]

Kahnweiler was used to this pressure and paid without complaining. He knew better than anyone that artists never showed any consideration for the plight of the dealer when they needed money. It did not matter whether he had financial problems, or faced clients who had not paid for their purchases. Whoever was in charge also acted as the banker in this profession. Even if it made him feel guilty, he managed somehow by making adjustments here and there. He was bound by his creed when he opened the gallery: he would always maintain that his task was to assume the responsibility for the artists' material concerns.

Léger also responded warmly to his offer. He would do everything to release his confiscated stock of paintings, but his current work, by contract, belonged to Rosenberg. Kahnweiler was patient and turned his attention toward new artists, notably outstanding sculptors. Lipchitz had received much attention when he exhibited his work at the Indépendants and was advised by Gris to sign a contract with Kahnweiler. Ossip Zadkin wanted to show him his new work. Kahnweiler finally met Laurens, who immediately won him over. He and Lucie often met Laurens at the Opéra Comique for performances of Gluck. A sympathy was born out of their conversations about music and sculpture. Laurens and Klee were the rare artists with whom he could really discuss music. These evenings spent with the sculptor, who had lost a leg to tuberculosis of the bone yet was basically optimistic, kindly and humble by nature, confirmed his first impression of Laurens's work in Geneva. In April, they drew up a contract that was renewable at the end of a year.

In the contract there was one thing that was different, only a detail, but of great importance. The name had changed from the "Galerie Kahnweiler" to the "Galerie Simon." André Cahen, known as André Simon, was one of Kahnweiler's dearest friends. He worked on the stock exchange in Tardieu's office, where Kahnweiler had worked when he first came to Paris. Kahnweiler went into a partnership with him in order to make a new start. The gallery carried Simon's name, but he neither worked there nor took any direct interest in it; he remained the backer. He loved the paintings shown there, and that was the extent of his involvement. However, his was the only name that appeared in the official documents deposited at the Office of Commercial Licensing. As a German citizen it may not have been possible for Kahnweiler to open a business in France. André Simon's participation gave Kahnweiler the necessary financial base and much needed moral support; his name and connections were Kahnweiler's guarantee. But Simon's role stopped there; he never interfered with the artistic policy nor with the day-to-day running of the gallery. There was a complete confidence between the two men.

Kahnweiler still had to find an address for the gallery, and this proved more difficult than finding an apartment. He had certain standards, and the small shop on rue Vignon was no longer acceptable. He planned a gallery on a different scale. The neighborhood became more important to him, as the location of galleries had changed since the war: more and more of them were opening on the Left Bank, in the Latin Quarter and around Montparnasse, and on the Right Bank between rue Laffitte and the Madeleine.

He wanted to be there. Through Amédée Ozenfant, an acquaintance whom he had met in Switzerland, Kahnweiler heard of a large space at 29-bis rue d'Astorg. On first inspection he had his doubts; these former stables appeared sinister. But there were high ceilings with skylights that let in an especially fine lighting for sculpture. Beyond the entrance hall were four large rooms, one after the other, with an office in the back and stairs leading down to the basement. With a little work it would be quite suitable. The very first visitors thought it had no charm, although eventually they would grow to like it. The gallery appeared to have been used as a warehouse for a glass wholesaler. Coming upstairs from the basement, which was used for storage, Kahnweiler presented the strange sight of first a head, then a torso gradually emerging through the floor.[11]

Everything was put into order as soon as Kahnweiler had moved in. The place still gave an impression of severity, which was in keeping with his conception of his role as an art dealer. Once again, there were no opening parties, no publicity, nor any demonstrations or events to bring the gallery to the attention of the art world. The place was all the more suited to him as it was close to rue La Boétie, where Paul Rosenberg and Paul Guillaume had their galleries, and most important, where Picasso lived.

The Galerie Simon opened its doors on September 1, 1920. Kahnweiler did not have to let anyone know that he was in business again; the whole art world was aware of it. Florent Fels lost no time congratulating him in terms that went straight to his heart: "If Picasso and Braque created cubism, you assured its existence." Accompanying this was a prospectus announcing the next issue of his journal of art and philosophy, *Action*, with a rate card for advertisements, just in case.[12]

Kahnweiler had not made a bad start, as his walls were hung with recent purchases and the results of the new contracts. The basement was filling up with sculptures. Ludwig Neumann, his uncle from England, had agreed to open a line of credit for 100,000 francs at the Bank of Jacques de Gunzburg and Co.; it had become available to him on April 2, 1920.[13] The carrying costs of the gallery were heavy but manageable. The monthly rent was 5,000 francs, Simon received a monthly salary of 1,000 francs and Kahnweiler 1,500 francs. There was a small monthly salary for François Fichet, who had been taken on as an errand boy; a monthly fee for Argus, the press clipping service; and office expenses. Then there were the bills for insurance, shipping, photographs, framing, the editing and printing of the books published by the gallery, and publicity for those publications. This did not take into account the taxes, the monthly stipends paid to artists in fulfillment of the contracts, and the cost of purchasing their works.[14]

The only thing left for him to do was to sell from the gallery, in France and abroad. Roger Dutilleul was one of the first people to visit him in his new location; he could be counted on and was a friend equally of the gallery, the dealer, and the artists. But with potential new clients Kahn-weiler had no hesitation about stretching the truth. To a New York corre-spondent he wrote that his was the most important gallery in Paris.[15] It was interesting the way he stressed the continuity between the Galerie Kahnweiler and Galerie Simon, the only difference other than size being the fact that his artists were now recognized as being of great stature. He offered works by Braque and Derain, but was careful to say that as far as Picasso was concerned he could provide no current works, only from the cubist and pre-cubist periods.

Kahnweiler made no secret of his desire to build solid and reliable working relationships with American galleries, which was where things happened, and also in other markets that were untapped, ignored, or misunderstood, such as the Swedish market. He remained convinced that the country was very promising, and that a following for modern art could be developed there.

In Germany Kahnweiler could always count on Alfred Flechtheim, his loyal friend, who would be joined in one of his galleries by Gustave Kahnweiler. In Prague his friend Vincenz Kramar was among those who initiated the great French collection of modern art at the Narodni Gallery. As soon as Kramar returned to Paris as a member of the official commis-sion charged with making purchases for the museum, the first gallery on his list was, naturally, the Galerie Simon. By the end of their stay the commission returned with twenty-seven paintings: Derain, Braque, Pi-casso, and le Douanier Rousseau were soon installed in the museum in Prague. It was the result of Kahnweiler's subtle influence.

The French government remained firm in its position: Uhde's collec-tion and Kahnweiler's stock must be subject to the same rules as other confiscated German goods. No exceptions would be made. The French people would not stand for it, especially when it concerned such types of painting. As he waited for the boom to fall, which now seemed inevitable, Kahnweiler took stock of another aspect of the situation: the art dealers who were his colleagues.

His indifference toward them should not be interpreted as disdain or contempt. At the same time he did not have much sense of corporate spirit. He belonged to the Art Dealers Syndicate, but was not outstanding for his participation. It did not interest him to mix with people who had the same professional title but who did not share his philosophy. He wanted his contacts with his colleagues to remain within the framework of his gallery. Ever since the beginning he sold them paintings, at first little by little; eventually, he would become the dealer's dealer. This development was inevitable, given the exclusivity clause in all his contracts: any person, dealer or collector, who wanted works by one of his artists had to go through him.

Kahnweiler did not believe that all dealers were the same. There were those he found offensive, and then there were others. Paul Guillaume was only twenty-seven and beginning to make a name for himself. Even before the war he had been an active supporter of the Ballets Russes and of African art. Originally he was interested in artists such as Giorgio de Chirico, Modigliani, and Maurice Utrillo. His taste was eclectic, but his natural inclination might have evolved even more if his close friend Apollinaire had not suffered an early death. Kahnweiler kept an eye on him and was right to do so, as in a few years Paul Guillaume would win over the man all Paris art dealers wanted as their client, the person who made periodic shopping expeditions in Montparnasse and rue La Boétie. This was Albert C. Barnes, collector by avocation, chemist and doctor by profession, who owed his new fortune to the discovery and marketing of the medicine Argyrol. He would eventually form one of the finest collections in the United States of paintings from the second half of the nineteenth century and the first half of the twentieth. Paul Guillaume owed his success to him.

Kahnweiler did not look down on private dealers, who sometimes made great discoveries and were generally a reliable source of information. Two in particular, both of Polish origin, were very enterprising in the realm of modern art. The first, Alfred Basler, always claimed that he was the first Parisian to buy a painting from his fellow countryman Moïse Kisling, as early as 1912. The other, Léopold Zborowski, also took an interest in Kisling, as well as in Chaim Soutine and Utrillo, but above all else he devoted himself to promoting and defending the works of Modigliani. [16] Kahnweiler knew both men quite well and found them unreliable, as he had to send countless friendly reminders about payment for works that in fact he had already sold to them. Zborowski, in particular, had no respect for dates, forgot to send back signed bills of sale, and let Kahnweiler's notes go unanswered. Kahnweiler wrote him: "I don't know how you order your business, but ours is organized in such a way that it requires prompt payment on the fixed dates agreed upon."[17] A futile letter. Not only did Zbo (as he was known) never make the first payment toward the price of the Derain he purchased from the Galerie Simon, but he had already resold it and received full payment, as Kahnweiler discovered when he met the client in question. It was difficult not to lose his temper, but for some reason Kahnweiler never broke off relations with the man. His patience with people was legendary, but there were limits—as shown by symptoms of a stomach ulcer.

The Rosenbergs were two well-known dealers, the sons of Alexandre Rosenberg, who had had a gallery dealing in objets d'art since 1872. He slowly made the progression from the Renaissance to the eighteenth century before becoming involved with impressionism. It was during this phase, at the beginning of the century, that Paul and Léonce worked with their father in his gallery on the avenue de l'Opéra for about ten years before they set up a gallery on the rue La Boétie. But the brothers quickly separated, each to open his own gallery independently of the other. They were also extreme opposites in character.

The painter Amédée Ozenfant captured them in a few words: "Paul an able businessman, the other an aristocrat of wonderful taste and completely incompetent in business. The same painting that one brother loved, to the point of ruining himself, would enrich the other, who hated it."[18] Paul would earn a fortune from the works of Picasso, despite the fact that they left him cold to such an extent that when he was hanging the show of October 1920 he refused to put *Nude in the Square* on his wall, saying, "I don't want any assholes in my gallery."[19]

Léonce, who was an ardent admirer of Picasso's cubism, proved to be incapable of selling it. Paul, on the other hand, sold high and was only interested in master works. He was a sharp businessman, but only that. He did not understand painting and was ignorant of art history to such an extent that his artists felt he could not care less what they painted. On the other hand, he had great intuition about the art market and was well-connected among the very wealthy. It was not by coincidence that Picasso's "worldly" phase, with his chauffeur, limousine, and big parties, coincided with the period when he was managed by Paul Rosenberg. The dealer only had a contract for first refusal, but it was enough to guarantee his advantage over all the others who were constantly courting the creator of *Les Demoiselles d'Avignon*.

Léonce Rosenberg was another matter. He was seven years older than Kahnweiler, and the comparison between them was inevitable, as they were often in conflict over the years and to a great extent they worked the same territory.

Still, there were important differences. Kahnweiler had his eye on long-term goals, and saw his work in a larger historical framework. Methodical, thoughtful, he loved his artists possessively and tolerated no other dealers. When he did not like the development of their work he said so bluntly, even if it meant a break. If he liked the work, he loved everything about it and bought everything without regard to public opinion. His tactics can be summed up in one word: patience.

Léonce was an impulsive man, who loved deals, grand gestures, and publicity. He was impetuous and often got into arguments with his artists when he disagreed with them. He also never hesitated to buy the works of an artist who was not in public favor. He loved painting and was ready to support it when he believed in it. But his tactics, which consisted of selling quickly, for as high an amount as possible, were really based on promotion and reputation. He never hesitated to intervene personally to defend his "stable" of artists in the newspapers, and even started publishing an art review in this spirit.

Frantic, irascible, and vainglorious, Léonce behaved like a spiritual adviser, embarrassed and angered his artists with his intrusive opinions, made them sign detailed contracts, and sent them verbose letters. Often tactless with French or American collectors, he tried to impress them by dropping demagogic sentences. He tried pulling the same strings in his writings about art. When he was writing to the French elite he always managed to work in a quote from Plato about "beauty" itself. When addressing collectors from the New World he always quoted from Ralph Waldo Emerson. He was quite wily: to war veterans he quoted Foch, and to a French Jew an appropriate but heavy-handed passage from Zola's "J'accuse."

Try as he might he would not succeed, and posterity would only remember his failure to make money, which is "the worst opprobrium against a businessman, who espoused every style that came along without being able to make any one of them his own."[20] For a long time Kahnweiler was mollified by Léonce's action during the war which enabled Kahnweiler's artists to survive for the duration of his exile in Switzerland. But later, in private, it did not take much for him to mutter his opinion of the man: "What an ass!"

It is easy to understand why it was difficult for these two dealers to work together. They were opposites in their relationships with artists: one respected them, the other not as much. One would give critiques, the other gave intrusive criticism. One was a fine businessman, the other had a poor head for business. One was German, Jewish, and a pacifist; the other French, patriotic, and a veteran. One had a concept of cubism that he had formulated for himself, while the other limited himself to a qualitative appreciation of this style of painting.

These difficulties would hardly have mattered if Léonce had not made the worst decision of his career: instead of remaining on the sidelines during the terrible event that was about to befall Kahnweiler, the sequestration of his stock, he pushed himself to the forefront. He joined those who wanted to hasten the process. During the war, when he had supported the artists from the rue Vignon gallery, he had no doubt aspired to become the champion of cubism. Kahnweiler's return to Paris threatened to undermine his efforts. There was no doubt that if Kahnweiler recovered the stock of his gallery he would dominate the art market. Thus, Léonce supported the auction. When people warned him about the disaster of flooding the market, he answered that on the contrary these historic sales would proclaim the triumph of cubism. Everywhere in Paris he could be seen and heard rejoicing about this long-awaited event. Roger Dutilleul was nauseated by his behavior and Gris had the same reaction.[21]

Léonce's behavior revealed his naiveté about business: no great ability was required to know that the market could not absorb such a deluge of paintings from the same school and period. Léonce did not care; he continued advocating the sale with such energy that he was appointed the expert adviser of the auction. It was a mistake that would cost him dearly.

By the end of 1920 Léger was completely involved with defending Kahnweiler. He requested and set up meetings with lawyers, the administrator for sequestered goods, and even the public prosecutor. Everything seemed to be going well, since they all reassured him that his case deserved sympathetic treatment and an equitable solution was being sought that would satisfy all parties involved.

Léger reported, "Zapp says that the court will try to interpret the law in our favor."[22]

Kahnweiler could not ask for more, and he and his wife were optimistic as the old year waned. Every action taken by Léger drew the same favorable response. Kahnweiler was brimming over with energy and projects. He had several books going into print. He had solicited most of his artists, along with writers and poets, for publication under the imprint of the Galerie Simon. Meanwhile, German publishers had agreed to bring out his own books on Derain and Vlaminck along with *The Rise of Cubism*, which he had revised and expanded. The commercial side of the gallery was very active: between November and December he sold Léger's *The Aviator* for 1,800 francs to Librairie Kundig de Genève,[23] and five Vlamincks for 15,750 marks to Goldschmidt and Co., in Frankfurt.[24] When the couturier and art patron Jacques Doucet agreed to buy a Braque which Kahnweiler did not quite know whether to call *The Apricots* or *The Peaches*, he set his limit at 4,500 francs, above which he would not pay. Kahnweiler accepted the bid on the spot, saying it was "Just to be nice and for the sake of selling you your first Braque." He then immediately tried to get the collector also interested in Derain.[25]

Kahnweiler was caught in a whirl of activity, such as purchasing works from Signac for the sum of 12,000 francs, without saying whether he intended to keep them for his private collection.[26] At the behest of a Swiss collector he agreed to negotiate with artists Metzinger and Dunoyer de Segonzac, whom he did not represent and never wanted to, for the purpose of transmitting the client's offers.[27] In his newfound enthusiasm he made carbon copies of his letters out of anything at hand, even the back of a friend's wedding announcement.

By 1921 Germany was still reluctant to pay the reparation stipulated in the Treaty of Versailles, and was being coerced. The outcome of this conflict was foreseeable. Since the French government could not go into Germany to seize its assets, they would seize all German assets in France, without exception. They proceeded ruthlessly: The Heilbronner Collection of Medieval Art, the Worthe Collection of Chinese Art, and the Uhde and Kahnweiler collections of modern art would be confiscated for reparation. The die was cast.

In March the Kahnweilers decided to move from their cramped apartment in Auteuil and away from the sixteenth arrondissement, which they found very dull, to a house on rue de la Mairie in the nearby suburb of Boulogne-Billancourt. There they had the pleasure of a garden where they displayed Manolo's sculptures, and the first one installed was *Seated Woman*, a large statue in stone dating from 1913.

Kahnweiler did not want his spirits cast down by the forthcoming auction. He continued making studio visits and purchasing works for the gallery. From Braque's studio he took fifteen paintings and one drawing for 27,600 francs, a sum that would be paid in three installments: 10,000 francs down, 10,000 francs in one month, and the balance two months later. It was a method of payment that he wanted to make routine, rather than enter the entire sum as a debit, in order to balance his books.[28] In Derain's studio he found sixteen paintings and six drawings that he bought for the sum of 36,200 francs, in three payments.[29] He shared the works of Léger with Léonce Rosenberg, except for very large or very small canvases. Gris's whole output was under contract to him. Léonce had made the artist pay the deficit owed his gallery.

Kahnweiler's usual rounds of studio visits did not prevent him from making little detours along the way to satisfy his curiosity. That was how he discovered the works of José de Togorès, a promising young artist who, like all Catalans, considered Manolo a master. But Kahnweiler upheld his old principle: the true art dealer knows how to choose, thus how to refuse. Therefore when he visited the studio of a young artist who had been highly recommended to him, he looked at each canvas in turn and quietly went on his way without a word to Joan Miró, the twenty-eight-year-old painter from Spain. He decided against him, and it was final.[30] When Fernande Olivier, Picasso's old friend, wrote to him about Miró, Kahnweiler warned her not to have any illusions. Even in the name of the Bateau-Lavoir, and the memory of "the heroic years" they shared, he would not give Miró a contract. It was useless of her to bring his works to his gallery. Because she insisted, he sent the young artist to his dear Léonce.[31]

"What's the meaning of this painting?" With this supposedly ironic question, *l'Intransigeant,* Paris's most popular evening paper, set the tone for the auction of sequestered goods. The people who frequented the gallery on rue d'Astorg were forewarned: the press coverage would be mocking and sarcastic. Beneath this headline the papers reproduced a picture of Picasso's *Violin, Glass, and Newspaper,* and the caption can be imagined. Fortunately, there was a catalogue for the sale.[32] In the letters exchanged between Uhde and Kahnweiler, they would both sum up their situation in one word: *Hinrichtung* (execution); that was how many viewed the experience. Wilhelm Uhde would stoically comment that somehow one does survive, while Kahnweiler drained the bitter cup, saying he had "the pleasure of attending my own execution."[33]

Uhde's collection went on the block first. It was minor in scale and was disposed of in one session: seventeen Braques, five Dufys, three Laurencins, one Gris, one Léger, five Douanier Rousseaus, and assorted odds and ends. The sale would bring 168,000 francs. As a reference point, according to the archives of the Louvre, *La Mort de Sardanapale* by Delacroix was worth 800,000 francs at that time.[34] But Uhde remained calm in the face of events and showed great wisdom. He saw it as a validation. Where he had once had a collection, now he had a catalogue— like any other visitor to a museum. "I now have the catalogue of the Uhde collection as a memento of those happy years in Paris. I can overcome the pain of my loss because the pleasure of acquiring the collection remains."[35]

Reading these words made Kahnweiler think, but they brought no solace. He owned many more paintings, and he was not a collector but a dealer. He could not make himself consider the situation as a dispassionate intellectual: the stock of his gallery was his livelihood, his flesh and blood.

At the beginning of the year he had received the news of his father's death. He knew that he had been sick and they had communicated at a distance, but he had hoped to see him again someday. Then had come the news that really dealt him a terrible blow: the date of his sale had been set for June 13 and 14, 1921. That was only the beginning of his ordeal.

His firing squad, as he thought of them, was made up of four men: M. Zapp, the liquidator of sequestered goods; Bellier, the executor; the head of the auction house; and the expert in charge of the catalogue and of making the estimates, Léonce Rosenberg. He was doing the unthinkable, "he had no shame."[36] Nothing could have stopped Léonce, neither the anger of the artists nor of his colleagues. He even had the temerity to send the sale catalogue of the Uhde collection to Juan Gris. The bitter irony of the gesture was not lost on the artist, who no longer harbored any illusions about his former dealer: "He is proud of his new job as auction appraiser."[37]

Not all artists had Gris's self-control. In the exhibition rooms of Hôtel Drouot, even before the sale began, there was a serious incident. It was so amazing to the public that each witness remembered it differently.

It was Braque who lost control. His strength, his courage, his relationship to Kahnweiler made him a natural leader who spoke for other artists. Braque had been disgusted by Léonce's role in this sale, which was going to be a catastrophe for everyone. His responsibility for the whole scandalous procedure was all the more galling in that he was setting himself up as the art dealer of the cubists.

In the dusty sales rooms comments of all sorts were flying. But from artists the barbs were aimed at that "bastard Léonce." The atmosphere was charged with tension when the despised Léonce finally appeared. In one leap Braque seized him by the collar and shook him like an old rag. They were shouting and screaming when Braque started kicking him in the backside as he ran. Amédée Ozenfant tried to separate them and received a punch in the stomach by Braque that sent him flying into the arms of the collector André Level. "You are defending that bastard!" Braque shouted. He grabbed Léonce, accusing him of having failed the most elementary duties of a self-respecting art dealer, and for an answer received the ultimate insult: "Norman pig!"

The painter, who had had some training in boxing, was pummeling him, and the stunned art dealer cried for help: "He has gone mad! He is crazy!"

Matisse arrived at Drouot in the middle of the fight, and on being told by Gertrude Stein what had occurred, he shouted out with decisive conviction: "Braque is right! This man has robbed France, and we all know about those who have robbed France!"

The fight would have gone on except that the parties involved found themselves at the police station; but no complaints were filed. It was not followed by a duel, which would have been indecent for these two veterans after the horrors of the war. Sickened by the whole situation, Braque decided to abstain from attending the auction. He preferred the peace and solitude of Sorgues to Drouot, and resigned himself to never again seeing some of his early works. As a result of this incident Léonce Rosenberg began taking boxing lessons. The Kahnweiler sale thus started in a terrible atmosphere under the worst auspices.[38]

On June 13, the first day of the sale, the attendance at the auction resembled a friendly reunion at rue Vignon. It was the first time many of the people had seen each other since the war. Kahnweiler knew that he could count on them, even lean on them for support if necessary. The problem he faced was that the French were a minority in the salesroom. On the whole the artists were against this auction because of the unusual circumstances, not on principle.

Kahnweiler could also read the catalogue as a summation of his career; and there was nothing to be ashamed of. Everything in his possession had been seized and catalogued. There were no mistakes, and he took pride in everything listed, except for a few things: two Metzingers that he had accepted as part of an exchange, and four or five canvases from a fashionable painter he had been weak enough to agree to keep in the back room.[39] It was a handsome catalogue and a unique exhibition, as the contents of his storerooms had been transformed into a gallery on a larger scale, such as he had never dreamed of having. In the salesroom, while waiting for the first blow of the ivory gavel, two art dealers were talking:

"The one thing in favor of cubism," said one, "is that some very intelligent people believed in it."

"But really," answered the other, "how do you know that Apollinaire, Cocteau, and Salmon were not pretending just for the fun of it, to fool their friends?"

Reputations were made and ruined on that day at Hôtel Drouot. It was the first public auction of modern art on such a scale. Rumor placed Derain very high, way above other artists; those who were professionals and knowledgeable let novice collectors eager for inside information know that they would be wise to invest in him. Thus he became the most acceptable of these subversive artists. The art dealers of the Right Bank found him the most "saleable" to their clientele, who had barely recovered from the fireworks set off by the fauves.

A large crowd showed up for this awful drama. There were art dealers, artists, collectors, writers, poets, art critics, journalists, mere curiosity seekers who wandered in: Durand-Ruel, Amédée Ozenfant, the Rosenberg brothers of course, Bernheim-Jeune, Joseph Brenner from New York, Paul Guillaume, Lipchitz, Goldschmidt from Frankfurt, Zborowski from Montparnasse, Gimpel, Jacques Doucet, Jean Paulhan, future surrealists Paul Eluard and André Breton, André Lefèvre, Alfred Richet, and numerous others who came to attend the sale from Stockholm, Zurich, Geneva, and London.

The auctioneers mispronounced foreign names so consistently that people wondered if they were making them up or doing it on purpose. The catalogue of this first sale had so many lots listed that Léonce did not always bother to identify the artists whose works were on sale. He listed a Braque or a Picasso at random, but the prices were just about the same.

Tristan Tzara, special representative of the dadaist group, was horrified by this shoddy procedure, but he was overwhelmed by the public viewing of the works and the quality of the audience present. He had intended to buy much more than he did, but he consoled himself with bidding on Picasso's collages, which he considered one of the great inventions of modern times.[40] Jean Paulhan, the shy secretary of the Nouvelle Revue Française, obtained *Violin*, a collage by Braque, for 170 francs. The painter Charles-Edouard Jeanneret, who had not yet become Le Corbusier, bought many items, but not for himself. He was acting as the agent of the Swiss banker Raoul La Roche, who had been convinced by Jeanneret and Ozenfant to buy a collection of modern art which would one day become the pride of the Kunstmuseum of Basel. He bought works by Braque, Picasso, and Gris, and spent only 50,000 francs; it would be one of M. La Roche's finest involuntary investments. Amédeé Ozenfant bought the wonderful collage by Braque, *La Clarinette*, for 470 francs (selling it to Nelson Rockefeller in 1952 for 8,000 dollars).[41]

Again the nation was too prudent. The representatives were all there because they were still obsessing about the scandal of the Caillebotte Collection, when the authorities from the Beaux-Arts had watched complacently, or even with pleasure, as impressionist paintings were bought by foreign collectors. They did not want to make the same mistake this time, but neither were they prepared to act. The curators of the national museums were uneasy at being pulled in both directions—by the academics of the Ecole des Beaux-Arts on the one hand and the advocates of the explosive avant-garde on the other. They hesitated to use the right to preempt works and turned most of them down; thus they garnered an insignificant number of them. They committed a serious error in not recognizing the special circumstances that would have allowed Kahnweiler to have certain works exempted from the sale, or to have certain works protected from leaving the country.

In the course of the sale twenty-two Braques, twenty-four Derains, nine Grises, seven Légers, twenty-six Picassos, six van Dongens, and twenty-three Vlamincks were sold, for a total of 216,335 francs. Braque's prices held their own, since *Violin* went up to 3,200 francs. The works of other artists also commanded a fair price, except for works by Picasso and Vlaminck, which had low appraisals. But the winner, if anyone could be said to have come out on top in such a fiasco, was André Derain. His paintings were bid up to anywhere between 2,800 francs and 20,000 francs. The *Portrait of Lucie Kahnweiler* went up to 18,000 francs. There was a great deal of bidding over the painting, and it was with a real pang that Kahnweiler saw it sold to Paul Rosenberg, who bid for it with suspicious fervor. It was as if he wanted it only in order to give the knife another twist in his colleague's wound.

Kahnweiler himself was not present at the sale—he would have found the experience unbearable—although he was represented in the room. After finding out that he was not allowed to buy under his own name, he decided to form a syndicate composed of Louise Leiris (his sister-in-law), Hermann Rupf, the German art dealer Alfred Flechtheim, Gustave Kahnweiler, and himself. At Drouot they used the name "Grassat." They were careful not to compete with Bernheim-Jeune, who was the most enterprising and would walk away with an impressive number of Vlamincks. The syndicate did not have those means at its disposal, and being thus limited, did not bid past a certain point. To maintain Braque's prices the syndicate bought eleven out of twenty-two in the sale. They also got all the stone sculptures, models, and bronzes by Manolo, for which there was little bidding. It enabled Kahnweiler to say proudly to Manolo, "We really protected you."[42]

There was very little bidding on paintings by Gris, and eight out of nine were bought back by the syndicate. They also bid for three Derains, three Légers, one van Dongen, and two Vlamincks. They did not get any Picassos; prices were too high. Kahnweiler was convinced that these paintings would be sold either in the rue d'Astorg gallery or by Flechtheim in Germany, especially the Vlamincks. Kahnweiler had wanted desperately to buy more, but the syndicate did not have the funds. Léonce Rosenberg bought very little, only a few Légers, because he also did not have the means.[43]

The press, true to its nature, was surly, hateful, and malicious. It did not understand the situation, so it became abusive. Kahnweiler was presented as a common speculator, a stock market investor who strayed into the artists' studios, a dealer in inflated reputations, fabricating adulterated paintings that he put over as masterpieces to the unsuspecting French. Just before the sale the house newsletter, *La Gazette de l'Hôtel Drouot*, which might have been expected to remain impartial, was feeling self-congratulatory about the preponderant number of foreigners in the audience for the sale of modern art.[44] The honor of the nation was safe as long as the French knew how to resist this perversion of art.

The second part of the auction was scheduled for November. Thus the summer brought a welcome respite from this descent into hell which had undermined Kahnweiler's morale. No matter how things stood, he closed his gallery for August. There was no one in town. The Kahnweilers spent some time in Rome under very different circumstances than those they had experienced in August 1914.

When they returned the capital was still lethargic, and the house in Boulogne was as quiet as the quietest section of Paris. He and Lucie sat for their portrait by Gris. Kahnweiler wanted to forget what lay ahead, as if he could not take another disaster. But very quickly it was November and the fateful event was upon him.

The auction was scheduled for Thursday the seventeenth, in room number 6. Again the art dealers, collectors, and critics flocked to the sale. People knew or recognized one another, greeted one another with warmth or reserve, like opening night at the theater. The audience even stamped its feet so that the auction would begin on time. Columnists who were there to cover the event had their pieces written beforehand, and, knowing what to expect, watched things unravel with open pleasure. Just by listening to these bizarrely dressed people with their thick accents, who did not hide the fact that they were experts and collected art, they harvested a treasury of one-liners, such as this exchange between an elderly man and a younger person: "They have a lot of imagination but very little talent. In my day . . ."

"In your day they had a lot of talent and no imagination."[45]

The atmosphere was charged, and again there was an outburst just before the sale. This time it was not a match between Léonce and the boxer Braque; now Léonce had another opponent. In the exhibition room, talking about the auction at Drouot, he and Basler started calling each other names.

"Dirty Pole!" said Léonce.

"Austrian swine!" answered Basler, just as loudly.

Spiteful public rumors had spread the story that these two had called each other "dirty half-breeds" in writing. Kahnweiler, who had a good laugh at this (and he had few occasions for humor), did not believe a word of it.[46] The name-calling suddenly took another turn when Basler's cane came down heavily on Léonce's skull and Léonce's fist flew out in search of Basler's nose. Louis Vauxcelles could not let this incident go by and called it the art world's "new style"—which had nothing to do with aesthetics.[47]

According to him, in the soporific atmosphere of the auction room only foreign dealers bought these cubist paintings at ridiculous prices. He found the auction boring, sad, and torpid until the Vlamincks: "Paintings finally appeared among these lugubrious geometric practical jokes. Ozenfant, overwhelmed, began to sob uncontrollably in the arms of Jeanneret."[48]

In fact, this time it was Vlaminck who came out the best in purely commercial terms, along with Derain, whose works were still in demand. When the latter's works went on the auction block there were a lot of comments from the audience: "He is everything except a cubist." "He never wants to do the same thing twice, except for painting badly." "The 'New Testament' of modern painting is 'copy one another.'" "What one looks for in the works by the cubists, and what one ends up liking about them is still the tradition." "In one hundred and fifty years people will be seeking out Derain the same way that today we look for Fragonard, and he will be as expensive."[49]

In his report to Derain, Kahnweiler confirmed the fact that the prices realized were lower than those of the first sale, that his prices had remained at a respectable level, and that the syndicate had been able to buy about ten of his canvases. The most important among them were *The Italian Woman* and *The Checkerboard*. But he could not hide his pessimism about the third part of the sale, especially considering the present economic situation.[50] In a similar letter to Braque, Kahnweiler sent him the catalogue with the list of prices obtained without expanding upon the relative success of Derain and Vlaminck, believing as he did that the auction had been bad for everyone. Instead he preferred to relate what Basler colorfully termed "my epic battle with Léonce."[51]

Braque would understand easily just by reviewing prices, and he would learn the extent of the fiasco from the newspapers. Vauxcelles derived a mean-spirited pleasure in driving home the nail: "Collectors of Picasso were gleefully rubbing their hands because they could buy the works of the great man for the price of the stretcher. The art speculators were making a face that what had been worth three thousand francs a while back now sold for fifteen louis [three hundred francs]—frame included."[52]

During this second auction the gavel came down on a total of thirty-five Braques, thirty-nine Derains, fifteen Grises, ten Légers, forty-six Picassos, sixty Vlamincks, twenty-seven van Dongens, and a number of their gouaches and drawings, amounting to 175,215 francs. It was a ridiculously small sum. Kahnweiler's syndicate could buy only twenty-five canvases, whereas André Breton, whether acting as Jacques Doucet's agent or for himself, bought ten. Kahnweiler's sorrows knew no limit, as he then had to suffer the sarcasm of the press, who were jubilant about the relatively few French buyers in the audience. Some publications maliciously insisted on referring to him only as "the German, Kahnweiler" (in twenty years, under Nazi occupation, it would become "Kahnweiler, the Jew") and to remind their readers that on his wall at home hung *Portrait of a Man* by Derain, which was of none other than Landru, the infamous murderer.[53]

This was not the most irritating aspect of this sordid business, which still had surprises in store for him. Léonce Rosenberg once again amazed him. A month earlier, in October, they had had an extraordinary epistolary exchange.

"All this is good publicity for the cubists. It's one compensation for your losses," Léonce said in all earnestness.[54]

"I am too cast down by the misfortune that has befallen me to see it in such an objective manner," Kahnweiler answered with his consummate sense of litotes.[55]

But Léonce would stop at nothing. He had been asked to exhibit in London the sculptures by Laurens that he owned; he wanted to offer them to Kahnweiler first, "at cost with ten percent added," out of courtesy for "a fellow defender of cubism."[56]

He considered himself Kahnweiler's equal in the struggle for cubism, he who caused the liquidation which brought cubism to the verge of bankruptcy. Kahnweiler was too overwhelmed to speak his mind. He simply refused the offer and argued that Laurens was not being represented fairly.[57] In his letters to Derain he spoke of his bitterness:

"The Rosenbergs are bastards. To think that Léonce is now making grotesque proposals. I am convinced that had they not meddled, an agreement with the government could have been reached. On top of all this, Germany is giving me trouble about reimbursing me for my losses. They won't even recognize their debt to me, using the pretext that I refused to serve in the army."[58]

He had expected it, just as he had been prepared for the Rosenbergs. At this time he was still wondering whether Léonce was evil, or just plain stupid. In his naive incompetence Léonce seemed convinced that only at public auction could the cubist painters find their true values. He also believed that it was the only way to cultivate new collectors. He would have preferred Kahnweiler to reopen his gallery in Bern rather than near rue La Boétie; since events turned out differently, he was determined to flood the art market with the stock of the rue Vignon gallery in such a way that the new works he owned by cubist artists would quickly find buyers. Thus in October, according to a logic that escaped everyone's grasp, he put 381 canvases from his own gallery up for sale at the De Roos Auction House in Amsterdam.

By November the expert appraiser at the Kahnweiler auction was on the verge of bankruptcy. To Kahnweiler's amazement, this man without any sense of pride came to him to explain that he could not pay his bills; what should he do? This turn of events evoked Kahnweiler's pity: he was aware of a number of things few people knew. He had it from reliable sources that Léonce, penniless and crazed, had approached Vlaminck directly to buy his work, and approached Bernheim-Jeune about their Dufys because he only wanted to buy what was saleable.[59] Kahnweiler also knew that Léonce had sent concrete offers to Flechtheim, with whom Kahnweiler had a special business relationship in Germany, so that they could work together in selling Matisse, Picasso, Derain, Utrillo, Braque, Gris, Leger, and Valmier. Flechtheim sent the original letter to Kahnweiler, scrawling at the bottom in pencil the ironic comment, "What do you think, my friend?"[60]

Kahnweiler did not know what attitude he should take, as he was not a man to rush in or to cause a scandal. Despite everything, Kahnweiler continued to sell him Légers of the dimensions specified in his contract, but Léonce could not pay for them; he dragged his feet and made endless excuses. Clearly this was a drowning man, but instead of pushing his head under and holding him there to speed things up, Kahnweiler preferred to extend a helping hand. It was not out of compassion for the man but because one liquidation sale was enough. The cubist artists would never recover if the Léonce Rosenberg gallery were forced into a bankruptcy sale. That would be too many in one year. Kahnweiler advised him to arrange for a schedule of payment. By applying to the court Léonce could obtain the benefit of an ad hoc ruling, a sort of moratorium for war veterans whose business had been ruined by the aftermath of the war. Thus Léonce obtained a respite of ten years to pay his debts, which amounted to 90,000 francs.

Léonce Rosenberg felt that he was losing faith in cubism, so he dropped his artists and only bought what he could sell. Kahnweiler's only consideration was to prevent Léonce from flooding the art market again. That was the disaster to be feared. As for the rest . . .[61]

Léonce, discouraged, came to see Kahnweiler in the gallery: "You don't feel that we have worked for nothing?" he asked Kahnweiler, who was rendered speechless, less by the question than by this *we* which pretended to link them together.

"You are to blame for everything that is occurring now, the eclipse of cubism and the rest of it," Kahnweiler answered, smiling, before telling him some basic truths.

"I swear to you I never pushed for the sale of your stock. Those are all artists' fabrications."

This was a vain denial, since Kahnweiler was well aware of Léonce's role in the downgrading of cubism and the prices of the artists.[62]

At the end of the year, when he took stock of the situation, Kahnweiler discovered that, even with the two disastrous auctions that would forever stamp the year 1921 in his mind, not everything had been negative. Among his artists, Braque had renewed his contract for another year, although Laurens wanted his freedom, as he did not want to discuss his finances with anyone. Vlaminck sent recent canvases and watercolors at the pressing request of the dealer, who also continued buying from Derain: fourteen canvases, seven watercolors, and two sanguines for 50,000 francs.[63]

In its outreach to foreign countries the Galerie Simon had started working with the J. H. de Bois Gallery in Haarlem (Holland). In both the United States and Germany the economic climate made it more difficult. In New York, Joseph Brenner had difficulty convincing Kahnweiler that the prices he set for the exhibition of Derain and Vlaminck were much too high. These artists were unknown on the other side of the Atlantic, and Brenner wanted to encourage new collectors to become involved, as there were so many Derain paintings on the market. But Kahnweiler remained adamant. His prices were not negotiable and Brenner had to accept them or give up having the exhibition.[64] The problems were of another sort in Berlin. The art market had been going through hard times since October with the first devaluation of the mark. The situation was tight, and competition had increased. When Kahnweiler learned that the Scandinavian art dealer, Halvorsen, wanted to sell his Braques, Derains, and Vlamincks on the German market he immediately sent him a letter of protest: "You have the whole world in which to sell your paintings!"

Halvorsen was willing to oblige him. But in exchange he asked that Kahnweiler influence Flechtheim in Berlin to buy the Matisses he needed from Halvorsen. For other works by Matisse, Flechtheim would buy directly from the artist, and for the Cézanne drawings he needed Kahnweiler was willing to act as an intermediary.[65] Thus the problem was solved to everyone's satisfaction.

This type of transaction would become more common, a sign of a time of crisis. Kahnweiler could no longer devote himself only to the artists and works he represented. He had to create business in order to live.

The only area where Kahnweiler felt completely free was in his publishing venture. During the year six books were brought out under the imprint of the Galerie Simon, which was considerable for a firm that did not specialize in publishing. Kahnweiler persuaded his friends, artists and writers, to work in collaboration even if they held divergent views.

The books he published were of a similar format, between twenty-eight and forty-eight pages, in editions of 112 copies, with 12 presentation copies, 10 printed on Imperial Japan paper, and 90 on Holland van Gelder. One hundred copies were signed both by the writer and the illustrator. Each work was a notable literary event. *Ne coupez pas Mademoiselle, ou les erreurs des PTT* (Don't Cut Me Off, Operator; or the Mistakes of the Phone Company), a philosophical tale by Max Jacob, was the first work illustrated by Juan Gris. André Malraux's *Lunes en papier* (Paper Moons) was his first published book, and it was illustrated with six woodcuts by Léger, which was also a first for him. *Communications* was a collection of poems by Vlaminck which he also illustrated. *Les Pélicans* (The Pelicans) by the adolescent Raymond Radiguet (two years before his great success with the novel *Devil in the Flesh*) was illustrated with engravings by Henri Laurens. *Le Piège de Méduse* (Medusa's Trap), a lyric comedy, was the only work by Erik Satie published in book form and the first to be illustrated with woodcuts by Braque. The last work, *Coeur de Chêne* (Heart of Oak), a collection of poems by Pierre Reverdy, was the only book Manolo ever illustrated.

From this list and the perspective of time, it becomes evident that Kahnweiler was also a notable publisher. He had the ability to discover writers and works that he matched with great artists. It makes one wonder what he would have done with the imprint of the Galerie Simon if he had had the means and if he had devoted himself to publishing with the same passion and ambition he had for art. At that time he simply followed his instincts by publishing what seemed "real poetry" and "good writing," as there is "good and real painting."

Kahnweiler had smiled on reading the inscription mocking biblio- phile speculators that Radiguet wrote in *Pelicans*: "From the typescript of this work two carbon copies were made. They are the second edition!" Malraux was only twenty years old, and he penned something even longer in the school notebook that he submitted to Kahnweiler. In his uniform slanted handwriting he wrote as a subtitle: "A little work containing the relation of several little-known struggles, as well as a journey among common but strange objects, told with respect for the truth." He then appended two notes for the reader. If Kahnweiler enjoyed the first warn- ing, "There are no symbols in this book," he must have been surprised by the second: "If certain boring situations require that this book be read out loud, we wish to inform the reader from the very first page that we recommend it be done with a nasal twang."[66]

The books were not uniformly successful, and some remained on the shelf for a long time. Among the first subscribers were the fashion de- signers Paul Poiret and Jacques Doucet, the lawyer John Quinn, the art dealer Paul Guillaume, and author-editor André Gide. Fortunately the gallery did not rely on the sale of books to survive.

During this time Kahnweiler was also waiting for the third part of the auction to be announced. Ironically his informant was none other than Léonce Rosenberg, who periodically reported that the state might set the date for June, then it was October, unless July would be better. Léonce kept warning him, "Consider yourself lucky and don't complain because it could be much worse. The state does not give a damn about these cubists. If it becomes a problem, they will sell it all as one lot through a hostile art dealer." This was too much coming from the mouth of Léonce. To Kahn- weiler he seemed unbelievably two-faced, since he delayed the payment for the monies he owed Kahnweiler (4,500 francs) but at the same time pushed for the auction at Drouot.[67]

Léonce disagreed with Kahnweiler about the value of cubist paint- ings and blamed the weak market on the economic situation, not on the Drouot auctions. He believed that the only solution was to sell cubist works for whatever the limited audience was willing to pay. He went so far as to affirm that the buyers from the future auctions would become collectors of cubist artists and faithful followers of the Galerie Simon. In other words, from Kahnweiler's misery some good was sure to come.[68] Léonce believed that to survive this period of crisis, it was sufficient not to be in debt and to buy works at a discount; that was the secret of success in their profession.[69] But when Kahnweiler asked for repayment of his debt and suggested he observe a strict schedule of payment in business dealings, Léonce answered with great detachment: "Unfortunately, today in the luxury trade, there is no fixed date of payment, not because one does not want to pay, but one cannot due to circumstances."[70]

It was simply, "Patience, be patient, dear colleague." Everything would come out well in the end, and when business picked up, art dealers would again buy from one another. Patience was characteristic of Kahnweiler even in times of crisis, but with Léonce he found his resolve flagging. At times he wanted to quote Chateaubriand: "You have to be sparing in your use of contempt as there are so many deserving people."

Kahnweiler had another interpretation of the existing condition of the art market: the state was killing the goose that laid the golden egg. Cubism represented a sizable sum in terms of export, and the blindness of the French authorities was beyond comprehension. He believed that the art market had to be left alone, to catch its breath, to absorb the works of his artists. Everyone would benefit from such a policy: artists, dealers, collectors, even the government, if it had more sense. Kahnweiler, among others, had asked people in high places to use their influence to push back the date of the third liquidation sale until November 1922. The market was at its lowest in years, and this brief span of time would allow collectors to return and create a demand again.[71] It was a futile effort.

On July 4, 1922, room number 7 of Hôtel Drouot was packed with people who wanted to be present for Act Three. This sale was plagued by vicious rumors, and opponents no longer used the term paintings. They said "cubes" instead. All the old arguments from previous sales were resumed, while the audience repeated Vauxcelles's allegations that Léonce would show up wearing chain mail and armor, Basler a helmet and gas mask, Braque his boxing gloves, and Kahnweiler a cane (*Kahn*) weighted (*weiler*) with lead.[72]

Far more serious was the conflict between Vauxcelles and the painters Ozenfant and Jeanneret. The critic had expressed his disgust with cubism everywhere, using his own name and his various pseudonyms, such as Pinturicchio. The two artists decided to drag his name through the mud using the same tactics. In an article of unusual venom they insinuated that he was paid by the other camp, that he was so venal, so greedy it was no secret among art dealers. They knew him to be a compulsive liar when he wrote that the market for cubism was ruined by the Kahnweiler sales or that collectors of Picasso could pick up works for the cost of the canvas: "21,150 francs was expensive for a stretched canvas!" Ozenfant wrote in his response published in one of the critic's newspapers.

Jeanneret accused Vauxcelles of playing a double game of extreme hypocrisy. In the art review he edited, he was quite complacent about cubism, but when he published elsewhere under different pseudonyms, he was cutthroat in his attacks.[73]

There were the minor events leading up to the auction. People no longer protested when employees at Drouot held paintings and drawings upside down. In this atmosphere of complete indifference only Kahnweiler made himself heard.

By the end of the liquidation sale, fifteen Braques, twelve Derains, six Grises, eight Légers, ten Picassos, thirty Vlamincks, and gouaches and drawings were disposed of for the sum of 84,927 francs. Vlaminck's prices again withstood the test of the auction. As for those of other artists, there was a certain distress, even if such and such a Léger went for 800 francs. The Kahnweiler syndicate was able to buy even less than André Breton, who acquired one Léger and three Braques.

In order to forget, Kahnweiler had to immerse himself in his work until the inevitable fourth and last liquidation auction. He closed the gallery, and he and Lucie went on vacation with his partner André Simon. They headed for Austria, Zell-am-See in the Kitzbüheler Alps. They made many stops in Germany on the way there and back. The contrast between the respective plights of the two countries struck him.

In Austria he threw himself into mountain climbing, swimming, sailing, and rowing on the lake near the lovely village where they stayed. The country was economically distressed because of the indolence and fatalistic resignation of its population up and down the social ladder. He saw no hope of economic recovery. There was misery in the cities and in the countryside, although a measure of comfort could be found with the devaluation of the crown. By contrast, Germany seemed to be the scene of great activity, though he added to his judgment a serious reservation: because the economy was artificial, if it were not stabilized by an international loan in the near future, Germany would be headed for disaster. Even on vacation Kahnweiler could not leave business interests behind. He stopped in Munich to see the Raphaels and some admirable El Grecos, as well as German polychrome sculptures of the fifteenth century; he also bought a beautiful Pietà.[74]

It was not difficult to come back to the reality of Paris. He felt that with the exception of the auction at Hôtel Drouot, 1922 was a good year for the Galerie Simon, largely due to a general quickening of activity.

A new gallery had opened, founded on the most original principles. The Percier Gallery on rue La Boétie had a capital of 250,000 francs, and was created in the same spirit as the "Peau de l'Ours" association, which had supported young artists before the war. In both cases there was the same animating spirit and collectors with the desire to see works exhibited. The six original shareholders were Messrs. Tournaire, Pellequer, and Bonnet; Alfred Richet (the secretary of a company that imported coal); André Level (secretary of the Marseilles docks company); and André Lefèvre, a financier originally from Granville, intimate with bankers and stockbrokers of the capital, who had been influenced by Kahnweiler in the formation of his taste and his selections. An artist described him as "only a carbon copy of that clear-sighted dealer."[75] This statement sold short Lefèvre's character. Among his friends, Level and Richet shared his philosophy: they did not buy paintings in order to resell them at a profit but to bring support to the artists they valued and to defend art that was to their taste. Speculation was anathema to them; they were collectors at heart. The Percier Gallery, which was located in a shop, was probably the only gallery that regretted making any sales. Separation from a painting was painful.

In describing his friend André Level, Alfred Richet would give the psychological traits of the ideal art collector: a man for whom the intrinsic value of the painting was the only criterion by which he arrived at a decision. The collector who was only interested in contemporary artists, the cubists in particular, acted according to his intuition rather than by cultural reflex, by predilection rather than rules. Despite all the influences that shaped him, "he himself explored the depth of his preferences."[76]

Kahnweiler valued Level all the more for his idealism. He would be happy with ten or twelve collectors of the same mettle as Lefèvre, Level, and Richet. But the reality of the 1920s was more down to earth. By the end of 1922 Durand-Ruel had died. Although almost penniless at the end, in his storerooms he had hoarded eight hundred Renoirs and six hundred Degas.[77] Vollard, by contrast, was in the best of health. His only problem was that the gallery on rue Laffitte was condemned for the right of way of a street. Where would he move—to Matignon, to Montparnasse, to Saint-Germain? It could be taken as a sign of the times, but he bought a town house in the seventh arrondissement, believing that he was important enough for people to come to him at his home. But the situation was to prove fatal.

Léonce Rosenberg seemed crushed by problems. He was bitter, disappointed in his artists and their lack of gratitude, and he became interested in the rising values of real estate and industry. For him the era of contracts had come to an end. He had had it with buying ten paintings and selling only two or three of them. He would not renew any contracts, "even with the Pope," preferring to buy paintings individually from two or three artists, no more. During this period he could not afford to repay Kahnweiler the 750 francs he still owed him.[78]

Everyone was hard up for cash at this time, even the Galerie Simon, despite the 20,000 marks in indemnity the German government finally paid Kahnweiler. Everyone thought that was only the first payment. There was the expectation that a revival of the market for luxury goods would include the art market. While living in expectation, so many opportunities were missed. Kahnweiler was heartbroken to learn that *Les Demoiselles d'Avignon* had been removed from Picasso's studio. The fashion designer and art patron Jacques Doucet carried it off, having been well advised by his scouts, André Breton and Louis Aragon. He had paid quite a price: 25,000 francs.

Kahnweiler's finances were affected by the temporary downturn of the German and American markets. In New York, Brenner sold only one painting from the Derain exhibition and owed 8,000 francs to the Galerie Simon.[79] The three Vlamincks and the Gris sold by John Wanamaker, the art dealer, only brought the gallery 5,900 francs.[80] It was very little compared to the gallery's balance of credit at the Comptoir National d'Escompte, which was only 19,070 francs.[81]

Kahnweiler became more demanding and less flexible than ever about terms when his artists were shown abroad. When Samuel Katznelson was planning to open a gallery in New York and wanted a stock of paintings, Kahnweiler offered Derain and Vlaminck paintings at a 33 percent reduction. But in return he wanted a guarantee that 25 percent of the paintings would be purchased during the appointed time. Take it or leave it.[82]

The problem was not restricted to the United States. The Swedish art dealer Gusta Olson, owner of the Svensk-Franska Kontsgalleriet in Stockholm, conferred with Kahnweiler about a Derain exhibition and the "correct" price for that market. Olson got quite a shock when back in Sweden he received a list of prices: from 1,300 to 13,000 francs. He thought these prices were too high for his clientele, but Kahnweiler refused to budge. According to him those were the "right" prices, which applied to the highest as well as the lowest figures. He wanted the prices maintained and would lower them only in specific negotiations. But events proved Olson to be right for his time: from the exhibition not one painting would be sold.[83]

Times were hard in Paris, and Kahnweiler began selling, from the back room, works other than those by gallery artists. He had no heart for it, but the stimulus was the debit of his current account with Baron Jacques de Gunzburg: 296,290.80 francs, which was alarming.[84] At the request of Robert Delaunay he acted as agent for the sale of a painting to a collector;[85] the same for a Manet, a Seurat, and a Sisley which proved to be a forgery; and he attempted to sell to Jacques Doucet a large and important canvas by Raoul Dufy from 1914, left with him on consignment.[86]

He chafed at having this second string of works, and it disgusted him. At this time he bought from Léger's studio an oil painting entitled *Woman in an Interior*, which he would only be able to resell six years later to Baron Gourgaud. He was a new collector along with Etienne de Beaumont, the Princess de Bassiano, and the writer Edmond Jaloux, in whom Kahnweiler tried to cultivate a permanent interest in the works of his artists, specifically Derain. Kahnweiler even arranged terms for installment payments to make these clients more loyal to his gallery. Edmond Jaloux, whose eyes were bigger than his stomach, would pay 9,000 francs for *The Church* by Derain over a period of six months or more.[87] A collector from Lyon, M. Vautheret, bought two Derains for 22,200 francs, with a down payment of 5,000 francs and the rest spread over a five-month period. Henceforth these arrangements became standard practice,[88] especially with collectors of the works of Derain, whom Kahnweiler was pushing since he fetched such high prices at the Drouot auctions. He could not carry enough Derains; he was always in need of more works:

"Were you able to work well? I hope that you will bring back with you work you found satisfying, and that I will have an important series of paintings. What I need are some nudes. They can be found everywhere except here—Bernheim-Jeune has stacks of them. Anyway, perhaps you will have some for me this fall."[89]

He decided for the first time to organize exhibitions in the gallery. The paintings and drawings of the Catalan artist José de Togorès proved a great success, which was helped by the catalogue essay by Max Jacob. His show of "unknown" artists was simply in the spirit of the gallery's reputation. It consisted of paintings, watercolors, and sculptures by folk artists, which were not for sale, but on loan from the collections of friends such as Malraux, Basler, or Raynal. Finally the large exhibition of forty-five paintings by Elie Lascaux was a statement of his intention to become involved with the new generation of artists, those who were born after the turn of the century.

For a long time Kahnweiler was convinced that a dealer could represent only his own generation, perhaps two generations at the most. But even with this guideline he could not find what he needed. At the Salon d'Automne of 1922 he stopped for a long time in front of a large Léger, a beautiful panel by Braque, and two Matisses which resembled a Bonnard he rather liked. He dismissed the rest as filler, paintings he had seen before, probably last year in the same show. Dufy was too stylish, ideally suited to Bernheim-Jeune. The worst in his opinion was Dunoyer de Segonzac, whose works he generally disliked, but the paintings in the show he found especially abominable: "thick paint, false Courbets, badly painted, already warping, disgusting."[90]

He used to escape this nightmare briefly in the studio of his friend Gris. Now he visited the studio almost on a daily basis since he had managed to convince the artist to move out to Boulogne near him. Kahnweiler lived at 12 and Gris at 8 rue de la Mairie, just a house away. They shared meals, and the two households went out together to films and restaurants in the neighborhood. They were rarely apart, and it was amazing to people that such a harmonious understanding could exist between an art dealer and a painter. They did seem to be in agreement, rejecting abstract art as well as expressionism. If anyone would want to write parallel biographies about them, it would be amazing to see the aesthetic development in Gris, and the similar direction of Kahnweiler's thinking. They both evolved toward greater purity, rigor, and simplicity, all of which were components of a classical cubism.

Kahnweiler could depend on Gris, the way Durand-Ruel did on Renoir. His loyalty made up for the difficulties caused by the other artists, such as Manolo, who promised to send paintings for an exhibition and never delivered. Yet Kahnweiler was never late in mailing the monthly stipend check. He could no longer represent him if there was nothing in return, especially now that business was deteriorating. Manolo, who could not make the payments on the house he had just bought, displayed a disarming commercial naiveté as usual. He received the small sum of 350 francs a month from the Galerie Simon. He wanted a larger stipend but he could not even meet the obligations of such a small sum. He was two years behind in relation to the dates of delivery stated in the contracts. In Kahnweiler's opinion it was not humanly possible to catch up. He had been prepared to raise the stipend to seven hundred francs, but now it was out of the question.

"We cannot ruin ourselves, and you wouldn't want us to do that either." He wanted to deduct what was owed from his monthly stipend, arguing that he had to balance his accounts for his partner André Simon. Manolo seemed never to hear, or refused to understand, always returning with the complaint, "You want me to work and live on 350 francs a month?" He then drew up minute accounts in which he became confused and promised forty-two pieces of sculpture in seven months. That was not acceptable either; it would be done too hastily and would be detrimental to his work. Kahnweiler reminded him, like a great lord, of how he had taken on his work before the war regardless of profit or loss. But now he was inflexible about the terms of the new gallery: "You have to manage somehow, Manolo, these are hard times for everyone."

That was not the end of his troubles with Manolo. He caught wind of the sculptor's acceptance of commissions for monuments in Arles and Sévérac to pay the mortgage on his house. Kahnweiler felt caught in a vicious circle he could escape only by severing relations, or at least pushing back the date of Manolo's exhibition.[91]

1923 was the year of the last liquidation sale of his stock, but also the year he parted from some of his most valued artists. There had been a gradual buildup of tension between him and his artists caused by problems of the art market, the competition from other art dealers, and the aesthetic direction taken by the artists themselves. First there were Derain and Vlaminck, who had never been cubists, properly speaking, even though their relationship to Kahnweiler and their work from 1910 made them part of that wave. Their current development left him behind and did not interest him. They had grown too far apart and their paths had diverged from Kahnweiler's. Now Vlaminck even reproached Kahnweiler for having led him into error. "Kahnweiler, when I consider the fact that you showed me a sheet of white paper with some charcoal markings and a piece of newspaper glued to it and you said that was something! The worst of it is that I believed you."[92]

Derain was also maintaining his distance, and like his friend, questioned the terms of his contract with the Galerie Simon. Braque was simply leaving to sign a more profitable contract with Paul Rosenberg and was moving from Montmartre to Montparnasse. Some people saw this as symbolic of the future. Even Léger was taking liberties with his contract, and Kahnweiler had to bring him back into line. Nothing serious, but it augured ill. Kahnweiler noticed these little warnings because he was sensitive to detail. He valued Léger, the man and the artist. Léger was the energetic traveling companion who, in defiance of his vertigo and terror, followed Kahnweiler up dizzying trails in the Tyrolean Alps. He was the man who left the key to his studio on the door and who, from the midst of all those canvases leaning face against the wall, that steel helmet from the kaiser's army, or the signpost giving directions to the trenches in German, always greeted him at any hour with an outstretched hand and a loud, "Bonjour Kahn!" He was the only person who ever called him that.[93]

But whether it was Derain, Vlaminck, Braque, or Léger, none of them undermined him the way Manolo had for the last few months. Everything he touched suddenly became complicated. The exhibition of Manolo's sculptures and drawings went very well, but the promotion was very expensive. To make critics attend, Kahnweiler sacrificed his integrity and presented small examples of Manolo's work, little terra-cottas, to prominent critics such as Louis Vauxcelles, to give them a taste of the show.[94]

He made the overture because Manolo remained unknown. His work sold periodically, as did that of Togorès, to an important art dealer in Barcelona, Luis Plandiura. In France it was much harder to put Manolo's work across.

Worst of all, Kahnweiler had to fight on both fronts: the public, which had to be made to understand Manolo's work, and the artist himself, who had to be made to listen to common sense. There was no doubt that for all his naiveté, he was completely sincere in his protestations: he pulled his hair, he whined, he rolled his eyes—it was unbelievable. Kahnweiler's letters had an exasperated edge to them—he did not know which was harder to bear, the ravings or the artist. His letters from 1923 were not typical and are certainly revelatory of the relationship between dealer and artist.

> Pay attention, my dear Manolo, I am not put out because I know you lack business experience, otherwise I would be in a state of rage over your letter. As you are so very far behind schedule for the minimum you owe me, I am forced to reduce your monthly stipend. You are late in making your deadline even as you are promising me that you will catch up. But as you are having money troubles I agreed to give you 800 francs a month again. You promised me three other stone sculptures, but if you are not paid, you will keep these three sculptures. But Manolo, please do me the favor of reading your contract and think about it: you owe me all of your production.[95]

The artist replied with incoherent arguments. He acted as if he did not understand French, but despite his errors in spelling and syntax he spoke and wrote it well. He did not want to admit that since the beginning of their relationship he had been doing less and less. The art dealer wanted him to honor the contract and guarantee that he would provide a minimum of eighteen sculptures and thirty drawings a year. To make Manolo understand this he had to always be prepared to show a degree of patience that could scarcely be believed.

> I am going to force myself to answer calmly. It is difficult under the circumstances, I assure you. I write you that you do not have the right to keep the three stone sculptures, and you answer that yes, you agree, you will just put them in your garden somewhere unless I pay you separately for them. But I have been telling you that you cannot keep them, so I wonder if you think that I'm a complete fool. What if I told you that the Galerie Simon's money was doing fine in the bank and was going to stay there. But haven't you any sense of moral obligation? Why do you think that the Galerie Simon faithfully sends you a check on the thirtieth of every month? . . .
>
> I have proven my loyalty to you under all circumstances. But I also insist on your loyalty in relation to me. I don't like your trying to make me pay for what rightfully belongs to me. Believe me, my friend, I don't enjoy writing this. If I am being hard, I am sorry. I am trying to control myself as best as I can. Let me say once and for all, observe the contract or that's the end of it between us.[96]

With his other artists the break was made more quickly and neatly. They wanted more, they always wanted more. Their demands were encouraged by the rivalry of dealers and growing reputations. Kahnweiler remained firm: it was out of the question, out of principle and from lack of means. Braque did not understand why he did not earn as much money as Picasso! Derain and Vlaminck let their success at the Drouot auctions go to their heads. Léger always had a cash-flow problem. It was inevitable. Braque and Léger signed up with Paul Rosenberg, Vlaminck with Bernheim-Jeune, Derain with Paul Guillaume. That May, the Galerie Simon organized a group show of gallery artists. The exhibition was a swan song.

It was a hard blow for Kahnweiler, as hard to take as the fourth and last act of his tragedy at Hôtel Drouot. The date of the auction was set for May 7 and 8, 1923. That was the end, he felt, in every sense of the word.

The poet Robert Desnos attended the sale as a reporter for *Paris-Journal* and was appalled at the way it was conducted. Paintings were piled haphazardly, drawings were rolled or folded between cardboard, and others were hidden behind the stage, where they could not be seen, grimy and wrinkled. The auctioneer ridiculed the merchandise; the assistants held the paintings upside down, treated drawings roughly, and glued stickers on the front of works with contempt.

Desnos could have sworn he saw the imprint of a shoe on a canvas. This carelessness, that even the experts shared, enabled the poet to buy a charcoal drawing, described in the catalogue as being 37 by 46 cm and by Braque. After buying it he realized that the drawing was in fact much smaller, and that it was signed on the back by Picasso. The attribution to Braque was completely random.[97]

This fourth auction would bring in the sum of 227,662 francs. In addition to the books of Editions Kahnweiler, sculptures by Manolo, fourteen collages by Braque, various gouaches and drawings, forty-six Braques, thirty-six Derains, twenty-six Grises, eighteen Légers, fifty Picassos, and ninety-two Vlamincks were sold! The loyal friend Roger Dutilleul, who had seen the beginnings of the rue Vignon gallery, did not want to participate in this pillage and only bought three Légers, including a *Landscape* from 1914 and the famous *Kitchen Utensils*.

The Ministry of Finance and the Commission on War Reparation earned a total of 704,139 francs from the Kahnweiler sales, which dispersed hundreds of modern paintings from before World War I. French public opinion was indifferent to the event. In May 1923 the reform of secondary school education was the main concern, along with the beginning of the French occupation of the Ruhr valley and the murder of Marius Plateau, editor of the ultrareactionary newspaper *L'Action Française*, by anarchist Germaine Berton. Art, much less cubist painting, was of little concern to anyone. There was no sympathy for the confiscation of the goods of a German citizen, even if his wife was French, even if he was a francophile.

Those involved with art who followed the development of events understood that Kahnweiler was the dealer of the cubist artists, that his gallery formed the common ground they shared, and the liquidation of his stock was a historic event. The war had splintered the informal bond linking this group of strong individuals and had dealt the first blow. The sale had finished the dispersal.

Daniel-Henry Kahnweiler felt stripped naked. He had been despoiled, everything was gone, sold off, sacrificed. Had he listened to Picasso and taken out French citizenship, probably none of this would have occurred. All he could do now was to try to recover some small things of sentimental value to him. The dealer Georges Aubry bought a lot which contained books, prints, and documents from the Kahnweiler Gallery, so he offered to buy them.[98] That was nothing. Fortunately Roger Dutilleul had a surprise for him. At one of the sales he had bought a lot that contained the major portion of the archives of his gallery, and he gave them back to Kahnweiler, who was very moved by his thoughtfulness at a time like this.

Kahnweiler was thirty-nine years old, and after sixteen years of experience and vicissitudes he could say, "I was the art dealer of the cubists." He could claim it but not prove it because from this period, which people were already calling "heroic," he had nothing left. He could show the annotated catalogue of an unbelievable exhibition, such as there never would be again, and bundles of his correspondence with his artists and collectors. There was nothing but packets and documents, parcels of memory that were destined to become a part of art history.

SUNDAYS IN BOULOGNE

▭ It is customary to be bored in France on a Sunday. But during the twenties no one was ever bored in the Kahnweiler home at 12 rue de la Mairie in Boulogne-Billancourt. Boulogne-Billancourt was a small town, its residential area surrounded by the Renault, Farman, and Bleriot factories on one side, and sculpture foundries and workshops on the other. Daniel-Henry Kahnweiler, convivial host and friend of artists and writers, would hold open house every Sunday afternoon for informal gatherings that lasted late into the night. People danced, laughed, and sang, but most of all conversation flowed. Every Sunday repeated itself like a refrain; Armand Salacrou, then a young playwright, recalled: "We waited for those Sundays in Boulogne as a reward for getting through the week, and the week that was beginning was already brightened by it."[1]

Lucie Kahnweiler, nicknamed "the Gracious Berrichonne," greeted all new arrivals.[2] The perfect hostess, she was in charge of arrangements for the open house, held in the garden during the summer and the drawing room during the winter. The guest list was unpredictable, but there would always be many people. The chairs were covered with needlepoint Lucie had made from sketches by Juan Gris. She loved having a large circle of friends, and considered them her extended family. The distinction was blurred because her sister, Berthe, had married one of the gallery artists, Elie Lascaux, while her other sister, Louise, married Michel Leiris, a writer published by the gallery.

Kahnweiler, as host, would stand next to Lucie. He was in his forties, had put on weight, and had great presence and authority for his age. He dressed only in well-cut dark suits from Burberry's or Old England.

Despite his financial problems, Kahnweiler had just traded in his Renault G-S for the latest model, a 10 CV "de luxe" sedan. When the garage man handed him the bill, he examined it, then said in all seriousness, "The baggage rack seems very expensive to me."[3] They continued to spend summer vacations in Germany, Austria, and Switzerland for the mountain climbing expeditions they were so fond of, but now they also started taking cures at Bains-les-Bains in the Vosges Mountains, their only concession to age.

Kahnweiler was now a well-known personality in Paris artistic and intellectual circles. He was already considered the mentor of cubism and its best "critic," having written a history and analysis of the movement. He had a reputation for devoting himself completely to his artists, even when he received no recognition for his efforts. Yet he set down inflexible rules for both artists and collectors. For those he cared about he took on the responsibility for everything. He would find an apartment or a studio, negotiate leases, pay the cleaning lady when the artists were away from Paris. He took on all these tasks, and did them well, but sometimes he could be pushed too far, even lose his legendary self-control. When the wife of a gallery artist one day asked him about her different options for their upcoming divorce, he exploded, "How the hell would I know that! Consult a lawyer!"[4]

On Sundays in Boulogne, however, he was no longer the dealer on rue d'Astorg, but another man entirely. In the garden there was no talk of money or contracts. Salacrou, fifteen years younger, was much impressed with Kahnweiler's intellectual authority and took him for a genuinely wise man, a philosopher.[5] This was due to the fact that, unlike most art critics at the time, Kahnweiler had a true international overview of contemporary art as it was being created.

He disliked German expressionism, finding the art generally disappointing. It had not lived up to the originality of cubism. He believed that it was an extension of fauvism—but mainly of its purely decorative aspects—and much of the work was influenced by Derain and Matisse, who had been exhibited in Munich.[6] Franz Marc's enthusiasm was touching, but his animals were all stylized. Kandinsky was decorative in the oriental mode. Kahnweiler found it unbelievable that he could have written an essay entitled "Uber das Geistige in der Kunst" ("On the Spiritual in Art") when nothing was so completely "unspiritual" as his work. August Macke seemed to be the weakest artist of the group. Paul Klee was the saving grace, the only one to rise above the others.[7]

As for futurism, he dismissed it as being already outmoded before it began. All the uproar created by Marinetti and his friends did not deceive him. Kahnweiler believed that futurism should be reduced to its common denominator: the Italian variant of expressionism.[8]

And the subject of the Ballets Russes threw Kahnweiler into a rage. As was his habit he was more radical and outspoken against it than anyone else. The Ballets Russes was a catastrophe. He did not mean Sergei Diaghilev's enterprise, which he admired, but rather its nefarious, destructive influence on his artists. Diaghilev was asking Picasso, Gris, and other artists to do the set designs and costumes for his productions.

The offer was seductive: they would be participating in the latest trends and would be earning more money more quickly then they could with their oil paintings. After all, they had to make a living. But Kahnweiler felt that they worked for Diaghilev at the expense of their art. Each set decoration was painted to the detriment of several oil paintings. Worse than that, Kahnweiler thought that when they returned to the easel their work had deteriorated perceptibly.

Kahnweiler could not be convinced otherwise. Art was one vocation and set design another. For him, Diaghilev was a devil and a scourge.[9] He led artists astray from their true work. And for what? If there had not been a scandalous protest, would Picasso's designs for *Parade* matter to anyone? He knew these artists very well in any case; they did not give a damn about the theater. Their friends were poets, not actors. The Ballets Russes was just another myth.[10]

Kahnweiler always pointed out that it was difficult to find a great artist who had created a great stage set. The art was too ephemeral and of mixed purposes. But what made him angry was the fact that Gris allowed himself to be persuaded by Diaghilev instead of pursuing his own work. "Gris is working for Louis XIV," he would lament.[11]

The big, heavyset Russian with dark eyes would drop by Gris's studio to discuss the finishing touches for an important commission, such as the sets and costumes for "La Fête Merveilleuse," which was to be performed in the Hall of Mirrors at Versailles. The Kahnweilers attended the performance, of course, and in good faith they found it splendid. But as a friend and neighbor who witnessed the meetings between Gris and Diaghilev, Kahnweiler was convinced that Gris was squandering his talent. The artist, who had to work in Monte Carlo, home of the Ballets Russes, promptly came to the same conclusion. These were not his people; he felt nothing for the stage or for dancers and actors, the gossip and the factions, the backbiting and the displays of affection. Just as Kahnweiler said, he could not wait to get back to his own studio to find some peace and to work in solitude. He even came to believe that the experience was detrimental to his work: when he sent his next paintings to the dealer he said, "Don't hesitate for a second to destroy them if they don't come up to the standard of the rest of my work."[12] Kahnweiler would never take such drastic measures, but he did not hide his poor opinion of the recent works.

Painters express themselves with their hands; but on Sundays in Boulogne it was a time for talk. The conversations varied according to the subjects Kahnweiler expounded. But, from whichever direction it was approached, from the most abstruse critical analysis to the most minute detail, everything came back to art.

People laughed and argued at these gatherings, but they never got out of hand. Everyone knew and appreciated one another. There was a common spirit that made it a family. Here Braque's fist or Basler's cane would never encounter the nose of a Léonce Rosenberg. It did happen that the conversation would become anxious when one of the habitués was in trouble, as was the case during the André Malraux scandal.

Kahnweiler was beginning to understand the young writer. He was attractive, intelligent, slightly crazy, and definitely out of control. Ever since the gallery had published his first book, he had been recommending his writer friends to Kahnweiler, setting himself up in the role of literary adviser. No one took it very seriously: it was not as if Kahnweiler needed literary advice, or the gallery had the means to pay someone to oversee its publications. Still, biographies and studies of Malraux[13] have perpetrated the myth of his precocious beginnings in publishing ever since.

Malraux had helped Kahnweiler secure a profitable sale, which was welcome during these difficult times. He had entrusted the dealer with the sale of a painting that belonged to his family, *The Wine Festival* by Le Nain. Kahnweiler needed 25,000 francs to acquire it, and as it was more than he could afford, he organized a syndicate for the purpose. His partner, André Simon, bought a three-fifths share, the Flechtheim Gallery one-fifth, and Kahnweiler one-fifth. When he sold the painting for the high estimate, his gallery would receive a 10 percent commission on the purchase price and the rest would be divided according to the shares held. Malraux was paid 18,000 francs down, which he wanted in cash because of an emergency.[14] That was the real beginning of the Malraux affair, which would be the subject of intense interest on Sunday afternoons in Boulogne.

It seemed Malraux had gone to Indochina to explore the ruins of Angkor Wat, and could not resist the Khmer sculptures. He was caught red-handed, along with his wife and a friend, and the authorities confined them to house arrest while they waited to go on trial. Then in July 1924 he was brought before the court in Phnom-Penh, charged with the destruction of monuments and the smuggling of bas-reliefs. He defended himself against the accusation of pillaging protected sites by claiming that he was on a special mission for the French School of Far Eastern Studies.

The idea of Malraux as an archaeologist caused great hilarity at Boulogne on Sundays. But no one laughed when the verdict was handed down: three years in prison, and five years of banishment from the country. While waiting for his appeal he was again confined to house arrest. The most damaging consequence of the case occurred while he was awaiting sentencing, when it was publicly disclosed that Malraux was associated with art dealers "from across the Rhine" who trafficked in archaeological pieces. [15]

In *The Royal Way*, his famous novel published six years later, Malraux would portray Kahnweiler in his true role, naming the German dealer Cassirer. But during the trial, it was assumed Kahnweiler was the art dealer referred to in the court of appeals.

The dossier consisted of the correspondence between Kahnweiler and Walter Pach, the American artist and art critic who was one of the organizers of the Armory Show before the war, but who also acted as an agent for paintings and objets d'art in New York. He was the supplier for several important collectors, most notably John Quinn. Did Malraux go to Indochina as the common agent for a New York collector? That would have ruined his budding reputation. At any rate, Kahnweiler was too cautious by nature, too scrupulous and insistent on business being conducted in the proper and correct form to have incited Malraux to trafficking. When Malraux had told him about his plans and asked to be placed in communication with Pach, he had helped him but gave a strict warning: "Whether on a mission or not, the export of works of art from Indochina is strictly forbidden!" But he could not repress the essential character of his young author, who was an adventurer in every sense of the word. What was bound to happen, had happened.

Kahnweiler was furious at even being mentioned as part of the case. He bitterly reproached Max Jacob for bringing such an unreliable person to the gallery, and used the incident to insist that in the future he not abuse his right to recommend writers. Luckily everything was quickly settled. A petition by writers and intellectuals, many of whom were

Sunday regulars at Boulogne, was published in the *Nouvelles Littéraires* to protest this unjustified and harsh sentence. It must have been effective, because by the end of 1924 André Malraux had boarded a steamer for Marseilles.

On Sundays in Boulogne people talked about everything and nothing. If Kahnweiler had kept a guest book at the garden gate for people to sign it would have read like the catalogue of a publishing house or an exhibit of modern art.

The surrealist poet and playwright Antonin Artaud, barely thirty years old, attended the open houses. Kahnweiler had published his first volume of poetry, *Tric trac du ciel* (1923), in which the symptoms of his mental disorder, his creative genius, and the ascetic pain of his experiences could already be discerned. He was introduced to the group by Elie Lascaux, who would illustrate his book. Artaud was a pathetic young man whose suffering was visible on his face. It was rumored that he took laudanum. There was something appealing but very disturbing about him. One night he made Armand Salacrou accompany him back home, as he was afraid of crossing Paris alone. As they parted, Artaud said, "The surrealists suffer with a Sunday soul, while it is my everyday soul that is in pain."[16]

Kahnweiler would always feel great affection for Artaud. In addition to writing, he was an actor working with Pitoëff and in Charles Dullin's troupe; he was desperately seeking to create other forms of theater. At his request, Kahnweiler helped him to find backers to produce his performances. He tried sending them to the Vieux-Colombier Theater to attend a performance of Calderón's *Life Is a Dream*.[17] Only once did Artaud disappoint him, and that was by reselling a painting of Masson's that Kahnweiler had let him have at a negligible price (1,200 francs), a friend's price if the cost of framing, the luxury tax, and the size of the work were taken into account.[18] Artaud had said that he loved it. He was quickly forgiven by Kahnweiler; after all, he was Artaud.

Armand Salacrou had just turned twenty-five when he became a regular. There were three people he idolized: Lugné-Poë, publisher Gaston Gallimard, and D. H. Kahnweiler. They had met in Masson's studio and Salacrou immediately had been impressed by the man who had discovered Picasso, Braque, Gris, and Léger, and was also the publisher of Apollinaire and Max Jacob. Having just arrived from his hometown of Rouen he could not help but be dazzled by this man who was interested in every manifestation of contemporary creativity. He had even read James Joyce's *Ulysses* in the original! Henceforth Kahnweiler took an interest in the career of the young dramatist, and every time he bumped into him asked if he had any manuscripts for his "publishing house."

"I only write plays!"

"I'd like to see them."

Kahnweiler was patient but persistent, and at their next encounter he continued in the same bantering tone.

"So why won't you show me your manuscript? Any reason?"

Finally Salacrou fetched the manuscript from the desk of Charles Dullin at the Théâtre de l'Atelier, where it had lain untouched, and handed it over to Kahnweiler. One week later, Kahnweiler said that he would publish it with illustrations by Gris.[19] In 1924 Kahnweiler published Salacrou's first book, *Le Casseur d'Assiettes* (The Breaker of Plates), a one-act play which would not be staged for another ten years.

Even as a publisher Kahnweiler was unique, in that once a book was published he did not forget it and go on to other things. He hoped that this play by his young hopeful would appear on the Paris stage. When he learned that the book had been submitted to Lugné-Poë, an old friend who now presided over the fate of the renowned Théâtre de l'Oeuvre, he sent him a letter of recommendation in which he predicted that Salacrou had the true temperament of a man of the theater, and would become one of the most important playwrights of his generation.[20]

Another regular was Erik Satie, an odd little fellow, half-Norman, half-Scottish by birth, inventive and mystical by nature. He quit his courses at the conservatory in order to join the army, then became a pianist, playing in the cabarets of Montmartre, which is where he met Debussy. He had a reputation for being a dabbler and a dilettante, a marginal character who was both original and sarcastic. He looked like the people in the background of paintings by Toulouse-Lautrec. Some described him as a solitary individual given to explosive fits of anger, who nonetheless brought back humor to contemporary music.[21] Others thought that he looked like an undertaker or, at best, a bank employee in the most conservative establishment, with his white beard, his old-fashioned pince-nez, a bowler hat, and a black umbrella that matched his coat.[22]

He had to make a special effort to attend these gatherings in Boulogne, as he lived in the far-off suburb of Arcueil. By now he was nearly seventy years old, and was considered the venerable elder of the group. Kahnweiler always addressed him as "our dear maestro." At his funeral in 1925 nearly every regular of these Sundays in Boulogne took part in the procession. They had witnessed his extreme suffering in his last months. Lost in the crowd, Kahnweiler walked side by side with Gris, neither dreaming that two years later, in similar circumstances, one would be burying the other.

Of the group, Kahnweiler was especially fond of Ilia Zdanevich—Iliazd as he was called—future publisher of art books. Before World War I he had been intimate with the futurists, and now his circle of friends consisted mostly of the dadaists, but it did not matter much. He was the inventor of a new language called Zaoum.

Elie Lascaux had been brought into the gallery by Max Jacob, and as Kahnweiler's brother-in-law he was literally a "member of the family." His work did not fit into any school. His technical skill consisted in being able to paint a naive landscape that was reminiscent of folk art. On the surface his work was the opposite of anything that would appeal to Kahnweiler. But according to writer and critic Michel Leiris, his art was at once spontaneous and mannered, capable of capturing the ephemeral on canvas. Though Lascaux's work had so little in common with the other Galerie Simon painters that Kahnweiler was suspected of nepotism in showing him, it quickly found its audience.

The sensitive Henri Laurens appealed to Kahnweiler as much through his art as through his sweetness of temperament, his modesty and simplicity of character. He was a man who loved his craft like an artisan. He believed that working in plaster, in clay, in stone was superior to any other occupation. He had respect for his tools and his materials and never felt better than in the quiet of his studio. His drawings were very fine, as were the collages he made during the war, and his sculptures were quite removed from any abstraction. Laurens loved to watch them as he turned them around, revealing the thousand lines of their contours. He would have liked to have seen them integrated into a landscape or architecture, or placed at certain focal points. Kahnweiler, who always felt modest in front of a painting, could recognize himself in the humility with which Laurens spoke about his work.

"When I start working on a piece, I only have the vaguest idea of what I want to make. For example, I have an idea of a woman, or of something to do with motherhood. But before it becomes the representation of anything, the sculpture is a plastic act, or more precisely, a sequence of plastic manifestations expressing my imagination as determined by the nature of the material. That's what constitutes my work. I give it a name only when it is finished."[23]

It sounded so simple. Aside from a brief falling out, Laurens would remain "the Sculptor" for Kahnweiler and the gallery during several decades.

Generally, groups gathered around Gertrude Stein and Alice B. Toklas at rue de Fleurus; but the two women also enjoyed the trip every Sunday to Boulogne, where they were among the regulars. Kahnweiler was entranced by Stein's personality. She seemed to have mastered her emotions and was able to register all external events with disconcerting ease. He would never forget the time a fire caused by a blocked chimney broke out in her home. Everyone panicked at the thought that the paintings in her famous collection could be damaged or destroyed. The concierge, the police, the firemen ran among her usual guests. In the midst of this confusion, as they were prying loose the tiles on the roof to put out the fire, Gertrude Stein was imperturbable and continued the conversation with the person next to her as if nothing out of the ordinary was occurring.[24]

Kahnweiler also happened to be the publisher of her first book to come out in France: A Book Concluding with: As a Wife Has a Cow (1926), illustrated by Gris, and two years later A Village, a play in four acts with lithographs by Elie Lascaux. Kahnweiler saw her as a unique writer who was attempting to accomplish in literature something very close to what the cubists had tried in painting. She did not invent new words or a new syntax, but experimented with existing material in such a way that she conferred on words an extraordinary density. He found similarities between her work on language and the experiments of Carl Einstein or James Joyce. As with Gertrude Stein, their search was in the same spirit: to distinguish within their art form what was unchanging from what was ephemeral.[25]

There was also Marcel Jouhandeau, a priest defrocked even before he was ordained, a young teacher who left Guéret in the Creuse to better describe with cruelty and detachment the details of daily life there in his novel La Jeunesse de Théophile. In 1925 Kahnweiler paid him a one-thousand-franc advance for the rights to publish the collected tales Brigitte ou la Belle au bois dormant, with illustrations commissioned from Marie Laurencin. This was an unusual team: the author was not publishing his first work with him, as had the others, and the artist illustrating it was not from his gallery.

Also present was the surrealist poet André Breton, who was at the time a valuable agent and adviser to arts patron Jacques Doucet, a fashion designer who would drop in at rue d'Astorg to buy mostly André Masson.

Efstratios Elefteriades, better known simply as Tériade, and his accomplice, Maurice Raynal, who wrote art criticism for *l'Intransigeant* under a joint pseudonym that was a well-known secret—"The Two Blind Men"—were also regulars. And so were painters Suzanne Roger and André Beaudin, her husband; and poets Pierre Reverdy and Georges Limbour, who had published his first book with Galerie Simon.

One of the most colorful characters to attend these Sunday afternoons in Boulogne was known as Baron Mollet, the former secretary to Apollinaire. He was neither a baron nor a secretary, though Apollinaire had once hired him to do some clerical work. In that capacity he had even refused to answer the mail, but they remained friends. His real name was Jean, which he found too common; "the Baron" was better. Some people even believed it. He was about fifty—quite resourceful although always without a sou. He was the personification of a jack-of-all-trades, master of none. People said they knew him in turn as a glass cutter, theater manager, law clerk, and even the salesman for a music publishing firm for several years. Reputedly he was outstanding at all endeavors, but no one quite knew exactly what work he did. He was one of those beings who live only in the present. To that extent he resembled his friend Manolo, who had originally introduced him to the circle. Kahnweiler liked him because he was a funny and moving person, even pathetic at times. Baron Mollet knew everyone, and it was rumored he had worked as an art dealer in a previous life; therefore Kahnweiler proposed that he act as an agent for the Galerie Simon. He would borrow a painting now and then and sell it to one of his wealthy friends, earning a 10 percent commission.[26]

Juan Gris, whom Kahnweiler simply called Jean as if there were only one in the world, was there almost every day so that his presence on Sundays was a foregone conclusion. He was a wonderful dancer, a person of natural elegance in all his movements. He was always in charge of the record player and gave tango lessons to any of the ladies who asked. As a young man he had entered dance contests. Even Kahnweiler, who had to admit that he had no sense of rhythm and was a trial to Lucie on the dance floor, would join in when Gris started the evening's dancing. Of everyone present Gris had the qualities Kahnweiler valued most: generosity, loyalty, austerity, and a classical spirit. This Spaniard seemed to him most German in his values and in his meticulous ways. Kahnweiler always praised him more than any other artist in his letters to collectors, and he could have applied to Gris the words Baudelaire used to describe Delacroix: "For such a man, endowed with such courage and passion, the most interesting struggles are those waged against himself; there doesn't have to be a wide horizon for the battles to be important; revolutions and the strangest events take place beneath the heaven within a man's skull, in that narrow and mysterious laboratory of the brain."[27]

These Sundays in Boulogne would not have been the same without him. Sometimes he would take two or three people from Kahnweiler's garden next door to his place, to show them his studio. Gris's home was more peaceful, despite his sudden fits of temper and his domestic scenes with Josette. He lived in a three-room apartment on the third floor, with a studio above in a converted attic. He delighted in the incredible light because the roof had been replaced with great panes of glass. From the windows of his apartment he could see all the way to the hills of Saint-Cloud. This was far removed from the filth of the Bateau-Lavoir. His apartment was much smaller than Kahnweiler's residence, but there were fewer people in his family. Kahnweiler's house was crammed with the people living there—his wife, both of his sisters-in-law (and eventually his brother-in-law Michel Leiris), Renée the cook, and Fernande the maid.[28]

Often in attendance were the Swiss Romance poet Charles-Albert Cingria; the Belgian poet Paul Dermée; and, of course, Kahnweiler's partner, André Simon. There might also be Tristan Tzara, the dadaist from Zurich; and the surrealist poet Robert Desnos, who was anticipating the publication of his poems, *La liberté ou l'amour*; the painter Gaston-Louis Roux, who would be under contract with the gallery starting in 1927; the Chilean poet Vicente Huidobro, author of *Square Horizon*; and a well-known collector and psychiatrist who was inspired to invite Gris to lecture on his work to the "Philosophical and Scientific Study Group" at the Sorbonne.

The surrealists did not congregate as a group in Boulogne, but Artaud and several others attended regularly. There were two groups, those from rue Fontaine (Breton's home) and those from rue Blomet. The first group consisted of the orthodox surrealists around Breton. When he sent Kahnweiler his *Surrealist Manifesto* in October 1924 Kahnweiler immediately replied, thanking him and asking, "You know how much I admire what you are doing. I would be glad to have you among the poets I have published, a selection which you have often praised. If you have anything that you could send me, I would be delighted."[29] These overtures brought no results. Kahnweiler remained hostile to surrealism in the visual arts, although not in its literary form. He dismissed Salvador Dali as well as Max Ernst and René Magritte. It would take him years to become accustomed to Miró, as he made not the slightest effort to come to terms with his painting. He had been indifferent when he made a studio visit in 1922.

Six years later, attending an exhibition of Miró's work, Kahnweiler would call it "very pretty," but he believed that the artist was going around in circles, that he was trying to perfect something that should be spontaneous.[30]

Kahnweiler always kept in mind something that Vlaminck had said, which seemed very pertinent: "The surrealists are people who have a telephone installed and then cut the wires." He found it a clear statement of the sons' rebellion against the fathers, which is natural in the course of things; but he preferred to think, as did Braque, that painting was not an art form to be used as a catchall, and that the poetic content the surrealists sometimes claimed to put there was most often only "literary" in the most pejorative sense of the term.[31] They were making the mistake of replacing simple objects from everyday life used by the cubists in their paintings with extraordinary and startling objects.

In the group of young surrealists of rue Blomet, a dissident center that rejected the dogmatism of an André Breton, there were two men with whom Kahnweiler became closely linked: André Masson and Michel Leiris. André Masson would become one of "his" painters in the long run, despite the highs and lows in their relationship. Michel Leiris, whose work would stand apart in French literature, would become a lifelong friend, in addition to being his brother-in-law.

It was Kahnweiler's other brother-in-law, Elie Lascaux, who had first shown him the paintings of André Masson. Then, at the urging of Max Jacob and Michel Leiris, Kahnweiler paid a visit to the rue Blomet studio. Masson was a man of great erudition, who had read enormously and knew the German romantics, and the qualities of his intellect came through in his paintings. Kahnweiler thought that he was the only major painter to come out of the surrealist movement. Masson would never betray his ideals, thus demonstrating that he had transcended surrealism, remaining first and foremost true to himself. Kahnweiler would always refuse to allow him to be labeled or placed in the context of a movement. He insisted on this in order to prevent Masson's work from being grouped with more orthodox surrealists, such as the Dali of melting watches and illustrative paintings more suited to post office calendars.[32] The key to Masson's work was metamorphosis: everything started from a point and returned there.

When Kahnweiler met him for the first time at home, he discovered a young man who sought to become an artist. He did not have the material means, the balance and stability, nor the harmony that would enable him to devote himself to his art. His home was big but very poor, and for a while he and his wife were forced to entrust their baby to Lucie Kahn-weiler in Boulogne for reasons of health. At night he worked as a proof-reader for the *Journal Officiel* to earn a living. During the day he found it difficult to concentrate on painting because his studio was next to a noisy factory. It became quiet only after six. As Kahnweiler discovered, Masson had been marked by his experiences during the war. By a strange coinci-dence he had followed a path that was the reverse of Kahnweiler's: at the outbreak of war he was in Switzerland and rushed back to France to enlist. Severely wounded in the trenches, he was cured in the Val-de-Grâce hospital, where he stunned the staff by refusing to take advantage of his respite. "I want you to discharge me. I want to leave for India, I've had it with Western civilization."[33] He was placed in a padded cell, but not for long. He found it hard to make the people around him recognize the fact that he was at war with the whole world. He would say that during this period men had lived in a surrealist way without knowing it.[34]

He was quickly adopted by everyone on Sundays in Boulogne. Kahn-weiler got him to sign a contract with the Galerie Simon as early as October 1922. Masson was especially taken with Gris because of his fondness for the tradition of painting and his insight into the paintings of Fouquet, Le Nain, or Watteau; reproductions of them were tacked all over the walls of his studio. "I could not imagine that someone who so loved humanist art could create such inhuman paintings," he would later say.[35]

His meeting with Kahnweiler was decisive and put an end to a frenzied life of license and pleasure. Masson would never forget it. "You can imagine what it meant for an artist who could only paint on the run; I was half-crazed. With Kahnweiler, I had the stability needed to begin painting seriously, really seriously, with the opportunity of thinking only about painting."[36]

It was a dream come true for Masson, who immediately thought of having Yves Tanguy, one of his surrealist friends, benefit from it. Kahn-weiler was won over the moment he met Tanguy and offered him a contract, which placed the artist in a painful situation vis-à-vis his friend Roland Tual, who had newly opened a surrealist gallery. He hesitated, then decided to remain loyal to Tual; Masson concluded from this that Tanguy was more of a surrealist than a painter. He had better luck in introducing Kahnweiler to Michel Leiris.

Leiris, who was twenty-one in 1922, became a permanent witness, personal and professional, to the life of Kahnweiler. They were outspoken with each other about everything, but Leiris made it a matter of honor never to interfere in decisions about the gallery.[37]

He was discreet, courteous, and enigmatic; he would become a poet, an essayist, an ethnographer, and the secretary-archivist of the Dakar-Djibouti Expedition. He came from a Parisian bourgeois background, and his poetry was influenced by Max Jacob. He was unstable, and for several years remained without any definite profession. The surrealists found him passionate about writing, honest to a fault, and remarkable for his sense of integrity.

He described himself in 1935 in his autobiography *L'age d'homme* (Manhood) as: "Physically of average height, on the short side, with a straight nape of the neck, protuberances on his broad forehead, with the complexion of someone who blushes easily. His head seemed too large for his slender body. He was an elegant, meticulous dresser. He looked as if he stepped out of a bandbox."

Literature was Leiris's principal activity. What is a writer? Whoever likes to think, pen in hand. He had written few books, but, as might be expected, Kahnweiler had been the publisher of his first work, *Simulacre* (1925), a collection of verses illustrated with lithographs by André Masson. He himself was not well known, but he disdained both the successful author and the *poète maudit*. As a young man he traveled widely, especially in Europe and Africa, but he did not possess Kahnweiler's facility with foreign languages.

This ethnographer by profession had a revelation about growing old, at the age of nine, on seeing the birth of his nephew. He thought that nothing resembled a brothel as much as a museum: "The same dubious side could be found there, and the petrified side." In both cases it was a matter of archaeology and of prostitution. His encounter with Masson and the surrealist group on rue Blomet was decisive for him because it enabled him to write "something readable." But he claimed that he was only capable of writing autobiographically. His work would be the long confession of a man in an endless psychoanalysis which would lead him as far as possible into the realm of sincerity. He would mull over the self to the point of nausea; his one goal was to get beyond it. The day when he would finally be emancipated, perhaps he would write a novel. Meanwhile he refused to use language only to record his ideas. Language should bring forth ideas. He was obsessed by love, death, the struggle against suffering, and suicide.[38]

On Sundays in Boulogne he was in his home, which was also the Kahnweilers', chatting with his colleague Georges Bataille, who would also publish his first book, *L'Anus Solaire*, with Galerie Simon. The young men discussed a project. They would like to start a new movement called

Yes, which would have an ambitious scope, "entailing a perpetual acquiescence to everything and which would have an advantage over the *No* movement of Dada, by going beyond the bounds of a puerile, systematic, and provoking negation." They even discovered a place to house the movement and its publication: the bar of a brothel on rue Saint-Denis; but the project went no further.[39]

Along with the regulars on those Sunday afternoons were visitors who would return and others who were merely passing through. There were friends who rarely attended and those whose absence was felt by all. Max Jacob had recently withdrawn to the monastery of Saint-Benoît-sur-Loire. In his quest for God he found consolation in his work and the memory of true friendships, such as the devotion of the Kahnweilers. He claimed to be disgusted by the sordid values of modern culture, overwhelmed by the artistic triviality and lack of integrity in his peers. He hated Paris, but he returned there periodically, especially on Sundays when he could drop by Boulogne.[40]

With his friends he made up for the vows of silence in the monastery and, in turn, became lyrical, inspired, and satirical. Josette Gris, who had walked by his side at Apollinaire's funeral, recalled being startled as he leaned over to her and whispered, "Now *I'll* be France's leading poet."[41]

Braque was never really a part of the circle, as he lived in the south and his ties with Kahnweiler were from a distance. Picasso was another subject entirely, because he had been taken up by another group. He always remained true to himself, selling a great deal to Paul Rosenberg. But after 1923 he was slowly drawing nearer Kahnweiler. Still, he rarely attended the gathering in Boulogne, choosing to remain apart. For one thing, people were always talking about him, his artistic development, his fame, his fortune. For another, he could not stand Gris, who was at home there. Picasso was always full of sarcasm and withering phrases, not all of them reserved for Gris. He repeated everywhere that when Max Jacob would pay him a visit he put glue on the soles of his shoes in an attempt to take away drawings that might be lying on the floor. It was a demeaning exaggeration, but like most things out of Picasso's mouth, not without a grain of truth. All of his friends knew that Max Jacob was often so destitute that he had to sell the drawings given to him by friends.[42]

By evening in Boulogne, Artaud would perform his imitations and Gris, who was interested in the occult, would lead a séance. As darkness fell over the house a few guests would stay on for supper. The butcher shop on the corner was open Sundays, and a frugal dinner of pork chops, salad, and cake would be served. Kahnweiler's taste reflected his background, that of the upper bourgeoisie, but he was experiencing financial hardship which he never showed. He was so circumspect that Salacrou became aware of it only twenty years later. Right after dinner the surrealist members from rue Blomet would wait in front of the town hall for the streetcar that would take them home to the fifteenth arrondissement.

By bedtime D. H. Kahnweiler was often overwhelmed by these Sundays, which were celebrations of talent and friendship. But he was not blind to the fact that the festivities veiled a crisis, of which each person was part. One evening, dejected, he wrote Vlaminck, who had found refuge in the country at Rueil-la-Gardelière: "You seem to have such a marvelous life, the only true way in the end. You are the only one among us who had the courage, the good sense, and the opportunity to lead a life that is not artificial, a life that is *true*. I envy you."[43]

Life on rue d'Astorg was becoming more difficult every day, but not enough to overwhelm Kahnweiler. His faith was his strength. His convictions formed a bulwark against adversity. He had to fight on every front: rival galleries, his artists, collectors, and the banks.

He knew where the rival galleries stood, and he was not afraid of Léonce Rosenberg. But Léonce's brother, Paul, was someone to contend with, not as an art dealer, but as a businessman; nothing could put him off. He knew only one language, money, but he knew it fluently.

There were many more galleries now, and whatever style they espoused and however they named themselves, they showed artists Kahnweiler would have wanted for his gallery. Galerie Vavin-Raspail exhibited Klee; the newly opened Galerie Pierre, started on rue Bonaparte by Pierre Loeb, was extremely active since Masson already had had a show there; Roland Tual's surrealist gallery represented Yves Tanguy. Henceforth Kahnweiler would have to work with them. The volume of business was unfortunately not very considerable, but Kahnweiler had never worked so hard. For secretarial help, for the organization and daily running of the gallery, he took on as an assistant someone in whom he had complete confidence, who was in fact the perfect second-in-command—his younger sister-in-law, Louise Leiris.

Kahnweiler had adapted the premises on rue d'Astorg to his needs. He had transformed those ancient stables and given them his own personality. Every time that he passed by his old place on rue Vignon (now a candy shop), he could not conceive of how so many paintings had been contained in such a small space. He was thinking of the thousands of works in the inventory of confiscated property. It was true that there were few large works during that period, but all the same . . . .[44]

He was never a dealer to tell artists what to do, but the limitations of the gallery and the entrance to the storage space below had forced Kahnweiler to avoid buying large paintings for fear that they would not fit.

Business remained within the confines of the gallery, and everything took place there—sales, negotiations, contracts. He disliked business lunches and dinners and refused to discuss money at home with Lucie, doing everything possible to prevent his home from becoming a continuation of his gallery. In one place he kept his stock, in the other his private collection, and he never mixed the two.

He saw people every weekday between three and six in the afternoon. The workdays grew longer by the week, between exhibitions abroad, answering requests for photographic reproductions, and so on. All this created an amount of work that was disproportionate to its immediate commercial return. Still, it had to be done. He had always been compulsive about answering letters the same day he received them, but now he stayed after hours to attack the stack of bills, answer the urgent letters from M. de la Rancheraye, who specialized in international shipping, from M. Pottier, the packer, or M. Fernandez, the framer. It had to be done immediately, yet it was a burden, and he felt harassed. When he saw art critics flitting from one opening to another, and young art dealers opening new galleries, he wondered who was buying the paintings. The market, it seemed to him, was still very weak.

Kahnweiler retained his faithful following of collectors, such as Dutilleul, who now followed the works of André Masson and Eugène de Kermadec in addition to Léger. The Russian collector Shchukin continued to buy art for his collection despite the consequences of the revolution, but he, too, was following new artists. When Kahnweiler learned from Picasso that Shchukin was looking for a Dufy, he tried to sell him *Turkish Rider* even below cost, so eager was he to get rid of this painting.[45] Vincenz Kramar, the Czech collector who had become director of the Narodni Gallery in Prague, would often come to Paris on buying trips. In 1923 he expressed his disappointment at the lack of recent works by Picasso, but he purchased 1,640 francs' worth of works by Vlaminck, Braque, Derain, and Picasso.[46]

Every time he received a shipment of paintings from an artist, Kahnweiler would write to the collectors who might be interested. When he learned that Francis Carco was working on a book about landscape painters, he suggested not only Derain, whom he already collected, but

Lascaux as well. John Quinn was introduced to rue d'Astorg by his agent on the continent, Henri-Pierre Roché, but he only purchased Picasso lithographs for one hundred francs, pieces from signed and numbered limited editions of fifty. Still, the introduction augured well for the future.[47] Dr. Reber from Lugano, René Gaffé from Belgium, and Dr. Roudinesco from Paris were becoming steady collectors. They bought a few well-chosen works. Young Baron Jacques Benoist-Méchin made regular visits to the gallery. Alphonse Kann, an enlightened English collector, dropped by rue d'Astorg in Kahnweiler's absence and left the following message: "What is the best price for the tricolor Léger as you come in the door?"[48] Kahnweiler contacted him immediately and sold *The Man with the Guitar*, a painting on wood, for 6,900 francs (for a profit of over 4,000 francs).

During this period numerous new American collectors appeared at the gallery: Maurice Speiser, a lawyer from Philadelphia; and Vickery, Atkins, and Torrey, art dealers from San Francisco with a special interest in the works of Vlaminck. In addition to foreign collectors, businessmen, professional men, artists, and French art patrons, there was another category of collectors he now ventured to interest: the aristocracy.

When cubism became fashionable, the circles around the Viscount de Leché and Count Étienne de Beaumont became fertile ground. This group was not familiar to him, but he had access to it through three personalities of the period. Princess de Bassiano lived in Versailles, but in fact was American. She was a cousin of T. S. Eliot, held a literary salon frequented by the young Italian novelist, Alberto Moravia, and founded and edited a literary review entitled *Commerce*. The Gourgaud family was another matter entirely: two distinct social strata, who infiltrated one another to form a new collection—that of the Baron Napoléon (prominent nobility from the Empire) and that of the Baroness Eva (Jewish-American bankers). Kahnweiler knew that Léonce Rosenberg had great success in bringing them paintings by Léger for their town-house walls, and that he sold them Gris's work at high prices.[49]

Then there were Charles de Noailles and his wife Marie-Laure, née Bischoffsheim (the daughter of a prominent banker), who were noted patrons of the arts. Their town house on place des États-Unis was very popular, and placing the works of his artists on their walls would have been a drawing card for an art dealer. Kahnweiler was prepared to make an enormous effort to sell them paintings, but he would not do just anything. When early in their relationship Charles de Noailles insisted that the dealer give shows at rue d'Astorg to two of his protégés, Kahnweiler remained inflexible: "We only show works that belong to us, and we show few artists as there are only a few good ones." Although he was sorry to start their relationship on a negative note, he would not compromise his principles even for someone of such social standing.[50]

The art dealer was different from the Sunday afternoon host. It was the law of necessity, and in the Galerie Simon Kahnweiler seemed to have a thousand different facets. When young Armand Salacrou was ready to buy his first painting, he had asked, "What is the price of that large canvas?"

"Three hundred francs," came the reply. Then focusing on the painting by Suzanne Roger, and recalling Salacrou's modest means, he immediately offered, "Two hundred seventy francs without the frame."

"Sold!" Salacrou became more daring during the Masson exhibit in 1924, which was a major event for the Sunday afternoon regulars. He dared to ask, "What is the price of *Les Corbeaux?*"

"Six hundred francs."

It was expensive for him, but in the catalogue Georges Limbour praised it as the most important in the show. He bought it.[51]

Kahnweiler had to adapt to these difficult times, while remaining true to his principles. He made many small compromises, so that he found himself in the uncomfortable position of working on commission. When in 1925 the city of Frankfurt planned to present an exhibition of French art from the nineteenth and twentieth centuries over a period of two years, he immediately contacted the people responsible in the ministry on quai d'Orsay, and to sound out the French art world.[52] When Professor Baum, director of the Museum of Art in Ulm, arrived in Paris to visit galleries and studios, Kahnweiler served as his guide.[53] When M. Silberger, an important collector from Breslau, was in Paris, Kahnweiler brought him to Ambroise Vollard's den. Later he took him to Paul Rosenberg, where he earned sixteen thousand francs commission for the sale of Renoir's *Vue de Venise.*[54] Curiously, when the critic Louis Vauxcelles wanted a third commission on the sale of the Douanier Rousseau's large painting *Sleeping Gypsy*, he went to the Galerie Simon for an equitable arrangement: fifty thousand francs for the owner of the painting, and fifty-fifty of the remainder to be divided between himself and the Galerie Simon.[55]

Kahnweiler had always insisted that he would never sell someone else's painting on commission; yet when his Spanish affiliate, Luis Plandiura, asked him for the favor, he had to make an exception.[56] His reactions were sometimes quite touching in his predicament. When a Belgian dealer asked him to buy a Chagall for him, he agreed to do it but implored the man to remove the canvas as soon as possible, as he did not want that sort of painting in his gallery, even temporarily. There were also terrible mistakes over painters he did not know well, such as Franz von Lenbach or Sisley, whose works turned out to be forgeries.

These were business matters he took on strictly to meet the expenses of running the gallery. His coffers were not empty, but he saw the future with a dim eye and wanted to be prepared. In 1925 he had at his disposal from the Gunzburg account a credit for the sum of 334,1534.60 francs, for which he paid interest of 6,624.85 francs.[57] The following year he applied for a credit of 325,000 francs from the French-Japanese Bank to be repaid in three yearly installments of 25,000 francs with 9 percent interest per year.[58]

People did not pay him on time, and he had to accept these delays. Furthermore, his uncle Ludwig Neumann in England was taking action against the administration of sequestered goods. In fact, his uncle was a financial partner of Jacques de Gunzburg and brought suit against the office of private interests and holdings which supervised the confiscation of enemy goods. He wanted to recover his initial loan-investment in the Kahnweiler Gallery in 1907. Alas, the court had turned down the request. His uncle continued to help him, however, without anyone suspecting it. Armand Salacrou was convinced that the British branch of the family had cut off all support to Kahnweiler when they saw that he dealt in "cubist horrors," and not in "Fragonard and Chardin."[59] Fortunately, Ludwig Neumann was more intelligent than that.

Kahnweiler represented the artists he wanted, but on principle he did not try to hold on to those who left the gallery by offering them more money. But he defended and encouraged them, even when his enthusiasm was not shared by others.

This was the case with Togorès. His work hardly sold at all, and in 1926 Kahnweiler could only offer him a stipend of two thousand francs a month. But when Togorès was violently attacked by the critic Florent Fels, Kahnweiler was more encouraging then ever: "To be attacked by Fels is proof of worth; he's a wretched person, a sad case, a venomous beast." He went so far as to use language he abhorred: "You'll come through, you'll show them! Despise critics the way they deserve, despise all critics without exception."[60]

Togorès felt reassured. He believed in Kahnweiler, whose compliments and encouragement were invaluable to him because he knew how

Kahnweiler could be critical when it was necessary. A word from Kahnweiler and his spirits were renewed. "Bravo! Bravo! Your paintings have just been delivered by Fichet. I like them very much. They have such a feeling of liberation; it's as if you had shed a leaden weight that had been smothering you, paralyzing you. They give off confidence and enthusiasm. My heartfelt congratulations. I am happy and all is well. It required great courage to make the leap and you have accomplished it. Onward, onward, you are again on the road to the greatness I have always believed was destined for you. I cannot say right now which of these paintings are my favorites. I like them all and will keep a few of them for myself and Lucie in Boulogne."[61]

He could not go any further, nor do more for the artist. When Togorès asked for more money, the answer was NO, absolutely not! He was not worth more than the two thousand francs monthly stipend in the current market. If the artist believed this sum was not enough, then he could break the contract; Kahnweiler would release him at the end of the month. But he could not go beyond that.

The prices of the works could not be dictated by the needs of the artist, but must be set according to their market value. Kahnweiler was more rigid about this rule than anything else. If he paid more than the sum he stated, he would have the dreadful feeling of betraying the financial interests for which he was responsible. He explained his position in a letter that could be considered the art dealer's breviary:

> Painting is a commodity like any other. It is priced according to the reputation of the artist. There is nothing artificial about this price, or, rather there should be nothing artificial if the price of the work is to remain stable, and then gradually increase. As with all commodities, there is the law of supply and demand. If the demand is weak, increasing the prices would create a disaster.[62]

Togorès clearly did not share this set of values. In his reply he brought up the cost of clothing, the rent for his apartment, the rising price of stretchers and canvas. It was a dialogue of the deaf and could only lead to a severance of relations. When this occurred Kahnweiler became much more critical of Togorès's work. He even regretted having had him in the gallery. But he would never admit to having made a mistake; he always said that Togorès took the wrong direction in his painting.[63]

He had the same reaction when Derain severed their business relationship, believing that after his period of great creativity, Derain also took a wrong direction. Derain had distanced himself from Vlaminck since the end of the war, and something was missing from their friendship. Their paintings evolved in different directions, as did the way they lived, Derain in Paris, Vlaminck in the countryside. After 1922 they scarcely saw one another despite a friendship of twenty years.[64] This distancing and silence was a sign of the crisis they were undergoing. For Derain, a stage of his life had come to an end when he left Kahnweiler in 1924:

> Monsieur Kahnweiler, in answer to both of your letters, I can only say that by dint of hard work and drive, I have succeeded in freeing myself of all obligations toward anyone else. I never want to lose this freedom again, and I guard it jealously to the point of not compromising it in any way by becoming part of a shop or a group in which yesterday's friends become today's enemies. Starting next year, just about all that I can do is sell you paintings if I have any to sell. With my best wishes.[65]

The heroic years were long gone. War, fame, and the economic depression had ruined everything. But Derain and Vlaminck were also leaving him because of their hostility toward cubism.

Even with Braque the separation was not easy. Braque believed, rightly or wrongly, that he should earn as much as Picasso, and Kahnweiler disagreed. If Paul Rosenberg offered him three times the price, then the door was open. They would always remain friends, but for the moment and even several years afterward the resentment and bitterness were mutual and ran deep.

Then the same separation occurred with Léger. Since 1924–1925, when he had showed *La Lecture* at Léonce Rosenberg's gallery, he was no longer the same man. "He stopped being the painter people talked about and became the painter whose works people bought."[66] A few months earlier his paintings could be bought for next to nothing at the Kahnweiler auction at Hôtel Drouot. But during the exhibition Léonce sold *La Lecture* to the Baron Gourgaud, and Léger left the ghetto once and for all. Léger went to Kahnweiler with the following ultimatum: "Paul Rosenberg is offering to pay me twice the amount you are paying me."

"Then I will raise my terms to meet his offer," Kahnweiler replied sadly.

Three months later Léger announced again: "Paul Rosenberg offered me twice the present rate you are paying me."

"My dear friend, I feel that it is a terrible mistake to inflate prices in this way, and I cannot match his new offer. You are free to accept Paul Rosenberg's contract."[67]

That was exactly what Léger did. In painting as in literature, with art dealers as with publishers, the relationship also involved friendship, cooperation, and the lure of the siren's song. How could the artist remain unmoved when finally he saw light at the end of the tunnel? Kahnweiler made arrangements to maintain a working relationship with Léger so as not to make a definite break. He agreed to a three-way agreement with Paul Rosenberg, to retain the rights to all works in small format. It created difficulties because he had few Légers to show his clients, but in the long run it proved beneficial.

Gris alone resisted temptation. Paul Rosenberg had paid him a visit waving his checkbook. By 1925 Gris was becoming well known to international collectors. The Swiss banker Raoul La Roche had just purchased his *Le Broc* for eight hundred francs from the gallery, through the intercession of Ozenfant.[68] And Dr. Reber in Lausanne had acquired a large canvas, 20 by 26 inches, *Compotier, Carafe et Livre Ouvert.**

But Kahnweiler still had trouble selling Gris's works. When the curators of the Fine Arts Museum in Zurich approached him to organize an international exhibition that would include thirty contemporary European artists, he failed to convince them to include Gris.

One day in 1925, feeling that everything was favorable, Paul Rosenberg offered to buy all Gris produced at the high market price. At Gris's usual protestations about being already under contract, the dealer exclaimed: "I will pay for your freedom!"[69]

He did not know his man. Kahnweiler was not disturbed by the offer, which was the action of a businessman, but he was disgusted by the tone adopted to approach someone as fine as Gris. The artist felt that he was in closer rapport with Kahnweiler than ever before, and appreciated the qualities he had praised since the start of their friendship.

Gris had understood that Kahnweiler would be completely frank with him, even at the risk of being cruel or offending him. When he was in Monte Carlo working for Diaghilev and seriously questioning his painting, Kahnweiler, instead of simply praising the works he received, had confirmed Gris's worst fears. He bluntly told him the bare truth. He believed that Diaghilev was having a detrimental influence on Gris, and when he received the shipment of paintings of nudes he was very upset by them. They were not up to the artist's usual standards, and Kahnweiler had written to him about it. Earlier, when he painted an apple, he painted

*Later it was sold to George Cukor and came on the market again, on July 1, 1987, at Sotheby's London, where it was sold for 185,000 pounds (approx. $330,000).

the platonic ideal of an apple; now he painted apples with worm holes, warts, and all. And the women, they were painted so literally, "they could be described."

Kahnweiler meant that as a criticism. The nudes were strong and muscular, their anatomy precisely rendered. He believed that this was the wrong direction for Gris and wrote as much. You had to be straightforward with a friend who had such doubts.[70] Gris would never forget.

In 1927 Masson returned from the south of France with new work. On receiving a shipment, Kahnweiler suddenly had a premonition that Masson had renewed his art, had worked through the impasse in which he found himself after his last paintings. In a burst of enthusiasm and haste, Kahnweiler opened the crates, cutting and scratching himself on nails and splinters. With bandaged fingers he pulled out the paintings one by one. He was dazzled by the originality, the freedom and lyricism of the colors. Masson had truly found his direction. This was the end of so-called surrealist symbols, the end of knives, doves, and clouds. That work had a poetic charm, and Masson had anticipated the surrealists. But Kahnweiler thought that they had been too self-conscious with their old workhorse symbols of dreams. Masson's cubist sense of construction became the forceful composition of the new paintings. Kahnweiler, who disliked shows, now felt he had good reason to put on an exhibit, and did so. He ordered frames and hung the paintings, but there was no reaction from either the public or critics. This total indifference he found even worse than spiteful attacks. Even Masson's surrealist friends had not bothered to come.

Marcel Jouhandeau, whose next book, *Ximenès Malinjoude*, was going to be published by Editions de la Galerie Simon with six engravings by Masson, arrived at the gallery to find it empty, and it made him quite depressed. He was disappointed in the work. Jouhandeau feared that his writing would be linked with the failure of Masson's art, whereas Kahnweiler was persuaded that the illustrations would be acclaimed as an artistic milestone.

"What a strange thing art is," Kahnweiler answered. "One of us had to be wrong." He felt alone standing before these paintings. Only one man seconded his opinion, and that was Picasso.[71]

At that time Tériade decided to interview the art dealer in his gallery, for a supplement of the review *Les Cahiers d'Art*.

When the critic entered the premises on rue d'Astorg, he shrewdly described the Galerie Simon as being halfway between an art office and a welfare office. No one strolling by could suspect what lay behind the door. He described Kahnweiler as a staunch, paternalistic defender of his artists, courageous in his loyalty, and gentlemanly in his way of concluding a deal. He was a systematic man: he gave value to paintings which had none when he bought them. Kahnweiler went through the required material for the journalist. He recalled the Salons, exhibits, critics and reviews, art history, the importance of French painting in Germany, Paris art dealers, the great collectors, the major collections, and the market with predictions. But he became impassioned when he discussed two generations of artists. He summed up his thoughts succinctly:

"Vlaminck, what a wonderful painter. He was so prolific, so inspiring, like the Nile replenishing the earth by overflowing its banks."

"But in the group of artists you represent, isn't Vlaminck an exception, due to his quality as a painter, and a divergent aesthetic direction?" Tériade asked.

"Not entirely. I buy paintings not according to their theories, but by their artists. I used to love the work of Derain. I don't like his current work as much."

"What of Matisse?"

"I think of the greatness of the Matisse of 1905 and 1906; this monumental phase could be a culmination. He went far with an art that was purely decorative, reduced to a two-dimensional surface."

"What do you think of the new generation, those born around 1900? Do you see a new spirit, new directions among them?"

"Yes, I see a poetic spirit which is quite new. Look at this painting by Masson. [Kahnweiler showed the fluid shapes of a cloud surrounding a series of small round forms.] There's a lyrical quality that cannot be seen elsewhere. There's an underlying poetic feeling within the structure of cubism, young artists are introducing a new spirit."

"You haven't observed a new development in the work of Picasso, such as in his last exhibition?"

"Of course I have," Kahnweiler replied. "Picasso is a prodigious artist who is dissatisfied the next day with what he painted the day before, and thus starts anew every day. There's something in his noble despair which produces such masterpieces. You can see that I believe in the new generation of artists just by looking on the walls of the gallery."

Kahnweiler gave him a private tour of the gallery, which Tériade found to be a place of monastic simplicity. "As you can see, I am not limited to a single style," the art dealer explained. "Among the young I select those who seem truly representative of the art of today or tomorrow. Togorès represents neo-classicism. It's in the same spirit as the sculptures by Manolo. Perhaps Juan Gris might be included in this category. Thus, it is Spain that has provided the necessary lucidity of intellect. Certainly within the context of cubism Gris does stand for a certain order, not a flabby order but a passion restrained by an extraordinary act of will. Yes, I like Fernand Léger. You speak of his theories. Everyone discusses Léger's theories, but what matters to me is the marvelous brilliance, the freedom, yes the freedom of his paintings which are so strong that they completely dominate the walls on which they are hanging. I admire the intensity of Georges Braque's work. He is such a patient master of the craft of painting. Masson is also a great painter. A new lyricism exalts his work. Suzanne Roger's work reveals an astonishing pictorial imagination. By contrast, Lascaux is a fresh and sincere talent whose work is so spontaneous."

The interview was about to conclude when a visitor suddenly opened the door of the gallery. It was Picasso.

"How pale you are, Kahnweiler," he said.

"I've just passed a dangerous hour under interrogation. That's why," he answered.

"But you have said only nice things about everyone," Tériade said.

"That is even more dangerous," Picasso said decidedly.[72]

By late 1926, the Sundays in Boulogne had lost their former zest and splendor. Now people were as tired in Boulogne as elsewhere, friendships became more distant. Kahnweiler had foreseen this some time ago.

The regulars had formed a core over the last year, consisting of the Leirises, the Lascaux, and the Massons. The Salacrous were no longer so close, the Grises were in the south. A sign of the times was that no one sang or danced anymore. It was solid, nonstop talk; Salacrou and Masson spent one entire evening locked in an argument about God.[73]

If the garden on rue de la Mairie had grown quiet and melancholy, soon it would be overwhelmed with grief and sorrow.

For several months Juan Gris had not been feeling well, and his physical health had deteriorated. His asthma attacks were becoming increasingly severe. From Hyères he stayed in touch with Kahnweiler through letters which were becoming shorter and more terse. He could barely work anymore and could only sleep under the influence of morphine. His correspondence with his dealer and friend was a record of his descent into hell. Gris could not stand it any longer. He needed five thousand francs to go where he would be able to breathe, just to breathe different air, anywhere else. Kahnweiler sent the sum by return mail, for which his friend was grateful.

But a few weeks later Gris still could not breathe. He wanted to move away from the sea, to a place fifty miles from Nice, at an altitude of sixteen hundred feet. He was drawn to the Basque country but feared he could not make the trip. He, who had always been so discreet in life and had used words so sparingly, now described his life in these terms: "The trip was fine, hoping for improvement. Best, Gris."[74] This telegram, from January 1927, was his last communication.

It was already too late. He was brought back to Boulogne shortly afterward. Kahnweiler received the friends who rushed to visit Gris on learning this news. But he lay stretched out, his breathing labored, and rasping. One evening in May 1927 Kahnweiler left the bedside and ran next door to have his dinner. The moment he sat down George Gonzalez, Gris's son, rushed into the dining room: "I believe Juan has died."[75]

That was how it ended. In a few hours the old regulars of Sunday afternoon all gathered at the foot of the bed for the wake. On looking around, Kahnweiler felt that he had already lived through this. He closed his eyes and the scene came to him. It was five years ago on Sunday with all his friends. Juan had tried to incarnate a character, in the theatrical manner of Antonin Artaud. He had stretched out on the sofa, and all the lights had been turned off for a few minutes. Then someone had turned them back on, but Juan had failed to reincarnate himself. He was still Gris, but the expression on his face seemed as if he had anticipated his own death. It had been frightening.[76]

Picasso was one of the first people at Gris's bedside. He appeared crushed, but was he sincere? Gertrude Stein was shocked by his presence and his show of sympathy. "Not you, not here! After all the horrible things you have said about Gris."[77]

Picasso told her he had had a premonition: "I made a black, gray, and white painting, but I didn't know what it was supposed to represent. But when I saw Gris on his deathbed, I knew that was my painting."[78]

The funeral took place on Friday, May 13, at 11:45. People gathered at the funeral parlor, then followed avenue de la Reine to reach the old cemetery at Boulogne, where he was buried. This was the first death among the pioneers of cubism. Gris was only forty years old, and more than one hostile critic, in mixed metaphors, wanted to see this as cubism's funeral as well.

The pallbearers were Kahnweiler, Picasso, Lipchitz, Maurice Raynal, and George Gonzalez. An art dealer, an artist, a sculptor, a critic, and a son; only the public and the collectors were missing. But the turnout was large: no one would have believed that Juan Gris had had so many friends. Lost in the crowd, Gertrude Stein was intrigued and asked Georges Braque, "But who are all these people? They are so numerous, they look so familiar, but I don't know anyone by name."

"Oh, these are all the people you see at the opening of the Salon des Indépendants and the Salon d'Automne. You see their faces twice a year, every year; that's why they look familiar."[79]

There was neither a sermon nor any speeches, but there were many wreaths. One of the wreaths perplexed everyone. In gold letters across the ribbon was written: "To Juan Gris, from his comrades in arms." No one knew what it referred to. Painters denied any knowledge of it. He had never served in the army nor joined any political party. The mystery was explained only later, when it was learned that Gris had been a Freemason, a member of the Voltaire Lodge in the Grand Orient of France.[80]

Following his wishes, Kahnweiler and Josette Gris destroyed the numerous sketches and mathematical calculations by which he worked out his paintings. He used to destroy them systematically as he worked.[81]

Kahnweiler would never forget Gris, the most faithful, kindly, and noble friend he had ever known. He feared that because Gris died so young it would be all the more difficult to make his work known. He had not had the time to enjoy fame, and he had suffered for his work.

For Kahnweiler, Gris would remain the ideal example of an art that did not pander to the viewer, of a classicism that was the opposite of seductive. He was the classical accomplishment of cubism, a painter with great unity and integration in his work. There were no fragments and detached pieces in his paintings, which were so structured, complete, and self-contained. He was the most classic of modern artists, the one who could reconcile the extremes of a movement: the renewal of tradition and originality.

He seemed to be the truest and purest of cubists, as he had not distanced himself from cubism as had Léger; nor was he as romantic or frantically autobiographical as Picasso; but he knew the relationship of the material world to man. By his talent he had greatly enriched this new rendering of the world that Kahnweiler defended with such passion. To the end of his life Kahnweiler would be devoted to Juan Gris, the artist and the man. A master with humility, who deserved more from life.[82]

He had died too soon, too quickly. On Sundays in Boulogne there was no more dancing.

SURVIVING THE CRASH

⊏⊐ Despite his basic optimism, Kahnweiler had been expecting it. Now he had to face it. On October 25, 1929, the New York stock market plummeted under circumstances already familiar: the same conditions had precipitated the crisis of 1882 in France and that of 1907 in the United States. Only this time it would last longer and was on a larger scale.[1]

What followed were six lean years. How could the luxury trade, to which the art market belonged, escape the effect of these economic conditions? The art market was linked to financial fluctuations and to the prosperity of collectors—American collectors most of all. The smaller galleries had to learn to live with the specter of bankruptcy. The market had turned so sluggish that M. Bellier, the expert in modern art at Hôtel Drouot, believed that the clock had been turned back a few years to when the popularity of cubism had only just begun.

Kahnweiler sometimes had the horrible feeling that everything was worthless.[2] What was the use of setting a price when no one was buying? As he attempted to adjust to a crisis, he remained hard at work, trying to keep his wits about him and face the situation head-on. He adapted Fichte's saying, "You have to strive to maintain your identity."

Everyone was in the same boat during this worldwide depression. Periodically there was an outburst of optimism, talk of a slight economic upturn. The possibility of war between France and Germany seemed remote. Traffic on the streets had returned to normal, and that was seen as a positive sign.

But the gallery was deserted, and Kahnweiler was constantly bored during business hours (10:30 to noon and 2:30 till 6:00). The day's transactions sometimes entailed no more than labeling all the photographs of works that Delétang had delivered in a stack and which Kahnweiler wanted to give to each artist. At one point the basement flooded, but fortunately it did not reach the oil paintings. In the haste of moving, frames and glass were left stacked on the floor and were damaged; but the worst was avoided since the insurance would pay.[3]

Between 1929 and 1933 the Galerie Simon did not organize a single exhibition. Kahnweiler's publishing venture was also much slowed down, bringing out only Carl Einstein's poetry and Georges Bataille's *L'Anus Solaire.* The other projects had to wait; there was no sense in surfeiting a reluctant public. Kahnweiler's own essay on Gris, published in Germany in 1929 under the pseudonym of Daniel Henry, provoked a harsh reproach from Christian Zervos in *Cahiers d'Art,* which he found infinitely painful, and which wiped out the memory of his well-received articles. The critic faulted him for having written a panegyric inspired by Gertrude Stein, which closed its eyes to all negative aspects, for having conveniently "forgotten" hostile criticisms of Gris, for having expunged anything detrimental to his reputation and only reproducing paintings carefully selected from private collections to impress the reader.[4]

Kahnweiler let it pass; he had other priorities. He had to remind clients of unpaid bills in more pressing terms. Formerly he would draw up his accounts each quarter, but now he went over his books every month. It was always a delicate matter, to know how to ask a client for payment. But Kahnweiler, polite and patient by nature, had to become harder. He needed the money.

In 1927 he had refused to sell a Derain at Drouot: "On principle I would never place a painting of mine on the auction block at Hôtel Drouot. Too many paintings belonging to me passed through there, in spite of anything I could do."[5] The wound of having his stock sequestered had not healed. But in 1932 he ruthlessly turned over for auction *Nude Wearing a Hat* by van Dongen, and a cubist still life by Kisling which he had consigned to M. Bellier. "There is no reserve on these paintings. No matter what price is bid, they should be sold at any cost."[6] The auction would bring 590 francs. In New York he worked with other dealers, Sam Kootz and especially Pierre Matisse, the son of the artist, who had a gallery in the Fuller Building on Fifty-seventh Street. He had reserved the rights to the first and second castings of all sculptures by Laurens.[7]

He had changed his attitude toward collectors. As early as 1925 he had said that salvation lay in gaining new collectors.[8] Now more than ever people who had never bought a painting before had to be brought to the gallery. If the crash of 1929 had destroyed some established fortunes, it had also favored the creation of new ones. Great art collections were amassed by buying at auction, or through discreet transactions with great families who found themselves in straitened circumstances. Paintings were the ideal investment because they represented a hedge against inflation and easily eluded government taxation.[9]

Kahnweiler's worst problem was the fact that even rich people no longer paid their bills. It came as a revelation to him. In Switzerland Dr. Reber had borrowed too much from the bank and, when they demanded repayment, he was forced to sell off, at low prices, certain works from his magnificent cubist collection.[10] In Paris even the aristocracy was having problems. The Duchess de Clermont-Tonnerre, who was supposed to buy a drawing, *Head of Young Girl*, and an oil painting, *Bather with Raised Arm*, by Picasso for 110,000 francs, changed her mind and canceled the sale. Kahnweiler made the counterproposal of 90,000 francs for the painting alone, with 10,000 francs down. But even this fell through, although the Duchess had signed a written agreement for the purchase.[11]

There was an even more delicate problem with the Princess de Bassiano, who had owed him 6,000 francs for three years now, and he could never recover this debt. After many failures, he decided to become litigious. He raised the threat of a civil suit, but as a demonstration of his goodwill he proposed a schedule of payment. He threatened but did not strike.[12]

One of his basic principles was always to avoid a permanent break or irreversible stance, because a good client in the past could again become a good client when conditions improved.

Not all collectors were problems, and he still had a faithful following: Dutilleul, Richet, Gertrude Stein. Dr. Roudinesco had so many canvases stashed away in his home and office that patients had trouble making their way from the waiting room to see him.[13] A wealthy young English collector, Douglas Cooper, had the intelligence and intuition to start a collection of cubist art in 1931 by meeting Paris art dealers and the artists themselves during a period when prices were at their lowest and the art market in some difficulty. Alphonse Kann devoted himself with his usual discretion and elegance to the building of a beautiful art collection. The measure of his success could be gauged when his house in Saint-Germain-en-Laye became "uninhabitable." He would bemoan the fact that curators and art dealers would come regularly to "pillage" his collections for exhibitions.[14]

There were still financial problems, however, and in the evenings in his office at the Galerie Simon, Kahnweiler was in a state of anxiety. The thirties were going to be years of hardship. He had to make fewer studio visits and more appointments with banks. He had to hang on in order to make it through these times. But events during the early days of 1930 made him dizzy. In a short period he had to twice request a postponement of his scheduled repayment of 25,000 francs to the Banque Franco-Japonais. Then, unexpectedly, another bill came due, and it was impossible to meet the payment. By the middle of January he did not know how he would finish the month. He was expecting important sums to be paid to him: 26,000 marks from Frankfurt, 18,000 francs from an impecunious aristocrat, 15,000 francs from a collector who was a friend, a regular on Sundays in Boulogne, and an equal amount from Marragall, the art dealer in Madrid.

These sums should have been paid, but he could not count on them. To cover himself during the two weeks he had only one solution, to ask his partner André Simon for a bridge loan of 20,000 francs to the gallery for the crucial period of time. Three-quarters of the sum would enable him to pay the quarter's rent and the rest would tide him over. On the fifteenth he had to make his payment to the bank. "It's only a difficult moment . . ."[15]

Eventually everything was settled. He obtained a six-month extension from the bank. But six months later he had to request an increase in his line of credit. At the end of the year he had to request another extension of his loans from the Banque Franco-Japonais due to delays in receiving payments from his clients. What he had to say to his bankers was straightforward: his sales were down to nothing and clients who owed him money kept delaying their payments.[16] It was a vicious circle with the implacable logic of a game of dominos.

Then 1931 started on the same footing as the previous year, leaving a bitter aftertaste. He had to ask André Simon for another bridge loan of 25,000 francs. Kahnweiler had tried everything to avoid this solution. But if anything, the situation was worse. To top it all off, he received a summons for immediate payment of his income taxes, and five days later he had to pay 10,000 francs on his dealer's license.[17]

There was no end to the pressure. Once, twice, three times he had asked for a postponement of six months on his schedule of repayment to the bank. His situation was so precarious because he was expecting a large sum to be paid by a wealthy collector whom he could not pressure and who was one of his best customers.[18]

Finally, during the summer of 1932, he had cause for high hopes and bright expectations: he received 300 pounds sterling from the executors of his uncle Sir Sigmund Neumann's will, and his second uncle, Sir Ludwig, underwrote with his own account the 400,000 francs balance owed to the bank by the gallery. Ludwig Neumann was an extraordinary man: when he visited the gallery with one of his "ladies," he invariably made jokes about the absurd paintings,[19] yet it did not prevent him from helping his nephew to succeed in his chosen profession against all odds. Kahnweiler would never forget his debt to him. No sooner had the uncle completed this transaction on his behalf than D. H. Kahnweiler again placed his business on the line by opening a new line of credit from the bank of Louis Hirsch, asking for a loan at 6 percent interest annually, which he would repay in installments until 1940, and immediately made out a check for 400,000 francs to be paid into the account of his uncle in England.[20] It was a matter of principle.

Uncle and nephew were very close. There was mutual respect, and they corresponded regularly. Kahnweiler's letters were forwarded to Sir Ludwig everywhere he went: the Carlton in Cannes, the Royal in Deauville, or the Ritz in London. Kahnweiler discussed everything with him in circumspect but well-reasoned letters, including his hopes and fears. He wanted his advice as an experienced businessman as much as he did his assets as a guarantee of his banking interests.

In page after page he discussed the specific nature of his luxury business: how he drew up his balance by the end of the month, what it meant to be wealthy in stock but cash poor, what the implications were for an artist and the future of his sales if he sold all of his works to one person (it would destroy his market value for ten or twenty years, and he might as well throw his work into the Seine), the unbelievable position of selling paintings to the Americans, to the English, to the Germans, but not to the French ("Nothing!"). He explained all these dilemmas. He could not sell at auction because it could cause a panic of selling by his collectors. It was a touchy matter turning down the requests of artists who had been with him for a long time for a raise in their monthly stipend despite the reality of the marketplace. Very proud and egotistical, Kahnweiler turned to his uncle for help only as a desperate last measure. But these exceptional requests were repeated so often that they could have become the rule; how many times could he repeat, "For the last time . . ."

His sense of shame gave a poignancy to his requests. It was almost palpable, the feeling that he was struggling to overcome his pride. Sometimes he even considered withdrawing his business completely to Boulogne-Billancourt as a private dealer within his own home in order to save the rental on the gallery. At other times he returned to work with renewed faith.

When his uncle expressed his doubts about the commercial soundness of such a venture he would reply with concrete examples to convince him of the highly lucrative nature of the profession: recently he sold to an American collector for the sum of 25,000 francs a painting by Gris which he had bought six years earlier for the sum of 2,000 francs. He also managed to sell for 2,000 francs a painting by Masson which he had bought for 100 francs three years earlier. These figures showed a good profit. His uncle responded to this sort of argument but the two men were not on the same wavelength. They did not have the same solutions to the same problems. Neumann was of the firm opinion that he should first reduce his stock, adapt to the economic crisis by understanding that those who formerly could pay would become more and more scarce, that he must reduce his bank debts and wipe out the interest payments. Kahnweiler tried to obtain a financial moratorium, collect the monies owed him, and then to hang on, with the sole aim of keeping the gallery afloat for as long as the economic crisis lasted. To survive became his obsession.[21]

These transactions remained his secret; no one knew about them. Kahnweiler, usually discreet, was secretive when it concerned gallery business. His role became more tenuous in relation to his artists. His situation grew desperate, and they seemed unaware of economic conditions in France and across the world, much less those of their dealer. The ones who were paid the least considered Kahnweiler a capitalist exploiter during the years when he supported them. But he could no longer continue this practice. It was not a question of price; the economic reality made it impossible. Complicated explanations ensued.

He could not renew the contracts with artists whose work he loved. It was not a cancellation of contract so much as a suspension. He could carry their paintings on commission only. He could not guarantee to purchase them.[22] He had no choice, and it was a cruel separation until better times returned.

He was relieved by the separation from Manolo, because he had strained the bonds of all normal relationships. Kahnweiler even wondered if the sculptor was not mentally deranged. Often he would ship his work express (an expensive method) from Spain to Boulogne, instead of to the gallery; when he did send work to rue d'Astorg, it was in August when the gallery was closed. Once he wrote on the customs forms "of no artistic value," which cost the gallery more money than if it had been declared as a "work of art" (it would have entered the country duty free and been taxed only when sold). Last but not least, he sold works directly to museums in Madrid and Barcelona without notifying his dealer.[23]

Kahnweiler had had enough. He was less bothered by the expense and inconvenience than by the lack of gratitude and loyalty from an artist whom he had always championed. At such times, seated deep in his garden in Boulogne where he spent his summer vacation in 1932 (the depression had eliminated the prospect of Italy), he thought about Michel Leiris and the young artist Gaston-Louis Roux, who had left France to join the Dakar-Djibouti expedition on Lake Tana: "They've got all the luck, those fellows."[24]

His break with José de Togorès was just as radical when it occurred, during the same period. Togorès also could not understand the impact of the economic depression. Kahnweiler tried to explain: the other day at the Drouot auctions a Utrillo, which had been purchased shortly before for 50,000 francs, was sold for 4,000 francs. That was the economic depression!

Togorès still could not understand why his dealer had reduced his monthly stipend from three thousand francs to two thousand francs. Kahnweiler advised him to save some money and count his blessings in having a small income: "I know people who used to have fantastic contracts and who are going hungry today."[25]

After several months the artist still did not understand. Kahnweiler decided it was time to separate, having just made a horrible discovery: Togorès was not a good painter. After eleven years he realized he had made a mistake. He would never admit it, ascribing this to a change in the artist's style and the decadence of the artist's work. But he still had to admit that it was bad. He had received a final shipment of paintings. He examined them and went over them again, hoping to attenuate his first impression. After all, it was not the first time that he had reservations about Togorès's work, and each time he had repressed his feelings to favor the artist's development. With each conversation, with all his diplomatic skills and tact he had expressed the hope that Togorès would return one day to the carefully-thought-out work of his early style. But it was in vain. On opening the crates and looking at everything minutely, from the small *Head of a Man* to the large compositions, Kahnweiler was overcome with a sense of disappointment. He could no longer hide his feelings. It was not the time for that. "I must tell you that I don't like them." He admitted that he was not qualified to judge the artist's work, but that he was unable to stand behind it in any way. Other dealers could sell his paintings, but he was no longer able to do so.

Daniel-Henry Kahnweiler at age 16, in Karlsruhe. (Photo: Galerie Louise Leiris)

D. H. Kahnweiler (seated) in Paris in 1904, with his friend Hermann Rupf. (Photo: Galerie Louise Leiris)

Kahnweiler and his wife, Lucie, in their Paris apartment on
rue George-Sand, 1912. (Photos: Galerie Louise Leiris)

Portrait of Kahnweiler by van
Dongen, 1907. (Photo: Musée
du Petit Palais, Geneva)

Portrait of Kahnweiler by
Derain, 1913. (Photo: Galerie
Louise Leiris)

Dinner during one of the "Sundays in Boulogne," 1921. Seated, from left to right: Lucie Kahnweiler, Juan Gris, Zdanevich, Josette Gris, Fernand Léger, D. H. Kahnweiler, Jeanne Léger, and Vicente Huidobro; standing at far right: Louise Leiris. (Photo: Galerie Louise Leiris)

Kahnweiler at his desk in the Galerie Simon on rue d'Astorg during the 1920s. (Photo: Galerie Louise Leiris)

The Gris exhibit at the Galerie Simon, June 1928. (Photo: Galerie Louise Leiris)

Portrait of the rue d'Astorg group in the 1920s. Seated, from left to right: Vlaminck, Louise Leiris, and Alfred Flechtheim. Standing, from left to right: Kahnweiler, Gris, and Otto Waetjan. (Photo: Galerie Louise Leiris)

Portrait of Kahnweiler by Picasso, 1910. (Photo: Art Institute of Chicago)

Portrait of Kahnweiler by Picasso, 1957, in a lithograph limited to fifty copies. (Photo: Galerie Louise Leiris)

Portrait of Kahnweiler by
Juan Gris, 1921. (Photo:
Galerie Louise Leiris)

Portrait of Kahnweiler by Derain, 1913.
(Photo: Galerie Louise Leiris)

Portrait of Kahnweiler by
André Masson, 1946.
(Photo: Galerie Louise
Leiris)

Portrait of Kahnweiler by
Beaudin, 1946. (Photo: Galerie
Louise Leiris)

André Masson. (Photo: Galerie Louise Leiris)

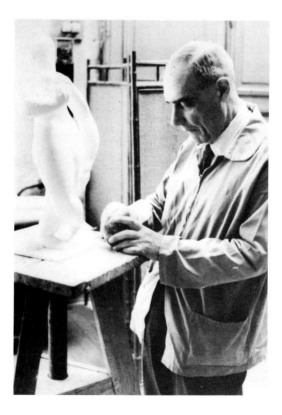

Henri Laurens in his studio in 1952. (Photo: Galerie Louise Leiris)

Juan Gris in 1926. (Photo: Galerie Louise Leiris)

Fernand Léger in the final years of his life. (Photo: Galerie Louise Leiris)

Georges Braque in his studio, 1949. (Photo: Roger-Viollet)

Kahnweiler and Picasso photographed by Edward Quinn at "La Californie," 1956. For Picasso's seventy-fifth birthday, the art dealer had given him a grandfather clock.

Kahnweiler photographed by Brassaï in 1952 at Saint-Hilaire, before *Woman with Open Arms,* Picasso's sculpture in cement and gravel. (Photo © Gilberte Brassaï)

Kahnweiler and Picasso in the garden of "La Californie," 1956, photographed by Edward Quinn.

Kahnweiler at The Priory,
his property in Saint-
Hilaire, photographed by
Brassaï in 1962. (Photo ©
Gilberte Brassaï)

Picasso between
Kahnweiler and Michel
Leiris in Mougins, 1967.
(Photo: all rights reserved)

Kahnweiler in 1960, photographed by Brassaï. (Photo © Gilberte Brassaï)

Kahnweiler and Maurice Jardot
during a Léger exhibit in Rome,
1963. (Photo: all rights reserved)

Louise Leiris in her
gallery during a Masson
exhibit, early 1982.
(Photo: Carlos Freire)

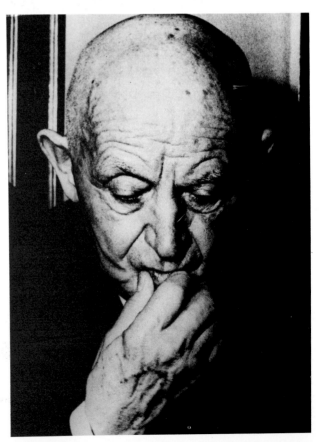

Kahnweiler in his office on rue de Monceau, before Picasso's *Nude Beneath a Pine Tree* (1959), photographed in 1962 by Brassaï. (Photo © Gilberte Brassaï)

A wise man who has no doubts. (Photo: Ingeborg Sello)

"I hope that you will find other galleries capable of selling your work and that we will always remain friends without doing business together."

Their relationship remained friendly, but the painter never understood the situation. When Togorès sent a collector to the Galerie Simon a few days later he requested that the art dealer not denigrate his work as the client could prove helpful to him.

"But I don't think badly of your paintings," Kahnweiler protested. "I am just not the right person to represent them."[26]

After that, what more could be said?

The separation from Masson was much more painful, even though it proved to be only temporary. Kahnweiler truly admired the work and liked the artist; he told all his clients, "Masson is the most important painter of his generation, and I am convinced of it. He is on the threshold of great fame. His canvases are not expensive as yet."[27]

It was Masson who decided to break the contract. For months there had been a rumor in the art world that Masson was ready to "dump" the Galerie Simon. Kahnweiler heard it several times and quickly went from being worried to a state of anxiety. He asked the artist to deny the rumor publicly once and for all. Masson refused to do it for the simple reason that the rumor was true: Paul Rosenberg had offered him more money. Even with Kahnweiler's great solicitude on his behalf, the artist could not resist his rival's offer. Kahnweiler countered with the proposal to continue his monthly stipend for another year, or if Masson preferred, he was prepared to buy every painting for cash based on a new rate to be agreed upon. He was prepared to do anything to keep the artist and would have made any sacrifice. But it was all in vain, and Masson changed galleries.

Kahnweiler was overcome with sadness. The gallery was his life, the artists his children. He had tried to be more than just a dealer for Masson, more than for any other artist of his generation. When his exhibition opened at the rue La Boétie Gallery he could not refrain from going to see it. He was somewhat disappointed but did not voice his opinion, lest it be said he was jealous. Clearly his "artist" was now self-consciously aspiring to a place in the Louvre, and Paul Rosenberg was responsible for turning his head by hanging his work between Corot and Delacroix. Masson's work had become self-conscious and so deliberate, whereas his art, his talent lay in its spontaneity and hallucinatory quality. It was distressing to see.

For three years they did not write one another, and then little by little Masson made his way back. He had come to understand that Rosenberg was a businessman and only that, whereas Kahnweiler had also been a good friend, a connoisseur, and a man with whom he could discuss painting in depth, not someone limited exclusively to money matters.

Beginning in August 1933 the Galerie Simon offered Masson a contract, renewable every three months, which stipulated that he would be paid a monthly stipend of three thousand francs for the exclusive rights to all his work, including the rights to all reproduction. Masson remained free to work for the ballet and to accept commissions for illustrations. The monthly fee being too heavy to carry alone in relation to the economic situation, Kahnweiler found a partner in his colleague, Georges Wildenstein. Soon he alone would represent Masson, for life. The artist regretted his earlier mistake, and henceforth remained completely faithful.[28]

The depression had a clarifying effect. It placed people in predicaments that required making decisions and looking to the future. During this period, even in the midst of the crisis, the balance was not completely negative for Kahnweiler.

It seemed as if some artists had left only to return, and that distance from his gallery had given them a greater appreciation when they came back to him. After Masson, Léger slowly gravitated back to him, as he found Léonce Rosenberg's meddling intolerable. Rosenberg went so far as to specify that he paint hair on the head of the woman in *La Lecture*, as he was "always concerned about bringing the modernism of a work of art within limits of decency that were acceptable to his clients."[29]

As had happened with many artists, Léger first tried dispensing with intermediaries altogether. Collectors could buy his work directly from his studio, and he would be in charge of everything. But he quickly changed his mind and decided to return to the dealer of his early days, the one who had given him the means to work. An artist did not sell, he painted. To each his own job. A dealer had only one mistress, his gallery, and Kahnweiler could not conceive of the idea that the artists had any other mistress than painting.

For Kahnweiler the major historical figures of cubism were as classical as any of the painters in the Louvre,[30] and they should act accordingly. Even Picasso slowly was drawing closer to Kahnweiler. He had also distanced himself from the gallery; in fact, he had been the first to leave even before the economic crisis, when he became famous. He sold work to everyone, including the Galerie Simon. In 1929 Kahnweiler had even bought a large painting for the considerable sum of 125,000 francs.[31] Once removed from the social round, which he rapidly found vacuous, Picasso began renewing ties with his dealer from before the Great War. Kahnweiler also visited him more often at Boisgeloup, where he would rejoin the Leirises, Braque, and Christian Zervos. They started talking again. In 1932 Kahnweiler remained as dazzled by Picasso's painting as he had been in the days of the Bateau-Lavoir.

"I would like to paint the way a blind man would describe the shape of a woman's ass by touch," Picasso told him. He went to fetch two paintings of nudes he had just finished and showed them to him. Seeing them stunned and silenced Kahnweiler. When he recovered the use of speech he said, "It seems as if a satyr who had murdered a woman had painted this picture." When Kahnweiler left the studio he was overwhelmed by this giant's eroticism, neither cubist nor naturalistic, without any artifice whatever. Picasso was unclassifiable. As in the early days he left him breathless and dumb. That day Kahnweiler also had to visit Braque. There he was terribly disappointed, because the work showed that Braque was trying to renew himself and break out of his usual style. "It's like Picasso of 1926, diluted and without any strength."[32]

It was an irreversible decision. Kahnweiler, usually so tactful, could not suppress his judgment when it came to painting, even if it was peremptory. But before making a judgment he opened his eyes, he listened carefully, and he took the pains to learn about the painting or the sculpture in question. However, in regard to sculpture he had harbored a prejudice for several years now.

The economic situation was more unfavorable to sculpture than any of the other plastic arts because of the cost of materials. He remembered that before the war Modigliani, who had worked under Constantin Brancusi for a while, had to give it up because he was not strong enough to carve directly into stone, and also because it was too expensive for him. During a period of time Laurens himself had to give up working in bronze in favor of terra-cotta, as neither he nor Kahnweiler could afford to pay the foundry. But how could he make collectors understand that it did not lessen the value of the artist; the fragility of the material was the only drawback.[33] For the last few years he had tried to dissuade Manolo from using it while still praising the quality of his work: "It's a shame that you are a sculptor. Had you been a painter your work would have made you wealthy and celebrated. I would be able to sell it like pâté. But, alas, there are so few collectors of sculpture."[34]

But even this prejudice did not prevent Kahnweiler from visiting a sculptor whose ideas had intrigued him a few days earlier. He was curious about the work because he liked the man and believed that the art would correspond. He went to the studio with the same enthusiasm with which he had gone searching down the streets of Montmartre twenty years earlier. But no one was home. He stepped inside, because the studio door was wide open, but there were only sculptures inside. He looked at them carefully: the work was fine, sensitive, elegant, a bit affected.[35] Unfortunately, the artist was not present at the meeting; perhaps he would have explained it had he been there. They would often meet at numerous events. But Kahnweiler and Alberto Giacometti missed each other on that day the same way that Kahnweiler and Klee did before the war at rue Vignon when their paths crossed without their being aware of it.

Kahnweiler had more than a quarter of a century's experience of artists and the art market behind him. He had gained in confidence whatever he may have lost in his capacity for wonder. He was already being placed on a pedestal by some people. Alphonse Kann gave him intense pleasure when he spoke of "The Kahnweiler Period" to refer to cubist paintings of the years 1907–1914. Kahnweiler felt flattered when receiving compliments or being awarded honors, but excessive praise worried him—he felt pleased at being glorified, but panicked at the same time. He had the feeling of already being dead.[36]

His judgment was sharper and he spoke with conviction. When Fernande Olivier's memoirs, *Picasso and His Friends*, were published, he was glad to see that the Bateau-Lavoir had entered history, but he did not mince his words when asked about the truth of the portrait of him drawn by the author: a daring Jewish businessman, very Germanic in his method, who spent hours bargaining to wear out his artists and get the works at lower prices. When Kahnweiler realized that what could be termed a virtue was not complimentary under the author's pen, he dismissed her book with a wave of his hand.[37]

With the same certainty he put Sigmund Freud in his place, criticizing his *Totem and Tabu* as a grotesque work. The publication of Bronislaw Malinowski's anthropological study, *The Sexual Life of the Natives of North-West Melanesia* (1929) was the limit, and he thundered against the errors of the Freudians. Kahnweiler remained suspicious of psychoanalysis, especially when the surrealists got hold of it.[38]

Yet he also predicted for surrealist poet Robert Desnos a future as a great writer, and the same for Malraux. On receiving his autographed copy of *The Conquerors* on publication, he wrote Malraux a warm letter: "It's the best work published in years. . . . Beautiful and admirably clear, without needless color: everything in it works."[39] He was filled with the same enthusiasm when he discovered excerpts from *A Farewell to Arms* in the *Frankfurter Zeitung*, especially as the author, Ernest Hemingway, was a great collector of the works of Masson and a regular client of the Galerie Simon.[40]

The Kahnweilers rarely went out now both in order to economize and because there was less to enjoy. They went to the movies and to the theater. Kahnweiler thought Sergei Eisenstein's *Potemkin* very good and had loved *The Threepenny Opera* by G. W. Pabst, but he was disappointed in *La Vie en Rose* by Salacrou, which seemed a throwback to the turn of the century. What made a lasting impression was Antonin Artaud's lecture at the Sorbonne, if it could be called a lecture. It consisted of a lyrical description of a painting by Lucas van Leyden, frantic statements about the rotten state of the contemporary stage, a reading from *Woyzeck* by Georg Büchner, and exclamations and wild screams. The lecturer concluded with a sentence that said it all: ". . . Besides, clear ideas are dead ideas."[41]

There were two hundred art dealers of all kinds listed in Paris in 1930, whereas in 1911 the *Annuaire de la curiosité et des Beaux-Arts* had listed "only" a hundred and thirty of them.[42] When he had first started, Kahnweiler could count all of them on the fingers of both hands. But these numbers did not represent a proliferation of the art market; they indicated a greater movement.

New galleries were opening when many others were dying. Jeanne Bucher had been struggling since 1926 to show the cubists as well as the surrealists, abstract painters, and a number of younger painters such as Charles Lapicque. Another very enterprising dealer, Etienne-Jean Bignou, who sold impressionist paintings by Dufy and Lurçat, forged ahead and opened a gallery on rue La Boétie, and another one in New York, while becoming affiliated with Reid and Lefèvre in London. He had become international when everything had ground to a halt in France.

There were others who would be ruined by the crash, either in the immediate or distant future. That had been the case for Durand-Ruel during the economic crash of 1882 and the bankruptcy of the Union General, a bank which was a limited partner in his gallery. This time the crisis would put an end to the Galerie de l'Effort Moderne, undermining Léonce Rosenberg, who had already lost his moral credibility as a professional after acting as the expert for the Kahnweiler liquidation auction. His gallery still represented Herbin, Metzinger, Valmier, de Chirico, and Picabia. Despite his reduced circumstances, Léonce continued to publish his thoughts on art. His famous maxims were so imbued with elementary common sense that they brought out the skepticism of the most worldly collectors:

"Not to change is to grow old . . . Talent surprises, genius startles . . .

There's the true and the false, but there is much truth in falsehood . . . Other than that which is universal, there is nothing eternal . . . When art is the goal, it is never the final result. Each period has its art . . . The evolution of art is parallel to that of the human spirit . . . A cubist work is nothing more than an organism created by the harmony of all the senses."

Most of these were published as an anthology of epigrams.[43] When Léonce recounted the pioneering days of cubism, he minimized Kahnweiler's role and instead presented himself as the savior who sacrificed his own interests for the sake of the movement.[44]

Théophile Briant and Henry Bing closed their galleries, as did Katia Granoff, who reopened a year later on the Left Bank. At that time Christian Dior had not yet become interested in haute couture, and with his friend Jacques Bonjean opened a gallery in 1927. But a few years later, when his father lost his fortune in the crash, he would close it.

Kahnweiler had neither the fortune nor the stock nor the connections of Georges Wildenstein, who was not at all interested in artists, only in paintings.[45] Nor was Kahnweiler as business-minded as Paul Rosenberg, nor the gambler that Josse Hessel was. He was not as blasé as Paul Guillaume, who was awarded the legion d'honneur in 1930 as an editor and art critic, rather than as an art dealer. Guillaume was among the first to become interested in African art, although he preferred it to be antique. One day Francis Carco and journalist Georges Charensol saw him in the gallery squatting on the ground rubbing something in the dirt, and he said to them, "I am adding centuries to it."[46]

These times of crisis were not simply a matter of bankruptcy and liquidation. Beyond the commercial sphere, there was a political temper exacerbated by the rise of nationalism and a new xenophobia, and the restlessness of the unions which created a permanent state of tension. In the art world this was manifested by a resurgence of ideology that did not surprise anyone. An advocate of revolution that is "communal and personalistic," such as Emmanuel Mounier, would have liked to see all artists eliminated from "the academies as well as the Parisian scene, corrupted as they are by capitalist trusts, art dealers, and wealthy collectors."[47] This was not taken seriously, as it seemed natural coming from such intellectuals, and what people said did not matter. What was much more serious was the anti-Semitism.

According to dealer Pierre Loeb, during this period four art dealers out of five were Jewish, as were four out of five collectors.[48] The preponderance of Jews in the art world clearly had no adverse effect on the number and volume of transactions. Wilhelm Uhde, who had made the same observations, added art critics to the list and, generalizing about

Europe in general, thought it was extremely beneficial. He believed that without the Jewish influence the state of painting would be dull, and that it was their taste and instincts that led to the discovery of great paintings; thanks to the efforts of their agents, these would eventually become part of museum collections.[49]

As might be expected, the critic from the extreme right, Camille Mauclair, spearheaded a new crusade to "purify" the scene. His goal was not utopian; he was just a bit ahead of his time. He had not stopped denouncing the "Internationale" of the paintbrush, this School of Paris in which native Frenchmen were a minority. Before launching his attack on the German traders, the German-Jewish propagandists of art, the Soviet pictorials and the artistic hodgepodge of Mitteleuropa, he had the gall to write: "I am not in any way anti-Semitic, but it is not my fault if the great majority of critics and dealers of the avant-garde are Jewish, as if by chance."[50]

In this chorus of hate which set the tone for the reactionary press, the only surprise was the reaction of Louis Dimier, who though politically a supporter of the ultranationalist *L'Action Française* (and whose slogan was "France and only France"), nevertheless remained cosmopolitan in his artistic taste. But this exception proved very rare.

In 1933 the new German chancellor was the man the radio still called Herr Hitler. Germany was ruled by the National Socialist Party. But Kahnweiler always remained German at heart. He still admired his country, even as it was losing its head. Naturally he was against the Nazis. His country was that of Goethe and Schiller, Hölderlin and Wagner, not that of Goebbels and Goering. He was truly convinced that the Nazis would be quickly voted out of office. He believed in the present danger of a Hitler but not in Hitler's threat to the immediate future.

When his brother Gustave telephoned, saying that he had left Germany for France, Kahnweiler was incredulous and could only conceive of his hasty departure as a fit of panic. His reaction reveals another fear on his part: the sudden influx of new Jewish immigrants from central Europe into French society. It would destabilize a position so dearly won in the last quarter of a century. He feared it might give rise to a new anti-Semitism.

In the end Gustave Kahnweiler settled in England, first London, then Cambridge. His arrival among his Neumann cousins, who were closely allied to the monied elite and the gentry, caused the same reaction as Kahnweiler's: "What are you doing here? Stay in Germany, you have nothing to fear from Hitler."[51]

Gustave Kahnweiler left Germany at the same time as Alfred

Flechtheim, who had decided to settle in Switzerland at an early date. Flechtheim had had to close his galleries. From Paris, Kahnweiler recalled a large number of his paintings which were across the Rhine, his Grises, Massons, and Légers. He could not be careful enough; they would despoil him a second time. The shadow of having his stock sequestered in 1914–1918 would obsess him during this whole period of increasing risks right up until the outbreak of World War II.

He had always tended to minimize the impact of political events, but now he tried to anticipate them. He had been caught off guard once, but this time he would be proven correct as things developed. In a few short years, 417 works by Oskar Kokoschka would be branded "degenerate" and confiscated by the German state.[52] The Germany of autos-da-fé was beginning to seriously worry European intellectual circles. In Paris Mauclair was denouncing Gris and Uhde as "Jews," although the first was Catholic and the second of an old Protestant family, while in Berlin Hitler's "Brownshirts" were setting fire to its culture. Soon enough Heinrich Heine's premonition proved only too true: "When you start burning books, you end up burning people."

More than ever now, Kahnweiler followed the German press avidly. He needed to keep up, as he was more interested in the reactions of the artistic community than in day-to-day political developments. He knew that Carl Einstein, avant-garde poet and aesthetician, would struggle with every means available. But what of Robert Musil, whom Kahnweiler admired so much? He had never met the writer, but had read him with great interest. In June 1933 a Ministry of Information and Propaganda headed by Joseph Goebbels was created. When it became clear that Goebbels had complete jurisdiction over all cultural activities, Robert Musil understood that he could no longer live in this new Germany: "It was difficult enough for me under the old regime," he wrote.[53]

Artists did not feel any easier than writers. What did it matter that Chancellor Adolf Hitler was a painter, passionate about monumental architecture? Reading *Mein Kampf* was enough; everything was there. There was nothing ambiguous in his statements; all of Germany's troubles were caused by the Jews, or the Reds, or the Social Democrats. "Theater, art, literature, films, the press, posters, window displays, have to be cleansed, stopped from exhibiting a world that is rotting, in order to be placed in the service of a moral ideal that is a principle of the state and of civilization. The world belongs only to the strong who put into practice total solutions; it does not belong to the weak with their halfway measures."[54]

Diseases, contamination, pollutants . . . he used the vocabulary of pathology to denounce "the insane and decadent excesses that we have learned to accept since the beginning of the century under the concept of cubism and dadaism."[55]

By October 1932, shortly after the National Socialist Party of German Workers won a majority in the municipal council at Dessau, the Bauhaus had closed its doors. The director moved it to Berlin where it was shut down indefinitely the year Adolf Hitler took power.

Under pressure to leave, thirty thousand refugees chose to go to France. Kandinsky, who had taken out German nationality papers in 1928, now moved to a house in Neuilly, near Paris. But for him as for other refugees, France was even worse. It was the only place where he could see himself living because it was the cultural capital of the world, but he bitterly resented his position as a tolerated guest; fifteen years after the Treaty of Versailles, anti-German feelings were still rampant in French society, not to mention the thinly disguised xenophobia and anti-Semitism.[56]

Germans were not the only refugees in Paris. Eleven years earlier, Mussolini's rise to power had also driven intellectuals into exile, men such as Lionello Venturi, professor at the University of Turin, who gave up his chair in art history to be spared the necessity of pledging his allegiance to the new regime and had fled to Paris for the greater benefit of the history of impressionism.

In artistic circles German refugees were the most numerous, the most active, the most noticeable because Germany for years was the "second" center for the study and criticism of art. Many of them headed straight for the Galerie Simon as soon as they arrived to ask for Kahn-weiler's help. He always welcomed them. For them he was a man of great influence in a world where people were not accessible. He knew people, their ways and manners, and the right doors to knock on. His recommendation was taken seriously, and his card acted as a reference. He never abused his power of recommendation, and used it efficiently even if persistently. He was a wonderful ambassador for these refugees whether they were artists, university professors, collectors, or art dealers.

For Paul Westheim, the talented journalist and art critic of high repute, longtime editor of *Kunstblatt*, Kahnweiler spoke to Malraux, now working for the publishing house of Gallimard. The refugee needed the advance as much as he needed to deliver a political message, by writing a book on the relationship between the National Socialist Party and the artistic and literary community. It would be an eyewitness account about the Nazis taking power in the strongholds of culture. But Malraux had to turn down the project on behalf of the Gallimard editorial board. Kahnweiler was not discouraged, and he knocked on other doors, that of Jean Paulhan, editor of the *Nouvelle Revue Française*, and that of Emmanuel Berl, editor in chief of *Marianne*. A series of articles, rather than a book, would have satisfied him just as well. Paul Westheim was not one of his friends, properly speaking, but Kahnweiler respected him and everything that he had accomplished in Germany, and therefore wanted to "lend a helping hand."[57]

Sometimes a simple service that was of small consequence to the dealer relieved the new refugee of considerable difficulties. A high police official from Berlin who fled without a penny, for example, managed to save his furniture and paintings and wanted to have his Pinturicchio appraised and verified in order to sell it. Kahnweiler immediately intervened with his colleague Georges Wildenstein.[58]

Of the people who had to flee Germany there was one person, aside from his brother, with whom Kahnweiler stayed in contact, a man he was prepared to do anything to help—Alfred Flechtheim. After going to Switzerland the art dealer settled in England, but his spirit remained on the continent.

Of all the artists he had exhibited in Germany or who were under contract to him, Flechtheim was especially fond of Paul Klee. In the interest of both parties he did not want to leave the artist stranded, as this might affect his ability to work. For seventeen years, from the beginning of the century until the end of the war, Klee had suffered from having to work without ever being able to support himself financially. His situation had begun to improve when he signed an agreement with the Goltz Gallery in Munich and, five years later, one with Flechtheim. The solution was simple; Flechtheim wanted Kahnweiler and the Galerie Simon to take on the responsibilities of the Flechtheim gallery by assuming the contract with Klee for exclusive representation of his work.

Kahnweiler was favorably disposed to the proposal despite his natural reservations on principle: he preferred to handle only those artists he had discovered. But once he overcame his reluctance he was pleased. Since their initial silent encounter at the rue Vignon gallery, the two had met during the war at the home of their mutual friend Hermann Rupf. The paintings Kahnweiler had seen then were not exactly overwhelming, but they had intrigued him because they were so antithetical to cubism. He soon learned to decipher them, and grew to like them. He thought that Klee was the only artist to have influenced the School of Paris without having ever lived in Paris. He believed that the surrealists found in Klee the qualities they could not see in the cubists. When he was asked by Alfred Flechtheim and Hermann Rupf to represent Klee, he was glad to accept.

Kahnweiler and the artist had many interests in common. Along with painting, music was as important to one as to the other. Klee was of half-German, half-Swiss parentage, and had left his beloved Düsseldorf in 1933. He returned home to Bern, where he still had a measure of financial independence. Between a Germany that had vowed the destruction of the Bauhaus and the Switzerland of his childhood he did not hesitate in making his choice. His "exile" bothered Kahnweiler, who was persuaded that to win over Paris, Klee had to live in Paris, or at least in France. Klee was the only artist of the Galerie Simon not to do so. Kahnweiler would adjust, making his first visit to the artist at home in his small apartment in the Elfenau quarter of Bern. Klee painted in his living room surrounded by all his furniture just as he had done in Munich. He would entertain guests by playing chamber music, he the violin, his wife at the piano. Their playing was of concert caliber—both had been members of orchestras and had professionally performed Bach, Beethoven, and Mozart.

Kahnweiler felt at home in this strange studio, in the apartment of this unusual man who wrote with his right hand and painted with his left, who was a friend of Arnold Schönberg in Munich but preferred playing Haydn. He never tried to be innovative or modern as he discreetly used pieces from the past as well as from the present. He wrote methodically; his life was ordered and calm. He never named his paintings as he worked on them, one at a time, but once a month he baptized them collectively.

He was a strange, lovable man. Only much later would Kahnweiler learn that Klee was making a descent into hell. As the Nazis were taking command of Germany he began to show the first symptoms of multiple sclerosis. When the Wehrmacht invaded Europe, he was overcome by the disease. For seven horrible years his paintings would become increasingly sad and anguished.

Back in Paris, Kahnweiler wrote to him and their correspondence would last till the very end, even when the artist was no longer able to hold a pen. At first the tone of their exchange was aesthetic, but very quickly the dealer was led to discuss the "art market" and "money." Kahnweiler had bought for his own collection some watercolors and the famous painting *The Arrow in the Garden,* done in oil on canvas, which had first introduced the dealer to Klee's world. But he did not have an easy time trying to sell Klee's work. It was too expensive, just too expensive, he would grumble. It was a hard time for the market in general, the atmosphere was not favorable to art, and rumors of war did not help matters. Still, it was the price of a Klee that made a prospective buyer pause and hesitate. Most of the time it was Klee who fixed the price in a precise and calculated way, and Kahnweiler made it his business to try to reduce it by one-third for the French market. But often it was still too much. He fought to have Klee's paintings shown in the Jeu de Paume and the Musée de Grenoble, and in exhibits in Copenhagen, Brussels, Lucerne, Chicago, New York, and London, where they often met with great success. In Paris, however, no matter how prominently he featured the work in his gallery, his efforts were in vain. He himself had said that you cannot force people to look at paintings, much less buy them. Klee's work was difficult for the French public to place, either in relation to cubism or to surrealism. The shows drew large crowds, but the reviews were lukewarm and the sales mediocre at best. At any other period his prices might have been acceptable, but at present there was a crisis.[59]

The economic depression reached its lowest point in the spring of 1935. For several months at a time Kahnweiler could not sell a painting to a Parisian. Only foreign collectors bought,[60] and even the Americans, who flocked to his gallery in ever greater numbers and wanted to see everything, made few purchases. The Masson and Klee exhibitions brought him more prestige than money. The wife of Joseph Caillaux, former president of the cabinet, had purchased two engravings by Klee, *The Gorgons* and *Swan Devoured by Tigers*.[61] He needed many more sales like that. To make up for it, he acted as a guide to the curator of the Royal Museum of Fine Arts in Copenhagen, a job that took him to Matisse's and Laurens's studios, and to a few galleries. The curator had been looking for a Braque for the museum, but Paul Rosenberg's prices were too high. Kahnweiler took him directly to Braque's studio, where he bought a *Gueridon* for 30,000 francs. Kahnweiler received one-sixth of the transaction as his commission.[62]

Earning these small sums was easier and more certain than his usual, more ambitious plans, which were now fruitless. A significant indicator of the times was the trouble Kahnweiler had in selling an interesting historical artifact, of enormous importance to any collector of cubism. It was a ceramic tile painted by both Picasso and Derain in July 1914 when they were in Montfavet near Avignon. This beautiful piece, tastefully mounted, looked like a fresco; in reality it was a testimony to the end of their friendship. Kahnweiler could not sell it in the same way he would have done with a painting. Even the New York dealer Pierre Matisse could not be persuaded to take it.[63]

The economic depression also had a psychological effect on people. It affected the way they lived. The Kahnweilers went out less; he traded in his car only when forced to do so because the motor threatened to give out. Their summer vacation had turned into a nightmare because they could no longer go to Italy, Switzerland, and Germany. They spent a dreadful summer in Brittany, where Kahnweiler was confined to an easy chair in Trébeurden as the result of an attack of sciatica after swimming in the ocean. The following summers of these depressed years during the thirties he took no risks and remained in his garden at Boulogne-Billancourt until a time when things would improve.

At the moment such prospects seemed to be in the realm of fantasy. The only two people working in the gallery now were he and Louise Leiris. It was the minimum staff and they did everything. Kahnweiler then had to decide to make severe cuts in the monthly stipends he paid his artists, such as André Masson. He tried to explain to Pierre Matisse the way in which he was revising the terms of his contract with Masson (the retail price of Masson's paintings had gone down by one-third): "I believe that the only sound policy at the present time is to sell the works of young artists as cheaply as possible in order to continue having a reliable market, instead of waiting for the one person who will pay more. I am sure that it is the solution for this market."[64]

With others, such as Gaston-Louis Roux, who had only recently signed up with the Galerie Simon, he severed his contractual obligations entirely. The way he terminated the contract gave the artist no recourse: "I have something very sad to say: I will no longer be able to buy your paintings. As you might suspect, it is not a question of sales, but simply finding the money necessary to make purchases. I was able to manage it until now, but I can no longer do it. I don't have to say that your paintings have nothing to do with this decision. I like your work as much as ever, but I cannot buy either your work or that of anyone else."[65]

The number of artists in his gallery was shrinking visibly. What a terrible blow to absorb just before Christmas 1933! The few Grises and Massons his friend Rupf purchased at low prices gave him the liquid assets to maintain these artists on the market. But these were lean times, and Kahnweiler could not hold out at such a pace. He had to find a way to survive, to keep the gallery going, and also to prepare for the future. When this economic depression came to an end, which artists would still be in his gallery? He could not wait until then; it would be much too late. He had to forge ahead now. After examining the problem from every angle he came to a solution that would benefit all of them: to form a syndicate to help artists.

Kahnweiler did not want a secret society, just a "small organization," as he called it. The idea was straightforward: to ask a number of collectors to commit themselves firmly to pledge a certain sum over a period of a year for the purpose of buying the works of young artists. In return the subscribers (for that was what they were) would derive many benefits, especially that of buying at the lowest prices. The dealers and artists would benefit from the arrangement. It would enable artists to continue working, help a sluggish market to show signs of life, and create interest in sales by the gallery, no matter how modest, even if the art dealer received no commission.

The concept evolved slowly in Kahnweiler's mind. In private and under a seal of secrecy he discussed it only with the young artists involved: Kermadec, Roger, Roux, and Masson.[66] The collectors who might be interested in this art investment scheme included Armand Salacrou. To Georges Wildenstein he presented a simple outline of his plan without going into specific details. Each person would pay a stated amount each month, and the gallery would act as the receiver and distribute the sums to the artists involved. By the end of the year each subscriber would have the right to purchase a certain number of paintings (starting at 125 francs for the smallest size) according to how much they had paid into the fund. The Galerie Simon would take a percentage, but it had to pay like any other subscriber to buy paintings. The organization acted as an anonymous art patron. Kahnweiler hated the idea of payments over time, but it was the most direct—albeit complicated—solution.

This Artists' Mutual Aid Union became a reality due to the goodwill of several collectors, including Alfred Richet, André Level, and Alphonse Kann. Salacrou took out two subscriptions, each one entailing a monthly payment of 2,000 francs.[67] It was a volatile business, difficult to manage because each payment had to be invested, but on the whole it proved very effective. It worked so well that Kahnweiler began thinking about including an artist he had always dismissed: Joan Miró. In April 1935 he asked Miró point-blank: "What is your financial situation at the present time? Are you free or are you under contract to a gallery?"[68]

Kahnweiler did not hide the fact that he had a proposal in mind for him, but did not say anything specific that would break the seal of absolute secrecy. No one must know about this. Kahnweiler's obsession was reinforced by the possibility of misunderstanding in a business where inconsequential information could create serious financial repercussions.

Although Kahnweiler now claimed that Miró was an important artist of the younger generation,[69] it would be difficult to imagine any other motivation for him than the purely financial one, and everything in his relationship with the artist seemed to confirm this. Ever since his first visit to the studios on rue Blomet over ten years before, he had made a disdainful grimace at the sight of Miró's paintings. More recently, in 1932, after a visit to Pierre Cole's gallery, he did not hide his poor opinion of the two artists who were featured there: "Dali is always the same careful maniac and for me, very Ecole des Beaux-Arts." As for Miró, he was "very Catalan in a vulgar sort of way, as might be expected. His subjects were also completely idiotic."[70] When Miró dropped by the gallery to ask how he was doing, Kahnweiler answered so dryly, so cursorily as to cut short the conversation. He thought of Miró as a small eccentric.[71]

Kahnweiler's offer might be interpreted as proof of the artist's development since the war, but that was not the case. A month before making the offer he had described Miró as a "minor Catalan realist painter, not without talent, but who was influenced by André Masson into becoming a surrealist. He was a talented minor painter unaware of his own limitations and who undertook artistic adventures well beyond his powers."[72]

Kahnweiler had asked Pierre Matisse to share the contract with Miró.[73] The economic situation was forcing him into contradictory actions that he detested. He was asked to explain his actions at length to a young man with whom he started corresponding in 1933. This was a London collector, Douglas Cooper, who, along with F. H. Mayor and J. F. Duthie, became the triumvirate that inaugurated the Mayor Gallery on Cork Street in London.

Kahnweiler was unfamiliar with contemporary English art aside from the works of Ben Nicholson, an artist he liked who never failed to show him his latest work when passing through Paris.[74] He discussed painting and the whole art market with Cooper. Kahnweiler felt it would be a long hard struggle to separate the wheat from the chaff, and to distinguish between painting and non-painting. For him abstract art was a dead end. And if English collectors preferred Max Ernst to cubism, it did not say much for their taste.

Kahnweiler refused to take his ledgers home for bedside reading. Once he was home he forgot all unpaid bills until the next morning, remaining faithful to his habit of keeping his home and his gallery separate. He was an enthusiastic reader of Malraux's *The Human Condition,* which he thought was his best writing to date.[75] He was also quite dazzled when he read the manuscript of Georges Bataille's *Blue of Noon,* which Michel Leiris had passed on to him. It made him regret suspending publications by the Galerie Simon. To relieve his frustration he gave Bataille's manuscript to André Malraux to recommend its publication to the editorial board at Gallimard.[76]

It was not the first time, nor would it be the last, that Kahnweiler would appeal to Malraux for a worthy cause. Malraux had achieved fame and a position of influence. He always claimed that he would never forget his first editor. Kahnweiler had warmly recommended the manuscript of Michel Leiris's journal of the Dakar to Djibouti expedition, which was finally completed after two years spent in Africa.[77] Malraux also recommended artists to Kahnweiler. One day he sent over canvases by Engel-Rozier, whom the *Nouvelle Revue Française* wanted to please. Kahnweiler hated them on sight, but he explained to the artist that economic conditions prevented him from . . . That was one way to use the crash. But the editorial board at Gallimard also knew how to refuse.[78]

The publication by Harcourt, Brace of Gertrude Stein's *The Autobiography of Alice B. Toklas* came as a pleasant surprise, but also as an irritant. He was happy for his friend, who at the age of sixty and after thirty years of writing had finally won recognition for her work. Her success was enormous, and she was caught up in a whirlwind of lectures, public appearances, and innumerable offers from every side. Kahnweiler had twice published her and was feeling self-congratulatory, even if her current best-seller overshadowed all her other work. He became quite angry because many readers believed that this fictional memoir was history, and thus a major eyewitness account of the heroic years of cubism. He was almost as indignant as he had been with Apollinaire. There were so many errors among the accurate details. He found this all the more exasperating because Gertrude Stein had asked him to read the manuscript before publication. How could she publish that he had made a fortune in London many years before opening his gallery on rue Vignon in Paris, or that Wilhelm Uhde had been a German spy in 1914, as the scandal sheets of the period had proclaimed? It was regrettable, but it did not affect their friendship.

At times like these Kahnweiler stayed at his desk in his office at the back of the hopelessly empty gallery. Despite all opposition he still knew that he was right. His happiest moments were the most unexpected.

Robert Goldwater, a professor from New York University, refused to leave Paris without greeting "the famous Kahnweiler" and proceeded to listen for several hours as Kahnweiler lectured on art history as it applied to art dealers and critics.

He was even most pleased with the fact that slowly over the years he had renewed his friendship with Picasso. Now Picasso dropped by the gallery on rue d'Astorg so often that Kahnweiler started taking notes on their conversations after each visit. Painting was their main topic of conversation; they pursued it whenever they were together, oblivious to everything else around them.

"Fundamentally, what is an artist?" Picasso wondered in February 1934, when the place de la Concorde was red with blood after pro-fascist riots. "He is a collector who wants to build up a body of work by creating for himself the works that he wants. That's how I always begin, and then it turns into something else."[79]

Their conversations would refer to current events in the cultural sphere, such as an exhibition of Italian painting at the Petit Palais, which Picasso found horrifying. "It appeals to the lowest instincts! You like that work? You admire all that glory and those high prices?"

Kahnweiler explained his point of view and defended his favorite Italian artists. The art dealer was as composed and reasonable in his views as the artist was irrational and extreme, each according to his temperament. Kahnweiler wanted to be sensible and give things their just due. He recalled that when he was young he despised the Renaissance, but as he grew older and acquired some sense of historical perspective, in time he learned to appreciate what was important about the Renaissance artists. This was high-minded, but Picasso was not going to be convinced so easily.

"Of course, you want to buy cheap and sell high. That's why you admire Caravaggio, Titian, and all the rest. I'd trade all of Italian painting for a Vermeer van Delft. That's an artist who said what he had to say without thinking about anything else."

"I'll grant you Titian," Kahnweiler conceded. "But Tintoretto, that's someone else, and Masaccio, Caravaggio. And what about a painter like Giotto, what do you think of him?"

"It's all decoration, just horrible. It's manufactured to decorate churches and apartments."

"I believe that what is most important about painting is its creative interaction with the external world," Kahnweiler said. He launched into lengthy explanations that elaborated the theoretical writings of his days in exile in Bern. He pursued his thoughts: "Yes, it's evident that Giotto or Masaccio or Caravaggio renewed perception of the external world. Even Vermeer would not have been possible without Caravaggio."

"Yes, but in Vermeer you don't find all this reminiscence of antiquity." Picasso continued to mock Kahnweiler's fascination with Italy, then headed for the door, as once again they had whiled away the afternoon with discussion.[80]

In these lean years, which left Kahnweiler with free time to talk about his interests, he had two friends with whom he could continue these day-to-day conversations about his two preoccupations of the moment: Picasso for painting and Vlaminck for politics.

In 1934, after the treaty between Poland and Germany, Vlaminck was convinced that war was again about to break out, and offered the same reasons as in 1914: human stupidity and egotism. In this debate Vlaminck had the advantage of having been right the first time over Kahnweiler, days, months, and even years before war had been declared between France and Germany.

"Listen, Kahnweiler," he said, "if those in power were suddenly convinced that war were impossible forevermore, in the present state of things when they count on war as the only solution, they would all go mad! They would be insane with anguish at the thought of not being able to order things so that they could continue to live in a closed world or else of not being able to reorganize the whole world on an egalitarian basis, dependent on individual generosity and mutual goodwill."[81]

These arguments continued from conversations to long, dense letters punctuated with exclamation points to give the arguments even more dramatic impact. Although it was an epistolary exchange, it maintained the dialogue between the two men, one answering the other by return mail. They were in agreement on the ills besetting the world but not on the remedy for them.

Kahnweiler was emphatic about saying what he had to say when it was his turn: "I admit to having been in error in 1914. Mea culpa! But so what? Do you want me to say that I don't regret it? Had I been *clever* perhaps I could have saved some of my worldly goods. I would have been a rich man, and I am not. But then I did not take part in what I considered a crime. You more than anyone else know that is something. I paid for that liberty with all my possessions. That was fair. I am no more optimistic about the future than you are. I believe war is possible. There are a thousand dangers just as horrible I see threatening us. Fascism—it would be our fiercest enemy as it is in Germany. Fascism would prevent all of us—you included—from working, writing, exhibiting. Hitler's victims file in to see me at the gallery. I see every important German artist hounded into exile. (They are not Jewish; they are only artists.) My family has left Germany. The galleries belonging to Flechtheim have all been closed down, and Flechtheim himself is now in London. I don't believe that these events will be restricted to Germany."[82]

Kahnweiler criticized Vlaminck for his lack of clarity in defining the problems. Vlaminck's inventory of wrongs was jumbled, even if essentially correct. The artist mixed everything in a hodgepodge: cubism and jazz, the patricide Violette Nozières and Picasso. Moreover, it seemed the artist did not realize that in the eyes of the extreme right, such as Camille Mauclair, Vlaminck was considered an integral part of the modern movement.

The artist and the art dealer could not come to an understanding because Vlaminck seemed to rationalize the meaning of events that Kahnweiler saw clearly as profoundly anti-intellectual and anti-humanistic. It was no longer possible to withdraw to a place far from Paris in case of a general conflagration. Vlaminck was not so much identified with a school or a movement as with a certain style, part of a family of like-minded intellects from before the war who gathered in certain studios and vacation places and a certain gallery—whether he liked it or not! Kahnweiler promised him that the day fascism triumphed in Europe, that political party would classify him among those responsible for the decadence, along with all the others. It had already started, since his work, as well as that of Gris, Braque, and Picasso, was blacklisted as not to be shown in the new Germany. It was more than a taste of things to come; it was a warning he should not ignore.

Naturally Vlaminck disagreed, as he did not feel part of any group. To make his position clear, he used a curious metaphor, drawn from sports and from mechanics: "I am as responsible for cubism as the inventor of the bicycle is responsible for the motor in the automobile. The invention of the bicycle left a large place to man, who had to use his muscles to work the machine. The bicycle is a human, sporting instrument. But in the automobile there is nothing human; an idiot, an invalid, a healthy man can all equally attain any speed they want. Cubism is painting that anyone can do. Am I responsible for the literary ramblings, nightmares, and dreams of these little men, for their impotence and all their other diseases?"[83]

Vlaminck would take a more extreme position to make his point. He considered the bloody right-wing riots of February 6, 1934, on the place de la Concorde as the vanguard announcing "The Great Celebration" that was imminent. His feeling of urgency made him adopt an apocalyptic tone. He spoke like a man preparing for doomsday. At one point he even wondered if the impending disaster did not demand that he exchange his paintbrushes for the pen. This is exactly what he would eventually decide to do, publishing such pamphlets as *Tournants dangereux* (Hazardous Bends), as dark and grim and despairing as the leaden skies of his landscapes, so heavy over those hopelessly buried villages.

"The incurable patient," he concluded, "and that is what is so terrible, is mankind itself. The just and terrible punishment about to fall will set him right, will make him devour his excrement, his ego and vanity, his nastiness and hypocrisy."

This made a profound impression on Kahnweiler, who had often heard that Vlaminck was in the throes of misanthropy. But he realized that this was more serious. He disregarded the final postscript the artist placed on his writings: "My best collectors at the present moment are the Germans!" The tone and the state of mind of the artist had become more radical than ever before. The words he used were not those of bitterness, grudges, or even jealousy. His malady was much more serious. In some ways his words recalled the speeches and references that had appeared in Germany since Hitler came to power. It was as if Vlaminck were calling down with his imprecations a vengeance whose consequences he could not conceive, which would be tragic for the very people he had loved most.

In his replies, Kahnweiler attempted to explain his earlier criticisms. He had never tried to make him one of the artists responsible for cubism, only a member in spirit, even against his will, of the group from which it arose, which was a very different matter. As for the sales of Vlaminck paintings in Germany, Kahnweiler was in a position to know from experience that it was an artificial market. There were no exhibitions, sales were all clandestine, and investments were made by people who would not give their names. The art dealers who sold his paintings on the other side of the Rhine did not stand for anything: they were salesmen without allegiance, faith, or rules, who only wanted a quick profit and would do anything for a good business deal. These were not things that mattered according to Kahnweiler.

Kahnweiler had joined the anti-fascist camp. That was the priority through which every other decision was filtered, and the ultimate arbiter to which he referred everything. It was a bitter pill to swallow, as it was for all of his friends—Malraux and the others—who joined ranks under the banner of a watchdog committee of "anti-fascist intellectuals."

Ever since the Treaty of Versailles Kahnweiler had been aware of the serious mistakes made by France and Britain, even though he could understand all the benefits derived by the communist Internationale from the situation in France. Even if this vast political movement evidenced all the maneuvering and manipulations dictated by such political flux, in the years to come Kahnweiler defined his actions according to one man, and only one: Hitler. He was the man to defeat. Everything else was of secondary consideration. Kahnweiler did not care if that played into the hands of Soviet communism. His stance was not essentially political, but humanitarian. For him it was simply about matters of the intellect, and about the future of civilization.

He regularly met refugees from the triumphant Third Reich and followed the German press on a daily basis, so he knew the condition of the arts and letters in that country by the end of the twenties, and to what state of moral misery it had been reduced after two years of pressure from the Nazis. He was convinced that if they were not stopped, they would destroy Europe. The barbarians were at the gates, and he acted with full knowledge of that fact. The time for compromise had come and gone. France and Britain were the last bastion of democracy in Europe, in spite of everything. In such an atmosphere the least sign of protest was cause for celebration, such as Arturo Toscanini's refusal to return to Italy. It was balm to soothe the wound.[84]

Kahnweiler was a supporter of the Republic for his own good reasons. France was a nation that had granted him and his extensive circle of friends the freedom to follow and practice whatever they liked—painting, philosophy, poetry, literature. It had made him want to shout, "Vive la France! As long as it lasts!"[85]

⫼

COME WHAT MAY

▭ It was "Vive la France!" for lack of anything else. But that universal bastion of democracy was beginning to show its weakness. There was nothing positive in the downfall of Laval's cabinet, nor in the breakup of the league of Action Française. There was still rioting going on, and at the least provocation turmoil would break out in the streets. Kahnweiler placed all his hopes on the publication of the program drawn up by the Popular Front. His position was the opposite of some of the bourgeoisie, who said, "Better Hitler than the Popular Front."

The economic situation had improved since the dark days of 1931, but instability still reigned. Now there were people in the galleries, but fewer buyers than visitors.[1] The Artists' Mutual Aid Union began to show signs of slackening. André Level and Alfred Richet were faithful to the principles of the organization, but Alphonse Kann did not renew his subscription. Fortunately André Lefèvre had just paid four thousand francs for the last quarter.[2]

The organization hung by a thread. Political events frightened property-owners in France. The Mutual Aid Union was rapidly diminishing in size; Salacrou did not even answer Kahnweiler's inquiry as to whether he was still a subscriber.[3] But Kahnweiler in his gallery was more determined than ever not to give up and pull down the metal shutters.

To promote his young artists, he asked André Malraux to edit a series of small books on new artists, to be published by Gallimard. A patron, whose name he would keep confidential (with his usual penchant for secrecy) would finance works on Beaudin, Borès, Kermadec, Lascaux, Roger, Roux, and others. Kahnweiler was so persistent that it raised the question of whether he (or perhaps André Simon) was the financial backer in question. He would commit himself to buying a set number of copies for the gallery on publication. Again, all his work came to naught. That seemed to be the final result of all his projects to keep his gallery alive.[4]

There was always America, which still had a monopoly on buying, in dollars and in large quantities. But Kahnweiler was not about to change his tactics, bound as he was to his gallery in Paris. He was unshakable in his belief that his paintings had an intrinsic value, and therefore would only sell at a price that would enable him to replace his stock while making some profit. "Their price today is what their price was yesterday," was his answer to anyone asking for a better price.[5]

Kahnweiler refused to bend his principles to meet the changing situation. Once he had an idea he kept to it, both in his commercial dealings and in his aesthetic judgment. When everyone around him praised the Matisse exhibition, he would temper their ardor with his own chilly reaction: "It's only Matisse, and it's not overwhelming." He would invite people to visit the library of the Senate to see the decor painted by Delacroix, which *was* overwhelming.[6]

He pursued his defense and praise of "true painting" and of authentic cubism with intensity. He could be momentarily lulled, but little was needed to awaken him and put him on the alert.

In the spring of 1936 he received news from London that threw him into a fury. It seemed that the Mayor Gallery, whose schedule of shows he had been following through his dealings with one of the directors, Douglas Cooper, was preparing an exhibition of the second-generation cubists— Gleizes, Metzinger, Valmier, Herbin, and others. It was April 1, but this was not a joke. He received word of it from Alfred Flechtheim.

Without a moment's hesitation, Kahnweiler picked up his pen to ask—more accurately, to demand—that they not do it. He knew that he had no right to make the request but he felt morally obliged to interfere. Considering the rapport between their establishments, he had always advised them as a business connection, and as an informed friend, to exhibit only works of the highest quality to the detriment of quantity. Did they not understand his point? He went on to explain his request.

Twenty-five years before, when Braque, Picasso, Gleizes, Metzinger, and their cohorts were all one and the same in the public's mind, he had fought to draw a distinction between them. In time collectors finally understood that there were great painters on the one hand and, on the other, camp followers, wretched devils, mere imitators. Time had done its work. In order for the four greats not to be shown on the same walls with them, Kahnweiler had refused to send paintings to the Salon des Indé-pendants and the Salon d'Automne. In Germany critics and dealers had seen the light, since his friend Flechtheim had severed relations with Herwarth Walden, who allowed the four great cubists to be confused with the *ersatzkubisten* in his review *Der Sturm*.

By this time England was the only country left in doubt, because modern art had only recently made its appearance there. But what would be the sense of his maintaining close relations with a new and promising gallery such as Mayor, if it were to be the first to destroy his long and patient labor? Kahnweiler was beside himself. It did not matter to him that Cooper and his friends exhibited the works of Cocteau and Soutine, of Dali, whom he loathed, or Max Ernst, whom he deemed minor. They were what they were, that is, only themselves. But the by-products of cubism were vile imitators. Hanging their works next to the historical cubist artists would deceive and mislead the public, and even worse, it was a dangerous confusion that could only be prejudicial to "his" artists. The public could not decide for itself. Its need to be directed gave the art dealer the true measure of his responsibility. "Therefore, please give up any thought of this show!"[7]

"It's our business," was essentially the reply sent by the Mayor Gallery, which was offended by Kahnweiler's unsolicited interference. The directors wanted to alter the scope of their exhibition and specified that they were not completely committed to these artists either, but they wanted to include them in their show for purely historical reasons. They belonged to the movement by simple chronology and it would be futile, or worse, gross negligence, to omit them.[8]

Kahnweiler could not accept this explanation and returned to the attack. Their business was also his to the extent that he had the power to refuse to lend them the works of Gris and Braque that they requested for the exhibition. The proximity to the others would spoil these works. He had principles he wanted respected at all costs. If the Mayor Gallery and the Galerie Simon were to continue their cooperation, then the Mayor Gallery had to learn to respect these principles. Meanwhile, they should distance themselves from these artists. He was not about to give up.[9] But he was already too late. The paintings were there, ready to be hung. They were a fact and the artists who had painted them were also real. They could not be passed over or denied.[10]

Kahnweiler might have lost the battle for a cause dear to his heart, but he had the last word, not as a menace but as a warning. The gist of it was: in the future, please refrain from making such dreadful blunders. You owe that to your public. Since you are not present on the premises from morning till night to explain the difference between a Braque and a Metzinger, they will rely on the authority of the gallery and confuse the works, and visual laziness will do the rest. Not just anything can be hung together, grouped on the walls of a gallery.

What Kahnweiler really wanted was to make them admit that they had organized the exhibition just to please Léonce Rosenberg. After all, these second-rate cubists were *his* artists, and if Villon and Le Fauconnier were not included in this show it was merely because Léonce did not have any of their work at the moment. But the die was cast and what was done was done. Kahnweiler could not answer for Braque if he ever got wind of this affair. It was a lesson for the future: never show these artists! "You are destroying my life's work by doing this, and I could never consent to it."[11]

In May 1936 the leftist Popular Front swept the second round of the legislative elections. Finally Léon Blum's socialist experiment was about to begin: collective bargaining, the forty-hour week, dissolving the opposing organizations. These programs were soon initiated despite the opposition, and in less than a month everything was decided.

D. H. Kahnweiler was overwhelmed by the victory, as it was unexpected. France had again become an adult as a nation. A few days before this triumph he had been disillusioned: "Human stupidity is fulminating in Paris," he told Picasso. "People already see themselves as dispossessed and completely ruined. As if seventy-two communists would be able to impose their ideas on an assembly of over six hundred elected deputies."[12] Kahnweiler rejoiced as a citizen but not as a person who sold art. There was a sharp drop in the market when, on March 7, Hitler denounced the Treaty of Locarno (which set the terms for French-German reconciliation and reparation) and the military occupation of the Rhineland. Again it became impossible to sell anything. The French, at least, were no longer buying.

There was no prospect for immediate improvement; there was only the foreign market on which Kahnweiler placed his hopes. In the early days of June, France was living through the workers' occupation of factories and other demonstrations that ran the risk of turning into rioting. Kahnweiler chose to ignore these strikes. The situation was full of unexpected developments, but it was only a superficial manifestation of things. You could not see the forest for the trees. The real troubles awaiting

France, both internally and on the international front, were of a different and more complex order, and could not be settled by rioting in the streets.

He thought he could escape solely political issues by concentrating on art, but in June 1936 everything in France was politicized. Along with some friends he attended two evenings of lectures and discussions on the communist view of art, organized by the Maison de la Culture. He was shocked by the very title of the program, "Realism and Painting." He expressed his anger to Masson, who was as anti-fascist as he was but had never doubted the reactionary stance of the Russians in regard to culture. "The problem is poorly formulated," Kahnweiler pointed out, "as can be seen in the title of the lectures. But at least it lets you know what to expect." At the same time there was an exhibition of the works of Gustave Courbet. They were advising painters to make pictures " 'in the manner of Courbet,' as if that made any sense. I've always held such views to be abhorrent, and I believe it expresses a petit-bourgeois pretentious state of mind. Paintings for the proletariat! But the proletariat is worth every bit as much as the bourgeoisie. Why this condescension? The finest works of art should not be too fine for the proletariat. The average bourgeois has no idea of what's going on in art to start with. Those who develop a grasp of it have been slowly introduced to the work. Why not lead the workers to an understanding of art? I did it during the war when I taught art classes in Bern. I spoke to the workers about cubism, among other things, often lecturing with slide projections, and I can tell you that rarely has there been a more attentive or more eager audience. But the idea of asking artists to create mediocre works for mediocre people, so as not to be bothered explaining a higher form of art, that is a disgrace!"[13]

Kahnweiler had always been an elitist in art, but he was unique among art dealers and collectors to the extent that his principles were not restricted only to the elite of the bourgeoisie, but included the proletariat as well. This was the basis of his rejection of any concept of "art for the masses."

In July 1936 the Popular Front had been in power for several months in Spain: Republicans, socialists, communists, and the unions were all united against fascism. The new president of the republic, Manuel Azaña, was powerless to neutralize the extreme tensions gripping his nation. The slightest thing could have tipped the balance toward total violence. That catalyst was provided by the assassination of monarchist deputy Calvo Sotelo on July 13. It was a signal for a counterrevolution. Five days later civil war broke out. World War II actually began on that day, and not three years later.

On the day Sotelo was assassinated, Joan Miró wrote Kahnweiler, reiterating his invitation to come to Spain to join Raymond Queneau and Michel Leiris.[14] Now that was obviously out of the question. The Republicans were on one side, Franco's Nationalist forces on the other, and the country was thrown into the most terrible of ordeals.

Masson, in Catalonia, wanted to send his paintings to Kahnweiler, who dissuaded him: it was too dangerous. No insurance company would cover the damages of a civil war, especially at a time like this—and particularly for shipments from Spain. Revolutions were like the forces of nature; there was no recourse in case of loss. "Give them to Georges Bataille when he returns home," Kahnweiler advised Masson.[15]

That was the surest mode of transport, and Kahnweiler awaited the paintings with impatience. Masson had become exclusively Kahnweiler's. On September 1 the Galerie Simon had to break the contract with Georges Wildenstein, whose enthusiasm had cooled because of Masson's lack of commercial success. Kahnweiler felt that it was better this way, despite the added cost.

Taking advantage of his new independence he mounted an exhibition for the beginning of December, "Masson in Spain, 1934–1936," bringing together seventy-four paintings, drawings, pastels, and watercolors. He could not get over the success of the show. The gallery had never seen such crowds since the end of the war. It was unhoped for. Louis Aragon was exultant, and discussed it with Bernard Groethuysen, the German reader for the Gallimard editorial board. At the exhibition the critics René Jean and Paul Westheim met the members of the Spanish Embassy. There was an unknown young Swedish woman who suddenly burst into tears and had to leave the exhibition, weeping copiously, completely stricken. People could not tell whether hers was an aesthetic reaction, or one of disgust before the sight of such carnage.[16]

Among the visitors to the Masson exhibition, Picasso remained in the dealer's office after closing to continue their conversation. It was unusual because this time, instead of painting, the two men discussed politics—the civil war in Spain. It could not be avoided. Picasso found himself in an unreal situation, since he had been named as the symbolic director of the Prado by the Republican government. The museum now stood empty; the collection had been evacuated as a security precaution.

When Picasso departed, Kahnweiler jotted down the conversation in a notebook, as was his habit. It was dark outside. The France of a newly devalued franc and of the suicide of Minister of the Interior Roger Salengro in reaction to the accusations against him was nearing its first Christmas under the Popular Front.

One evening in 1937 the Rupfs invited the Kahnweilers to the Drouant Restaurant in appreciation of their hospitality. It was an unforgettable evening in every sense of the word. The art dealer had lived in a state of crisis for so long that he had forgotten what dining out was like: "It was delicious, but I have to say that the price terrified me. I am no longer used to seeing so much money spent just to stuff your face."[17]

Business had picked up since Léon Blum announced a moratorium and a loan for national defense had been initiated. The Galerie Simon had not counted solely on the Masson exhibition to balance its books, even if the sales had been substantial and Kenneth Clark, director of the National Gallery in London, had purchased three drawings and the *Ibdès d'Aragon*.[18] Kahnweiler's principal clients were from the American market. Nierendorf, a New York dealer from Fifty-seventh Street, contracted to pay two thousand dollars a year for the purchase of works by Klee. In exchange he obtained from Kahnweiler, now officially known as Klee's manager, the exclusive rights to sell his paintings for the next three years.[19] The agreement was binding solely for the works of Klee.

In the United States Kahnweiler began working with a dealer recently installed in New York, for whom he felt great admiration and friendship, all the more sincere since it was mutual. Curt Valentin, a thirty-five-year-old who worked out of the Buchholz Gallery, was reputed to be very inventive and a little given to drink. He had been drafted as a young man into the German army during the war; the one pleasure he derived from the experience was being stationed in Charleville, the town where Rimbaud had lived. Curt Valentin's character revealed itself only gradually. His appearance was deceptive: he had a profoundly melancholic streak, which he masked with easy banter.[20] Of all the associates Kahnweiler had worked with over the last thirty years, Valentin was the person he respected the most. In working with him he felt on familiar ground, and in complete accord. They shared the same ideas about painting and about how to defend their cause. Kahnweiler did not hold back when praising him to artists: "He is a young man working in the same tradition as Flechtheim, that is to say, representing only a few artists, but devoting himself to them completely. He knows that success in painting does not occur overnight. What he loves, he clings to and never abandons."[21]

It was not just a coincidence that made Kahnweiler compare Valentin to Flechtheim. His old friend had just died. His estate presented a real headache to the London lawyers who had the heavy burden of settling it. He and Kahnweiler owned numerous paintings together as partners, especially the works of Klee. It was almost impossible to make the lawyers understand that they had been friends since 1909, as well as business associates, and their friendship had been the basis of commercial transactions for which there were no written records. [22]

Spain was a field of carnage, aflame from one end to the other. Kahnweiler was optimistic that the Republican victory in Guadalajara would lead to the liberation of Madrid and their ultimate triumph. Franco, who was head of the military junta, could only win with the intervention of Germany with massive shipments of men and weapons. But the situation had not yet deteriorated to that extent, and if France and Britain could continue negotiating, the Spanish Civil War would not lead to a worldwide conflagration.

"As for me," Kahnweiler confided to friends, "I stopped worrying about politics a long time ago. Come what may. Even if it's time to perish, then let us die."[23]

He remained as much a pacifist as ever. There was no cause worthy of his taking up arms. But this did not diminish his intention of defending the cause in his own way. "Any anti-fascist demonstration will always find me its ally," was his reply when solicited for a London exhibition of German artists banned by the Nazi regime.[24]

In April 1937 the struggle of the Spanish Republican forces became the major preoccupation of artists, replacing in urgency the plight of those persecuted in Berlin or Vienna. Oskar Kokoschka, the expressionist, sent them a specially designed poster all the way from Prague, where he lived. The art critic Christian Zervos and his wife stepped up efforts to rescue works of art belonging to the Spanish Republicans. Kahnweiler sent paintings and drawings by Gris, Borès, and Manolo to Tristan Tzara, who headed a Committee for the Defense of Spanish Culture. They would be exhibited in Scandinavia. The art dealer turned over his 33 percent of the price of sales to the Fund to Help Republican Spain.[25]

Kahnweiler was extremely affected by the participation of his friends in the war. The art critic Carl Einstein's involvement was total, and not on a symbolic level. He threw himself headlong into battle, dropping articles in progress, abandoning contracts with delivery deadlines for several manuscripts and projects for his newly established publishing company. He simply left everything behind and went to Spain.

Headed by a legendary hero, a figure who symbolized the Spanish anarchist movement, the Durutti battalion, a column of 3,500 men, left the front in Aragon to join the battle for Madrid. The leader, Buenaventura Durutti, was the man who shouted rhythmically, "We are not afraid of ruins. . . . We are going to inherit the earth. . . . We carry the new world, here, in our hearts, and the new world is growing this very moment."[26] Carl Einstein was a member of his battalion, and Kahnweiler was overwhelmed by his letters from the front, stamped with an authenticity possessed by no other narrative of the war.

In Paris it was the time to prepare for the Great International Exhibition. The committee in charge of the event commissioned Fernand Léger to find an idea for it. He had been awarded the Legion of Honor medal a few months earlier, though he rarely wore it. Kahnweiler, on hearing the news, bitterly remarked that he was the only artist from the original rue Vignon group that had accepted the award.[27]

Léger came up with an old concept for the International Exhibition: paint the city in different colors. He had already discussed it when he was on leave from the front at a bistro in Montparnasse with Leon Trotsky, who was so carried away by the project that he envisioned a polychromatic Moscow.[28] Léger wanted to supervise three thousand unemployed workmen in painting the houses of central Paris: one street all blue, one green, one yellow, a tricolor Notre Dame, and at night this would be swept by spotlights from planes flying over the capital. Oddly enough, this project was not even considered . . .[29]

The Spanish Pavilion was preparing to create a project with Picasso. It was unthinkable that he would not react in his own way to the civil war, and that these tragic times were not recorded in his works. The *Peintures Sauvages* that Miró painted during this period expressed his reaction to events; and a young French painter in his thirties, Pierre Tal-Coat, was so completely shaken that his work was even more violent, as can be seen in his *Massacres*.

At the beginning of the war the Republican government commissioned Picasso to paint a mural for the pavilion. He made several sketches, having often said to Kahnweiler, "When I start [a painting] I have to have an idea but only a vague idea."[30]

On April 27 the German air force made his idea very specific. In support of the Nationalists they bombed the holy place of the Spanish Basque country. Guernica was annihilated. Two thousand dead. Picasso's painting, also called *Guernica*, was a cry of outrage against war. It did not exalt warriors; it wept for the victims. In the painting the bull is the symbol of the invincible spirit of the Spanish people. Kahnweiler considered this work Picasso's first contribution to the cause of peace.[31]

In July 1937, when the International Exhibition opened in Paris, the sculptor Paul Belmondo, traveling beyond the Rhine as part of a French-German cultural exchange, could see other works by Picasso in different circumstances—in the collections of anti-Nazis who had to hide them in their basements.[32]

In Munich there was the strange spectacle of two parallel exhibits: one, which had little success and drew almost no attendance, represented the new art of the Third Reich; the other, contrary to the organizers' intent, was not empty for a second. This was the exhibit of "degenerate art." The Nazi Ministry of Culture wanted to show these works for the edification of the masses, meaning to stigmatize Judeo-Bolshevik culture, represented by these works, and it drew upon the holdings of museums and galleries. The public was thrilled—not in four years had they seen gathered together the works of Ernst, Chagall, Beckmann, Kirchner, Dix, Klee, Kandinsky, and others. The show was scheduled to travel, and the duration of the exhibit at each stop was cut short, with guards posted at strategic points to urge the crowds to move along each time a group gathered in front of a work. The most popular was the section called "Insult to German Womanhood," where *La Belle Jardinière* by Max Ernst and other assorted nudes could be seen.[33]

In January 1938 business seemed to have picked up a little at the Galerie Simon, which exhibited the recent works of Klee. Among the visitors was a man who introduced himself to Kahnweiler as Louis Carré, who wanted to buy a number of paintings with prices ranging from 1,800 to 7,500 francs.

The son of a clockmaker and jeweler, Louis Carré was a lawyer by training, and had published two indispensable reference books on gold and silver collecting. He had just opened his own gallery on avenue de Messine in partnership with Roland Balay, under the name of Balay and Carré. Intuitive, methodical, thorough, compulsive about the arrangement of his gallery, he considered himself a publisher of artworks, rather than an art dealer, a term he considered vulgar.

Although his gallery had opened recently, he was not entirely a novice. Having left the bar to take up his father's business in Britanny, he had moved the store to rue du Faubourg-Saint-Honoré during the twenties, and still feeling restless, he had taken up African art, started attending auctions at Hôtel Drouot, and organized the sale of the André Breton–Paul Eluard collection of contemporary art.

Painting came as a revelation to him in 1933, after seeing an exhibition of Toulouse-Lautrec's works. He launched himself enthusiastically into modern art, and began to direct his attention toward the American market. He was a neighbor of Le Corbusier, who urged him to visit the Galerie Simon, where he immediately purchased certain works by Gris, seen by chance leaning against a wall, and some Klees on exhibit. He became a new member of this closed circle of dealers specializing in modern works.[34]

Daring was needed to start a venture into the modern-art market in 1938. The economy had improved, but the luxury trade was still precarious. Kahnweiler was optimistic, because he had a feeling, if not an innate conviction, that the artists he represented and their works in general were about to enjoy a triumphant success. They were noticed by the public, singled out, and put into a special category. In addition to Americans, the English and Scandinavians had started to buy them seriously, which was a positive development. For the last year a major breakthrough had occurred, due entirely to his strategy of keeping prices low. He felt that prices were about to rise, that it would happen soon, and that everything would turn out well, "except for complications of war."[35]

That was exactly when the war started. On March 12 German troops invaded Austria, and Hitler annexed it to Germany. The market shut down and the decrease in sales was considerable. Kahnweiler remained optimistic, giving a positive interpretation to every development, even the worst. "People who live at the foot of Vesuvius become used to it, and Europe seems to have become accustomed to living on the brink of a volcano."[36] Hitler was a fact, and one had to make the best of it until such time as he could be gotten rid of.

During this period the Nazis stripped Kahnweiler's fellow countryman Wilhelm Uhde of his German nationality for having published *From Bismarck to Picasso*. The idea of placing these two names next to each other on the cover of a book was sacrilegious, without even taking into account his defense of "degenerate art." It was by coincidence that the authorities promulgated a law authorizing the confiscation of degenerate art for the benefit of the Third Reich without any compensation—from museums or private collections open to the public. Kirchner committed suicide; 639 of his works were confiscated. This was a dramatic turn of events but not cause for despair. "These occurrences are really ugly but so many things have already been decided," Kahnweiler believed.[37]

He wanted to assuage his apprehensions, while the national museums of France were already crating and packing certain works to be placed in secure storage far from the capital. Even for the least alarmist of collectors, this was a sign that had to be taken into account.

* * *

The year 1938 saw Republican Spain cut into two sectors by the Nationalist offensive, and the fall of the Léon Blum government in France. Somehow Hitler had all the European ministers of foreign affairs in his pocket at the Munich Conference.

There was economic recession and moral depression as the fear of war and the fall of the stock market in the United States again reduced the art market to a trickle. Kahnweiler tried to explain to his artists that if their works did not sell it had nothing to do with the quality of their art. He could not make Masson understand that if the exhibition of his work in London was a failure, it was caused by the fact that the opening coincided with the German annexation of Austria by Hitler.[38]

Kahnweiler found it very difficult to make his artists understand the connection without offending them or being blunt about it. If they left the gallery they would eventually return, but he wanted to avoid the kind of confrontation that would make it impossible to turn back. Kahnweiler continued to pay his artists their monthly stipend as best he could, from 2,500 francs (Masson, Borès) to 1,000 francs (Kermadec) to maintain his involvement and keep the gallery active.

If the art market of the thirties was ruined by the depression, 1939 would prove even worse. It was an unbearable year: Barcelona was taken by Franco's forces, the German army marched into Bohemia, Madrid fell, Albania surrendered to the Italian army, Germany and Russia signed a nonaggression pact, and people speculated about the impending invasion of Poland by the Wehrmacht. It was not possible to see paintings under such circumstances. Even the Swiss art market failed. The only painting to be sold at the highly popular Borès exhibition in Bern was *Enfant au Clair de Lune,* which Hermann Rupf purchased out of friendship for Kahnweiler and to lend his support to the movement.[39] It was a futile gesture. If the only important sale that took place in this neutral country, which everyone believed was sheltered from the storms of Europe, was this single transaction, it was nothing to be proud of.

At the end of June a sale organized by Theodore Fischer was held in the Grand Hotel of Lucerne. It was an auction of some 125 pieces of modern painting and sculpture from German museums and private collections. The sale was held in disrepute because there was no doubt that the works had been pillaged and had escaped the flames in the courtyard of the central fire station in Berlin. Even the Nazis had understood that an international auction would profit the war machine more than a symbolic auto-da-fé and they had decided to sell off their "degenerate art" in neutral territory.

The auction raised a storm of protests, but only made Kahnweiler smile. Just fifteen years earlier the confiscation and sales of his stock of paintings, auctioned by the hundreds, had not aroused such an outcry. Several weeks before the opening of the first sale, there was threat of a boycott. There was no doubt in anyone's mind as to who would benefit from the proceeds of the sale. The auctioneer Fischer had to appeal to his European colleagues. He sent them a mailing denying and denouncing the rumors. He reassured everyone that proceeds from the sale would go to German museums and would enable them to buy other works. But few believed him.[40]*

That summer of 1939 affected Kahnweiler in a number of ways. One evening in June he was dining with Klee at a country inn not far from Bern. He already knew that the artist was afflicted with multiple sclerosis. Throughout Klee's good-humored conversation he had to take a drink with each mouthful to help him swallow without making a terrible grimace. Paul Klee was pale, emaciated, his eyes glazed and unrecognizable. Kahnweiler felt the proximity of death. The titles he gave his latest paintings were very somber and tragic. Now that the disease had reached his arm, he could no longer hold his beloved violin, nor paintbrush and pencil.

Kahnweiler concealed how upset he was. It was painful just to look at his friend. On his canvases the delicate fine lines had thickened, and yet his work gained in serenity and order. The subject was impending death. Klee was the hero who made a strength out of the fate that befell him; he was the artist who knew how to present the fundamental problem: "Art doesn't represent what is already visible, it makes things visible." Kahnweiler refused the categories in which so many critics and art historians wanted to place Klee—among the expressionists, the Bauhaus movement, the surrealists. Klee's work was completely different, something apart. His natural modesty of character, his distrust of the techniques of painting, his stance as the "honorable opposition" of cubism transformed him into the eternal romantic.

They bid each other farewell with great warmth, because Kahnweiler had to return to Paris. It was the last time they were to see one another.[42] On the train home Kahnweiler remembered the last paintings done by Gris, who revealed neither his physical pain nor his mental anguish when he warned "sickness hardens painting."[43]

During the six years Klee was ravaged by the disease, Europe was

* A good many of these paintings would eventually end up in the Art Institute of Detroit or the Museum of Modern Art in New York, donated by German refugees settled in those cities who originally purchased them in Lucerne.[41]

also stricken. Kahnweiler noticed these signs of the times. The Old World had turned another page. Two great men who were symbolic of the art world for him suddenly disappeared one after the other.

In London the genial Joseph Duveen, the consummate art dealer, had also disappeared, but he left behind a reputation greater than that of an art merchant. He had become a patron of the arts, donating paintings to the Tate Gallery and financing the museum's expansion. Besides, it was not simply under the name of Duveen that he was mourned on both banks of the Thames, but as Lord Duveen of Millbank, after the name of the thoroughfare dominated by the imposing facade of the Tate Gallery. (Duveen, the dealer in art that was the rarest, the most ancient and valuable, had built his success and credibility on the fame of Bernard Berenson, the most respected expert in the realm of Italian art. He had been Duveen's expert adviser for thirty years. In 1987 an investigation revealed that a contract had been drawn up in absolute secrecy between the two men, and that Berenson received 25 percent of the profit cleared from the sales of paintings whose authenticity he guaranteed.)[44]

The other great man who died was Ambroise Vollard. He was riding in his black Talbot convertible on the road to Pontchartrain one weekend in July when his chauffeur lost control of the vehicle. The steering wheel broke. The art dealer never reached his country house at Tremblay-sur-Mauldre. He was taken to the hospital in Versailles. "A lawyer, a lawyer," were his last words. Out of superstition he had not revised his last will and testament since 1911. He left a legacy of four thousand canvases to his family and to the Galéa Museum on condition that they would be sold off little by little, every ten years, and that a number of paintings would be donated to the city of Paris.[45]

Kahnweiler mourned his passing, which came seventeen years after Durand-Ruel. Gone were the two men about whom he always said, "They were my only mentors."

Inevitably, war broke out. The armored divisions of the Wehrmacht had invaded Poland. London and Paris had declared a state of emergency and were on the alert against Berlin. The British Expeditionary Force, numbering 150,000 men, landed in France a few days before the Russian army invaded Poland, which brought about its surrender and division between the Germans and the Soviets. France was in a state of mobilization, the National Assembly had approved the military budget, and the government outlawed the Communist Party and its organizations. In

September 1939 Daniel-Henry Kahnweiler was overwhelmed with anguish on reading the newspapers in his small back-room office on rue d'Astorg. He was in complete despair; this was the end. There was nothing he could believe in any longer. His pessimism matched that of Thomas Mann in his darkest moments. "I am too old to live through another war," Kahnweiler said. "I no longer have the will to live."[46]

Nevertheless, whatever the outcome of present events he had already taken precautions. Having been despoiled of all his possessions once was enough. He was not going to have history repeat itself. During the last days of August he had shipped some fifteen paintings by Juan Gris to his brother-in-law Elie Lascaux in the countryside near Limoges. He so wanted them in a safe place this time that he risked sending them via the postal service.

Kahnweiler was completely prepared to move, and had packed 154 paintings, a sealed case containing drawings, and 62 watercolors by Klee in a smaller container. His basement storerooms were far from empty, naturally. But he felt that he had halved his risk of being ruined. "It's a relief all the same to know that everything I own is not at the mercy of a single German plane," he said.

On September 20 he loaded a truck with his possessions, and with his family had headed for St. Léonard-de-Noblat in the area of Limoges. His plan was to wait there or leave for a distant country until the end of the war, sometime in the future. He chose to wait in peace, calmly. Five years of enforced idleness in Bern had left him with a bitter memory of exile, and that was enough. He truly believed that the Nazis would be defeated from within by a general uprising. A Nazi-dominated Europe was inconceivable to him. Passive resistance was not yet a familiar position, but the air-raid sirens did not send him to the basement scurrying for shelter. There was no question but that he "would prefer to die in [his] bed if possible."[47]

For now he only thought about how to survive. The Kahnweilers had a sum of money at their disposal, just enough for the family to live on and to support a few of his artists for a period of time, if the war did not last long.

He no longer ventured to make predictions, having been so mistaken in his judgment in 1914. He relied on radio broadcasts; he was constantly turning the dial on his set. He read and reread the editorials in the newspapers as if they would provide an answer to the problem. The people around him, whose political judgment he trusted, were of the opinion that the war would end in the autumn of 1940 at the latest.[48] Even from

Switzerland his friend Rupf echoed the general hope of his fellow country-men: "France will save civilization and put an end to this gangster, this adventurer called Hitler."[49]

Kahnweiler lived on hope. At times this hope was firmly grounded when it concerned his business. But he often wondered if he had not deceived himself, like all his artist friends, if he had not lulled himself with illusions. He refused to believe that if the extreme right came to power in France, they would adopt the same political and racial policies as the National Socialists in Germany. He was a man of the left, who believed in the Republic. He had faith in France, and it never occurred to him for a moment that the state and government, like men, could abuse people's confidence.

Kahnweiler tried to maintain his balance. Earlier, when the notion of a general mobilization was only a rumor, Salacrou and Picasso paid him a visit on rue d'Astorg and found him in his office. He seemed calm and self-possessed, but after discussing stories with them about people who had been arrested and interned in concentration camps, he said of the Nazis: "If these people succeed, I know that in perhaps two hundred years they will rediscover everything that we have loved. But as for me, I should just drop dead. I would prefer to die."[50]

Kahnweiler was on the edge of a breakdown. After the initial shock, he recovered slowly—was somewhat less nervous—but he suffered from insomnia. He devoted his sleepless nights to reading, writing, reflection. Kahnweiler was taking stock and using every moment allotted him. He wanted to become detached as if he were entering a period of meditation. He instinctively may have been preparing himself for a period of exile as long as the last one. He was jotting down notes for a book he wanted to write on "the evolution of painting from 1914 to 1939,"[51] and pondering certain fundamental issues: "Why did the great lesson of cubism not bear fruit? Why did the generation of painters born around 1900 admire the achievements of cubism without following it at all, nor even understanding it completely?"[52]

There were some people who resisted the war and others who were depressed by it. For Kahnweiler it was the source of an endless sorrow. He had been naturalized as a French citizen in 1936, but now he felt so powerless and helpless against the ideas of those who proclaimed themselves the new masters of Europe. Rarely had the values he held, which he considered the sacred values of mankind, been trampled down with such rage, such vehemence and violence; it left him speechless.

When he wrote to his brother Gustave in Cambridge, to Rupf in

Bern, or to his cousin Henry Wolf in London, he was forced by the censors to use French instead of German. Everyone he met nowadays and those he spoke to all seemed to be special cases, as if the war had made each person's situation an exceptional one.

Picasso, who could not decide whether to remain in Paris or return to work in Royan, was depressed, sour, sarcastic, and feeling demoralized. Masson was in the opposite mood when Kahnweiler visited him in Lyons-la-Forêt one Sunday. He was cheerful and only concerned with his paintings.[53] Hans Arp told the story of how he lived in a surrealistic atmosphere when he first arrived in London. He went there for the opening of an exhibition of his works, and everywhere he looked he saw how thoroughly his gallery had publicized the show. His name was everywhere. Then he suddenly understood that for the Englishman on the street who had to find shelter quickly when the air-raid sirens sounded, the letters ARP had the prosaic meaning, "Air Raid Protection."[54]

One morning Alice B. Toklas and Gertrude Stein were on the phone, urgently needing Kahnweiler's help. "Come over, right away!" They had made a lightning raid on their Paris apartment to take paintings back to Bilignin, where they would be safe. Kahnweiler went to rue Christine, where the women were living temporarily. He arrived just in time to find Alice in the hallway, stooping over the portrait of Madame Cézanne, one foot on the frame, trying desperately to remove the canvas. Kahnweiler, with less violent methods, used his expert hands to free the canvas. Out of their collection that was the only painting they wanted to take with them, along with the famous portrait of Gertrude by Picasso.

"You should also take these small Picassos," he suggested. "They take up little room and are easy to hide."

But they refused. Gertrude and Alice had faith. Events and fate would prove them right. Four years later, when they returned, they found every painting in place.[55]

In these times of trouble Kahnweiler was always ready to lend a helping hand. Friends and collectors knew that they could count on him, whether to find a shipper, an agent to get works of art through customs, or to locate an expert. Sometimes the calls for help were tragic. In November he went to great expense for the cause of Paul Westheim, who had become one of the editors of the *Paris Tageszeitung*, an anti-Nazi German-language daily. He was in France but held in a detention camp along with other refugees. He was one of the first people to be stripped of his German nationality by the Nazis. For thirty years he had supported French art in Germany and now he had to be saved, set free. Kahnweiler asked a number of artists and celebrities to write to the Sixth Bureau of the Ministry of the Interior to speed his liberation. That was the least that they could do for him, he who had so long struggled for their art beyond the Rhine.[56]

If only for this sort of effort he wanted to keep his gallery open at a time when his colleagues were seriously thinking of closing up shop because of the situation that had put them out of work. He now thought that it was important for them to maintain a high profile. It was not a practical idea, but he firmly believed in the morale value and its effects on people. His friends encouraged him to do so, especially those who now lived in the country and used the Galerie Simon as a meeting place. They were comforted just by being surrounded with paintings.[57]

Winter had set in and Kahnweiler could be found less often on rue d'Astorg. Despite the demands of administering the gallery and the endless problems brought to his attention, he attacked the necessary paperwork with cool efficiency. He closed the premises at five o'clock, as soon as it became dark. A few faithful clients passed by regularly: Alphonse Kann, André Lefèvre, and Roger Dutilleul. They bought a few Klees and some small things. Kahnweiler sometimes felt that they came simply to verify that their dealer was faithfully manning his post. But otherwise, the lights of the gallery attracted no one. Everything had ground to a halt. Even the Artists' Mutual Aid Union no longer existed, not only because of the dispersion of the people involved, but because for months now they had lost heart. What had been created to meet the needs of a period of crisis was not up to a time of war.

In a state of total uncertainty, Kahnweiler knew that there would be no business in the next few weeks, and beyond that he saw a complete blank. He even wondered if it would be possible to continue doing business with Scandinavia and the United States, which were his two last lifelines. The day these markets closed down would be the end of him.[58] At the same time he rushed to send shipments to New York lest he miss the last American boats leaving port. These were works sent on commission, which he considered so many bottles cast into the sea, but they were still better than nothing. Even this option was coming to an end; ships flying the American flag would certainly avoid French ports soon. He could not use companies of other nations because the war had caused insurance rates to rise 6 percent of the value of the merchandise being shipped.

More than ever the artists of his gallery were divided into two generations. There were "the old ones," comprising the generation of the "heroic" period of cubism, who came regularly to gossip with him and had free time on their hands. Their reputations made them attractive to American dealers. But "the young ones," artists born at the turn of the century, were shunted aside as too hard to sell. They could not even defend themselves, because many were still eligible for mobilization.

Despite the moral disintegration during the bleakest period of 1939, Kahnweiler still clung to a few things that gave him pleasure—the paintings of André Masson and the books of Michel Leiris.

The works of Masson had a strong and faithful following, including not only the gallery's old regulars but also new collectors such as the psychoanalyst Jacques Lacan, who was so enthusiastic about Masson's *Mythologie de la Nature* that he purchased the *Fil d'Ariane* as well.[59] Kahnweiler visited the artist regularly at Lyons-la-Forêt and did not hesitate to speak his mind to Masson. When he liked the work he would say so, and the same when he did not. On his return to Paris, he could not repress the urge to communicate his thoughts about the work he had seen. These "metaphysical" paintings were a necessary development of his work, but there was something lacking, an element he needed to integrate which would strengthen it. "You have put so much into them. As Goethe used to say about part two of *Faust:* 'How I have *hineingeheimnist* [stuffed mysteries into it]!' "

In other words, the viewer needed an explanation in order to grasp the work, which was not the case with *Le Labyrinthe*, in which he could enter naturally into the mythology. Having said this, Kahnweiler noted that this was not the last word, and a second viewing of the series of paintings might change his opinion.[60] But Masson knew him well enough to appreciate the worth of his criticisms, even if he might revise them later.

Michel Leiris was of the same mind, since Kahnweiler was his brother-in-law and had been his publisher. Overcoming many obstacles, Editions de la Galerie Simon had published his *Glossaire, j'y serre mes gloses*, illustrated with lithographs by André Masson. The poetic anthology was a veritable catalogue of terms that had lost their common usage or original meaning. Leiris virtually destroyed the vocabulary in current usage and, showing its meaninglessness, reconstituted it in his own fashion, which was that of a poet. By means of puns and other word games he dissected sentences as a surrealist, starting from this basic assumption: by a monstrous aberration mankind believes that language was created to facilitate mutual communication. Only Leiris's writings seemed able to lift Kahnweiler from his perpetual gloom. They were a celebration of wit for minds stupefied by war propaganda, the news, and the outpouring of clichés by those who monopolized public media.

During the year Leiris published another work with Gallimard, which Kahnweiler had enjoyed in manuscript: *L'Age d'Homme* (Manhood). By its power and authenticity it rose above the genre of autobiographical writing. Kahnweiler was even more profoundly affected by this book than he had been by Leiris's other writings, despite his deep distrust of psychoanalysis. He lost himself in the pages of "the age of manhood" to escape the age of iron to which the enemies of "degenerate art" wanted to reduce him and his friends.

The beginning of the year 1940 saw a cold spell settle over Paris, as people listened to the news of the fighting on the Russian-Finnish front, where it was infinitely colder. Kahnweiler and his wife no longer went out in the evenings or on weekends. On the rare exceptions when they did venture out, he regretted it; either the film was bad, or the play by Salacrou was disappointing, considering the success it enjoyed with the public. Kahnweiler seemed to have found his nirvana in Boulogne, at home seated across from Lucie on the sofa in the library with the drapes pulled, the windows shut, the shutters closed.[61] Their last refuge from the barbarism surrounding them and threatening to sweep over them at any moment was their passion for reading English novels—such as Dickens—to each other to forget the misery of the age. In between these novels they would return to the company of Manon Lescaut, young Werther, and Fabrice del Dongo. Kahnweiler called them the eternal heroes because these characters enabled the novel to survive as a genre, by becoming a part of their historical period; they had a life infinitely more intense than that of great men.[62]

In this seclusion he had created, Kahnweiler discovered a writer he had never even heard of and, like the English themselves, never read: Anthony Trollope. What attracted Kahnweiler was the author's mastery of English provincial life. Trollope had created an imaginary county inhabited by characters who represented their society, their world, and history through situations that were universal enough to transcend time. His works came as such a revelation that Kahnweiler even thought about writing an essay on Trollope.

Naturally he never did. Kahnweiler could not even jot down on a piece of paper his sundry thoughts and the facts concerning the development of painting in the last twenty years. He had started work only to encounter an old dilemma. "I am an art dealer, I know all the artists and I am the friend of a few, which makes it difficult for me to say what I think. If

I praise them, people think that I am promoting my gallery, and when I am critical I hurt my friends."[63] This would also be the beginning and the end of the memoirs he wanted to write. But at that time he was in no condition to write. When one lives day by day unconsciously waiting for news, it is possible to work, but not to think. Even his work, in 1940, seemed incongruous. The last thing people thought of was painting. Even art speculators were busy with other things. He could not be satisfied with the American market, and very quickly the Swedish market was becoming impossible.

His connection in Stockholm with dealer Gusta Olson made him believe that he could exhibit the young artists of rue d'Astorg in the face of the storm and against the tide. Kahnweiler did not even wonder if they would be well received or if they would sell, only whether they would ever reach their destination "safe and sound." Ever since the Swedish government had started placing limits on currency exchange, people no longer bought paintings. It was easy to understand that they had more urgent problems. Thousands of young people had volunteered to help the people of Finland after the Soviet invasion the year before, and now Sweden was being threatened with an attack from Germany. Olson, who believed the worst would happen, nevertheless continued to work on the exhibition with the same energy as his friend Kahnweiler a thousand miles away.[64]

Kahnweiler did not possess a keen political sense. In April, when Germany invaded Denmark and Norway, he still believed that Hitler would be defeated.[65] It was Rupf, who had only now grasped the dimensions of the drama being enacted at the front, who succeeded in making him understand. One by one he dispelled his illusions: No, there was no such thing as two Germanys, only one unanimously united behind the Führer. There was no silent opposition that was capable of a coup that would reverse the situation and bring back democracy.

Those hopes were extinguished long ago. Switzerland was filled with German refugees recently arrived. They talked about what they had witnessed and experienced. What they said was beyond anything one could imagine: the degree of repression, the detention camps, the persecution, the propaganda. "We are in the midst of barbarians," they said. "This is not the time to watch and wait."

Kahnweiler was numb. He no longer referred to "Hitler" but to "that raving maniac." Rupf's conclusions were of an even broader perspective. "When you consider that the Greeks created the first democracy in Athens two thousand five hundred years ago and that Germany is today living without a constitution, with no liberty . . ."[66]

Kahnweiler slowly adjusted to the painful idea that his Germany no longer existed.

He had never known the neighborhood around the Madeleine to be so bleak. Paul Rosenberg, who had opened a gallery in London two years earlier in association with J. Helft, had now permanently settled in New York. Uhde, having been burned once in the sequestration of his collection in 1914–1918, now prepared to move his collection to safety. In this he showed foresight: his apartment on rue de l'Université would be one of the very first to be looted by the Nazis when they entered Paris. Peggy Guggenheim also packed up her collection, but it was too large to move the paintings (by Gris, Magritte, Miró, Léger, Klee) and the sculptures (by Laurens, Henry Moore, Giacometti) by simply hiring a moving man. Léger had informed her that the administration of the Louvre would store them in a secure place somewhere in France. But at the last moment the museum decided not to give priority to modern art; this collection did not deserve to be saved. The Guggenheim collection finally was stored in the barn of a chateau near, of all places, Vichy, due solely to the efforts of her friend Maria Jolas.[67]

Although Kahnweiler remained at his observation post he also prepared a refuge for his family in the Limousin region. "I don't want to leave, if there's any chance of being able to remain in Paris," he wrote Picasso the same day that the battle of France started.[68]

Even if he was the only one, he had believed in Germany to the very end. Now he placed his faith in France up to the last moment. His persistence was therapeutic. His attitude was commercially self-defeating because of the cost of keeping the gallery open, and he was motivated solely by his sharp sense of duty and loyalty. His communications abroad had been cut off, and there was no way he could receive money from New York even if they had sold his paintings, as the United States government had frozen all French assets.

It was a strange atmosphere of things perceived and things known that were part of the mood of the times. The art historian Pierre Francastel was finishing a book denouncing the falsification of Nazi racist theories in painting. The publication of *History of Art as a Tool of German Propaganda* had to be deferred for several years "for reasons of circumstance."[69] Kahnweiler's friend Marie Cuttoli, a collector, brought him a Gris for expert appraisal. He had to believe that this crazy war had spurred even the most mediocre forger because this forgery of a collage had been completely painted in tempera, down to the famous paper with faux-bois pattern that Gris used in the original. In this area too, traditions were being lost.[70] Artists had all been conscripted into the Camouflage Department. High above, painter Charles Lapicque flew over France with the writer Antoine de Saint-Exupéry, studying the light and the intensity of blues and reds during his numerous night flights.[71] On the ground Fernand Léger was trying to apply pressure on his friend Huisman of the Ecole des Beaux-Arts administration, so that his crew working on camouflage would be recruited only from among good artists. "I know that you have your own opinion about this commission on camouflage. But don't forget that IMAGINATION is a quality possessed by the 'moderns' rather than those from [the Académie des Beaux-Arts on] rue Bonaparte."[72]

On May 10, 1940, the front was located along the river Meuse. The French lines were suddenly broken by the German blitzkrieg divisions. Kahnweiler canceled his visit to Masson at Lyons-la-Forêt and to Braque at Varengeville. "I don't think that it's the time to go driving on the roads," he wrote.[73] It was a mild euphemism, because he was afraid of leaving the gallery. It did not prevent him from advising every artist who visited to get as far away from the capital as possible: "A painter is not a businessman who has all his stock in one place and wants to stay in his shop."[74]

The French lines along the river Somme could not hold against the onslaught, and soon the lines along the river Aisne and the lower Seine were also breached, and Rouen fell. On June 11 the French government had fled to Tours and Paris was now an open city. It had never appeared so quiet. Kahnweiler suddenly felt serene because the calm was so wonderful. Neither he nor his family had suffered from the air raids. He had stayed in the basement. He felt smothered down there—even the least claustrophobic tolerated it poorly; they felt that they were stifling. However, they were among the living while aboveground things were horrible. Kahnweiler felt more fatalistic than ever and started using André Maurois's expression: "Each person in particular doesn't have more of a chance of being struck by a bomb than he has of winning the big prize in the lottery."[75]

Kahnweiler was terribly worried about Masson, who had notified him of the impending delivery of a batch of paintings—not one had shown up. As it turned out, they were safe in the most unlikely place. Masson had left Lyons-la-Forêt by train and after a hundred incidents was caught in Rouen during an air raid. When he arrived in Paris, fearing that he would not find a taxi there after midnight, he simply left his paintings in the baggage check of the Gare St. Lazare.[76]

In Paris on June 12 it was six o'clock in the morning when word came over the radio that the French army was in full retreat on all fronts. Now Kahnweiler felt the end had come. He had no gallery, because there was no country. The Kahnweilers prepared to flee Boulogne, having waited until the very last moment. Now they set out for the Limousin.

They had to find other ways than the general path of flight. If they took Highway 20 to Limoges, they would be trapped, Kahnweiler felt, by the flood of refugees. After two hours on the road they managed to reach la Croix-de-Berny, less than ten miles away, in the tide of ambulances and trucks and cars with mattresses on top and vehicles piled high with pathetic possessions. He fled a defeated France by making his way on small country roads, through Malesherbes, Sully, Bourges, Guéret, and finally to St. Léonard-de-Noblat in the Haute-Vienne department. A few miles beyond the village lay "Le Repaire," a former abbey, the home of the Lascaux.

Here night was falling, everything was quiet. There were not even any refugees sleeping by the side of the road, having run out of gasoline. The next day the Germans would march into Paris.

Kahnweiler needed a few days to recover. Marshal Pétain had sued for the terms of an armistice. Churchill announced to his people the terrible news from France, promising them blood, sweat, and tears. Kahnweiler was bewildered, and he tried to understand how the defeat had happened, what could have led to such a horrible undoing. Powerless to grasp a situation that was completely beyond his comprehension, he shared his doubts with his scattered friends.

"It is hard to imagine the future. . . ."[77]

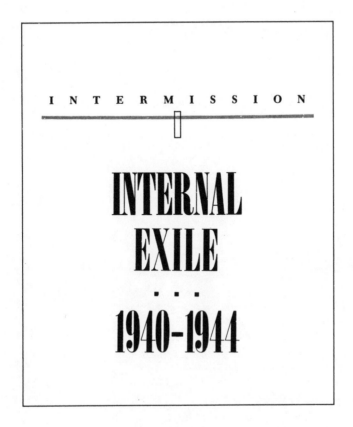

INTERMISSION

INTERNAL
EXILE
. . .
1940-1944

☐ "Paradise in the shadow of the crematoriums." This terrible phrase was often used by Kahnweiler to describe the four years he spent in the French countryside during the German occupation. It expressed the daily reality of the war for him. The Gestapo must have compiled a voluminous dossier on him: he was of Jewish origin, a draft dodger during World War I, no longer of German nationality, openly anti-Nazi, and a major promoter of "degenerate art." He somehow survived in spite of everything, and for four years he read, wrote, and thought in the invigorating fresh air, first of the province of Limousin and then the region of the Lot.

There was nothing like war to force one to recover one's health, as Kahnweiler needed to do. Le Repaire-l'Abbaye was close enough to St. Léonard-de-Noblat to replenish the stores with ease and fetch newspapers and groceries. As gasoline was difficult to obtain, Kahnweiler used his car only when absolutely necessary. Every day he walked the four-mile round-trip to the village to get the news about the outside world. He spent half the day away from home, cutting across fields and talking to the Miauletous (as the inhabitants of Léonard-de-Noblat were called), despite their indifference to world events.

The autumn weather was magnificent in this region, but the winters were harsh. He could not even warm up in the sun because the wind was so cold and biting. But he felt more at ease than in Boulogne-Billancourt, which had become sinister and deserted since the total destruction wreaked by the Allied bombing of 1942.

Often in the afternoon he would linger in the municipal library, absorbed in books that he would never have discovered in other circumstances, whether the subject was the origins of Christianity (in which he had a passionate interest), the foundations of Europe, the early days of the Limousin, and especially the medieval troubadours, particularly Bertran de Born, whose works he could slowly translate from their old dialect but which the young people in the library could not even understand.

The evenings were spent listening to the few existing programs on the radio. They seemed to be using a different language, one codified by the censors. The broadcasts from London so dear to him were not noted for their subtlety either. The airwaves had been adapted for the war, and information was a weapon of propaganda. Only music could not be tampered with, but the few concerts broadcast were difficult to receive without interference.

Kahnweiler had recourse to the Lascaux's library, which was well-furnished, diversified, and intelligent. But he was in a state of shock from recent events and could not at first make an effort to think, much less concentrate his attention for even one hour. Then he would often speak, and people would listen.

They could not re-create those Sunday afternoons in Boulogne, but there was something of the atmosphere. The great Gris was gone. Léger and Masson had become exiled to America, and Picasso and Braque had stayed in Paris to work. Klee had died on June 29. And Carl Einstein had also died, a fact Kahnweiler at first refused to believe. He started asking everyone he saw to confirm it, and heard that Einstein had said, in the spring of 1940, "If the Gestapo ever come after me, I'll drown myself."

That was exactly what happened in July. He was interned in a camp in southwest France near Gurs along with other foreign refugees. He had been set free during the German invasion, but he could not make the connection to find a boat sailing for the United States, and it was out of the question that this former volunteer in the Durutti column would find asylum in Franco's Spain. His despair made him slash his veins and plunge into the river Pau. Kahnweiler was in a state of grief. He would never forget Carl Einstein; they had been friends for over thirty years. He knew that others did not share his opinion, but he believed that Carl Einstein was one of the greatest writers in the German language and the most important art historian of his generation.[1] One day long after the war, on Carl Einstein's tomb in Boeil-Bezing in the Pyrénées Atlantique department, Kahnweiler would dedicate a plaque honoring the poet, the historian, and "the freedom fighter."

Le Repaire was probably the most intellectual spot in the Limousin. It had the highest concentration of writers, poets, and artists per square yard. Someone started calling it "The Sanctuary" and named Kahnweiler "The Sage."[2]

Raymond Queneau and his wife, Janine, Michel and Louise Leiris, the Lascaux, André Beaudin, Georges Limbour, Georges-Emmanuel Clancier, Suzanne Roger, Patrick Waldberg, Georges-Henri Rivière, Jacques Baron, and Frank Burty-Haviland, previously habitués of the cafés of Montmartre and Montparnasse, had become enthusiastic country folk. Some actually lived there, others were staying for a while, and some were only passing through. Even though he was only fifty-six years old at the beginning of the German occupation, Kahnweiler cut the figure of a patriarch with his peaceful demeanor and philosophic speech.

"The knowledge and subtlety of Kahnweiler's conversation made his listeners forget for a moment the anguish of the times," Clancier recalled.[3] "He seemed to have transported his whole world to that remote corner of the Haute-Vienne, his friends and even his paintings, since canvases by Gris, Picasso, and Masson transformed the former abbey into a strange and marvelous museum in the fields."[4]

During the day the small group was busy carving walking sticks. They combed the village for vestiges of Romanesque art, and took long walks on trails and through chestnut groves, all the while keeping up an endless flow of conversation. Queneau had developed a passion for palmistry, and Michel Leiris, who regularly had to make the round trip to Paris, brought news of the latest works by Simone de Beauvoir (*L'Invitée*), by Louis-René des Forêts (*Les Mendiants*), or Maurice Blanchot (*Aminadab*). Others discussed new manuscripts submitted to the Gallimard editorial committee, the literary life of the capital under enemy censorship, the art exhibits, and the latest developments on the Eastern Front.

Georges-Emmanuel Clancier, a local poet who was introduced to the group by Elie Lascaux and Raymond Queneau, discovered this whole world when he met Kahnweiler. He was struck by the fact that the anxiety surrounding all political discussions seemed to vanish when the circle gathered around Kahnweiler. Whether they were in the drawing room of the abbey, walking in the countryside, or at the inn of Monsieur Petitjean, whenever Kahnweiler spoke a sudden sense of peace would descend on the group. He spoke about recent events with a certain detachment and never even mentioned returning to Paris. It was as if he had settled in the country for a long stay.[5]

When he was not in conversation, he was writing. He was not prepared to start work on the book he wanted to write about Gris. Desire was not lacking, but his notes had been left behind in Paris, and without them he could not set down a single line about painting.[6] They were not necessary as a reference for his thinking on art, but he needed them as a stimulus.

At first, feeling so stunned by the death of Carl Einstein and such grief at the horrors of current events, Kahnweiler could write only about his reflections on life and death, religion and philosophy, and recent developments. He expressed his feelings with common sense and reserve in the dozens of long letters he exchanged with such friends as Marcel Moré, or the musicologist, conductor, and composer René Leibowitz. He wanted to have faith, to believe in transcendental values that expressed an ethical conscience as much as a rational and aesthetic one. He wrote to Marcel Moré, the most philosophical of the power brokers on the Paris stock exchange:

> It is in this union, it seems to me, which I experience before a work of art, that I can know what saints must experience in their union . . . with God.
>
> In contemplating a work of art we can momentarily escape the isolation to which we are condemned the rest of the time. We are united with humanity, with everything, with God.
>
> You can see that this concept is the opposite of my purely hedonistic idea of art, and how feeling tickled by jazz is not to be compared with this union. . . . Where we disagree is most apparent, unfortunately, in your idea of history. With all the goodwill in the world I cannot envision as a divine tragedy what appears to me to be a miserable comedy for which actual events are a sinister illustration. Your example, the fate of the people of Israel, only confirms this idea for me. I cannot believe that God would use as His instrument these paltry magic tricks by wretched fishermen to carry out His will.[7]

History appeared to him as an incoherent sequence of dangerous events that inevitably led to nothingness in the great beyond. Kahnweiler conceived of the world as made up of people at each other's throats in the name of human stupidity and viciousness. Above all he refused to accept the idea of progress in this constant turmoil, whether the progress of a Picasso over the paintings in the Lascaux caves, or the progress of Kant over Heraclitus. Humanity changed but did not necessarily improve. His mission, his duty, was henceforth defined very pragmatically: humanity had created a "treasury" composed of books, works of art, and other testimony, and he understood that he, Kahnweiler, must devote all his energy toward increasing that treasure. He knew that mankind had never been so close to the abyss, and the least little shock would engulf humanity as well as its "treasury."

The horror of war, which reached him as a dim echo, was for Kahnweiler the measure of all things. It made moral degradation of people and their urgent appeals for help relative. He received a plea from Antonin Artaud, his friend for twenty years, who wrote him from the asylum at Ville-Evrard, where he was incarcerated for insanity: "You understand the horrible war I wage against Evil from here in a state of agony from the daily and nightly mutilations inflicted on me by the Initiated. I hope it stops because I cannot go on. I have no doubt whatever that the moment you receive this letter, you will not hesitate a second to drop everything and follow me with your whole family and that you will come to see me right away as one does to visit a sick friend with whom one is going on a definitive voyage."[8]

These words froze the very blood in Kahnweiler's veins. It made him realize that he had to choose his words carefully. He could not speak about the "wholesale destruction of humanity" with someone like Antonin Artaud just as he could not speak of hell with someone such as Max Jacob. "Hell? But I have seen it! I have seen it!"

At Le Repaire life followed the course of the seasons, while in Paris the German occupation seemed, at least superficially, not to have changed anything, or very little. The artists who did not leave continued to work, and art dealers continued to exhibit them. These activities were not strictly supervised by the officials, and it even seemed that they were completely indifferent.

In the "Propaganda Office" at the German headquarters there were separate departments for literature, the theater, the press, and radio. Visual art was not important enough for them. Any exhibitions had to obtain the approval of the censors. The show's catalogue had to be submitted, and if the censor did not approve of the artist or of the work, he simply crossed out the name or the title. To prevent open conflict, people were careful not to support the so-called "degenerate art" denounced in *Mein Kampf.* Gallery directors were implicitly pressured to avoid at any cost, either in their choice of artists or of works, anything that was suspected of being Marxist, pacifist, Judeo-Bolshevik, expressionist, or abstract. This self-censorship appeared benign but dared not call itself by name. During the whole period of the occupation, cubist paintings by Picasso and Braque, as well as works by artists practicing an even more "subversive" form of art, were exhibited in the four corners of the city without publicity or official recrimination, even if one-man shows were not allowed. The most daring members of the art market were not afraid of the "Propaganda Office"; their real threat came from the collaborationist press, so eager to pounce on and denounce anyone who strayed.[9]

The two men representing both the Vichy government and the German authorities, who had free reign in this area, were not mean-spirited people. Louis Hautecoeur, appointed by Marshal Pétain to become the secretary general of the Beaux-Arts, was a moderate man. Whether from his office in Paris, on rue de Valois, or from the Hôtel Lucerne in Vichy, this former chief curator of the Luxembourg Museum issued a new policy, which was to respect the tradition of French art in keeping with the national revolution. As for Count Franz Wolff-Metternich, director of the agency for the protection of the arts created by the German military administration, he was more concerned with preventing the staff of other agencies from ruining the flower beds of the formal gardens. Jean Cassou said that this art historian, a specialist in medieval architecture, was "the perfect colleague and gentleman,"[10] which was high praise.

Everything would have gone well in this best of all possible situations if the German occupation force and its French satellites were not obsessed with the "dejudaicizing" of art galleries and collections.

Twenty years earlier Kahnweiler had been stripped of all his possessions because he was German. Now they wanted to take everything he had because he was Jewish. He still felt German in every particle of his being, although he was a Francophile. But he never felt Jewish; intellectually he was always more interested in Christianity than in the religion of his ancestors. Anti-Semitism was something that he had only experienced in slight ways in secondary school in Stuttgart or in the mutterings of art buyers at the Hôtel Drouot auctions, but he had never suffered directly from its effects. If for some people France was the country that shamefully dragged a Dreyfus through the mud, for Kahnweiler it was the country with the courage to rehabilitate the man.

He had only come across true hatred of the Jews in 1936, during the period of the Popular Front, when the pamphleteers of the extreme right, *Gringoire* and *l'Action Française* in the lead, were denouncing Léon Blum's cabinet as a red chamber, or a socialist Sanhedrin, and the deputy Xavier Vallat was lamenting to the Chamber of Deputies that this ancient land of the Gauls was henceforth to be governed, even if for the first time, by a bespectacled, Talmudic leader. A few days after Roger Salengro's suicide, Kahnweiler had confided to Max Jacob, "I had not known that I was Jewish. No one had told me, and the fact of being Jewish was of no importance to me because I don't believe in the theory of 'races.' Now I'm learning that I was wrong, that I am Jewish and that there are 'races.' It won't make a 'patriot' of me, and I don't have any inclination to become a martyr; I have every intention of returning blow for blow. The most effective way of doing that is to support those who think I am the same as they are—the parties of the left, the Popular Front—and to struggle alongside them against the common enemy, 'fascism,' to call it by its ordinary name."[11]

Four years later, fascism was victorious, and France was ruled by Germany. In October 1940 the Vichy government hurriedly passed laws which finally destroyed Kahnweiler's few remaining illusions, the supporter of the Republic blinded to everything by the values and laws inherited from the revolution of 1789. These laws defined the status of Jewish citizens, who were now excluded from society and banned from the government bodies of the state, the bar, and the legislature. Soon a Commissariat for Jewish Affairs was created to regulate the administration of this legalized racism. Camille Mauclair, who thought that Montmartre and Montparnasse needed a clean sweep of its denizens, had his wish fulfilled beyond his wildest hopes. Everything was ripe for pillage.

On June 30, 1940, five days after the full enforcement of the truce, Hitler ordered the seizure of art collections in France; those belonging to Jewish owners had priority. His decision was made after reading the report by his Minister of Foreign Relations, who substituted the term "transfer" for "expropriation." Officially it was motivated by the need to extract a guarantee from France during the negotiations for peace.[12]

Two weeks after that the German occupation administration in France issued a law forbidding the moving, changing, or transfer of ownership for any movable work of art without written authorization and forced collectors to declare all objets d'art with a value of over one hundred thousand francs. During this same period, the German ambassador Otto Betz, a former professor at the Beaux-Arts, submitted a detailed list of the names and addresses of fifteen Jewish art dealers whose property was to be searched immediately.

This complex politic of plundering is explained by two directives from Dr. Kummel, director-in-chief of German museums. One is dated September 18, 1940; the second, January 20, 1941. The French people it concerned, from the most obscure collector to the administration of the Beaux-Arts, would only learn of them after the war. Confidential documents of approximately a thousand pages, printed in an edition of only five copies, these texts were complete cultural charts of the occupation, and had been ordered by Joseph Goebbels, the Minister of Propaganda and Information. They presented the wholesale plunder of the French cultural heritage as a measure adopted to protect and conserve it; masterpieces at risk had to be transported to Germany for safekeeping. At this time France was still divided into two zones—the Free and the Occupied—and secrecy was necessary so that people such as Kahnweiler, who had found refuge in the free zone along with his collection, would not attempt to ship works overseas or across the Channel. To reunite the artistic holdings that the advances of the Wehrmacht through Europe had scattered to all corners of France, they had to respect the nationalist feelings of the Vichy government and those collaborators who were really more French than European no matter what they claimed.

These reports recommended three methods of investigation: the recovery of all works of art taken by the French after World War I, or that had changed hands as the result of any transaction; then the search for all or any works of art related in any way to the history of the Reich since the fifteenth century; then, the outright confiscation of property belonging to Jews and Freemasons.[13] The German military command insisted on the "legality" of any procedure. In the first two categories they sometimes used a system of compensation, exchange, or purchase, which appeared fine and in proper order even if the prices involved in these transactions were disproportionate to the real value of the objects in question. In the third category they would go so far as to confiscate Jewish collections in the name of "safeguarding property without any known owners." This was in fact the case, since these owners had first been imprisoned or deported.

In November 1940, in the Jeu de Paume, German soldiers were piling up crates of paintings brought there by trucks from all around the country. They were in high spirits as they worked in anticipation of the arrival of Hermann Goering, Field Commander of the Reich, head of the war economy, and an avid collector. They were hanging the paintings from collections they had looted so that he could make his choice. It was a private exhibition in the true sense of the word. It was on two floors, and would have looked like a Paris opening if it were not for the random nature of the works gathered there. The moderns were placed in a separate room at the end, so that the "degenerate art" could not contaminate the healthy art. These diseased works were used to make trades with art dealers in Germany, Holland, Hungary, and France for Italian paintings of the eighteenth century that the air marshal so dearly loved. Paul Rosenberg's gallery on rue La Boétie alone would "provide" him with some two hundred paintings.

Finally Goering arrived in civilian dress, a pachyderm covered with an overcoat that reached down almost to the ground, wearing a felt hat. In his right hand he held a walking stick that he used to point out details in a painting. In his left hand was a big cigar. Following him was Andreas Hofer, his art expert and curator of his collections, and then came officers in full uniform.

Goering was impressed and took his time examining each piece. There were so many works and not enough wall space. He would return two days later to continue his visit, happily playing the connoisseur discussing the comparative merits of this and that artist.[14] When asked about his taste he gleefully mentioned Cranach, and that he owned fifty-two of his works, then Corot, Delacroix, Ingres. The Führer, for whose collection he was also selecting works, had broader taste and did not hide his admiration for Derain.[15] Goering always asserted that modern art disgusted him, as did the impressionists. But an inventory reveals that all these protestations of principle were not borne out by the reality of the selection he made for his collection. There was *Lady in a Park* by Watteau; *The Little Girl with Shuttlecock* by Chardin; *The Little Girl with the Buddha* by Fragonard; but also *The Bathers* by Cézanne; *La Seine, The Woman with the Rose*, and *Reclining Nude* by Renoir; and, a glaring inconsistency, a horror for a man of his position, *La Place du Carrousel* by that Jew Pissarro![16]

"Aryanization" was another neologism, all the more horrible because it was put into effect during the occupation. It became a program of "dejudaicizing" all businesses whose owners were French Jews. At first the proprietors were removed and replaced with temporary administrators. During the second phase the Germans tried to replace the head of the business with someone who was a sympathizer in order to promulgate German interests within the firm.

In the neighborhood where the galleries were located, the policy of Aryanization was in full force. On rue La Boétie, the Paul Rosenberg Gallery was under the management of Octave Duchez. The Bernheim-Jeune Gallery was sold to a notorious anti-Semite who was none other than the office manager of Darquier de Pellepoix, the Commissioner of Jewish Affairs. He paid only two million francs for the business when experts had placed its value at fifteen million francs.[17] The stationery he used, due to the paper shortage, had the heading Bernheim-Jeune crossed out and replaced by the new name stamped in ink: "Saint-Honoré-Matignon."

In the Georges Wildenstein Gallery, one of the former employees, Roger Decquoy, was appointed the manager. He had been a well-known representative of many German collectors before the war (dealers, collectors, museums) and had to swear up and down before the Commissioner of Jewish Affairs that he had never been connected in any way with the former proprietor. The terms of the sale became difficult in this case when the government audit office declared that it could not evaluate even approximately the stock of the gallery. The sum of 9,654,455.65 francs listed as the gallery's capital was the only figure available for the purchase of the stock.[18] The basement storerooms of Wildenstein, the most dynamic art dealer in the business, were even better stocked than German experts had imagined.

Another dealer, Martin Fabiani, left France during the German invasion and found asylum in Portugal, the trunk of his car loaded with paintings. He spent several months in Nice before resurfacing in Paris and, at the request of a Jewish colleague, carried on business as usual at his gallery on avenue Matignon. When the owners returned after the liberation of France, he turned over the gallery to them.[19] Nevertheless Fabiani remained one of the art dealers with the greatest volume of sales in Paris during the occupation.

Louis Carré had to vacate his premises on avenue de Messine according to the terms of an old lease, and he could not gain access to his funds in the United States, where they had been blocked by a freeze on assets decreed by Franklin Roosevelt. He proposed to André Weil that he take over the gallery on avenue Matignon for the duration of the war, while Weil was in retreat in a village in the countryside. He would sell the existing stock for him and assume the cost of running the business according to terms clearly defined by contract. He was allowed to mount exhibitions of French paintings in the classical taste.[20] Carré, like Fabiani, was known as one of the art dealers who made a fortune during these difficult times after the war. Louis Carré explained that, on being demobilized in 1940, he was reluctant to go into exile. "I thought that I could be useful to certain artists. I probably would have gone abroad if I hadn't known that Picasso was remaining in France." During the occupation his exhibitions were very successful because censorship was fairly loose. He exhibited Maurice Denis, Dufy, Matisse, Maillol, Roussel, Rouault, Vuillard, Dominguez, but never Léger, who had fled to the United States. During this period he bought out the studio of Jacques Villon and placed him under contract. He would always remember 1942 as a wonderful year for business.

This points out the fact that after the crushing defeat many young French artists tried to come to terms. There were growing numbers of shows, and openings became well-attended social occasions. These shows were an indication of the mood of the times: they exalted the unspoiled face of France ("French Landscape from Corot to the Present" at the Charpentier Gallery); they celebrated peasant life (Galerie La Boétie); they introduced new artists in the French tradition, represented by twenty artists from Bazaine to Pierre Tal-Coat, including Lapicque, Edouard Pignon, and three young colts from the Kahnweiler stable: Borès, Beaudin, and Roger (the Braun Gallery); they exhibited paintings by German soldiers on leave (Bernheim-Jeune Gallery). At Jeanne Bucher's gallery works by Léger, Laurens, and even Miró and Ernst could still be seen, but the German authorities drew the line at Kandinsky and made Bucher remove his paintings and gouaches. The Galerie de France was inaugurated.

The "Otto Office"—the Gestapo economic department that monitored the black market—had a section specializing in the trafficking of works of art. Only later, after the war, did it become known that this activity was a cover-up for the counterespionage missions of the Abwehr, but it was a particularly lucrative cover-up since it provided liquid funds for immediate use. The German department in charge of the confiscation of collections drew up a list of seventy-nine names and addresses of the most important Jewish collectors; the Rothschilds had nine separate listings.[21] Paul Rosenberg was on the list but not his brother Léonce, who had not earned this recognition of success. Louis Carré had refused to accept his stock and agreed to take only paintings that were saleable. He seemed just to be waiting for the war to end.[22] A visitor to Paris found him sitting in his vast empty gallery, the collar of his coat turned up because there was no heat, reading Plato while awaiting his fate.[23]

André Simon hid from these racial laws by vanishing into the countryside of Britanny. The future of the Galerie Simon, as well as Kahnweiler, depended on preventing its Aryanization. Kahnweiler wanted to circumvent a second confiscation of his stock, and came to an agreement with his sister-in-law Louise Leiris: the only way to recover the gallery on the best terms was to have Louise buy it back. She was Catholic, French, and solvent, so there should have been no obstacles.

At the beginning of 1941 she appeared at the office of the Commissioner of Jewish Affairs to present her request as a purchaser. The transaction was almost concluded when an anonymous letter put everything in doubt again. "She is Kahnweiler's sister-in-law," could be deciphered from the jumble of letters cut out of newspapers and hastily glued on the page.

Louise Leiris did not let herself be discouraged, however. She returned to plead her cause before the Commissioner of Jewish Affairs. "Of course, it is true, I am Kahnweiler's sister-in-law. But as you can see, I am clearly Aryan and I have worked in that gallery since 1920, for over twenty-one years. Who better than I should buy the gallery?"[24]

Her statements were verified and her financial assets were checked. A private agreement was drawn up and registered on July 16, 1941, and approved ten days later. The Galerie Simon was capitalized to the sum of 240,000 francs, and Louise Leiris would buy the whole business, without the lease, for the sum of 73,460 francs.[25] The sequestration was lifted by the Commissioner of Jewish Affairs, but Kahnweiler, more cautious now, kept his paintings in the Limousin. Henceforth the gallery would be called Galerie Louise Leiris (it was the third and last change of name) and would be allowed to carry on more or less normally.

At the height of the war paintings again became a solid investment. The sudden increase in forgeries of modern paintings bore witness to this. The auctions at Hôtel Drouot were in full swing. Prices were stable: a cubist painting went for around 100,000 francs.[26] In November 1942, on the eve of the Allied landing in North Africa, a still life by Picasso was auctioned for 32,500 francs.[27]

Roger Dutilleul bought paintings by Borès, Kermadec, and nearly a million francs' worth of works by Picasso from the Galerie Louise Leiris. His nephew, Jean Masurel, whom he had introduced to modern art, purchased 17 Épices, an oil painting on silk by Klee. The Marquis de Momereu acquired a pair of Picasso paintings, L'Araignée de Mer and Les Soles, for the sum of 300,000 francs.[28]

The question remains—was art being sold to the Germans during the occupation? After the fact, most art dealers would claim that they had refused to have any dealings with them. Yet a number of German officers used to frequent artistic circles in civilian dress. Also, agents would buy for German clients, both dealers and collectors. This situation gave rise to a complex network of middlemen, some of whom were suspicious characters indeed. Thus a dealer could honestly claim never to have seen a German military presence in his gallery and not to know the ultimate destination of his paintings. In order to be able to refuse to sell paintings that might be wanted by a German client, as a precaution Louise Leiris went so far as to change the titles on the labels.

From the Limousin Kahnweiler stayed in constant contact with the gallery through the Leirises, whom he saw every day. They told him the news on their round-trip journeys between Le Repaire-l'Abbaye and rue d'Astorg. It was safer than letters, which were subject to random examination by the censors. It was important that he not lose touch with Paris. The ever-intense competition had become even stronger during this "reorganization" of the art market. The new dealers had financial backing and worked with a network of people acting as agents.

Picasso was like everyone else: he needed money regardless of his profound and long-standing friendship with the Leirises and the genuine respect he felt for Kahnweiler. Picasso was as productive during the occupation as he had been in the period between the wars, if not more so. "There was nothing else to do," he would explain. Just the fact that he was casting his sculptures in bronze at a time when the occupying forces were rounding up all bronze statues to melt them down for the war industry does not make Picasso a Resistance hero, as some people claim. Nor were his still lifes painted during these dark years a protest against the near famine condition of the civilian population any more than Jean Anouilh's *Antigone* was a call to resistance. In 1942, when some of Picasso's paintings came up for auction at Drouot, the event was announced and publicized in the collaborationist newspaper *Je suis partout*. Picasso illustrated special editions of literary works, opened his atelier for visits by Ernst Jünger and Gerhard Heller (German officers), and his work was exhibited everywhere in Paris with or without his knowledge. This artist who had painted *Guernica,* the supporter of the Spanish Republican forces, only concentrated on being able to work. [29]

An artist of his stature could not stop working. He would not have known what else to do; in fact, there was nothing else *to* do. The German occupying authorities in France wanted to make everyone believe that the arts, literature, and Parisian life had never known such a flowering as during this period under the jackboot, and they were not about to muffle an artist with Picasso's international standing.

Such a man, such an artist, Kahnweiler often said. In fact, none of the artists in whom he believed and continued to support had ever disappointed him. None succumbed to the temptations proffered by the hand of the barbarians. By contrast, those who had already betrayed their art, in his eyes, would betray it again. [30]

In 1941 the propaganda office had the idea of bringing French artists to tour Germany. They wanted to persuade the world that in spite of the war and the occupation of France, artistic cooperation (that euphemism for collaboration) was a reality on both sides of the Rhine. The French artists asked to join this group were told that they would only have to visit a few artists' studios in Berlin and Munich in exchange for the release of French artists who were held as prisoners in Germany. Five sculptors, Paul Belmondo and Charles Despiau among them, and seven painters, including Derain, Vlaminck, van Dongen, and Dunoyer de Segonzac, were persuaded to participate in this propaganda tour.

In the art world of Paris, feelings ran high: to exhibit work was one thing, but to go along blindly with the enemy's propaganda, when they are occupying your home ground, was inappropriate to say the least. Whatever these artists had hoped to accomplish by it, the situation was terribly unfortunate. But among the Resistance, the reaction was even more extreme. As a result of his joining this tour, Derain's name was placed on a list of collaborators to be executed or brought to trial on the day of liberation, a list that was communicated to and published by *Life* magazine.[31]

Kahnweiler was disgusted. What mattered most to him was the fact that three of the seven painters involved were the very first artists he had hung on the walls of his gallery in 1907. Certainly people changed in thirty-five years, but all the same . . . At St. Léonard-de-Noblat, where he bought the newspapers every day, he read even the collaborationist press, if only to remain informed about the thinking of his country's new masters. During this period the art critics, whose opinions dominated current taste, were even publishing books. Lucien Rebatet, of *Je suis partout*, published a book with the anti-Semitic title of *Les Tribes du Cinéma et du Théâtre* (The Tribes of the Cinema and the Theatre), followed by *Les décombres* (The Ruins), in which he gleefully buried the proponents of modern art. The *Paris-Soir* critic, Fritz René Vanderpyl, published *L'art sans patrie, un mensonge-le pinceau d'Israël* (Art without Nationality, a Lie: the Paintbrush of Israel). The critic of the prestigious review *l'Illustration* published Henri Bouchard's article on "The Life of the Artist in Present-Day Germany."

John Hemming Fry's book, *Decadent Art under Democratic and Communist Rule*,[32] was an indicator of the times. It condensed all the hatred and all the harbored grudges of those dark years. The author believed that he had discovered solid proof of America's aesthetic decadence in the Museum of Modern Art in New York and the crass intellectual levels of its founders. In England this corruption was demonstrated by the establishment's defense of Jacob Epstein's *Christ in Bondage*, commissioned by the authorities for Hyde Park. In France it was the worship of Cézanne by "neurotic charlatans," an expression that the author used to designate art dealers as well as collectors of the works of the "Master of Aix." He wrote that "the major cause of chaos in France is that the French spirit is being poisoned by an ideological miasma of Jewish origin."[33] He believed that only war and tyranny could stimulate art with happy results, to judge from earlier historical examples such as the Italian Renaissance, the war between Athens and Persia, and ancient Egyptian art. It should not come as a surprise that the book, which was originally scheduled for publication in June 1939, was stopped by French censors who insisted that the author make changes and at least suppress the conclusion. But finally it was published in its original form under German censorship.

Bookshops and newspaper stands were filled with ideas of this sort. It neither surprised nor offended Kahnweiler anymore. He had few illusions about a whole segment of the art world, both critics and artists. But what about the rest? What could he think of them when they blindly went on goodwill tours of Germany at the same time that a decree banned Jewish artists from receiving prizes and traveling scholarships; when the Petit Palais was exhibiting busts of Hitler; and a hundred thousand French workers were preparing to leave for Germany under unthinkable living conditions.

His indignation exploded at the beginning of the summer in 1942 when, with great fanfare, an exhibit of the sculptures of Arno Brecker opened at the Orangerie. In 1924, on his first trip to Paris, Brecker had visited Kahnweiler on rue d'Astorg in order to show his work. A few years later he exhibited his work in the Salon d'Automne with the help of Alfred Flechtheim, and in June 1940 he stood on the esplanade of the Trocadero surveying a deserted city, standing next to his Führer. The French artists who made the notorious trip to Germany attended the opening. The worst was in store. A few days after, Robert Brasillach gave a speech in praise of Brecker at the Théâtre des Arts Hébertot. And then there was a "Salute to Brecker" by Jean Cocteau that leapt from page one of the weekly *Comoedia:* "I salute you, Brecker. I salute you from the elevated realm of poetry, a realm that knows no national boundaries, except that each artist brings to it the treasures of his nation."[34]

Only days later Kahnweiler was horrified by another decree printed in all the newspapers: every person of Jewish origin was forced to wear a yellow star sewn over the chest of his clothing. It was a return to the Dark Ages. He thought that he had lost all illusions until he received through the mail the June 6, 1942, issue of *Comoedia*, which contained a new article by Vlaminck on the nefarious influence of cubism. Only this one attacked Picasso directly and placed the blame on him. The former fauve painter was showing his fangs and dragging his Spanish colleague through the mud, calling him impotent, a plagiarist, and holding him responsible for the decadence of French painting.

It was no longer disgusting; rather, it was sad. Eight years earlier, the letters Vlaminck had written Kahnweiler had made him fear the worst. And now the worst had occurred. Even after the armistice, how would people be able to forget this?

At Le Repaire, in 1942, Kahnweiler spent the days strolling and reading. In the evenings he was alone at his desk after having written a great deal. He had kept his correspondence—mystical and Christian with Marcel Moré, philosophical with Hermann Rupf, musicological with René Leibowitz—up to date. He wrote with a fine hand and packed his lines tightly, both on postcards and writing paper. Work on his own book had come to a halt; after writing two or three pages it all seemed idiotic to him. Without his papers and notes, he was afraid his memory would deceive him. He had run dry, desperately dry. It had been almost twenty years since he had taken up the pen to compose a work of such scope. Gris had died and cubism was already part of history. He did not feel that he could treat the subject lightly, in an illustrated booklet. Either he would do it thoroughly or not at all.[35]

He could have written on current events and his reactions to them, but these topics did not really interest him. He could have revealed the full membership of the current Salons that were such a valued part of Marshal Pétain's society. But twenty lines was ample for that. As for other subjects, the egotism and the futility of men's actions only made him feel more strongly than ever the pettiness of mankind, not in relation to God, but in relation to the universe.[36]

As Kahnweiler struggled with the book on Gris, he also began to outline a work on the origins of modern art, which he hoped would come more easily. His friend René Leibowitz followed his progress step by step through their correspondence. At first Kahnweiler addressed himself to the reasons for the so-called hermetic nature of modern art, and the division between official art and free art.[37] Kahnweiler wanted to show the unprecedented evolution of modern painting: its broad variety, its false obscurity, its eclecticism, its hypothetical decadence. His starting point was a precise definition of painting, of sculpture, and of architecture to show the need for this development. The true reasons for the gap between the "moderns" and the "academics" were not, from his point of view, the ones people generally believed. To claim that the "moderns" were ahead of their time was not to give an explanation but to make a value judgment. To discover the sources of this new concept of the world required reaching far back into history.

At this stage of his research he was frustrated by not having access to sources that would have given his ideas a more scientific basis. The local library was crammed with interesting books but contained nothing on art and only the most ancient books on the great civilizations, all dating from the library's founding around 1880. His first outline of the work on the origins of modern art took an autobiographical turn that he had wanted to avoid, having criticized many writers on art for being "discursive."

He set down his pen because he was not satisfied with what he was doing. He could not concentrate, and he felt that he was only repeating himself. During this same period, two historians destined to be among the most prominent figures of the French school of history were each writing a major work while deprived of notes, writing paper, and their valuable references. Marc Bloch, a resister, who was condemned to be executed by a German firing squad, defined while in hiding his ideas on his discipline in *Apologia for History or the Profession of Historian;* and from a prison camp in Mayence, then in Lübeck, Fernand Braudel devoted himself to *The Mediterranean and the Mediterranean World during the Reign of Philippe II.* But Kahnweiler was not a scholar. Since his exile in Bern twenty years before, he had not had a second to himself to think or to write. He had lost the habit.

Numerous false starts eventually brought him back to Gris. Racine used to say, "When I have made my outline, then my play is written." Kahnweiler had found the form and knew how to write the book. By linking his name with that of Gris, he was following in the wake of Baudelaire and Fénéon, of Delacroix and Seurat. If he achieved his goal, then people would speak of Kahnweiler's Gris for a long time. He differed from his predecessors in writing neither a monograph nor a biography but a hybrid work; he was writing his own memoirs through Gris's life, his experiences through the narrative of their friendship. The two lives were parallel chronologically, since Gris had arrived in Paris just before Kahnweiler, and his life as an artist was part of the twenty years Kahnweiler spent as an art dealer.

His plan was straightforward. There were three sections: the man; the work; the writings. Feeling quite able to discuss and analyze Gris's paintings without any notes, only with his past experience and his aesthetic sense, he began the manuscript in the middle. Then in the course of writing he turned to Gris the man, reserving for last the artist's writings, his letters and lectures.

Kahnweiler placed his whole being into the work. One can hear his voice distinctly on reading it. The book is in his words, using his expressions, his references, his cosmopolitan culture, his likes and his dislikes. It would be an exaggeration to say he had essentially written *The Autobiography of Juan Gris* in the manner of Gertrude Stein's *Alice B. Toklas*, but the work is as informative about the dealer as it is about the artist. Kahnweiler draws a parallel between cubism, which breaks with the conventions of perspective, and dodecaphonic music, which breaks with the scale, cubism being no more of an optical effect than atonal music is a matter of acoustics. Other parallels are established between the Empire style and the Bauhaus; the narrative elements of a painting and its composition; the lyrical poetry of Heine and *The Book of Painting* by Cennino Cennini; *Tristan* by Gottfried de Strasbourg and the idea of the sacred in the visual arts.

These pages were written in the sober, lucid style Kahnweiler used in *The Rise of Cubism* and other writings during World War I, but enriched by experience and the perspective of maturity. In twenty years of commercial activity and intellectual inactivity, his thinking had become set and narrow and had not evolved, but his writing was more dense and suggestive. The second section, devoted to the work of Gris, was the richest. Kahnweiler arrived at a clear definition of cubism. He presented it as the desire to portray objects in their permanent reality, whereas impressionism depicted the ephemeral reality. Kahnweiler defined "lasting" as that which is not merely a style of the times. The cubist painter presents the colored forms of the external world with a precise rendering of the volume and mass of the solids, not the space they occupy. He distrusted the effect of light in paintings. He recalled the mischief it wrought on some impressionist paintings, citing the shadow plays of Monet, who carried his easel on his back in pursuit of the changing light, playing hide-and-seek with clouds. For the cubist painter, light is only a means. For ever-changing daylight the cubist substitutes an invented light that is not ephemeral, and he replaces the appearance of form with the inherent qualities of an object. He replaces the aerial and linear perspective of the Renaissance with a closed and limited space, having a fixed shallow ground, which highlights the physicality of the object in question.

Some of these intuitions had been in his mind since the 1920s, and finally Kahnweiler expressed them. He was adamant about showing that, contrary to the widespread misconceptions generally held, neither Picasso nor Braque was directly influenced by African sculpture. If there is a strong resemblance between these two arts, their development was independent. Yet Kahnweiler granted that the study of African art was part of their background.

He also believed that cubism could only be analyzed and understood by taking into account parallel developments in the theater, literature, architecture, and music of the same period. There had been a general movement and it made no sense to separate one art form from the others in order to make it stylistically representative of the times. For Kahnweiler the basic premise of this development was discernible by the end of the nineteenth century when the discipline of traditional painting was eroded by the attacks of the impressionists, just as in music the tonal system had trouble resisting the assaults waged on it by Wagner, Richard Strauss, Mahler, and Debussy. Both art and music continued under attack until there appeared two geniuses, Pablo Picasso and Arnold Schönberg.

Kahnweiler quickly dropped his equanimity when it came to giving praise to those people who brought about decisive transformations in art, or when he discussed Cézanne, "The Great Architect of Color." He freely expressed his disdain for the Douanier Rousseau, who first composed painted surfaces, and for Gauguin, whom he held responsible for the false direction taken by impressionism and later also by fauvism. If Gauguin's influence had been limited to the school of Pont-Aven, to the nabis and Picasso's "Blue Period," it would have minimized the harm he did. But Kahnweiler found the natural extension and continuation of his work in abstract painting. His influence could still be felt everywhere: that was the reason Kahnweiler attacked him.

Kahnweiler did not need the notes and materials he had gathered to write this book. What he had to say about art he carried wholly within him—so much so that, after the war, when he published *Juan Gris, sa vie, son oeuvre, ses écrits* (translated into English in 1947 as *Juan Gris: His Life and Work*), one critic called it a catchall. Kahnweiler admitted that he had wanted to write down all he had to say about art, because he was not sure of surviving the war.

By 1943 France had lost the fiction of two zones, and it gave rise to curious incidents. Félix Fénéon, the anarchist of the Bernheim-Jeune Gallery, who had become bedridden during the last five years, still wanted to leave his art collection to Russia. But now it had become an obsession for him. Suddenly he came up against political obstacles from the Vichy administration.

At the Salon d'Automne there was a whole room dedicated to Braque, with twenty-six paintings and nine sculptures. Among the visitors were Ernst Jünger, a writer serving as an officer in the occupation army. He was so moved by the curved lines and the rich blues Braque used that he suddenly felt as if he were leaving the surrounding chaos behind. Taking out a little notebook he wrote in his diary: "I have the feeling that painters, like all artists, instinctively continue to create in the middle of catastrophe the way the ants in a half-wrecked anthill continue to work."[38]

Meanwhile life continued uneventfully at Le Repaire—long strolls and writing every day made the war seem a long way off. Then one morning, Michel Leiris rushed down from Paris to inform the Kahn-weilers: "All our friends are warning us that you will be arrested at any moment now. You must flee. We have found a refuge for you with friends in the Lot-and-Garonne. You must go there right now."

They agreed to do so, but after a moment's reflection exclaimed, "No, we won't leave! We are happy here, come what may."[39] They refused to change their minds although they knew very well that the country was being mercilessly given over to the German and French militia and collaborators, who were conducting round-ups of hostages and anti-Jewish raids.

Sitting in his apartment on quai des Grands-Augustins in Paris, where they had just moved, Michel Leiris was becoming very worried, and for good reason. He was more concerned about his brother-in-law than about his own safety. He had only been a registered member of the Communist Party for six months in 1926 when all the surrealists had joined in one block. He traveled in the literary and artistic circles of Paris, but that could not be the reason for the police to conduct an investigation of his background. "Leiris, isn't that a name changed from Levy?" they asked him before finally giving up.[40] If the French investigators had been less obsessed with finding out who was Jewish, half-Jewish, or quarter-Jewish, they might have discovered what Picasso and everyone else seemed to know—namely, that the Leirises were hiding in their home Laurent Casanova, who had collaborated with communist leader Maurice Thorez before the war. He had been imprisoned in 1940 and had escaped, living clandestinely in Paris since March 1942. It was Casanova, always precise with his information, who had told Leiris: "Your brother-in-law Kahnweiler had better vanish."[41]

Without a word to anyone, Leiris started looking for false passports.

Because of the laundry marks on his linen they chose the pseudonym of Daniel-Henry Kersaint. Another militant communist, Francis Cohen, managed to obtain false papers for them. When Leiris placed them in his hands, Kahnweiler took them with an air of resignation: "If it makes you feel any better."[42]

His proverbial optimism had disappeared. The Vichy government had placed the yellow star on him and had stripped him of the French nationality he had been granted by the Third Republic. He somehow still believed in his luck. Only a serious incident could have frightened him, and that is what now occurred.

At the end of August 1943 at Le Repaire-l'Abbaye, Jeannette Druy, a young woman hired by the Leirises to help with the housework, was reading under a tree one afternoon. Suddenly two strangers wearing dark blue suits stepped out of the shrubbery and, speaking with a strong accent—they could have been Alsatians drafted into the German army— asked, "Do you know where we can find Monsieur Kahnweiler?"

"He is not at home," she answered.

Without another word they left. When everyone returned from their afternoon outing she told them about the visit.

They were not alarmed because they were only civilians. But at four o'clock in the middle of the night there was a violent pounding at the front door. The men had returned, in uniform this time. It was the Gestapo. No one had heard or seen a thing because they had left their car, with headlights turned off, back on the road. The Leirises and Kahnweilers were immediately locked in the drawing room. They did not interrogate Kahnweiler; they asked only practical questions: "Is Monsieur Kahnweiler hiding any paintings? Any weapons?"

"No, there is nothing here."

They searched the whole house for over three hours. They even examined the well. Much later they would find out that an anonymous letter had been sent by the daughter of a neighboring farmer who was also a mistress of the head of the Limoges Gestapo, accusing Kahnweiler of hiding weapons for the Resistance. Naturally the Gestapo found cubist paintings, which they ignored, but they took cash and jewelry, including Kahnweiler's watch.

"You are lying to us!"

They were furious but their search had not been in vain; their pockets were full. There was no doubt that they would return soon.

This did frighten Kahnweiler. The letter, the brutality, the tension— it foretold the worst. He had been careful to place his prized paintings with a neighboring country squire. But even if the soldiers were not interested in the paintings they found, they could so easily have destroyed them in a fit of temper.

By dawn the Kahnweilers had packed their bags, and accompanied by Michel Leiris, they visited Dr. Barriere, the mayor of St. Léonard-de-Noblat. He had always behaved so well toward them. Now they wanted to show their gratitude by saying farewell and to inform him of the hour of their departure. Thus he knew how much time to allow before warning the authorities, which was his responsibility.

That evening the Kahnweilers went to Limoges to stay with a niece of Elie Lascaux. At four in the morning they stole out of town to catch the train, and after a brief stay in Agen they finally reached Lagupie, a hamlet between Marmande and la Réole in the Lot-and-Garonne department. They were welcomed with open arms by the Petits, a young couple of farmers, whom Michel Leiris had met when he had been demobilized in 1940. Then the Kahnweilers went on to Gascony, and life in the country-side continued as before.

Paris in 1944 was a city of two worlds. In the one, Kandinsky, Nicolas de Staël, and Magnelli were being shown at the Jeanne Bucher Gallery or on the walls of L'Esquisse, a small gallery near the Seine; and on quai des Grands-Augustins in the Leiris's new apartment, Picasso's one staging of his only play, *Desire Caught by the Tail,* was performed by Albert Camus, Jean-Paul Sartre, Dora Maar, Raymond Queneau, and Simone de Beauvoir, with an audience that included Braque, the photographer Brassaï, and Jacques Lacan.

In the other world, the periodical *Je suis partout* published Lucien Rebatet's denunciation of the scheming of artists belonging to the Resistance while his colleague Camille Mauclair published his book *The Crisis of Modern Art.* He was finally satisfied that the art market had been cleansed: there was not a Jewish person on the horizon, whether among dealers, artists, critics, and even collectors. He believed that this sanitizing should be pursued even further: "Then aesthetic debates could be carried on again with courtesy and knowledge among honest Frenchmen."[43]

Kandinsky, Maillol, and Piet Mondrian died during the year. But the two deaths that dealt a real blow to Kahnweiler were those of Robert Desnos, who was deported to the Terezin camp in Czechoslovakia, and, most of all, Max Jacob.

The news of Max Jacob's death, like that of Carl Einstein, left Kahnweiler speechless with grief. He died as he had lived, completely true to himself. In his monastery at St. Benoît-sur-Loire, he was the only one to sew a yellow star on his monk's robe. He wanted to be faithful to his Jewish origins, and to demonstrate his solidarity with the persecuted in a gesture that was Christian in spirit. His arrest in February and internment in the camp at Drancy roused an extreme concern among his friends. Jean Cocteau and a few others who had influence among the German cultural set tried every means to save him, but they were already too late; Max had fallen sick in Drancy from the conditions in the camp and died in the arms of Jewish detainees condemned to be deported.

On August 1, 1944, only two months after the Allied landing in Normandy, when Avranches had been liberated after heavy fighting and Soviet troops had reached the Vistula River, pedestrians witnessed a strange scene on the terrace of the Tuileries. The soldiers of the Wehrmacht were trying to pack their trucks with 148 crates on which were stenciled: Braque 24, Foujita 25, Picasso 64, Vlaminck 11, and so on through Manet, Dufy, and Cézanne. They were being transferred to the train station, but their destination was not Germany, where these "degenerates" were forbidden by law, but Czechoslovakia, where they would be stored in a château filled with other goods confiscated from occupied territories. They were destined to be sold as soon as possible to foreign dealers in exchange for goods needed for the Third Reich's war economy.

On August 2 five boxcars were officially sealed. The convoy was delayed because antique furniture was much more difficult to load and pack carefully, especially since these soldiers did not have the skills of professional movers during this time of defeat.

It was a veritable museum on wheels crammed into five cars. But for several weeks the workers belonging to the Rail Resistance did everything imaginable to delay its progress; from attacks to derailments, sabotage, strikes, and slow-downs. These works of art had to be prevented from leaving France at all cost. The train had to be delayed until a force from General Leclerc's army arrived to take charge of it. If the train left the country its precious contents would be destroyed by Allied bombing attacks. The commandoes arrived at last; ironically, their leader was named Rosenberg. In the train they had "liberated" there were numerous paintings stolen by the German occupying forces from the gallery of his father, Paul Rosenberg, then exiled in New York.[44]

In October 1944, after having spent four years in the countryside, the Kahnweilers decided to return to Paris instead of Boulogne. When the Leirises had moved to quai des Grands-Augustins they naturally were also thinking of their relatives and friends, and the two sisters and brothers-in-law continued living under the same roof after the war as they had before. Louise Leiris had recreated the Kahnweilers' bedroom with the same furniture and same paintings. For a while the Kahnweilers had considered being independent, but they gave up the idea. Lucie's health was visibly worsening. Kahnweiler knew that she had cancer, and he could not bear the thought of living without her.

On October 6 at the first Salon d'Automne of liberated France, Kahnweiler and Roger Dutilleul warmly embraced one another. Picasso witnessed this reunion. He was there for two reasons: he was also exhibiting seventy-four paintings. When some people wanted to eliminate a few that did not fit on the wall, Kahnweiler shrugged his shoulders, merely saying that they were not reducing the number of canvases of the artist, but of the communist hero of the Resistance. Picasso had officially announced his allegiance to the "party of the persecuted" which, in turn, quickly proclaimed him their hero, much to the artist's annoyance. It was true that during the war Picasso did not have an outstanding record for clandestine activities to help the Resistance. As Picasso never pretended to be a member of the Resistance, no one would have dreamed of reproaching him for anything that he did had the Communist Party not suddenly placed him high on a pedestal. Even before the war Picasso had a weakness for the worker's hat, and Man Ray said that his membership had been "a feather in the Party's cap."[45]

That was how the man who painted *Les Demoiselles d'Avignon* found himself heading the committee of the National Front for the Arts (painting, sculpture, engraving) with the task of drawing up a list for the arrest of those artists and critics who had served the enemy during the occupation. Even if those accused could defend themselves before their peers,[46] Kahnweiler was sorry to see Picasso taking this direction. Committees and political offices were not for artists, and especially not for someone of his genius. Kahnweiler felt that he had returned to Paris a few weeks too late to prevent Picasso's joining the Communist Party, and by the time he saw him, the decision had been made.

Picasso was now a political militant, even though the man had always been antagonistic toward any discipline or doctrine; his paintings were there to prove it. When he had something to say, he painted. He did not have to speak to the secretary general. Later the situation would reach the ultimate absurdity when Picasso was praised by the Communist Party, which had just officially endorsed a painting style antithetical to his own. Meanwhile, in the Soviet Union his canvases remained confined to museum basements.

Certainly Kahnweiler did not deny that Picasso was a man of the left. He recalled the conversation they had had right after he completed *Guernica*:

"I think that you are in complete sympathy with the communists," Kahnweiler had ventured.

"And who do you think came to the rescue of my country? The Russians!" the artist had replied.[47]

But to go from there to becoming the public hero of a party advocating the dictatorship of the proletariat was taking a big step.

Between the two wars, when Picasso lived on rue La Boétie and Kahnweiler was his neighbor on rue d'Astorg, they had met almost every day. They resumed that relationship now that Kahnweiler lived on quai des Grands-Augustins and Picasso had his studio on the nearby rue des Grands-Augustins. Kahnweiler acquired the habit of dropping by to see his friend, and they discussed the only topic that mattered to both of them: painting. It was always a meandering, random conversation, even though when Kahnweiler returned home he jotted down the main subject and tried to give it some continuity on paper. These were Talmudic conversations between two men, aged sixty and sixty-three, who spoke not to convince the other but for the friction of the exchange of ideas.

Among other things, they discussed those viewers who did not like the way Picasso painted faces, but loved his recent landscapes. Picasso had a ready explanation for this: "Of course it's the same situation as my nudes and my still lifes. But in looking at the faces they see that the nose is crooked while there is nothing that disturbs them about a bridge. But this 'crooked nose' was painted on purpose. Do you understand I did it in such a way that they are forced to see a nose? Later they will see or come to understand that it is not crooked. What I did not want was for those viewers to only see the 'lovely harmonies and exquisite colors.' "

These conversations between them continued right through all the celebrations when France, in the joy of liberation, almost forgot that the war was not over. Every day Kahnweiler at home rushed to jot down his notes for history whether it was his thoughts on the expressionistic aspect of Grunewald, or a comparison between a Raphael drawing and the firm lines in a Cranach.[48]

Outside the studio the reality was less inviting, as the whole country was going through a period of settling accounts. The purges of the darkest period of the war were followed by the purges of the liberation. At least those members of the Resistance who wanted to turn back the clock to build a healthy new state were doing it in a country free from foreign domination. Though the Resistance of certain regions, such as the Limousin so dear to Kahnweiler, did not behave well the day after the victory, this was nothing compared to the bloodletting, the shame and disgrace caused by the purges of the darkest years.

Kahnweiler found it slow and mild as retributions go. After all, to forbid showing the artists who thought it fine to become tourists in Germany was truly a lesser evil, with few consequences. The banned authors would soon enough republish all their works with the major publishing firms of Paris; the artists, too, would quickly resurface.[49]

In the neighborhood of the galleries quite a few exiles returned to take possession of their property and stock, or what remained of it, while waiting for the search committee to recover from Germany all the plundered works. Some dealers who had prospered greatly during the war could not hide the fact that they were worried. There were rumors flying in all directions. It was said that Martin Fabiani had just opened an exhibition of paintings by a certain Churchill, while the director of the Charpentier Gallery was refloating the treasury of the Communist Party.[50] It was true that both men had much to atone for. As for Louis Carré, his own spontaneous admissions before an investigatory committee resulted in a simple fine. But the committee for the confiscation of illicit profits would file away his dossier, finding after a close examination of his account books that there was "no evidence of collaboration with the enemy as concerned the sales of paintings."[51]

In point of fact the art world had more to fear from the years to come (the legal purges would last five years), because of confidential reports, which were all the more embarrassing as no one knew exactly what they contained.

The first one, called "The Rousseau Report," was drawn up by Theodore Rousseau, Jr., for the use of the American army and the OSS (precursor of the CIA). This investigation of the Paris art market and its relationship with the occupational forces would eventually be placed in the Goering archives at Stanford University. Rousseau concluded that nearly all art dealers sold work to the Germans, though never in a conspiratorial way or with a desire to collaborate. Only a minority of dealers had cooperated willingly, in a militant spirit, which corresponded with the overall pattern of the French under the occupation. Named among those who worked the most during the war were Martin Fabiani, Louis Carré, and Allen Loebl, a French Jew "protected from racial persecution by Goering himself."[52]

* * *

By 1945 the war had ended. A major portion of Bernard Koehler's collection was destroyed during the bombing of Berlin. Under the rubble thirty canvases by Klee were uncovered. Soon a shipment of some nine thousand paintings, confiscated according to the Potsdam agreement, would leave Germany for the United States.[53]

On rue d'Astorg Kahnweiler was back at his desk at the Galerie Louise Leiris. Business had picked up again. Kahnweiler was convinced as never before that the generation of painters who comprised the cubists were now the classics of modern art. In purely commercial terms, they should be considered as the impressionists had been twenty years earlier.[54]

Kahnweiler renewed his contacts with foreign dealers, Valentin in New York and Thannhauser in Germany. The latter had a surprise in store for him. After having offered to send Kahnweiler anything that he needed (books and drawings, for example), he received by return mail a list of a completely different sort (olive oil, sardines, corned beef).[55]

Feeling that he had been isolated for four years, Kahnweiler was eager to discover someone new. But he was generally disappointed by what he saw. Exhibits of the work of Edouard Pignon, Gischia, and others seemed to be "decorative neo-fauvism of poor quality." The opening of Sartre's play *No Exit* was successful, but *Le Malentendu* (The Misunderstanding) by Camus was less so. The press, ranging from *Action* and *Les Lettres Françaises* to *Carrefour,* had not entirely recovered.

To all his correspondents around the world who wanted to renew their relationship, Kahnweiler praised the courage of Louise Leiris. Without her the gallery would have been lost. He was unsparing in his admiration for her. However, this correspondence he maintained with such discipline for over forty years now took on a somber tone and finally became mournful. On May 14, 1945, Lucie Kahnweiler died of cancer after suffering horribly. Letters of condolence came from all quarters. Kahnweiler was in a state of profound grief; he seemed inconsolable. For forty years they had never left each other's side despite all misfortunes. He would never truly recover from her death. He even refused to return to St. Léonard-de-Noblat because it was so intensely associated with the three years when they were together there. For a long time he would go every Sunday to her tomb in Père Lachaise cemetery to think quietly. Their friend Gertrude Stein was buried very near her a year later.

Just before the summer of 1945, Kahnweiler's life was transformed by the end of the war and the terrible loss of his wife. At sixty-one years old, an age when others were planning their retirement, he was beginning again. He was an art dealer who had the privilege of becoming a recognized historical figure in his own lifetime.

PART

3

RECOGNITION

. . .

1945–1979

⬚

THE ACKNOWLEDGED MASTER

The short, bowlegged man with shaved head and protruding ears was engaged in a conversation while jingling the coins in his pocket. When asked about giving a special discount, he smiled and shook his head with the wry expression that means the same thing in all languages: no. Coming from a man of such principles, any token of generosity would be misinterpreted as a sign of weakness.

The conversation took place in one of the best restaurants in Paris. Kahnweiler ate the delicate dishes hurriedly. When his guest, who had lagged behind in the race to dessert, asked about his haste, the art dealer was taken aback at first and then, with a smile, recalled his youth.

"At the beginning of the century, when I opened my gallery, I worked alone and didn't close down for lunch. I had to take my meals, one franc for three courses and wine, as rapidly as possible. I have never been able to rid myself of this habit."

Paris, early summer 1949. Kahnweiler was entertaining Michael Hertz, a German visitor who would become one of the most important print dealers in his country. This was his first meeting with Kahnweiler.[1] At first Hertz had been disappointed by Kahnweiler's appearance, that of an average businessman. By the end of the conversation, however, he was convinced that Kahnweiler was a legendary character.

After four decades of experience in the art market, which had twice been interrupted by "events beyond our control," D. H. Kahnweiler now could finally live out the scope of his ambition. His success enabled him to own up to his faults; some people were so awed by him that they were ready to overlook his errors. He remained very much the same person he had been at the beginning of the century. But now his character was set; the sketch had taken on firm contours.

His qualities were easily defined. He was known for his loyalty, integrity, intuition, good judgment, independence, pride, keen intellect, and an extraordinarily diversified international culture. He was against any display of ostentation; he was logical in his thinking; he was stubborn; he hated waste and anything fashionable; he was meticulous about his person. Kahnweiler had high ideals for his profession and his mission in life, and he was defiant toward the state and art patrons.

His character flaws were of the same order. People used to say that he was inflexible, egotistical, puritanical, had no sense of humor, was extremely biased, dogmatic, elitist, and suspicious of the general public.

But a man should be understood rather than judged. If, as Malraux defined it, a biography is only a miserable little pile of secrets, some of these can be shown in a few anecdotes.

He had become rich, but his only luxuries were trips taken in the greatest comfort—the best hotels and restaurants.

He was subjected to numerous requests by curators, but he disliked giving paintings to museums because of his experiences during the sequestration of 1914–1918 and his horror at the plundering during 1940–1944. He felt that he had already given the state more than his share, and he had had no say about it.

Once when he was dining with the Rockefellers and the administrators of their foundation, he discreetly suggested to his colleague Maurice Jardot that he remove his wristwatch because with black tie he should be wearing a pocket watch. When Jardot pointed out that no one else at the table that he could see was wearing one, Kahnweiler dismissed them with, "That's because they don't know any better."

In 1946 he took *Les Cahiers d'Art* to court for reproducing works of Picasso without asking his permission and, naturally, without paying him a fee. *Les Cahiers d'Art* claimed in defense that the rights of reproducing the pictures had been given them verbally, free of charge, as a gesture of friendship by the artist himself. Kahnweiler brought out the contract Picasso had signed in 1912. He won. It was a matter of principle.

After World War II he had suddenly become a celebrity, a character. His artists were at last triumphant. He was to the world of modern art what Gide was to literature—"The Great Contemporary." It is true that fame begets fame. Right after the liberation the press announced that the existentialists were about to open a university in Paris for which large sums had already been raised. Jean-Paul Sartre was to be the dean and Maurice Merleau-Ponty, Simone de Beauvoir, Raymond Aron, and D. H. Kahnweiler were appointed professors.[2]

When the art review *l'Oeil* printed its first issue and needed a feature article for this historic occasion, the editor in chief, Georges Bernier, wrote a long profile of D. H. Kahnweiler under the title "The Time When the Cubists Were Young."[3]

When *Carrefour* published their survey of those who were "le tout Paris of the art world," they included Jean Dauberville-Berneim, David of Galerie Drouant-David, Raymond Nacenta (of Galerie Charpentier), Pierre Durand-Ruel, Louise Leiris, Denise René, Aimé Maeght, Gildo Caputo (Galerie de France), and featured Kahnweiler as the person "who was in an eminent if not preeminent position among his colleagues."[4]

Nevertheless, it was true that during the fifties he was atypical among dealers, a sort of dinosaur. *La Revue d'esthétique* published an "Essay on the Spontaneous Aesthetics of the Art Dealer," which contained nothing even remotely in accord with Kahnweiler's philosophy—on the contrary, it was a rather uncomplimentary picture.[5] But Kahnweiler paid no attention, and his rebuttal remained the same: when you have an idea you hang onto it. Whoever departs from this rule of conduct will inevitably be seen as following trends and being a dilettante, an amateur of no importance.

"The melancholic person cares little for other people's opinions, of what they consider good and true; he only trusts his own understanding. It's all the more difficult to convert him to other ways of thinking because his way takes on the character of a set of principles, and his constancy can degenerate into stubbornness. The changing fashion leaves him indifferent." These lines from Immanuel Kant were found in *Observations sur le sentiment du beau et du sublime* by Maurice Jardot, a man who worked with Kahnweiler for thirty years. Jardot believed that this quote defined Kahnweiler, except that he would replace the word "melancholic" with "serious."

Headstrong, dismissive, categorical—Kahnweiler was without question all these things. When Hôtel Drouot auctioned off the satirical drawings Gris had made for the press before he turned entirely to painting, Kahnweiler insisted on treating them with contempt, as works done for money, of no artistic interest. When Jean Paulhan published *Braque le patron* (Braque the boss) in 1946, Kahnweiler shared Picasso's rage. They dismissed this book as "literature" in its most pejorative sense, sub-Apollinaire, and based on such errors of chronology as stating that *Les Demoiselles d'Avignon* was painted two years after *La Route à l'Estaque*. "Braque the boss," indeed! Why not "Matisse, master of us all"! That gave them apoplexy, Picasso because of his sharp competitive spirit and Kahnweiler because of his personal convictions as well as his loyalty to the cubists.

When that same year dealer Aimé Maeght was preparing a major retrospective of surrealist painting, he asked for Kahnweiler's assistance. Kahnweiler turned him down because he did not want to lend his support to the term "surrealist painting," which was confusing, nor to a movement to which he strongly objected, despite his close relationship with such participants as Michel Leiris and André Masson.[6]

When he was asked along with Douglas Cooper to organize a cubist retrospective for the Venice Biennale, he featured the four great painters: Picasso, Braque, Gris, and Léger—but obstinately refused to include the works of "Metzinger and his consorts." He swore that any work of value made since 1920 derived historically from the cubists or else from Paul Klee, but certainly never from Gleizes or La Fresnaye.

Kahnweiler never gave advice; he handed down verdicts. He never expressed opinions; he made decisions. He knew how to listen to others, but in matters of art, the idea of compromise was completely alien to him.

"Thus Spake Kahnweiler." Michael Hertz saw the Zarathustra side of him. Kahnweiler did not excommunicate only the surrealists and abstract painters but also a certain type of work within a given artist's production. The works of Picasso's Blue and Rose periods were inferior in quality to those of his cubist period, Kahnweiler believed. In the course of their conversations, Hertz grew to understand that for Kahnweiler, expressing his opinion took precedence over everything.

"I was discussing the price of a major painting from 1938, *Le Labyrinthe* by André Masson," he recalled, "which I hoped to sell to a museum in the Rhineland. There was not another work of this quality of that date on the market. The price was right. When I agreed to take it, Kahnweiler said in a disturbing voice, 'You don't want to sell this Masson to a museum. It's a bad painting!' His determination to speak his mind was so strong that he didn't care if he sabotaged a sale from his own gallery, which is quite something for an art dealer."[7]

Kahnweiler was also opinionated about men who did not share his overwhelming passion for painting. Michael Hertz recalled the embarrassing failure of his effort to introduce Kahnweiler to C. G. Heise. It was at the opening of Documenta II, the exhibition of international modern art in Kassel, and these two men were the most renowned figures present. C. G. Heise had expressed a desire to meet Kahnweiler. Hertz, who knew both men well, volunteered to make the introduction. He was careful to refresh Kahnweiler's memory about C. G. Heise's life—he had been driven from his post as director of the museum at Lübeck by the Nazis. It did not matter. After a few seconds Kahnweiler turned his back on this man who had always refused to take any interest in cubism or Picasso.[8]

Marcel Duchamp considered himself and the viewer equal co-creators of a work. Kahnweiler did not go quite so far as to believe he was the cocreator of the works of his artists, but certainly he considered himself the principal witness of their creation. In this capacity he was being consulted more and more often, and he was much more casual and pragmatic than the official experts. When examining a questionable painting he became humble and proceeded very slowly. When he had a doubt, or when the authenticity seemed implausible, he would say that he was not competent to judge. Even when he was certain, he would make suggestions but never deliver a conclusive opinion as to authenticity. He harbored a profound distrust of "professionals" who, in some cases, were only self-proclaimed experts. Some of them were also art dealers, therefore *a priori* biased; their conflict of interest was unthinkable for a man such as Kahnweiler, who was so rigorously impartial that he postponed for a long time the publication of his writings.

Since the eighteenth century, expertise in attribution had been considered a specialty of the art dealer, while art appreciation and aesthetic discourse belonged to the gentleman, or the enlightened collector.[9] However, this traditional division between intellect and hands-on practical knowledge was being eroded due to certain rare individuals of the caliber of Kahnweiler, who were able to assume the dual role of dealer and critic. These were complete men of art, like well-rounded athletes able to compete in all Olympic events, or Renaissance artists with an equal mastery of painting, drawing, and sculpture.

Kahnweiler had a wonderful visual memory. When he saw a painting during his extensive travels that he believed was important, he made a mental photograph of it. He was a living catalogue. Rarely was a painting from the Alte Pinakothek in Munich or an extraordinary fresco in a small Florentine chapel mentioned in conversation that he could not describe precisely.

In 1959 Heinz Berggruen, an important dealer on rue de l'Université, felt that he had paid a million francs for a gouache by Léger (*The*

Typewriters) that might not have come from his hand, and he turned to Kahnweiler for help.[10] In a work by Léger Kahnweiler could immediately see whether the forms were too heavy or too flabby, badly composed or weakly rendered. But just as important was the signature, which, like a dedication, was often laboriously and painstakingly done.[11]

After Léger's death, Kahnweiler did not have the official right either to represent him or to assume the role of expert on his work, but his opinion counted heavily. One day, while visiting Drouot with Maurice Jardot to examine a gouache that had intrigued him in the catalogue, he found it suspect. When it was removed from the frame, he turned it around to examine the signature and the dedication. He did not recognize the handwriting, which made him all the more suspicious. Since he had not been brought in professionally, he kept his opinions to himself. But when the auctioneer asked him for his opinion, he answered that he did not like the gouache and that the Galerie Louise Leiris would not participate in the auction. The auctioneer took his opinion into account as that of an expert.[12] In a similar vein, when visiting a display of Picasso's works before an auction, he questioned the authenticity of number 22, *Le Journal*, a drawing the catalogue attributed to Picasso, and he wrote to the auctioneer, Alphonse Bellier, as well as to the expert adviser for the sale, Pacitti, just to warn them: "I have my doubts. . . ."[13] When his opinion was not a public declaration, he was more decisive in his pronouncements, especially when opposing the opinion of another expert. It was a matter of pride. For example, when his brother Gustave had just purchased a drawing by Picasso:

"I showed it to Christian Zervos," Gustave told him, "and he thinks it's a fake."

"Show me. No, it's real."

"Wonderful. But which one of you is right?"

"I am, of course," Kahnweiler answered icily.[14]

He wanted to be helpful, and was sometimes flattered to be asked for his advice if the request was within reasonable limits. One day he was asked to testify at a trial about a fake Picasso. He complied with Germanic punctiliousness and appeared early at the Palais de Justice. He had to wait for hours before being summoned before the court, and by then he had had enough. The painting was a wretched copy of horrible mediocrity even for an inexperienced collector, as Kahnweiler informed them in no uncertain terms. As it turned out, the painting was not really at issue, save as an example of the traffic in forgeries organized in Madrid by Léon Degrelle, the former Belgian fascist.[15] This was a political trial, quite removed from anything concerning Picasso.

Sometimes Kahnweiler was called upon to contradict the memory of his own artists, as was the case with Vlaminck. The artist judged as a forgery a painting an expert had authenticated as coming from his brush. In despair the expert asked Kahnweiler to intercede because the painting dated from the rue Vignon period. There was no doubt about it; Vlaminck had painted it even if it was during a time about which the artist's memory drew a blank.

"What's the meaning of this? What's the matter with you?" Kahnweiler asked him. Only then did the artist acknowledge the work.[16]

Sometimes Kahnweiler enjoyed provoking people, which always startled those around him who were accustomed to his taking art and artists seriously. In the middle of a public roundtable attended by critics, auctioneers, and artists who debated aesthetic concepts and scientific theories to combat the increasing problem of forgeries on the market, Kahnweiler caused a sensation by proclaiming with his usual good humor: "As for me, I have the solution. I photograph every painting that I buy before it leaves the artist's studio."[17]

When questions arose about the works of the Douanier Rousseau and people mentioned the names of some well-known experts, Kahnweiler announced, "I know of only one real expert on the works of Rousseau, and that is Picasso!" It was not a gratuitous joke: one day he had to ask Picasso to authenticate a painting by the Douanier Rousseau from a photograph sent by the Museum of Modern Art in Munich, which also had greater confidence in Picasso's eye than in an X-ray machine.[18]

Kahnweiler's expertise was most often solicited for important matters, controversies in which his opinion meant a considerable increase in the price of the work in question.[19] When the situation was obvious, the result of bad intentions, or when his own role as witness was put in doubt, he would drop all restraints and state his position. This happened in July 1954 during the Shchukine affair.

When the Russian museums lent thirty-seven paintings by Picasso for an exhibition at the Maison de la Pensée Française in Paris, Irène Shchukine de Keller, the daughter of the famous collector, living in Neuilly, wanted the sequestration of the paintings based on the fact that Sergei Shchukin had been dispossessed of his famous collection right after the Russian Revolution. Since the collection had been nationalized against his will, then let it be denationalized against the will of the Russian authorities! The judge in the case was embarrassed. It was a delicate problem. He had to clarify whether "the fact that paintings acquired by a foreign state over thirty years ago from one of its own citizens within its own territory according to a method of acquisition recognized by the legislature of that government and the aforementioned paintings now being exhibited to the public in France brings within our jurisdiction a conflicting claim upon them serious enough that the matter must be settled urgently."

The court refused to hear the case as it was not within its jurisdiction, but to avoid further problems the long-awaited show was canceled. Kahnweiler was indignant. There was no law concerning this case, nor should there be according to him. Establishing a precedent would be prejudicial, not just materially, but also psychologically. No one would ever dare to lend works of art to museums, exhibitions, or galleries in France. This claim was all the more outrageous as Shchukin's daughter had the effrontery to be greedy as well: she was laying claim to paintings her father never owned in his collection. Kahnweiler, who had up-to-date records, named them—*The Woman with the Guitar,* which he had sold to Gertrude Stein, and *The Young Girl with the Ball,* which he had sent to Ivan Morozov. In the course of an interview he asserted his principles:

"Since when," he asked, "does anyone contest a nation's right to its artistic and literary heritage? If we don't do the right thing and settle the question, all cultural exchanges will become impossible. The French, for example, could never send to Italy an exhibition of national treasures from their museums for fear of having them reclaimed on the pretext that Napoléon had carried them off to France."

He refused to consider this question as a political matter, or admit that it concerned the present government. Kahnweiler was all the more adamant about making his views known to the public. What he said would be decisive, because he was the art dealer who had had Shchukin's confidence, and he offered to give a press conference at the height of the debate.

"I am the person who sold these paintings to Sergei Shchukin," he said. "He made it clear to me that he intended to leave them to the Moscow museums in his will. The revolution only anticipated the realization of his wish."

"If he was so devoted to his country," a journalist asked, "then why didn't Monsieur Shchukin remain there himself?"

"No doubt because he feared for his own safety! Madame Irène Shchukine de Keller's claims are total fantasies. She is damaging cultural relations between countries."[20]

People listened. Kahnweiler's statements carried weight and the media featured him prominently because he was not only Shchukin's art dealer, he had had his own art collection confiscated by the state during the same period, though under entirely different circumstances.

He had become a legendary figure, and people were attentive to his opinions because he had begun publishing his writings after the liberation. Whether he dealt with aesthetics, cubist painting, or more specifically the position a given artist occupied in modern art, he seemed to have shelved once and for all his former compunction. He no longer used transparent pseudonyms, but now wrote under his own name.

Early in 1946 John Rewald, a young art historian from New York who was about to publish his *History of Impressionism,* and William Lieberman, secretary to Alfred Barr of the Museum of Modern Art, were proposing to translate Kahnweiler's *Der Weg zum Kubismus* (The Rise of Cubism). They considered it a major historical document and wanted to make it available to an American audience.[21]

After the war Kahnweiler's reemergence in the art world on a larger scale and his cosmopolitan background made him an international figure. He had never limited himself to working only within France, which he now found too small and narrow in spirit. In November 1945 he drew up an evaluation of the state of the arts in Paris for the London review *Horizon.* The article presented three ideas important to Kahnweiler. First he stated that there had been no observable new talent for the last five years, although he refrained from making any association between the decline in the arts and the political situation. Then he launched forth with a condemnation of abstract painters and other surface decorators. Finally, he refused even to consider, as the spirit of the times would seem to indicate, that New York had become the new Alexandria, the international art center supplanting Paris. He mentioned letters from those who felt exiled in New York and who could think of nothing but returning home. Kahnweiler was profoundly convinced that after the eclipse caused by the war and the situation right after the liberation, sooner or later Paris would once again become the artistic capital. He believed that foreign and French artists would eventually return there, and that the American adventure was only a passing episode. His faith in France had been greatly renewed as he had witnessed the nation's deep-rooted resistance over the four years of enemy occupation. Perhaps it would take a long time—ten, twenty, thirty years or more—but that was of no consequence. That was nothing in the life of a nation.

This article was soon followed by numerous others: "Should There Be a History of Taste?" (published in *Critique*); "On a Lecture by Paul Klee" (*Les Temps Modernes*); "Mallarmé and Painting" (*Les Lettres*); "African Art and Cubism" (*Présence Africaine*); "The Real Béarnais" (*Les Temps Modernes*); "The Subject of Picasso's Work" (*Verve*). In the article "The Rhetoric and Style in the Visual Arts of Today" (*Cahiers du Sud*), Kahnweiler defended the idea that the cubist repertory of style prepared the way for the development of contemporary painting, without in any way diminishing the standing of the work. "It would not be demeaning to Masaccio or Piero della Francesca to state that without Giotto their work would have been impossible." In "The Position of Georges Seurat" (*Critique*) he tried to demonstrate that this great artist died too young to have proven that he was as great as Cézanne. He did not have enough time to shed the techniques he had learned at the Ecole des Beaux-Arts and to produce enough work.

Most of these articles were collected in one volume in 1963 and published as *Confessions esthétiques*. Kahnweiler would continue writing articles, but his major work, which attempts to resolve the various elements of his aesthetics originating from his thinking during World War I, was *Juan Gris: His Life and Work*, published in 1946 and dedicated to the memory of his wife, Lucie.

Gaston Gallimard was his publisher for several reasons. Gallimard was to literature what Kahnweiler was to art, and the prestigious publishing firm employed numerous friends of the gallery, from Raymond Queneau to André Malraux. Gallimard and Kahnweiler had known one another since the 1920s when Gallimard purchased the rights to Max Jacob's book *Saint Matorel*.[22] On that occasion the publisher learned that Kahnweiler always read the fine print when he insisted that an omitted clause regarding translation rights be added to the contract. They were both shrewd businessmen.

On March 6, 1945, when the contract for *Juan Gris* was drawn up, Kahnweiler accepted the standard terms,[23] but he proved to be shrewder than Gallimard when it came to subsidiary rights. The negotiation between these two businessmen was the courteous encounter of the two sacred monsters of finance in the world of arts and letters.

The publication of *Juan Gris* was a major event. The book was serious, didactic, and painstakingly composed, with occasional lyrical or polemical passages; Kahnweiler's perspicacity was vividly expressed. The book enabled him to clarify certain basic premises, including such apparently simple questions as: What is an artist? What is great painting?

For him the artist was an individual who urgently needed to record his emotions. (Kahnweiler sometimes substituted for "emotion" the German equivalent "Erlebnis," which is closer to the idea of experience, the basis of all works of art.) By setting down his emotion on a surface plane, the artist created a visual image to communicate with his fellowman. Kahnweiler divided the creative act into several stages: internal emotion;

a mental image that is in flux and unformed; the urge to make it precise and concrete; the internal struggle of all real acts of creation; the materializing of an external image on the surface plane; and finally, the deciphering of the image. Art has the biological function of creating the world; painting communicates through a system of signs. If the viewer understands the work, it means that he has identified the meaning of the signs in the work. In this way Kahnweiler was in agreement with Masson, from whom he borrowed the idea that in a "great" painting the in-between spaces are charged with as much intensity as the figures that determine the composition.

The first time that a person saw avant-garde painting, he would understand nothing because previous experience had not prepared him for it. In short, he might as well have seen nothing. He would see only when he had reproduced or reconstituted within himself the image. It was an old idea Kahnweiler had been repeating for over thirty years and he would never stop reiterating: paintings only exist in the consciousness of the observer, in communicating with the artist and the emotion he wants to express.

Kahnweiler could even afford the luxury of recognizing his former errors. Unsparing toward his colleagues, whether critics or art historians, he agreed to correct himself on a matter of chronology. In 1920, in his theoretical writings, he had placed 1907 as a boundary of art history because of *Les Demoiselles d'Avignon*. Without detracting from the importance of that work in the history of the cubist revolution, he was now of the opinion that the real limit should be moved forward a few years to 1913. This would place it after "Analytic Cubism," in the period of "Synthetic Cubism." This transition between the two stages (and posterity would adopt his definition of these two concepts) marked the true break with the Renaissance tradition in painting and a return to the painting of the Middle Ages, but using other means for other ends. According to Kahnweiler, it was at that privileged moment in 1913, when the whole intellectual and artistic world was in ferment, that conceptual painting was born.

For the most part, the book was well received by the critics and the public. People hardly dared to object to Kahnweiler's explanation of Gris's work. He was too respected; he had too much authority and celebrity for people to be confident enough to contradict him. Even in private there were few criticisms. Only the sculptor Jacques Lipchitz, whom Gris had introduced to Kahnweiler on his return from exile in Bern, set down all his objections in a letter of twenty pages. He would not agree that the origins of cubist sculpture could be entirely ascribed to the cubist painters.

"As for me I don't pretend to have discovered cubism. I only claim to be one of the people who helped to develop it, to define it (I don't have any cubist portraits on my conscience! Supreme Heresy!) and I continue to build on it. I only want to show you how interconnected everything is and to show the dangerous nature of the ideas you have about the origins of cubist sculpture."[24]

In fact the artists concerned were better equipped than critics, both historically and psychologically, to question his assumptions. But it would take years before his aesthetics, his rejection of abstraction, and his chronological categories for the history of cubism were seriously contested. Only later with the rise of a new generation of art historians and the progress of serious research on modern art, would his position be challenged, the inconsistencies be shown up and errors in judgment pointed out: the unfinished appearance of *Les Demoiselles d'Avignon;* the idea that the cubists tried to be precise in their depiction of the position in space when they painted objects; and the rejection of decoration.[25]

At this period, however, D. H. Kahnweiler flourished, his reputation was at its zenith, his books and articles were translated abroad. Everywhere he went he carried the word of cubism triumphant. Invitations poured in—the art dealer/expert/historian had assumed yet another role, that of guest lecturer.

Traveling took up a considerable portion of his time, and the organizers of any event had a cheerful participant. He loved public speaking, recounting for the *n*th time the heroic epic of cubism, and defending his idea of painting before a large attentive audience. If the flattery became irksome at times, he was vain enough to tolerate it.

Kahnweiler's intellectual curiosity was insatiable and added zest to his traveling. His European culture and his knowledge of three languages enabled him to travel easily. At the beginning of the century, when he worked for his uncles in London, he would visit Paris every other weekend to attend exhibitions. In the same way, lecturing abroad served as a pretext to travel. A conscientious man who hated to waste time, he was never at ease with the freedom that came with vacations or tourism. It gave him an unpleasant sense of being aimless.

Art dealer Michael Hertz, who attended many of his lectures in Germany and Austria, had a vivid memory of those occasions. "The charm, the magic, and the sense of the setting with which he conjured up, as if for the very first time, the miserable little cast-iron stove with the pile of ashes in front of it in Picasso's studio on rue Ravignan, next to the enormous canvas of *Les Demoiselles d'Avignon . . .*"[26] Nor could Hertz forget the terribly "central European" aspect of Kahnweiler's character, a man for whom the fall of the monarchy on the Danube was the greatest tragedy of the century. One day while in Austria for a three-day visit and lectures in Vienna, they were at the reception desk of the Hotel Sacher to settle their accounts. The manager insisted that they consider themselves his guests. But Kahnweiler would not hear of it. The manager was equally insistent that such an eminent guest should not pay. Kahnweiler finally settled matters by thanking him for the rooms but paying for meals, telephone calls, and expenses. He whispered in Hertz's ear by way of explanation, "Austria is such a poor country, that's all we can accept."[27]

Kahnweiler's first trips after the war were in Europe, especially England and Holland, where he wanted to lecture and renew his gallery connections that dated back to the thirties. The museums in Holland were filled with beautiful works of the Flemish school, but where modern art was concerned the country seemed "sadly provincial." Judging from what was shown, there were two sorts of painters: pitiful academics, and followers of Mondrian, who wanted to be avant-garde and painted abstractly without any imagination.[28]

In Vienna he was received with every consideration. In addition to the traditional round of museum-exhibition-lecture, he had to preside at a dinner given by the French Institute, attend a Wagner and Mozart concert at the opera, and the next day dine with General Bethouart, the French High Commissioner in Austria. At a lecture on Picasso at the Albertina, one of the most important drawing and print collections in the world, he was overwhelmed when Professor Benesh introduced him not only as an art historian (which had become common) but as the embodiment of that line of art dealers who filled in the gap and assumed the role of patron of the arts of former times, vanished during the nineteenth century with the Industrial Revolution and economic development. This remark made him understand that his position in society had changed.[29] He was no longer just an art dealer.

In 1949 Kahnweiler traveled to the United States for the first time. He was invited on a lecture tour of art institutes in New York and Chicago, at Harvard and at Yale. Kahnweiler's visit made the front pages of the newspapers of the cities he visited. He impressed journalists with his enthusiasm and lucid analysis. They respected his courage in braving the Paris critics in the early years. Everywhere he went he became an ambassador of the avant-garde, the champion of his day, a man of quality, a gentleman with faith and conviction.[30]

His travels were overwhelming; he was the hero of the day. Through him "his" artists and "his" painting were being honored. Among all these peregrinations there was one which had a special significance, the one that took him, for the first time since the end of the war, back to Germany.

Since the liberation a number of Jewish intellectuals from central Europe, scattered throughout western Europe and the United States, rejected Germany and the Germans. Many who were German-speaking vowed never to speak or write in the language of Goethe, which was now, above all, that of Hitler. The pianist Arthur Rubinstein agreed to perform on the Dutch frontier in a concert hall rented by an audience of young Germans, but he refused absolutely to ever cross into Germany. "You have to show some respect for the dead," he explained. "In that country there were a lot of people who survived Nazism and who must have done *something* during the war." Gustave Kahnweiler would not return to their native city before obtaining his British citizenship in 1948, and only with His Majesty's passport in hand did he once again step on his native ground. American dealers of German origin had changed language in their correspondence: even personal letters were henceforth written only in English.

Kahnweiler did not share these feelings. He wanted to remain true to his origins: German by culture, European by choice, cosmopolitan by temperament. He refused to identify the new Germany rising from the rubble with its Nazi past. He rejected out of hand the idea of collective responsibility of the German people. Yet he was conscious of the problems this entailed. Michael Hertz recalled that when he visited him for the first time, in 1949, it was still necessary to first present a letter of introduction when a German wanted to contact someone of Jewish origin in Europe.[31] And even in 1964, when Kahnweiler had to give a lecture in Prague, he asked to speak in French even if few Czechs understood it, rather than in German, fearing that even the sound of the German language would be offensive in a country that had suffered so greatly at the hands of the Nazis.[32]

In 1947 he finally decided to make the journey in the company of the sociologist Raymond Aron, who had lectured at the University of Frankfurt in 1946, one of the few Jewish intellectuals from France to break the taboo by lecturing to an audience across the Rhine. Kahnweiler's decision sparked violent recriminations from his friend Douglas Cooper, the art historian who had been instrumental in bringing out the English edition of his book on Gris. He bitterly accused Kahnweiler of opportunism in his complacence toward a country and a people who invented and spread the

Nazi scourge throughout Europe. "You want to do business with them when the crematoriums have hardly grown cold."

Yet Kahnweiler was enthusiastic about the opportunity to return to his native country, which was provided by a young French inspector of historic monuments. Maurice Jardot had been appointed by the Beaux-Arts as a delegate to the military government for the region of Baden. He had been living in Freiburg for two years and wanted to introduce the new generation of Germans to modern art, have them discover the quality and diversity of French art, and attempt to compensate for the wrong done to their elders by the propaganda against "degenerate art." Jardot wanted to mount a major exhibition that would demonstrate the evolution of this work through the four major cubists along with Rouault, Matisse, and Chagall. He did not know any of these artists and needed Kahnweiler to locate the early works of Picasso and Braque. Kahnweiler decided to help the young man because he was impressed by the seriousness of the enterprise and its presentation. In October 1947 he gave two lectures in Germany, the first to the students at the University of Freiburg and the second among the paintings of the exhibition before a large and appreciative crowd.[33] There would be others, but this one was charged with symbolic meaning.

He had acquired a reputation as the dealer's dealer. Officially he was the technical director of the Galerie Louise Leiris, but everyone knew that he was the heart and soul of it. In addition, his principle of exclusivity now virtually transformed him into a wholesaler. Any gallery that wanted the works of Masson had to go through him. Léger was shared with Aimé Maeght's gallery. The same arrangement existed for Braque, whose prices were too high for exclusive representation. Then there was Picasso, who had returned to Kahnweiler. When a visitor, dealer, or collector paid the artist a studio visit and wanted to buy directly, Picasso would unfailingly repeat, "See Kahnweiler about that!" All transactions passed through his hands.

In the beginning, when he had started up again right after the war, things had been difficult because the Paris market was not enough to carry the gallery and exports remained mired in bureaucratic red tape. Even for the American market a million francs was a large amount for a Picasso measuring 14 by 11 inches.[34] Kahnweiler's immediate problem was not only how to sell, but also how to buy, not the second generation of artists such as Masson, but the "old timers" of the gallery, the Braques and the Picassos. These artists were now wealthy enough not to have to sell anything and were reluctant to do so. Taxes made it more difficult for him to persuade them as the tax people were very greedy when the artist sold and indifferent when the work stayed in the studio.

The situation improved rapidly in 1947. Kahnweiler had an exclusive on Picasso which was enough to keep any gallery busy, considering the extraordinary production of this artist; but he had also become the publisher of his lithographs, which were produced by the Mourlot workshop.[35] Michael Hertz, who specialized in the sale of Picasso's prints in Germany, claimed that at first museums, galleries, and private collectors from his country were the major buyers due to the traditional German passion for prints, and to the lack of interest shown by other markets—France was waiting to inherit them, England was asleep, and the United States, despite all the efforts made by Curt Valentin, was still untapped territory, judging by the remaining stock of Picasso prints discovered in Valentin's gallery after his death in 1954.[36]

Beginning in the fifties Kahnweiler started a ritual for paintings as well as prints on rue d'Astorg: with the arrival of an important shipment from an artist's studio, he would gather the major art dealers on a set day at the same time. The sale would proceed rapidly; given the competition, each person had only a few seconds in which to ask for the price and come to a decision.[37]

Kahnweiler sold to whomever he liked. However, he had preferences, whether friends or loyal colleagues or favored buyers. The sale might be a means of repayment, part of other business dealings, or simply for his own reasons. With him, people knew that the price was not negotiable. He hated haggling, and did not inflate a sum in order to then give a reduction. The price, which he established in agreement with Louise Leiris, was determined by the cost of purchase, the market value, his intuition and flair. In general, if he gave credit, the discount was forfeited, except for professionals. All dealers with galleries received a 20 percent discount; private dealers working out of their homes received less; and consultants even less. That was normal procedure. Each type of dealer had to bear the cost of different overheads. He saw no reason to treat someone who paid a lease and licensing fees the same as someone who did not. The old friends of the gallery who were not professionals also received a small discount, but it was done tacitly. In terms of power, he finally had the means to put into effect all his policies. There was no reason to deny himself.

In 1956, at the age of seventy-two, Kahnweiler, with over fifty years of professional experience, had not changed at all. He was true to his habit of closing the gallery between noon and 2:30 in order to return home for lunch unless he was expecting a notable visitor and had made reservations for a table at Lucas-Carton, not far away. He did not smoke, and remained as stubborn, dogmatic, and organized as ever. His priority in the morning remained, as it always had been, to answer his daily mail by return post.

Yet he was feeling his age. Though he remained mentally alert, his legs had difficulty carrying his weight and his hearing had weakened. He realized that he and Louise Leiris could no longer do all the work of the gallery. The volume of business was just too great. In ten years the paperwork had quadrupled due to the sales of Picasso lithographs. Right after they hired Jeanne Chenuet, they also took on a young woman from the country, Jeannette Druy, to help with the running of the gallery, the billing, and the labeling of works. They also needed help in the administration. Kahnweiler had to admit it after organizing the Gris exhibit at the Venice Biennale, which left him physically exhausted. The daily paperwork on rue d'Astorg had become unbearable, and he was pleased and relieved to have found someone ideal for him to work with.[38]

He had known Maurice Jardot ever since that famous exhibition in Freiburg in 1947. He had grown to appreciate his qualities and wanted to make him an assistant director, an equal in a triumvirate that would run the gallery. Everything that he knew about the man made him inclined to think that he had made the right choice.

Maurice Jardot, then forty-five years old, was from a small village in eastern France. He came from a background of peasants and shopkeepers, and as the son of the mayor of Evrette, his parents' ambition was to have him become an opthalmologist. He had a talent for drawing and took lessons in Belfort, later going to Paris to become a student at the National School of Decorative Arts in 1929. He received a degree in art history, then later took the examination to become a certified inspector of antique furniture and decorative objects. By the end of the war he wanted to discover German art, and he was commissioned to Germany for the "recovery" of stolen works. Stationed first in Karlsruhe and then in Freiburg, he was responsible for cultural affairs with the military delegation in Baden. When he returned to France in 1949 he was promoted to the commercial administration of the National Bureau of Historic Monuments.

As the commissioner in charge of the Picasso exhibit at the São Paulo Biennale, he worked closely with Kahnweiler, who was impressed by Jardot's organization of a major Picasso exhibition in 1955. Two years earlier, for the São Paulo exhibit, he had managed to get *Guernica* on loan; now the artist let him have the fifteen paintings he had just completed based on Delacroix's *Women of Algiers*, which would all be purchased by the American collector Victor Ganz.

Maurice Jardot was to become an important figure in the Galerie Louise Leiris. He was discreet, thorough, modest, hardworking, direct, and passionate about the works or the artists he liked. One evening in 1956 Kahnweiler invited him to dinner and suggested that he join the gallery, without mentioning a salary. It was that simple. He had made up his mind the previous year at the Picasso exhibit.

With Maurice Jardot's arrival in July another problem arose: the lack of space. There was not enough room to install another desk. The gallery on rue d'Astorg was no longer suited to the volume of business conducted there. Every time Kahnweiler wanted to show a painting it had to be brought up from the basement, which became risky when the subject was a bronze sculpture. Even the basement was inadequate. Some of Gris's works remained inaccessible because they had become blocked behind hundreds of others. Kahnweiler had often thought about moving elsewhere since the liberation, but he had not done anything about it.

On his way to the Nissim de Camondo Museum in the eighth arrondissement, Jardot saw a modern building under construction, right off the park, on the site of the former Rothschild mansion. On inquiring he learned that space on the premises could be purchased from the plans, and that the ground floor under construction was spacious, well-lighted with windows on the garden, and would perfectly suit their needs. Kahnweiler came to the same conclusion only after turning down a possible location on rue de l'Abbaye, which was unsuitable for two reasons: He did not want to have a gallery on the Left Bank and furthermore refused to have one fronting on the street. "I want people to come to see me, I don't want them to drop in because they were passing by," he told Jardot.

The inauguration of the new gallery in March 1957 was a great success, gauging by the number of people in attendance and the critical reaction. The guests were literally stirring up plaster dust because the building was still under construction. The date chosen for this event was loaded with symbolism. It commemorated the fiftieth anniversary of Kahnweiler's beginning as an art dealer; his first meeting with Picasso; the origins of cubism; and the seventy-fifth birthday of the painter of *Les Demoiselles d'Avignon*, which would occur a few months later.*

* As the greatest dealer of the century was celebrating the fiftieth year of his gallery, in New York, on Seventy-seventh Street, a businessman from Trieste, Leo Castelli, who would be considered the Kahnweiler of American art, was opening a gallery that would show Willem de Kooning, Jackson Pollock, Jasper Johns, Robert Rauschenberg, and others.

Of all the articles on the opening of the new premises on rue de Monceau, the most insightful was written by Alexander Watt, who asked Kahnweiler the big question: "If you were twenty-five today and your family gave you some money, what would you do?" The same thing, Kahnweiler answered. For him Paris was still the artistic capital it had always been. Abstract or not, his concept of his mission in life was the same: painters had to be supported, their work protected, their material problems settled. The dealer also had to be their friend. He could see that technically it would be more difficult now than before World War I. The worldwide expansion of the market, the development of a new kind of collector, the proliferation of new galleries, of artists and styles, and increased speculation in art had completely transformed the rules of the game.[39]

Other than that, nothing had changed. "People cannot change," he told Masson. "I love people more than paintings, and what I find most moving is observing that constant striving to be true to oneself, and realizing completely the potential of a personality."[40]

Instead of attending exhibitions, symposiums, listening to theories and criticism of contemporary art, Kahnweiler preferred driving through the countryside with Masson through the Gorges du Verdon in Provence and having the artist suddenly pull up on the side of the road and take a sketch pad and pencil from his pocket to draw a hawk in flight.

"I want to make a painting of these canyons as the hawk sees them," he muttered.

This spontaneous reaction by Masson was proof of the triumph of cubism for Kahnweiler. Everything had been turned upside down. For a twentieth-century artist to instinctively renounce the human perspective of the impressionists, a new system had to be invented. Between Monet working on several canvases in a field with haystacks, changing canvases every two hours and relying on a quasi-scientific understanding of light, and Masson trying to perceive as a bird in flight to express his feelings about the external world, it was necessary to overturn every established tenet of painting. Between these two artists there was a world: cubism.[41]

Nothing had changed, he said, yet his address book had become a cemetery of crossed-out names. Since the liberation Manolo (1945), Wilhelm Uhde (1947), and André Derain (1954) had died, as well as his dear friend Henri Laurens (1954). Disappointed that the Venice Biennale in 1950 did not award Laurens the Grand Prix in sculpture, Kahnweiler had participated in a banquet in Paris of 160 celebrities from the arts and friends and admirers of the artist to protest the offense. Matisse, recipient of the Grand Prix in painting, had generously shared it with Laurens. When it came time to make the toasts Kahnweiler had praised the modesty of the artist and his art, which was "great sculpture," that is to say sculpture where the spaces were as vital as the forms, a body of work that was coherent, complete, and sensual.[42]

Another person dear to him died, Curt Valentin, and it cast a pall over the summer of 1954. For years his New York associate had shown special care and consideration by sending him notes, catalogues, press clippings, and reviews. They had loved the same art, which would have been enough to seal a lifelong friendship. The funeral took place in the Italian town of Pietrasanta, and Kahnweiler had to deliver the eulogy. Speechless with emotion, he could not forget the extraordinary qualities of this man who was buried with a sculpture of Picasso, a bronze figurine he always carried with him.[43]

Kahnweiler also lost Fernand Léger (1955), who died at the age of seventy-four. Kahnweiler was completely unsettled, grieving for the death and resentful because the nation had not commissioned a major work by the time he died. Georges-Henri Rivière had wanted him to do his new museum, but he was too late.[44] He had just had the time to complete a mural for the dining room of Kahnweiler's country house.

Just before he died, Léger, feeling tired, had taken his wife's hand and said, "Don't listen to anyone else, and don't work with anyone other than Monsieur Kahnweiler. I have complete faith in him. He is the one who discovered me, who encouraged me, placed me under my first contract, saved me from starving. . . . It's thanks to Kahnweiler that I'm Fernand Léger."

After catching his breath he continued, "If you have any problems, don't go to a lawyer, ask Monsieur Kahnweiler's advice."[45]

Kahnweiler was shocked by the disappearance of this man whose art succeeded better than that of anyone else in placing itself squarely "at the juncture of the ethical and the aesthetic."[46] According to Kahnweiler, Fernand Léger should have been named alongside Braque and Picasso as a pioneer of cubism. Léger had been stimulated by their work, but always followed his own direction to arrive at different results. From their first meeting in 1910 until the end of his life, Kahnweiler had to fight against the accusation leveled at Léger more often than at anyone else, that of being "abstract." It was a commonplace cliché that critics would serve up again at regular intervals. His point of departure was always visual observation, even if it often disoriented the viewer by communicating structures and forms which no longer corresponded to the original visual perception. He depicted the external world in three dimensions, but his forms were simplified and massive. Whether the subject was the cylinder, the sphere, the cube, or any other basic shape, he only used light to heighten them to the detriment of the details of the subject.[47]

Of the four greats of the heroic period, there was still Braque. Kahnweiler continued to maintain friendly relations with him right up until his death in 1963, though they were never again on terms of such complete and open friendship as Kahnweiler had had with his favorite artists of rue Vignon, or rue d'Astorg, or rue de Monceau.

And there was Picasso, who had dominated his century and, since the beginning, the career of D. H. Kahnweiler.

KAHNWEILER AND PICASSO

☐ "Are you coming to charm me or to bother me?" Picasso asked over the phone when Kahnweiler announced that he was coming by the next day.[1] They had been together for over sixty-five years, with high and low points, interruptions and reconciliations, moments of intense anger and times of sincere friendship.

These two men were so different in origin, temperament, culture, and life-style. On certain points they were truly polar opposites. Yet on considering their relationship over the long term, it is evident that they never successfully made a clean break from one another despite the vicissitudes of the times and their immediate circumstances.

Even more extraordinary was that their relationship did not simply atrophy when Kahnweiler remained fixed down to the least little contradiction, while Picasso never stopped evolving, changing, adding new layers of contradictions to older ones.[2] Of the two, there is no question that the artist dominated his dealer. Picasso was fascinating, but he never became fascinated by anyone. He might be interested, amused, fond of, or seduced by someone, but never fascinated.

That had been the case when they first met at the Bateau-Lavoir, when their friends commented on the German's seriousness and the Andalusian's sense of humor. One wanted to take them to a concert while the other one was trying to get them to the Médrano Circus. The one treated everything concerning art very seriously while the other never hesitated to treat it as being of secondary importance. One day Picasso telephoned Kahnweiler to announce, "I bought Mount Sainte-Victoire!"

Kahnweiler wanted to know exactly which painting by Cézanne did he buy, incapable of understanding that he had bought the land itself: the Château de Vauvenargues at the base of the famous mountain, with all its lands, near Aix.[3]

Kahnweiler had always believed that a great artist, of necessity, was a great man. "Such a man, such an artist," was one of his favorite sayings. "Technical skills always fall short," he had said once, "if the man is petty and small. Picasso was a great man."[4] Now when he spoke of the artist he used and overused superlatives to the point of removing any credibility from his judgment. Even Picasso was embarrassed, as he confided to friends, by the excessive praise of Kahnweiler's lectures about him.

Yet Picasso was a complete artist, in the Renaissance manner. Drawing, painting, sculpture, engraving, ceramics—he endowed each medium with his creative genius, the same imagination and powers of invention that he put into his most celebrated paintings. Until the seventeenth century the artist was a complete artist, as Kahnweiler used to remind people. After Caravaggio, with few exceptions, the artist became only a painter. He devoted himself to the study of light for its own sake to the detriment of form. Sculptures were again made by painters in the nineteenth century with Daumier, Degas, Renoir. Picasso, following the fauves, renewed this tradition, but if he was primarily a painter he did not want to limit himself to working only on the surface plane.[5]

As he grew older he became a man who lived for his work, and in the last years of his life his work became more and more narrative. Kahnweiler never doubted that all of Picasso's art was essentially autobiographical. There remained the question of identifying the ring of truth in this perpetual confession. Kahnweiler believed that the key was in the direct quality of the narrative and Picasso's concern with the present. His awareness gave his painting a sense of spontaneity that is to be found in no other artist. He began with a vague idea and elaborated his subject as he worked on it, unless he completely changed his initial premise. He always knew how he would start but never how he would finish the work. This spontaneity explained the diversity of his work. It was not so much from a deliberate desire to create something new as from the freedom with which he followed the dictates of his genius.[6]

Picasso was the opposite of a theoretician; his art was the most human conceivable. He had never done anything but record his love in his paintings. His stormy emotional life was evident there in all its joys and torments. Those who saw only a colored surface and those who saw only a literal subject were equally mistaken. A painting came into existence only when the viewer collaborated with the artist and communicated with him in rediscovering the emotions.

It is surprising that Kahnweiler never wrote a book about Picasso, as he had for Gris. If Picasso was the painter he admired the most, Gris was the artist he loved the most. But that was not the whole explanation. Picasso was too large a subject for him. He would have gotten lost in it. This had happened to many qualified art historians, as can be seen by the immense international bibliography with Picasso as the subject.

Juan Gris was the artist who, in Kahnweiler's eyes, embodied in his work not only the development of cubism but also the Kahnweiler spirit. They shared a sense of classicism, discipline, and reserve. The work suited his aesthetic ideas perfectly. It was the ideal illustration. Even the artist's loyalty to Kahnweiler conformed to his ideal of the artist in relation to his dealer. The life and works of Picasso were not such a perfect match, nor did they permit such a perfect symbiotic relationship. Picasso went his own way part of the time. They often disagreed. They were less good partners than very good friends. Besides, not everything in the artist's work appealed to the dealer, so that had he ventured to write about him, he would have had to gloss over his reservations, his silence and even dislike of the "Blue Period" or the "Naturalist Period," that of the portrait of Olga, and the decade of the twenties, which he did not like as much as others. He compensated by increasing his praise of the Picasso he liked during his lectures and omitting altogether the bad aspects of his character: his egotism, the side of him that was hard, difficult, and unpredictable. There never would be a *Pablo Picasso: His Life and Work* by D. H. Kahnweiler. The artist felt bitter about that. It was in the same category as the idea that, all during the sixties, the record for the most expensive painting sold by the Galerie Louise Leiris was not held by Picasso, but by Léger for his *Adam and Eve*, sold for a million new francs (approximately $200,000) to a German dealer who wanted it for the Kunstsammlung Nordrhein-Westfalen of Düsseldorf. There were things that could not be overlooked, even by the artist who dominated his whole period.

For Picasso there were three Kahnweilers: the dealer, the ambassador, and the conversationalist. These were three functions Kahnweiler fulfilled completely and with special privilege. In the course of time their attitudes were quite set: one screamed, the other stopped his ears, and that was how they entertained one another. They had achieved that tacit understanding of two old troupers after years of doing their routine on the rounds of provincial stages. "This two-character play was their best collaborative creation," one of Picasso's biographers would claim.[7]

Each person played it his own way. Kahnweiler always complained that he did not have enough paintings and that Picasso made them too expensive for him to sell. He reproached him for giving away little things, or for selling directly to customers, which was in violation of the exclusivity clause in their contract. It was only a verbal agreement, it should be said, because after the contracts signed before World War I they were always content with a spoken understanding.

Picasso always complained that his art dealer was only a businessman. Since he had first come to Paris at the beginning of the century he was convinced that an art dealer was only concerned with swindling the artist he represented. He behaved toward Kahnweiler as he had done with his first dealer during his "Blue Period," his fellow countryman Pedro Mañach. He threw temper tantrums on principle. But basically they were in agreement about most things. They needed one another even if it was understood that Picasso would have no trouble finding another dealer while Kahnweiler would not be able to find another Picasso.

"Exploiter!" The word was thrown at him by the artist. Kahnweiler could not care less. True to habit, he let him speak and settled down to let the storm pass. His legendary patience was his defense but it was also his flaw. There was nothing he could do; he was one of the few who had witnessed Picasso's early poverty at the Bateau-Lavoir. It was folklore by now, but Picasso did not like to be reminded of it.

Françoise Gilot lived with Picasso between 1946 and 1953 and witnessed numerous scenes between these two men. She mentioned that Picasso always managed to impose his prices on everyone except for Kahnweiler, who always won in the end, obtaining the works at ridiculous prices.

"Oh, that Kahnweiler," he would sigh to her. "He's horrible. He's a friend, and I like him, but you'll see, he's going to get to me because he'll be after me night and day. I'll say no, and he'll bother me again the next day. I'll still say no, and he'll persist for a third day. Then I begin thinking, When is he ever going to leave me alone? What can I do to get rid of him? I can't stand the idea that he is going to pester me a fourth day. He will appear in front of me looking so sad, so tired that I'll finally say, 'I can't stand it any longer. I have to get rid of him.' In the end I will sell him all of my canvases just so that he'll go away."[8]

True, Kahnweiler was persistent. He would not budge until he got what he had come for. When Picasso was living in Paris, it all occurred without any problems. Kahnweiler would spend the day—and longer if necessary—in the studio. But when Picasso was living down south, Kahnweiler had to settle in. There was nothing Picasso could do against his immovability and persistence.[9]

Kahnweiler would stay calm. "Exploiter of the Bateau-Lavoir, me? No, no," he answered very simply, shaking his head. Without a fuss, or becoming acrimonious, knowing that he would never have the last word with a man like Picasso, Kahnweiler would let him win their artistic and aesthetic discussions to be sure that he would win the business discussions. After all, he was there to buy paintings.

That was also how he would answer to the reputation for being rapacious that Picasso had given him. "I don't bargain, I adjust the prices," he had tried to explain to Fernande Olivier, who had maligned him for being greedy in her memoirs about the heroic years.

"My possibilities were relative," he would explain, "because the collectors were few and far between. Had I paid more for the works, I wouldn't have been able to sell anything. From year to year, as Picasso's prices increased, I have always made it a rule to pay him more."[10]

To Picasso's mockery of this explanation of how he ran the gallery, Kahnweiler had to be more explicit. Hearing him rail against Yves Rouvre, a young artist the gallery had taken on, Kahnweiler replied in the following terms.

"You are quite right. I am playing with my dolly [that was Picasso's expression]. Now explain to me, if a dealer like me doesn't take on Rouvre, who will? You know as well as I do that for a young art dealer it would be very difficult to begin the way I started my gallery. As for Rouvre, who is going to provide a living for him? It's not me, it's you. With the profits from your paintings I am able to support the career of a young artist."[11]

Françoise Gilot believed that there was something of the toreador in Picasso's attitude toward people. In doing business, he was in the arena and never hesitated to use the red cape. For a dealer, the red cloth would be another art dealer. This strange attitude would make Kahnweiler really suffer in two separate incidents right after the war, before he became the master of the field.

Immediately following the liberation, when Picasso was much acclaimed, he had not yet given exclusive rights to his work to anyone. He used to sell to several dealers periodically, and two in particular, the

Galerie Louise Leiris and the Louis Carré gallery. It sometimes happened that Kahnweiler and Louis Carré were left waiting together in the hallway outside Picasso's studio. It was more than a test; Picasso always saw Carré first, leaving Kahnweiler alone to suffer. When the other dealer finally stepped out Kahnweiler kept an eye on him, trying to find the trace of a smile or a frown on his face to guess whether he had gotten what he was after. As Louis Carré was also a good actor he often played on Kahnweiler, especially if he did not succeed in buying the paintings he had wanted. Françoise Gilot claimed, "I've often seen Kahnweiler crestfallen at the sight. He had no control, it was stronger than he. It wasn't only a matter of professional jealousy. I believe that Kahnweiler felt possessive of Picasso and all of his work, more than the usual interest of an art dealer."[12]

This strategy put Kahnweiler through a trial he was not by nature able to endure. He was weakened by Lucie's absence, discouraged by Louis Carré's confidence and competitiveness, and disgusted by Picasso's cruelty, which bordered on being pure sadism. This was not the artist's intention, however: Picasso was simply hoping to weaken his defenses and make him increase his prices. But Kahnweiler refused to make this move until the market could bear it—especially the American market, which had lost some of its verve after Picasso's recent conversion to communism.

During this period the sale of works to Sam Kootz became the second major obstacle between Kahnweiler and Picasso. Between 1946 and the beginning of 1947 Louis Carré was having some difficulty selling his Picassos, so Kahnweiler decided to wait and maintain his paintings at a fair market price. That was when Kootz introduced himself to Picasso. He was everything that Kahnweiler found offensive in a dealer: he smoked a big cigar, had pockets full of dollars, and had the speech and mannerisms of a New York businessman. To make matters worse, he sold abstract art. Exactly what transactions took place when he and Picasso were closeted in the studio on rue des Grands-Augustins no one would ever know, but the visible result was that Kootz purchased several paintings directly from Picasso, bypassing all middlemen. This sickened Louis Carré as much as it did Kahnweiler. It was not the first time. But now there was an agreement that Picasso would refer all buyers automatically to the galleries of Carré and Kahnweiler.

Kootz had succeeded by sheer audacity. One day he drove up in an Oldsmobile, and in exchange for the car keys he took a large still life. Kahnweiler was floored by this procedure and could not grasp the fact that Picasso had consented. Kootz had to be Machiavellian to have gotten the upper hand. However, the rumor from New York was that he hung

Picassos in his gallery to attract new buyers so that he could sell them the works of his American abstract artists. Picasso could not be happier with the deal and used the situation to raise his prices.

Kahnweiler insisted on an explanation, and he got it in a succinct sentence.

"Now I have found a dealer who can pay my prices," Picasso said.

"Perfect. Maybe he can afford it, but I cannot."[13]

The issue was closed. Kahnweiler would continue to handle Picasso's lithographs. After a period of feeling discouraged, sad, and bitter, he decided to confront the artist once and for all. He returned to rue des Grands-Augustins. He did not even bother to ask for an explanation, but let his anger explode as he had never done before.

He shouted, "Have you gone crazy?"[14]

The artist was dumbstruck. Kahnweiler himself did not know why he had done it. It was his mood. He could not help it.

Kahnweiler felt that he had made his point. In the forty years that they had known each other it was the first time Kahnweiler had thrown such a fit, and it was worth it. But that was not the end of it. In 1947 Kahnweiler received word from his New York associate Curt Valentin that Kootz's New York exhibit of Picasso had been very successful. He had sold seven of the nine paintings shown, and was preparing to make another trip to Paris to buy more paintings from Picasso.[15]

Forewarned, Kahnweiler tried to head him off. He went straight to rue des Grands-Augustins and had a stormy argument with Picasso, who did not hide his intention of selling to Kootz. This time Kahnweiler would not let him get away with it, and insisted on his rights. Picasso reassured him that he would sell his work to the American only at prices that would be higher than the retail prices in a gallery, but Kahnweiler would not settle for this. It was a matter of principle, and he was not about to change his mind. The painter then pretended to be naive: "I don't see why I can't sell to Kootz."

"It's not advisable," Kahnweiler explained, "to sell to a man who is capable of selling cheap, if he should be in need of cash in the future. And in addition you are remiss on your agreement to your two long-term dealers."

Still, when he next visited the artist, there was the American dealer in the waiting room. Even if Picasso did make Kootz wait for two hours, Kahnweiler was not amused by this foolish behavior. Picasso apologized, admitted that he felt guilty, but continued to sell paintings to Kootz. This time Kahnweiler was truly disgusted by his behavior and let him know it in no uncertain terms.

Picasso finally stopped this little game when he grew tired of it. It was a cruel, capricious test but Kahnweiler came through with the exclusive rights to all Picasso's works.

Under the circumstances, it is easy to understand why a journalist discussing Kahnweiler's relationship with Picasso asked if he had been put through hell and high water. But Kahnweiler always judged human relations from a long-term perspective and preferred to overlook the negative incidents along the way.

"He was absolutely loyal. We have been separated in the course of life by wars, etc. But there's one thing I must emphasize: if all of Picasso's works pass through my hands as his dealer, and he sells to no one else, either collector or dealer, it is evidently an example of his great trust and loyalty. In the end, he does not need me. I am grateful to him. I have had nothing to reproach him for."[16]

Kahnweiler was the master of the "Picasso Business," as he used to say. The artist still played cat and mouse with his dealer, but they no longer argued over strategy, only over money. At last he had finally won Picasso's trust, and that was the most important thing. Kahnweiler worked with a free hand, as there was no doubt about his loyalty. From the beginning of the sixties Kahnweiler became someone the press would call "wealthy," someone whose fortune was never doubted, even if no one could precisely estimate what it was worth.

His attitude toward Picasso was very straightforward. He would buy everything the artist wanted to sell him. The discussions became more persuasive when Kahnweiler believed that Picasso kept too much for himself and did not sell him enough recent work—in spite of the fact that the artist turned over an enormous amount of work to him. One day he suddenly agreed to sell a hundred paintings in one fell swoop. His rate of production was phenomenal. A few years later, in Mougins, when they were sitting down to dinner, Picasso casually mentioned to Michel Leiris and Maurice Jardot, "Today I completed seven paintings."[17]

This never posed a financial problem for the gallery because buyers rushed over when they heard of the arrival of new works. Word of mouth was enough to spread the news throughout the art world.

On the occasion of Kahnweiler's eightieth birthday a columnist writing about his life and career summed up D. H. Kahnweiler in the following terms: the dean of European art dealers, the first impresario of cubism, and Picasso's personal ambassador to the world.[18] He was the medium, the indispensable screen that prevented someone as barraged with solicitations as Picasso from feeling completely harassed. Kahnweiler was in constant correspondence with him, and not a week went by without a long detailed letter that always began with "My dear friend." Picasso never felt at ease writing and was still uncomfortable doing so. Either he answered "his dear friend" himself in short telegraphic sentences, or, as happened more often, he made his wife write the reply. Kahnweiler's letters were all typewritten, with a narrative development that seemed to follow an epistolary form. Picasso's replies were written any which way on anything at hand, in charcoal or gouache or pen, on the back of his bills. The envelopes were even more interesting than his letters. The whole surface was covered with writing, and Kahnweiler was designated by a K or a DHK, followed by the name of the gallery, the address and city, often written in three different colored pencils when not painted by a brush. On the back was the return address: Picasso, Cannes, with a doodle.

There was always someone somewhere in the world who had a project, an idea, a proposal for Picasso. Only a few were serious. For some time now, Picasso had not left Mougins. He no longer came to Paris and never saw the rue de Monceau gallery, the one they called "the house Picasso built." Kahnweiler's telephone calls were among the few he would still accept even when working in his studio. In a general way his art dealer was one of the few people he still spoke to when he no longer spoke much to anyone.

They were in constant contact because, out of concern for honesty and impartiality, Kahnweiler communicated everything to the artist. At first he tried to be objective, hardly even venturing his advice. "This watercolor doesn't look right to me, but I am sending it to you at the owner's insistence"; or, "I think it is worthwhile to see this person." Little by little he stated his opinion and even helped make decisions. When Helene Weigel, Brecht's widow, who was the director of the Berliner Ensemble in East Berlin, asked the artist to make a portrait of Shakespeare, Kahnweiler could not praise her enough.[19] But by the end of the sixties requests came every day from all over the world, and Picasso could no longer even give a drawing to a friend without Kahnweiler stepping in.

The strangest assortment of requests came pouring in from all directions. An anti-racist group wanted a financial contribution, or a publisher friend wanted him to make a drawing. It was Nelson Rockefeller who wanted Picasso to make (in 1967) two sculptures, each six feet high, based on his drawings for the "Minotaur" (done in 1928!). Kahnweiler was startled because Alfred Barr from the Museum of Modern Art in New York communicated this request.[20] An American organization wanted to create communicated this request.[20] An American organization wanted to create a Picasso Museum. The *Nouvel Observateur* wanted Picasso to do their cover for the Christmas 1967 issue and then wanted to auction the original drawing to their subscribers, an idea which Kahnweiler found particularly offensive. A humanitarian organization would appreciate his financial support; a youth movement would like to have a drawing for their new publication; a Japanese man passing through Cannes would like to meet with him to discuss an exhibition of his work in Tokyo; Jean-Marie Drot requested an on-camera interview for his documentary film on Apollinaire; a record company promoting their Picasso symphony wanted to sell six large lithographs with the record; a Swedish critic wanted to meet the artist because he was writing a book about his work and thought that he could spend a few days in the artist's studio.[21] There was no end to it.

First, there were the Picasso exhibitions in France and throughout the world which were now multiplying rapidly. The artist almost never attended them but he wanted to know what the reaction was, how things went, and what was sold. Kahnweiler served as his clearinghouse. He sent the artist every catalogue and photo, especially those for major events dedicated to him such as the exhibition at the Grand Palais and Petit Palais in 1966–1967. Often it was the same little things that both artist and art dealer found very moving. As an example, for the great Paris exhibitions, the catalogue was too late for the opening and the printer had to implore the union for special hours. They said, "Yes, for Picasso we will work overtime." This was more eloquent than all the testimonials from celebrities in the art world.[22] When Picasso complained that his large painting for UNESCO was difficult to see because of a narrow walkway giving access to it, Kahnweiler went in person to the building to see for himself. He calmed the artist's fears. "The walkway is fifteen meters away from the painting. It is rather good, because when you walk in on it you see it differently, from above."[23] When, in 1960, Roland Penrose organized the most complete exhibition ever held on a living artist at the Tate Gallery in London, naturally Kahnweiler was in attendance and gave Picasso a detailed report as his special envoy: the number of rooms, the distance between paintings, the chronology of the hanging, the names of the dealers that Sotheby's had invited, the opening party held in a tent set up in front of the Tate with paella, flamenco dancers, and art critics singing his praises. Everything was there.[24]

Acting as Picasso's source of information was full-time work even during the intervals between exhibitions.

Yet, Kahnweiler could not influence Picasso's attitude toward *Life with Picasso,* a book written by his former companion Françoise Gilot in collaboration with the American art critic Carlton Lake. Picasso was furious about the content; his pride was wounded. According to him she told much too much, and it was not always correct, just like Fernande Olivier's book, *Picasso and His Friends.* Kahnweiler thought that the best policy was to ignore it, but most of Picasso's friends wanted to protest and drew up a petition, which he signed to go along with the rest. Where a stance of indifference would have been the best policy, there was now even more publicity for the book. Thus Picasso found himself publicly cast in the role of victim, which was an attitude that was the antithesis of his real temperament.

Picasso never forgave. Ten years earlier, when Gilot left him to marry the painter Luc Simon, Picasso flew into a rage over matters of inheritance for his children.[25] At the time Gilot, an artist, was also under contract to the Galerie Louise Leiris. Picasso demanded that Kahnweiler break her contract and finally forced him to sever all connections with her.[26]

Kahnweiler was often called upon to broach delicate matters with Picasso. There were two constant problems running through their correspondence: signature and authentication.

Between 1908 and 1914, the pioneering period of cubism, Picasso had the habit, along with Gris and Braque, of signing his paintings and drawings on the back and not on the front. The signature was not part of the painting as it intruded on the composition—at least that was the reason given by the artists even if Kahnweiler was convinced that they were trying to make their work more impersonal.[27] After World War II, when Kahnweiler became Picasso's exclusive dealer, collectors were always asking him to intercede with Picasso to sign his former works on the front of the canvas. For the collector, such a request was understandable if only for purely commercial reasons as a way of increasing the value of the piece. People who owned a Picasso liked having his name written across it.

In 1949 Justin Thannhauser had come to Kahnweiler with a serious problem. One of his clients, who owned *Screen, Bottle of Port, Playing Cards, and Guitar* from 1917, had come to see him in a furious state. He had read in the *catalogue raisonné* by Christian Zervos that Picasso had painted it on top of a Modigliani portrait of a boy on a night when the air raids lasted until dawn. The client had his painting X-rayed and, imagine, there was nothing underneath. Thus, he did not want it anymore! The dealer went to Zervos to ask for the source of the story and naturally it had come from Picasso. In turn Kahnweiler recounted this story to the artist and asked him to clear up the matter once and for all, not without adding, "I cannot explain the motives of this collector, whose behavior I find very strange."[28]

Determining the authenticity of a doubtful painting is a very delicate mission because a considerable sum of money is usually at stake. Kahnweiler knew how to handle the problem from experience, ever since an incident in the thirties. At that time, when he advised Picasso to bring charges for forgery, the artist had answered:

"How can I ever do that! I know what is going to happen! I will be sitting in the courtroom and the criminal will be brought in handcuffed, and it will turn out to be one of my friends."[29]

The implication of this joke, if it is a joke, must be understood in terms of Picasso's complete refusal to deal with anything concerning problems that occurred "after-the-sale." It did not interest him at all; he had better things to do. "I made the painting, that is enough. I can't be bothered with the rest of it," he would say categorically.[30]

Kahnweiler understood this about the artist, and knew that therefore it was left up to him. But the artist could not refuse to decide matters of forgery. Usually he would get around to it in a good-natured mood. Naturally, the more his prices increased, the more forgeries appeared, and after World War II fake Picassos flooded the market.

For Kahnweiler, courtroom experts had no credibility. He believed that the art dealer was in a better position to judge. The dealer knew the painter intimately and often saw works in progress, and thus had first-hand experience to document the work, which could be usefully supplemented by that indispensable tool for verification, the *catalogue raisonné*. If the dealer was no longer alive, the artist became the sole judge, on the condition that his memory was reliable. He should not say, as Picasso did about one of his paintings that had to be restored several times, "It's no longer by me."

This "no longer" threw everything into confusion for the New York dealer Saidenberg, and the Parke-Bernet auctioneer did not know what to do. What Picasso had said about the work had often been repeated, and the auctioneer was forced to withdraw number 86 from the catalogue of the sale in December 1961. But was it a fake?

Whenever he was in doubt Kahnweiler sent a photo of the dubious work to Picasso, or took it to him in person. The dealer, very cautious in his judgment, would say, "I believe it is real" or, "I don't like it very much," which were his favorite expressions. Even when he did not believe in the work at all, he still forwarded a photo. In 1960 two Spaniards brought him two paintings by Picasso's father. The subject was pigeons and they were dated 1892. They wanted to sell them to his son. The background was the Plaza de la Mercede in Málaga, and the signature was F. Ruiz Blasco. Kahnweiler was doubtful about them and even more so when they only asked for the negligible sum of five hundred francs for both paintings. They telephoned a few hours later to say that they had made a mistake and that they wanted 50,000 francs, which was much too expensive. But Kahnweiler conscientiously forwarded details of this proposal to Picasso to let him decide for himself.[31]

Little by little forgeries had become so numerous and so crude that Picasso could routinely judge them with a glance at the signature. Often it was enough to look at the back of the drawing to read the sticker with the address of some "modern art gallery" or other in New York, and see the so-called provenance. The forgers often made several copies of one original. It threw him into a state of despair. But Kahnweiler had a clear-cut policy: bring criminal charges. If they were not stopped they would only spoil the market. He had to take legal action if he did not want to force his clients and collectors to do it themselves.

Picasso's ambassador to the outside world was in fact one of his favorite conversationalists and the only person who had chatted with him since 1907. As for Kahnweiler, everything that Picasso said was of interest if only because it was *rare*. He had never written anything down, neither article nor book. True, he had written poetry and a play in his youth. But he refused to give real interviews. This lack of literary or journalistic information compared to the wealth of works of art transformed Kahnweiler from Picasso's art dealer into his interpreter. Thus he became the man people listened to and whose works they read because he was the man who spoke to the man who refused to speak. In private Picasso could be extremely talkative, but he clammed up the moment a microphone appeared.

Kahnweiler believed this artist had re-created the very grammar and syntax of art, and he would attempt to set down everything he said as if it were a historic pronouncement. Still, there were some sayings of Picasso's that Kahnweiler appreciated less than others, such as: "Every painter would like to be van Gogh but how many of them would agree to cut off an ear if that was the price they had to pay?"[32]

Kahnweiler did not only report, describe, and transcribe; he also had to interpret to avoid any misunderstandings. In 1937 Picasso had stopped by the gallery and, looking at a painting by Suzanne Roger, had said, "I think her earlier paintings were much better. I don't like all those parrots. Besides, I've just decided that I will no longer have any parrots in my paintings." When he left, the dealer typed out his notes, carefully dating them, and then explained, "Of course there were no parrots in the canvases. By this Picasso meant loud colors."[33]

Caravaggio remained a lifelong point of disagreement between them. Kahnweiler believed that he was the greatest of artists and that Picasso should give him the credit for the fact that in his work there first appeared that "Spanish realism" so dear to him: Saint Matthew's dirty feet, the bare legs of the dying virgin for which he was much criticized during his lifetime. That had offended people as much as his treatment of light. Picasso would not hear any of it, because he was not fond of Italian painting to begin with. He never stopped dismissing him with "Caravaggio is an art photographer. A floodlight on the right and a floodlight on the left."

Kahnweiler answered with, "If it was not for Caravaggio, and his innovations in painting, Velázquez, Zurbarán, Murillo, and Ribera could never have painted the way they did. The true painters never again painted as they had before Caravaggio. I believe that it is the greatest praise that can be accorded an artist. After Picasso also, painting would become something other than what it had been before him."

In June 1946 Kahnweiler and Picasso were discussing the decoration of Michelangelo's *Last Judgment* before returning inevitably to the subject of cubism. Kahnweiler was convinced that for Picasso only cubism had produced an honest painting, a way of painting conceived as a system of notation that invented signs and did not try to imitate reality. He placed this idea before the artist.

"You should say that in your lecture in Stockholm," Picasso answered. "You should speak the truth about all the artists in the Louvre since you know it. They are all prostitutes, pretty prostitutes but only that. It's not only cubism that has made paintings."

"You are being scabrous," Kahnweiler said. "You read what I wrote about Gris. You know that I say it very prudently. Otherwise people would take me for Marinetti, who wanted to burn down the Louvre."

"So what? You have to dirty your hands to get something done. You have to be dragged through the mud."

Kahnweiler wanted to place all judgments in the perspective of the history of art.

"Masson is right from his point of view," he said, "in believing that the cubists painted a cardboard world, but he is wrong historically. Of course only contemporary art is true art, honest because it is lyrical, free of tasks that are foreign to its real nature, tasks that are now assigned to photography, to films. But in the past it was not this way, and the artist's role of giving form to myths and his role as historiographer both justify and explain his former characteristics."

Picasso reacted as if he had heard but not understood as he repeated, "Yes, you can enjoy going to bed with a prostitute but you have to understand that it is still a prostitute."

On a January morning in 1955, in Picasso's studio, there was a genuine conversation that broke through their usual banter.

Picasso had shown Kahnweiler a new, very large painting from his *Women of Algiers* series. Kahnweiler was startled by the fact that this painting, different from the others in the series, was drawn in black and white. For lack of a better term he called it cubist.

"As for me, I feel that no one is going to like it," Picasso feared.

In spite of all the reassurances from his art dealer, the artist was discouraged. "Yes, when you used to buy things like this before 1914, yes," Picasso said. "But afterward, we, and by that I mean Braque and I—we led people into error with what we were doing. You yourself, if you had to choose between this painting and the others that are more finished, you would prefer the others. Oh, I understand, you would be right from a business point of view. Of course collectors always prefer crusty paintings, always."

Kahnweiler protested sincerely. Collectors had changed since those days when van Goghs were available. They did not buy with their pocket money any longer, and when they bought they kept in mind the fact that they might have to resell one day. Then a very finished painting would surely fetch a higher price at Hôtel Drouot.

"That is true," Picasso admitted, "that is how I bought my Cézanne painting of *l'Estaque*, which I don't like as much as my other paintings by him, or even the watercolors that he barely touched, but I bought it all the same because I wanted a Cézanne from this period. I know very well that people will always pay more for it. But it seems to me that people don't understand the artist's intentions anymore. They no longer appreciate the quality of a line that turns to meet another one."

"In that you are quite right," Kahnweiler admitted, "but I believe that it has always been this way. After all, is it really necessary that a collector understand that? What I find important, it seems to me, is their feelings. If they love a painting, if they are moved by it, that is what matters."[34]

Was this a dialogue of the deaf? Each one seemed preoccupied with expressing his own ideas and answered accordingly. Whatever topic they took up, each of them had his mind made up from the very beginning. Kahnweiler distrusted the artist's "culture," so instinctive, unbridled, and based on an altogether different frame of reference, while Picasso did not hide his distrust and defiance in regard to all theories in general, and art historians and critics in particular, who were busy categorizing and labeling the creative genius of the artist.

In April 1973 Kahnweiler awakened from his afternoon nap in his country house in Saint-Hilaire, thirty miles south of Paris. He heard the repeated loud ringing of the telephone in the distance. Louise Leiris went to answer it.

"What was it?" he asked.

"Picasso is dead."[35]

He had died of a heart attack after inflammation of the lungs. They notified Kahnweiler right after the family. He was stunned by the news. For a long time he had refused to even consider that Picasso might die. He would not see anyone, nor read articles, nor give interviews.

It was the end of a relationship that had lasted sixty-six years. The art dealer was so identified with his artist that, at Kahnweiler's death six years later, a newspaperman would write: "With Kahnweiler, it is Picasso we have lost once more."[36]

DOWN WITH ABSTRACT ART!

▭ "Abstract or not?"

Kahnweiler wanted these words printed on the belly band of his book *Confessions esthétiques*, when it was published in 1963, but finally Gaston Gallimard and his editor, Michel Mohrt, dissuaded him from it. The phrase was too ambiguous. But for Kahnweiler it was a clear refusal of abstraction on aesthetic grounds that he had formulated over decades, and it was just short of hatred.

This word may seem too violent to apply to someone as even-tempered and with such control over his feelings, yet D. H. Kahnweiler was a person who always took art and artists very seriously. His lack of a sense of humor in everyday life is all the more remarkable considering his intimate rapport with painting. He would not tolerate any jokes on the subject. Furthermore, he always believed that a true dealer was determined by his ability to reject and refuse, and not by his kindness. In his case, it was not even a question of choice, but of making a selection, a term he understood as harsh and implacable.

D. H. Kahnweiler practiced exclusion cheerfully. But as he had become a sort of "pope" of modern art, his judgment had the weight of an excommunication. It seemed that instead of diminishing with age, his position had intensified. Perhaps Kahnweiler had unconsciously taken a stand against the new developments in the art market as it defined itself between 1950 and 1970. The schools, labels, movements and countermovements, tendencies and undercurrents had multiplied immeasurably. Now galleries numbered in the hundreds and artists in the thousands. It was more than an increase, it was an invasion. In this confusion, styles were established and vanished in rapid succession. A young artist would have a known market price, supported by sales at Hôtel Drouot, with collectors and flattering catalogues, even before having had time to develop his art. Most of the time these artists disappeared as quickly as they had come into prominence.

Kahnweiler blamed this phenomenon, without going into a detailed analysis of the fluctuations in the art market, on its creation by false promoters, including art critics. For decades he used the word "cowards" to designate them. He would vary the term with "hideous cowardice"[1] or even "treacherous cowardice."[2] What Kahnweiler held against them was not so much their ignorance of art history as the fact that their thinking showed the "Wolf syndrome," named after the critic of Le Figaro, who spoke of Monet as a vulgar dauber of paint. The more he read nowadays the more he regretted that time when critics were virulent, authoritarian polemicists, and excessive in everything. Whereas then they showed a passionate and total commitment, now "They are so frightened of having the same thing done to them if they had spoken ill of X or Y who is now celebrated. . . . I prefer people whose ideas I don't agree with, but who defend their opinion, without any compromise."[3]

He was the dealer who represented two generations of artists, that of Picasso and that of André Masson, and later only made certain exceptions with Sébastien Hadengue and Yves Rouvre, a protégé of Masson's. Kahnweiler believed that he could only understand his own generation and perhaps, in some cases, the following one.

Aimé Maeght thought that Kahnweiler was wearing blinders to behave that way. His own criteria for making a choice were much simpler: "First you like it, then come all the good reasons for it."[4] It was precisely this eclecticism, so close in many ways to dilettantism, that Kahnweiler fought all of his life. It was enough that a great collector, his very dear friend Roger Dutilleul, had decided to extend his historical cubists to include the works of André Lanskoy, and after the war the works of de Staël and Bernard Buffet. But an art dealer could never deviate in such a way from his position.

After World War II the geography of the galleries in Paris had changed on both the Right and Left Banks, with the creation and expansion of the Galerie de France, and those of Louis Carré, Aimé Maeght, Denise René, Heinz Berggruen, Daniel Cordier, and René Drouin. If abstract art was born in the first two decades of the century in Paris, it did not really make its presence felt on the art market in Paris until after World War II. That was the reason for Kahnweiler's reaction; instead of remaining aloof, or losing interest, he renewed his attacks against it.

Galleries and Salons were filled with abstract art. In 1946 during the Salon des Réalités Nouvelles, the first exhibition had displayed over a thousand nonfigurative works submitted from all over the world, and thus announced the official launching of abstract art before the general public. Kahnweiler recoiled from it. He refused to send any works to an exhibition of "abstract art" and nonfigurative works. He would only relent if the name of the exhibition were changed. He would never betray the artists of the Galerie Louise Leiris by having them included in an exhibition that would make the spectator confuse them with abstract works which had no relation to them.[5]

In 1959, to satisfy his curiosity, he strolled through the Paris Biennale, the first exhibition devoted to artists between twenty and thirty-five years of age. He turned his attention from the abstract or *tachiste* painters to observe the public. He was struck by their passivity. Some liked the works, others did not. But there was no conflict, no protest or indignation. The audience's only reaction was to pause before a painting or to pass on their way. It confirmed his initial impression of abstract art: it had nothing to say.[6]

Kahnweiler consistently blamed certain artists for the vacuity of abstract art. First and foremost was Paul Gauguin, the starting point for ornamental painting. Then followed Kandinsky, who was not only a decorative painter but also a geometric one in the last years of his life. It made no difference that this artist preferred the term "pure art" to that of "abstract art," and that he also considered the term "decorative" to be insulting. Kahnweiler believed that all of his art was an error because he had started from a misunderstanding. He had understood nothing about cubism or fauvism nor even impressionism. As proof Kahnweiler referred to Kandinsky's notes in his journal of 1909, the passage in which he described Monet's *Haystacks* "as really being an abstract painting." It was common knowledge how painstakingly Monet had worked to capture the light and make the painting as true to life as possible. "Kandinsky was a very distinguished man," Kahnweiler recalled, "whom I liked quite well, a brave Russian painter, who was already making bad paintings in Russia and continued doing so in Munich."[7]

Usually when Kahnweiler attacked this artist, Mondrian was next in line, as also being responsible for making decorative panels. Mondrian was especially wrong about the meaning of cubism. He was making pseudo-paintings, incomplete in themselves because he was powerless to develop in them the signs to communicate his meaning. At the stage where he stopped—and it was impossible for him to develop his work any further—Mondrian confined himself to being pleasing when his ambition was to express "Beauty."

"This [painting] is hedonistic, in ordering the interplay of proportions and colors to please the viewer. There's no action, no radiance; it's only a brilliant surface with nothing more to it."[8] What did Kahnweiler think of Hans Hartung? "These are exercises of the paintbrush and the pen. He makes little sticks instead of sense."[9] And Alexander Calder? Kahnweiler thought that he never invented anything. He only worked on what Picasso had thought about in 1910, sculptures moving by a mechanism, according to him. But if Picasso had not made them, how could Calder have copied them? In *The Rise of Cubism*, Kahnweiler described Picasso's invention of a moving sculpture.[10]

Kahnweiler commented that "abstract expressionism" and American "action painting" was "infamous painting, of European descent, by the way." He was referring to European artists exiled to the New World for the duration of World War II, and the influence of Masson in particular. Although Pollock had acknowledged his indebtedness quite freely, Kahnweiler found his work and that of his friends completely uninteresting, since all of their experiments were new in name only, having been tried by the cubists as well as the surrealists. They were, in short, "absolutely deliquescent."[11]

In his opinion, Kahnweiler remained completely true to himself. His condemnation reflected his aesthetics. Accordingly, he might be considered either a man of limitations or else a man who was consistent in his thinking.

He blamed everyone—art dealers, critics, artists—for the appeal of the new and the desire to startle the bourgeoisie. Formerly, he would recall, artists were not trying to be original at any cost. They were happy to contribute what they believed to be missing. Nowadays "it was a bragging contest with each person trying to shout more loudly than the others." Kahnweiler never doubted that one day all of this pseudo-painting would be returned to where it belonged: in crates in the basements of the museum warehouses. They would be stored next to the academic painters of the nineteenth century. What did they have in common? They had been favored by the state and the public. In time the good would be separated from the bad. Meanwhile, contemporary works were of "sociological interest" and remained foreign to the realm of aesthetics.[12]

Not everything deserves to be shown. Those who have any doubt should know that of all those paintings he had seen in the former Luxembourg Museum at the beginning of this century, only those in the famous Caillebotte room remained. The other works, so praised by critics, the public, and art dealers, had finally found their true place—in storage.

His hostility was so violent and unremitting that people started wondering what abstract art represented for Kahnweiler. What did he understand by the term that he used as an insult?

It was understandable that for him art could only be representational, in the sense that he expected an artist to communicate his experiences through stylistic signs. The creation of a new pictorial language was his measure of the genius of a great artist. After a period of learning and adaptation, some of the artist's contemporaries would learn to understand the work. Abstract painting by contrast, offers nothing by which it can be understood.[13]

Of course Kahnweiler understood that these artists were also working within a system of communication, but he thought that they were making marks instead of using a code. They cannot be grasped although they are all more or less pleasant to look at. He was more responsive to the drawing than to the coloring. But he believed that drawing in itself was an abstraction because through a simple, black-and-white line, the artist captured a reality that existed in color and three dimensions.[14]

In his writing and in his speeches he used two words to condemn abstraction: academic and decorative.

For him, academics of the late 1950s were comparable to those of former Salons. The difference was that in the past people tried to seduce the viewer by pretty subjects, such as all the portrayals of nudes, whereas now it was the art object itself that tried to please.[15] When pressed by the art historian Meyer Shapiro to give a definition, Kahnweiler proposed the following: academic art is an art that uses forms taken elsewhere, and uses them either in contradiction to their meaning or without any meaning at all.[16] The older academics composed with the human form whereas the moderns compose with colors, and in both cases they are creating something with "charm." But they cannot create conflict. He saw the solution in the next generation, who, he believed, would rebel against their fathers in the same way that the cubists turned against the impressionists.[17]

His second anathema was decorative art, which he defined as the "deterioration into the ornamental that occurs whenever there's no longer an attempt to express an emotion or when there's a reproduction of a stereotyped symbol that is now devoid of any content and becomes only an aspect or a pleasing object."[18]

He believed that abstract painting was a form of calligraphy that failed to become a true system of notation evolving its own meaning. The proof was that on looking at the painting it stayed on the wall. It never moved because the viewer had no reference point on the surface plane and could not relate to it on the level of aesthetic consciousness. By contrast, a cubist painting moves, evolves, mutates when the viewer looks at it, and it is reconstituted in his consciousness. Many minor abstract painters had mistaken assumptions about the nature of cubism and its goals: some stopped short at the geometric forms, others focused on the apparent disorder, and still others believed that it was the deconstruction that made it cubism. All of these artists lost their way and for decades followed the wrong trail. For Kahnweiler a nonfigurative painting was non-sense; painting defined the external reality of mankind, and to ignore this truth was to reduce the work to the status of a decoration.[19]

If a new museum of modern art had been created during the sixties and he had been made the director, on what basis and by which criteria would he build the collection? *Les Lettres Françaises*, a cultural weekly, asked him. His selection would be ruthless, becoming more and more so as the number of painters increased and great artists became ever rarer. It was the only way to avoid having the paintings purchased every year by the state end up in storage, as was often the case. Each generation of curators believed that it was shrewder in making purchases than ever before, but it often could not go beyond the academic. Kahnweiler made a revolutionary proposal that did not stand a chance of being implemented: that the state should never buy the works of young artists. By fixing the age limit at sixty, for example, it would reduce the numbers of bad mistakes, since there would be a lifetime's work and reputation, and the standing of the artist to act as guidelines in making a purchase. At least it would guarantee a middling range of quality. Private collections that kept important works in France by leaving them to the state would act as a much needed filtering system. With the money saved, the state could purchase important works and masterpieces from auctions as they came up for sale. So what if some people seemed to have passed by the unknown young genius? Fashion's loss would benefit art history and, under this policy, the cultural heritage of France.[20] Kahnweiler was going against the mainstream of a whole period.

In 1969, during a long and in-depth interview, critic Pierre Cabanne backed him against the wall. "What I find extraordinary," he said, "is that since World War II, for the last twenty-five years, you have discovered only one artist!"*

"That is because there has only been one," Kahnweiler answered quietly. "Consider the nineteenth century in France. How many great artists were there before the impressionists? Twenty-five? Why do you expect it to continue that way? There is no reason why it should."

When urged to name great artists after Picasso and Braque he would name Masson, Beaudin, and Kermadec, adding that these last two artists were unjustly ignored by the public. Naturally his statement elicited the embarrassing question, "If I understand what you are saying, there are no great artists beyond those in your gallery?"

"Your question makes me sound ridiculous. But you could state it differently by saying: 'You have only taken on people whom you considered great artists?' That sounds more reasonable."

Clever and quick despite his eighty-five years, he also managed to avoid the other trap set by his interlocutor. No, he was not at all impressed by those painters of today who worked in the style of the fauves and the cubists. Those artists and styles were essentially part of their time, and their paintings had a meaning that they could not have today. And he added, "Fortunately, I never know beforehand what I am going to like."

* Sébastien Hadengue, born in 1932, and taken on by the gallery in 1960. Before Hadengue he had taken on Rouvre.

A WISE MAN
WHO HAS NO DOUBTS

☐ It was a Sunday during the seventies at the country house called "The Priory," near the village of Saint-Hilaire right outside of Étampes. Only the roofless Gothic chapel remained of the original priory for women. The handsome bourgeois house with slate roof was built during the *Directoire* Period. The drawing room on the ground floor opened onto the terrace. At some distance stood a farmhouse with its outbuildings. There were oak, pine, and birch trees with lawns and shrubbery. It was a fairly typical country house except that in front of the ivy-covered ruins of the chapel there stood a monumental sculpture by Picasso with arms outstretched to proclaim to all visitors the unique spirit of the place.

This was the country home where D. H. Kahnweiler spent two days per week, from Saturday afternoon to Monday morning; where he could catch his breath, think, and write a little. A guest who entered the house for the first time would be startled by the setting and the furnishings. Everything was as traditional as had been all his different apartments in Paris and Boulogne since 1907. Clearly it was proof that the modern spirit had not penetrated every aspect of his sensibility. In architecture, at least, he preferred the old.

The Priory, which belonged to the Galerie Louise Leiris, was opposite in spirit to a museum or artistic foundation. Poet Georges Limbour, a frequent visitor, wrote a telling description of the place: "It was a house for plain living, except that you encountered paintings there. Instead of going up to them to make a judgment or categorize them, at the least expected moment they would come forth like apparitions, crossing our path in the course of our meanderings around the house. Some seemed to be lying in wait in dark corners beyond the circumference of light cast by the lamps. This is the way to live with paintings. They interrupt our usual activity, capture our attention, and suddenly speak to us."[1]

Kahnweiler never paid much attention to the problems of hanging the work, and this was even more apparent in his country house than in the gallery (where Maurice Jardot now made it his responsibility). In Saint-Hilaire the works were randomly scattered throughout the house. On the ground floor, the famous portrait of Madame D. H. Kahnweiler (1921) by Derain hung in the drawing room. Above a fruitwood sideboard there was a still life by Picasso (1909), a gouache by Léger (1912), a landscape by Braque (1907), and a collage by Arp (1916), one of the few works by an artist not represented by the gallery. Across the room above a matching sideboard there was a painting by Gris and a sculpture by Laurens. On the mantelpiece was a terra-cotta sculpture by Laurens (1926), and reflected in the great mirror over it was a large painting from 1936 by Picasso.

In the library, behind the great work table piled high with stacks of papers, one wall was covered with bookshelves that rose from floor to ceiling with a library ladder attached. On the other walls there was a landscape by Beaudin (1961) and a nude by Kermadec (1933). Above the sofa at one end of the room was Picasso's imposing 1956 painting *Spring*, and next to it, a landscape by Masson (1952). Alongside it stood a table whose top was made of ceramic tiles by Picasso and whose wrought iron base was by Diego Giacometti.

The dining room was plain, quiet, with a serene light from the windows. On the wall hung a Klee from 1929 next to a Picasso from 1953. The paintings were on either side of a stone sculpture by Manolo from 1920. However, the most remarkable work of art there was the mural painted by Léger especially for the room, in clear bright colors, just before he died. In the attic, which had been transformed into a game room, there was a large painting by Picasso from 1965 which was hung above the harpsichord, across from the self-portrait with pipe by Vlaminck (1910) displayed on an easel.

Outside, overlooking the garden, was the immense cement sculpture by Picasso; and near the front door was a mermaid in terra-cotta by Laurens.[2]

These were treasures, and Kahnweiler always said that he must take steps to protect the house. Yet he never did. This attitude was the opposite of the one adopted by his brother Gustave. In England he had become a private dealer specializing in prints by Picasso and especially in the sculptures of Henry Moore, with whom he became close friends. As the owner of a sizable private collection (Picasso, Gris, Léger, Klee) he was in the habit of storing it at the Tate Gallery every year when he went on vacation. Finally, tired of his perpetual anxiety, he donated the collection, keeping only a few "little things," as well as an enormous statue by Henry Moore in the garden, which he could see from his window. It was too heavy for even the most daring thieves to attempt to remove!

It was in the shadows of the Priory ruins at Saint-Hilaire that Kahnweiler did his best work. His desk was buried under different piles of notes, on a variety of subjects concerning painting, all of which served to remind him of the task that he had been avoiding for many years: his memoirs.

This manuscript, which he never got around to writing, had become an obsession. His books were all written during periods of war, which had twice forced him to distance himself from his gallery. Was he waiting for World War III to start writing this long-awaited work? The problem was more complicated than simple writer's block; there was nothing that he could do about it, and it was not for lack of encouragement. Periodically his relatives and friends asked him about the proposed memoirs. He always answered evasively with a little smile.

He had received several proposals from publishers. As early as 1958, after spending an evening with Kahnweiler at Lord Amulree's in London, British publisher George Weidenfeld sent him a follow-up letter of encouragement. "If ever I write them, you will be the first to know!" Kahnweiler had replied without really believing it would ever happen.[3]

In 1975 Paul Flamand, editor in chief of Editions du Seuil and a close friend, and historian Jean Lacouture suggested that Kahnweiler tell the story of his life into a tape recorder.[4] But at the age of ninety-one he felt too old and worn out to begin on this sort of venture.[5]

Since the publication of *Juan Gris* in 1946 he had been entertaining the idea of writing three different books that resulted in his writing none: one on the business of selling art, a second on Picasso, and finally his memoirs. He had more or less gathered all the research materials he would need but he continued to write articles or short essays.[6] He was put off by the idea of autobiographical writing. In his eyes the genre presented the double dangers of falsehood and exhibitionism. In his book on Gris he had replaced with X, Y, or Z all names mentioned in the personal letters he quoted, even if the mentions themselves had nothing defamatory about them. Truly honest memoirs, direct and open, would be interesting but would bring down the wrath of his friends. How could he write about Léger, who always spoke about the abundance of his work and who worked very selectively? How would he write about Braque, who had become so uncommunicative that it was difficult just to speak to him? How could he describe Picasso, who was always talking but refused to be quoted or to have any notes taken in his presence? Remembering with pen in hand was difficult and painful. Kahnweiler learned this the hard way when Maurice Saillet asked him for an article on Reverdy and cubism in 1961. He accepted happily, but the writing gave him greater trouble than he could ever have imagined. He spent his time verifying every little detail. He burst into laughter on reading the memoirs of his colleague Martin Fabiani, where he was described in a few lines: "D. H. Kahnweiler, art dealer and collector, has made a name for himself in art history. His son is following in his footsteps."[7] Of course, Kahnweiler never had any children.

Kahnweiler managed some rough drafts of his memoirs but never got very far. They were primarily about Picasso. In making out his will on November 20, 1967, Kahnweiler was careful to state that he left his objets d'art, his paintings and engravings, his books and documents to Louise Leiris, and that only one other person had the right to read through his manuscripts—Michel Leiris.

Perhaps it was better that he never wrote his memoirs. D. H. Kahnweiler was a man who responded to human contact, who could speak lyrically, and he was a better lecturer than writer. He avoided introspection, whether in an intimate circle of friends or in total privacy. It was a question of modesty and upbringing.

In 1960 he finally made up his mind to speak about what he could not write, and agreed to talk out his memoirs. The idea was proposed by Francis Crémieux, a leading radio journalist. He became the medium who brought forth the truth Kahnweiler carried within himself. He would try to reach this venerable seventy-six-year-old gentleman by breaking down his reserve. The recordings were made in the most painstaking manner, as Kahnweiler recognized, without any prearranged topic, touching on whatever subject occurred to them. The conversations were taped either in his apartment on quai des Grands-Augustins, or in his country house in Saint-Hilaire, or in his office at the gallery.[8] He thought of it as a kind of autobiography, a general outline of his future memoirs which he still planned to write. Thus by telling his story very directly by speaking into the microphone, he gave his version of his life.[9]

These interviews, stretching over eight programs, were broadcast during the months of May and June. The series was extremely successful, and Kahnweiler became a popular celebrity. In the following year the broadcasts were developed into a book. Raymond Queneau and Dionys Mascolo were in charge of the project for Gallimard, and Kahnweiler was passionately involved with every aspect. The art-book format was eschewed because it would delay the publication too much, and Kahnweiler wanted to see it in the bookshops as soon as possible. He asked Michel Leiris, who had more experience in the matter, to help him find a title for the book; Leiris suggested, "Paintings of a Half Century," then "The Memoirs of an Art Dealer, 1907–1960."[10] They finally settled on *Mes galeries et mes peintres*. The book was published in England, the United States, Germany, Japan, Czechoslovakia, Poland, Sweden, and Finland.

"Hopefully it will come to pass!" were Crémieux's last words in the book of interviews. It was in response to Kahnweiler expressing the wish to continue the discussion in ten years. Indeed, the journalist would not forget this wish and in 1971 returned with microphone and tape recorder to interview an eighty-seven-year-old man who was tired, partly deaf, had a quavering voice, and tended to repeat himself. Kahnweiler again took up arms against critics, abstract art, the government, New York as the art center, art for speculation, the politics of museum acquisition, and concluded with a speech about Picasso as the dominant figure of the century. If his faith was still intact, his enthusiasm, his ability to persuade were not. Kahnweiler had grown tired in the interim.

Between these two meetings, Kahnweiler was the subject of an in-depth interview with Pierre Cabanne. In his home he also entertained the critic John Russell for an article in *Vogue* magazine. And he became the subject of a television documentary. Several months before the radio broadcasts Jean-Marie Drot devoted a program to him entitled "Memory, What Do You Expect of Me?" which was broadcast on February 14, 1960. Judging by the critical reviews that unanimously praised him for being a discoverer of genius, it was a success.

Drot did not merely interview Kahnweiler on his life and that of his artists; he placed him in a setting and directed him like an actor. Kahnweiler was a performer. The old gentleman, serious, heavyset, bald, his eyebrows like circumflex accents, narrated his adventures while walking in the snow at Saint-Hilaire with slow measured steps, soft-spoken, elegant and sober in his speech, all tweed and cashmere in dress. He was smiling when he recounted Manolo's adventures, but his composure and voice almost failed him when he discussed Juan Gris's character. Lost in thought before the flames of the fireplace, he stirred the embers distractedly. The director even persuaded him to return to the Bateau-Lavoir for the first time in many years. In a voice filled with emotion, he discussed the sad story of Max Jacob and the poverty of the studios in those days.

He spoke with the wisdom of a man who had shed all doubt. After decades of experience and professional practice, nuances were no longer part of his style. He always said that if after seventy-five years a person did not know where he was going, then his life was a failure. If one did know, then there should be no more of the indecision, experimentation, or maneuvering of a young man.

During his early years, as in mid-life, he had wanted to make the world receptive to certain profound truths. Now that he was an acknowledged authority on modern art, he had the means to carry out this ambition. He even had the supreme luxury of being at peace with his conscience, and of living according to his values.

What did he make of his other artists, next to such superstars as Picasso, Gris, Léger, and Masson? André Beaudin, for example, he considered a wonderful minor master of classical purity in his work, a worthy successor of Gris. It was a mystery to Kahnweiler that collectors did not appreciate Eugène de Kermadec's great works. Yet he was little known outside a small devoted circle of friends and collectors. It would come in time, as with Suzanne Roger or Yves Rouvre. Sébastien Hadengue represented youth for Kahnweiler. His paintings were never photographic, but fragments of the events of May 1968 could be found in his paintings. The artist had been on the barricades and among the protesters, but his earlier paintings reflected the anxiety, the hopes, and the enthusiasms of his generation.[11]

Whenever he discussed such and such an unknown artist from his gallery he was absolutely certain that one day justice would be done. They would be recognized for their worth, while 90 percent of the artists discussed and known at the end of his life would be completely forgotten in a hundred years. Even their works would have disappeared while people would continue admiring Rembrandt and discussing his work. Kahnweiler believed that modern art since Cézanne was condemned to remaining incomprehensible as long as people did not understand its nature as a system of notation. It felt as if he were writing a last testimonial in August 1969 when he added an afterword to the American edition of the interviews with Francis Crémieux, and signed it as if it were a will.

"I am too old to be able to watch the flowering of this new painting that I foresee. I have had the great satisfaction of seeing the triumph of my friends. One thing of which I am certain is that the plastic arts will not degenerate into childish games, but that they will continue to be for mankind that which is most precious. Besides creating man's external world, they will continue to give him the supreme joy of communicating with the great artists, of sharing their emotions. This is what is meant by aesthetic pleasure."

Even as Kahnweiler approached the century mark, his points of reference never changed. In politics his sympathies as a man of the left had remained intact; it was a matter of temperament rather than commitment to specific militant programs.

When General de Gaulle returned to political affairs in 1958, Kahnweiler voted against him. Yet he was not for Pierre Mendès-France either. Earlier, when Mendès-France was withdrawing French forces from North Africa after France had relinquished all claims to Indochina, the German art dealer Michael Hertz had a political conversation with Kahnweiler. As he recalled:

"I told Kahnweiler that considering the miseries of the war in Algeria, Mendès-France had the moral authority to order the withdrawal of the last French forces in North Africa. Kahnweiler looked at me in horror, raised his hands—a gesture that was typical of him when he wanted to emphasize what he was saying—and grimly asked me if I wanted the death of Pierre Mendès-France. Confused by the question, I finally gathered that Kahnweiler believed that a Jewish political figure should count on being assassinated if he relinquished two traditional French territories. I naively asked him if anti-Semitism still existed in France. He answered that as long as there were Jews there would be anti-Semitism, and France was no exception."[12]

When General de Gaulle granted independence to Algeria Kahnweiler could praise "the great man" in him. In the early seventies, when intellectuals in France began demonstrating against American intervention in Vietnam, Kahnweiler would lend his support, although he always reminded people that "in less than thirty years the Americans have twice fought to liberate France from the Germans."[13]

He signed a vast number of petitions for a variety of worthy causes: to protest the assassination of militants and leaders of the Union of Algerian Workers (October 1957); to renew a humane form of socialism in Czechoslovakia (1968); in favor of a reunion of the Commission for Peace in Vietnam (1967); for the freeing of Greek intellectuals and democrats imprisoned after the assassination of one of their colleagues in prison

(1967); in support of Angela Davis (1971); for reform of the state-run broadcasting system (1977).[14]

Toward the end of his life there was a decided return to his Jewish roots. Right after the October War in 1973 he signed a petition urging Arab-Israeli cooperation, recognizing the national rights of Israelis and Palestinians, and asking that the United Nations resolution of November 1967 be applied in full force.[15] He was outspoken against and critical of Zionism, but he remained a faithful contributor to numerous Israeli and Jewish charities in need of funds and remained a faithful patron all his life, although he was vehemently against Israeli "militarism" after 1967.

He was one of the very few in his group never to have joined the Communist Party. His basic convictions made him stay away until 1956; after that he was alienated by the invasion of Hungary and Khrushchev's speeches in the United Nations. Yet everyone in his immediate circle wanted him to become a member of the party.

Picasso, for one, was not only a member but a hero of the party. Still, if others were deceived, Picasso was not, and with his whole being he remained an independent spirit. In his home in the hills above Cannes, on the wall next to the telephone, was a list of private telephone numbers, including those of both Communist Party leader Maurice Thorez and "el Caudillo"—Francisco Franco.

Léger was also a member of the party, especially since he was married to Nadia, née Khodossevitch, very Russian and a fervent Stalinist. He was a latecomer to the party and joined less for ideological reasons than moral and artistic ones: his liking for crowds, for the masses, the urban world of workaday people. After his death, in his last will and testament, he placed the Communist Party and the peace movement after his "family" but before his "friends." Among the other key people in Kahnweiler's immediate circle during the fifties, Maurice Jardot was also a man of the left, but at odds with all the others because for the last twenty-five years he had been a Trotsky sympathizer, in opposition to the Stalinists.

Picasso often asked Kahnweiler about it point-blank. "Have you made up your mind to join the Communist Party? That would make me very happy, you know."

Finally Kahnweiler decided to speak out, instead of merely shaking his head or raising his eyebrows. "No, my dear friend, I don't believe I will join the Communist Party, because since the death of Stalin and the discovery of all his crimes . . ."

"I see what you're coming at," Picasso interrupted him. "That gives you an easy out, doesn't it? You're going to claim you're disgusted with Stalin and that solves everything."

"Not at all," Kahnweiler protested. "I've just come to realize something I never understood before, and that is, Stalin was a pessimist."

"What are you getting at?"

"Just that," Kahnweiler said. "A pessimist. I supposed he must have picked it up in his early years at the seminary. . . . He must have decided that evil is so well rooted in human nature that he could only eliminate it by wiping out human life. So, after studying the question very carefully, I have come to the conclusion that there's just too much of a contradiction there. On one hand, Marxism preaches the doctrine of endless possibilities of human progress: in other words, a doctrine based on optimism. Yet Stalin gives us the proof of just how false he thought that doctrine was. He was better placed than anyone to know whether optimism in that matter was possible, and he answered with a thumping negative by killing everyone within reach, apparently on the grounds that human nature was so bad, there was no other way of settling affairs. Under those conditions, how can you expect an intelligent man to become a Communist?"

"Typical bourgeois sophistry," Picasso grumbled.[16]

Kahnweiler had been an observer of the Eastern Bloc for a long time, and especially since the end of the war when he had had numerous occasions to lecture in Prague, Budapest, Warsaw, and Berlin. He had observed and listened to everything carefully. He concluded that the artist is happier in Eastern Europe to the degree in which he enjoys material well-being and economic security since he is not affected by the swings of the art market, nor collectors, nor the dealers' business troubles, and only lives on commissions from the government. Unfortunately this well-being has a reverse side: his individuality is crushed by the government and he has to work by and accept its guidelines, and by definition the state has no taste.

The controversy about Picasso's famous portrait of Stalin brought the point closer to home. For Kahnweiler it in itself summed up all the contradictions and ambivalences of the artist's commitment to a political party. After the death of "the Little Father of the People," Picasso had made for the cover illustration of the Communist periodical *Les Lettres Françaises* a truly conventional portrait, which could not be said to inspire either admiration or fear. But that was Stalin according to Picasso. Nevertheless it provoked an outcry of protest from the members of the party. Stunned by the reaction, the artist confided his disappointment to biographer Pierre Daix. "Here I brought this little bouquet to the funeral. No one liked it. It can happen, but usually people don't scold you because they don't like the flowers."[17]

But Kahnweiler's main criticism of the communist system vis-à-vis art he applied with equal intensity against capitalist regimes: the harmful policies of the state. He would have the state intervene in the arts only after a real upheaval that would revolutionize the schools and rouse the collective acceptance of a great style. Enlarging public art collections by purchasing old masterworks was to be encouraged. But the state should not spend money to help living artists, because this money would never reach the right destination; it would be wasted on people who were not deserving, who on the contrary should be discouraged because there were too many visual artists already. His opinion had little impact, however, judging by the purchasing policy of the majority of Western museums.

Kahnweiler thought that exclusion was all the more necessary in an age when social conformity was presented as a universal panacea. Just as he preferred the polemical and committed critics of the beginning of the century, he favored the museum curators and organizers of exhibitions who knew how to be merciless in making a selection. When he was criticized for refusing to lend paintings for exhibitions he explained that it was quite true he disliked lending certain historic paintings, such as *Still Life with Grapes* by Braque, which was much in demand but which could no longer be moved because the colors were mixed with sand. Furthermore, he was also fighting against a new development he found excessive: the proliferation of exhibitions, for the most part made up of the best works in catalogues of other institutions. All this not only left his walls bare, but also took up 80 percent of the time and energy of the gallery's staff.

He believed that one solution to the problem of the role of the state would be to adopt the practices of the United States. A private donor who left his paintings to a national museum could deduct from his own annual income not the price of the work originally paid by the donor but the current market value as estimated by experts. It would enrich the national cultural heritage, and the state could then devote itself exclusively, as it should, to purchasing works of renown. The deficit incurred by the department of taxation would be more than compensated for by the increased influx of visitors to the museums from abroad.[18] As he wrote, "It must always be remembered that it was through private initiative that the great collections of French art were formed in the United States and Scandinavia."[19]

D. H. Kahnweiler was deliberately iconoclastic, and that was his charm. If he had not been Kahnweiler he could have been an anachronism, two generations late. But his history, his confidence, his lucid intellect imposed respect.

He seemed to have an internal scale of values, according to which certain honors were acceptable and others not. In September 1963 he attended the funeral for Braque held in the courtyard of the Louvre. He told Picasso that he was offended by the ceremony. Near a row of colorful Republican Guards at attention, three generals and a colonel with drawn swords reviewed the troops before they filed past the catafalque. It was understandable; the government was paying homage to a great man. But this was an artist they were burying! What did this pompous and drawn-out ceremony have to do with art in general and the life and work of Braque in particular! During the whole ceremony Kahnweiler was lost in his own thoughts.[20]

Perhaps more significant was his attitude toward decorations, titles, and awards. He accepted with great pleasure the prize awarded by the Académie Française. Similarly he was profoundly moved when the government of Baden-Württemberg named him professor and awarded him an honorary doctorate from the University of Kaiserslautern (in the Rhine Palatinate). But in 1959 André Malraux, who had been appointed Minister of Cultural Affairs a year earlier, wanted to surprise his first publisher on his birthday: a promotion to the Legion of Honor! Malraux did not know his man. Kahnweiler even refused to fill out the questionnaire. For reasons of conscience he could not accept the gift. At seventy-five he had lived his life, and to accept the honor would go against all his principles. In a letter addressed more to his friend Malraux than to the minister, he tried to explain his feelings: "My whole past rises against such a possibility. You know my life. It's that of an independent man. Like Nietzsche I also believe that the state is 'the worst of monsters.' "[21] Although he was sorry to be such an ingrate, he asked Malraux to please take back his birthday present. For a man who was so proud and who enjoyed receiving honors, Kahnweiler could still surprise people.

As a publisher he only published what he considered worthwhile. In the years from the end of the war to 1968, the publication date of his last book, he brought out about fifteen books, all according to the same procedures established during the period on rue Vignon: *Le verre d'eau*, a collection of notes by Francis Ponge illustrated with lithographs by Kermadec; *Le Calligraphe* by Georges Limbour, illustrated by Beaudin; *La chasse au Merou* by the same author, illustrated with lithographs by Rouvre. There were also *Les Texticules* by Raymond Queneau with lithographs by Hadengue; Picasso's poems, naturally illustrated by himself; *balzacs en bas de casse et picassos sans majuscule* by Michel Leiris, with lithographs by Picasso; and above all the works of André Masson, *Carnet de croquis, Sur le vif, Toro, Voyage á Venise, Féminaire, Trophées éro-*

tiques, and *Jeux amoureux*, illustrated with his own engravings and lithographs.

His publications showed the same care and high standards as he devoted to his exhibits in the gallery. From the liberation of France to his death thirty-five years later, he organized over sixty exhibits, averaging two a year. And there were exceptional years, such as 1957, when he inaugurated the new gallery on rue de Monceau and held five exhibitions; and 1960, the year of his famous radio broadcasts, when he scheduled four.

These exhibits were always a major event. The most startling featured the works brought back from the United States by André Masson (1945), Picasso's works done in Provence (1948), the polychrome constructions and lithographs by Léger (1951), fifty new works by Picasso (1957), twenty-two paintings from Gris's studio made in the last two years of his life (1957), the eighty-nine drawings and gouaches by Léger done between 1900 and 1955 (1958), the stone sculptures of Henri Laurens (1958), the series of lithographs by Léger made for "La Ville" and the fifty-eight works for "Les Ménines" by Picasso (1959), the paintings and drawings for "Déjeuner sur l'herbe" by Picasso (1962), and Picasso's black-and-white and colored sketches (1971–1972). The catalogues for these exhibitions were usually signed and included essays by Kahnweiler, Maurice Jardot, or Michel Leiris. The gallery also called on its friends for other prefaces: Paul Eluard, Georges Bataille, André Frénaud, Georges Limbour, Raymond Queneau, Douglas Cooper, poets Jean Tardieu and Francis Ponge, and even the historian of the Middle Ages, Georges Duby, a close friend of Masson.

The aura around Kahnweiler and the prestige of the gallery made the public think of Galerie Louise Leiris as an institution in the manner of an American foundation, whereas it remained above all a commercial venture, and he an art dealer. In 1961 the gallery went public with a capital of two million francs, which consisted of a limited portion in cash and the major portion in shareholder contributions of stock. Ten years later the stocks were divided among the four partners of the gallery: Louise Leiris (32,725), Michel Leiris (5,785), Kahnweiler (1,090), and Maurice Jardot (400). The firm ranked among the top thousand export companies of France, holding 444th place.[22]

Kahnweiler remained the titular head and animating spirit but his great age rendered him less active. He came to the office every day but stayed for a limited amount of time. His routine remained unchanged: the morning was devoted to correspondence. Then he would see faithful old friends in his office and clients in a sparsely furnished room reserved for showing paintings. He never attended auctions, preferring to send Maurice Jardot and Louise Leiris. The last one he attended was on the special occasion of the dispersal of the André Lefèvre collection in 1964.[23]

He loathed opening parties for exhibitions and the auctions at Drouot, which were painful remainders of the sequestration of his stock. Besides, meeting his colleagues was not something he enjoyed. The social events that could still excite him and which he anticipated with great pleasure were concerts, lectures, and the exhibits in his own gallery.

All around Kahnweiler, people felt that there was a threat posed by the United States. It had produced a school of painting, the so-called New York School, that could rival the market of the school of Paris, and the number of galleries was rapidly multiplying on the other side of the Atlantic. The American tax system favored the collector. More and more contracts were being made directly between American dealers and European artists, and now New York galleries were opening branches in Europe, or else they were investing capital and controlling the stock of certain Paris galleries. In brief, a traditional client was now able to meet his own needs.

Kahnweiler thought this was nonsense. On the subject of Rauschenberg, Johns, de Kooning, and others, his beliefs had been set for a long time. When he said, "I don't believe that they are the great artists of their day," it was an understatement on his part. As for current prices, what appalled him most was to read in the ever-proliferating publications specializing in the American art market that André Masson's works would rise sharply during the sixties because of his influence on the works of Jackson Pollock! In 1965 he made a complete statement about the continuing crisis of the art market to Gilles Lapouge, who was writing a survey of the problem for *Le Figaro littéraire*.

> For the last four or five years people have said that business is slow. But I assure you that I have never felt it was slowing down in the least. When people speak of a crisis in painting I think of the crash in 1929. Compared to that the present problem is nonexistent. I would place the real crisis in the years before 1960 when paintings became an object of speculation. Today there are four hundred galleries in Paris, people say. I know as well as anyone that some are there to rent out their walls to anyone who paints, but that still gives you four hundred galleries which is far too many. I understand that there are twenty thousand artists in Paris; what does that mean? Each generation produces four or five geniuses at most. Today they launch a new

genius a week and people are amazed to discover that there are also failures. It takes genius a long time to come to terms and manifest itself. In the past artists were not in such a hurry. It wasn't at the age of twenty-two that they recognized their genius and they did not become wealthy at the age of thirty.[24]

To illustrate his point Kahnweiler cited Masson, who had only become famous since 1965 when he was commissioned to do the ceiling of the Odéon Theater, at the age of sixty-nine. Until his death in 1987, André Masson would become the personification of the "great" artist whose prices would rise spectacularly every five years by a common consensus among "specialists."

Every time someone spoke of a crisis in the art market, Kahnweiler would react philosophically and try to rebut even the most pessimistic arguments. He was one of the few individuals in the Paris art world who was able to place events in historical perspective. He refused to consider it a symptom of decline when he learned that his gallery exported only 85 percent of its previous volume of business to the United States, Germany, and Sweden.

He who had always wanted to be alone and separate from the rest of his profession rarely met his peers, except for the formal luncheons of the administrative board of the Committee of Art Galleries. He stood firmly by his old principles: to sell paintings at a reasonable price, they first had to be purchased at a low price from the artist. In this he was out of touch with the times during a period when his colleagues fervently believed that great art dealers made great artists and not the other way around.

Kahnweiler discovered a way to witness his own funeral as a historical figure, which was inspired by the example set by Picasso. He was celebrating his eightieth birthday in 1964. He read all the articles devoted to him, and the letters he received from every part of the world. He attended the celebration organized in his honor to appreciate the praise bestowed: "An exemplary life"; "The wizard of cubism"; "The great art dealer of the century"; "The source, the inventor, the promoter of modern art"; "The history of art has proven him right."

He was overwhelmed, exhausted, tired, depressed. He was beginning to feel his age, even if at the age of eighty he had made his first voyage to Japan. He had to lose weight because his knees could not support him. In 1968, when he turned eighty-four, he would repeat, "It's too long, too much. My time has come, I feel very old, people shouldn't live to such an age." He had hoped to die before Picasso.

"I feel that very few things are worth it. Perhaps I am only trying to convince myself of the fact," he confided to a friend.[25]

Four days a week, for two hours a day, he would come to the gallery in his wheelchair. He noticed that his daily mail contained numerous letters with black borders, containing the notification of yet another death. He could no longer take long trips or even his cures at health spas in Switzerland. He had grown too deaf to appreciate music. As early as 1967, after the last time he attended the performances at the Bayreuth Festival, which he had faithfully followed year after year almost as a ritual, he wrote to friends, "I loved every moment of it but all the same old age diminishes the capacity for ecstasy."[26] He could no longer listen to records except with a hearing aid, which distorted everything.

He was numbed by the monotony of his existence. Mentally alert, his intellect intact, he did not want to obsess about one question: is there life after death?

He often startled visitors by posing this question before settling down to a discussion about business or art. Deprived of almost everything, isolated to some extent by his deafness, more than ever before he found consolation in reading. Before World War II he had always been a great reader. When Raymond Queneau asked two hundred celebrities to list the titles of the hundred books that made up their "ideal libraries" for a survey he wanted to publish with Gallimard, Cocteau led those who listed additional titles with 352, and Kahnweiler followed with 179.[27] He still discovered works with the same enthusiasm as before, but now it was difficult for him to communicate it.

He never doubted. His art had triumphed and would continue to dominate. Time would complete his task. He was not concerned about the criticism leveled at him for being limited by his very discoveries in art, and therefore relevant only within those limits he set for himself; the critics reproached him for trying to create a goal for painting. He was convinced that cubism had put an end to traditional representation, and that painting must never be relegated to the function of being decorative. Its function, now and always, was to interpret the visible world and to re-create external reality. He appeared so fragile, but had the strength of his inner convictions. Questioning his ideas was enough to provoke an angry glance at the offender and for him to begin lecturing, reciting a chapter from his volume *Confessions esthétiques,* or recounting as if for the very first time the evenings spent by Picasso's broken-down stove in the Bateau-Lavoir.

He had succeeded in eliminating all doubts. He accomplished this quite simply by coming to Paris, opening a gallery, discovering future great artists, and hanging their paintings, which collectors promptly purchased. It all happened in such a straightforward manner. Yet, despite his enthusiasm and disarming candor, Kahnweiler had a horror of introspection. He could never explain how during the years of the crash of 1929 he managed to survive, taking care of his family and his artists without any client so much as setting foot in his gallery for weeks on end. When people asked him what he had learned from that experience, he always answered with one word: "Nothing."[28]

He believed that what had happened to him was too personal for there to be any lesson applicable to the new generation. His journey through life was a unique adventure despite its overall resemblance to the general pattern of that of his European colleagues. Even during the seventies he personified a breed of art dealer who was like a dinosaur in the art market. He was more interested in art than in the market, and able to discuss both subjects equally well.

He had not experienced great inner turmoil, having always done exactly what he wanted. He had never wanted to be an artist. Of course he had made some watercolors and collages to see how it was done, but he never cherished any illusions about the subject.

During the first days of January 1979, in Paris, one day at lunch Kahnweiler suddenly pointed to a bottle of white wine and said, "It's a present from Doctor Schneider."

It was inconceivable that his doctor would have offered him alcohol under any circumstances. Michel Leiris immediately understood that his brother-in-law, who had been mentally lucid, was now becoming "confused." The next day Kahnweiler insisted on eating ice cream. He was going through the same reaction as his wife, Lucie, had when she was near death, thirty years earlier, in the very same room. He said he wanted to watch the broadcast of *The Marriage of Figaro* on television. Then he lay down on his bed.

The room was his universe. On his right hung the portrait of Lucie by Derain. On the left was his own portrait by Beaudin, next to a Masson in gouache and sand. On the wall above him on either side of the bed were portraits of Lucie and Kahnweiler, drawn by Juan Gris. Facing him across the room, an oil painting by Léger hung above the armoire. On the antique dresser, between a Masson and a pencil sketch of Kahnweiler by Picasso, was a movable mirror. At a glance Kahnweiler could see his own reflection and that of the Picasso. From his bed looking out the two great windows he could see the barges moving on the Seine, but he paid no attention to them.

Between his hands he held a book by Cosima Wagner, the third volume of her diaries, covering the years 1878 to 1883. Since he could no longer hear her husband's music, he wanted to read about it. But he was shocked and revolted by the vehemence of her anti-Semitism. Of course he had known. But all the same . . . He had enough strength to be offended, even if he could not express it.

On January 11, at the end of the afternoon, he asked, "Where is Michel?"

The servant went to fetch Michel Leiris from the drawing room. They sat together by the window, chatting. Then Kahnweiler stood up, went to lie down on his bed, and closed his eyes.

That was the end. No one could bear to tell the servant's son who went in every day to bring him his reading material. That day, as on previous occasions, the boy brought him *Le Monde* and placed it next to the hands of the man who looked so old and so tired.

There were thirty people, and no speeches or prayers, at the funeral. It was very intimate; the news had not spread as yet. The art dealer Saidenberg, a friend from New York, took the first flight as soon as he heard the news, but even he arrived too late. At the gallery, in the office Kahnweiler had shared with Louise Leiris, no one else would ever use his desk. His armchair remained empty, the enormous painting by Picasso remained hanging behind the desk, and to the left his portrait by the same artist. On his desk his daily calendar remained open to that date in January 1979.

A few months before his death, at the Salon des Indépéndants, the room containing the exhibition of fifty cubist paintings was called "The Kahnweiler Room." Seventy years earlier there hung in that show two paintings by Braque "belonging to Monsieur Rahnweiler [*sic*]." Between those dates he had become known.

He had shown how he could write and count, sell and think, see and exhibit. As of no one else, it could be said that he was a man of art.

NOTES

ABBREVIATIONS

DHK: Daniel-Heinrich Kahnweiler
GLL Archives: archives of the Galerie Louise Leiris
n.d.: not dated

CHAPTER 1. MANNHEIM, STUTTGART, FRANKFURT

1. Letter of DHK in reply to an inquiry about his family name from Louis Kahnweiler of Chicago, June 19, 1964, GLL Archives.
2. Gustave Kahnweiler, author interview, London, 1986.
3. DHK, *My Galleries and Painters. Interviews with Francis Crémieux* (New York: Viking, 1971), p. 21.
4. Ibid., pp. 23, 24.
5. Herbert Franck, "Kahnweiler unverkaüfliche Bilder," *Schöner Wohnen*, March 3, 1961.
6. DHK, *My Galleries*, p. 19.
7. Ibid.
8. Ibid., p. 20.
9. Pierre Cabanne, "Interview with DHK," *Lectures pour tous*, November 1969.
10. DHK, answer to *Almanach Flinker*, 1961.
11. DHK, correspondence with Réné Leibowitz, February 20, 1942, GLL Archives.
12. Gustave Kahnweiler, interview, op. cit.
13. DHK, "Ein Selbstportrait," *Das Selbstportrait: Grosse Kunstler und Denker unserer Zeit erzahlen von ihrem Leben und ihrem Werk* (Hamburg: Christopher Wegner Verlag, 1967). See also DHK, *My Galleries*, p. 22.
14. DHK, "Les grands collectionneurs suisses au début du siècle," *Bulletin Skira*, No. 5, Geneva, 1967.
15. Gustave Kahnweiler, Michel Leiris, Maurice Jardot, interviews with the author. Correspondence, GLL Archives.

CHAPTER 2. PARIS, LONDON, AND BACK

1. Paule Chavasse, "Le cubisme et son temps," six broadcasts on France III, 1961–62, INA Archives.
2. DHK, *My Galleries*, p. 25.
3. Ibid., p. 23.
4. Interview with Michel Leiris.

5. Chavasse, op. cit.; DHK, *My Galleries*, p. 26.
6. Chavasse, op. cit.
7. Ibid.
8. Ibid.
9. DHK, *My Galleries*, p. 24.
10. DHK, "Ein Selbstportrait."
11. Henri Perruchot, "Scandale au Luxembourg," *L'Oeil*, No. 9, September 1955; Jeanne Laurent, *Arts et pouvoirs*, Université de Saint-Étienne, CIEREC 1983; John Rewald, *Histoire de l'impressionisme*, Albin Michel, 1955.
12. Werner Spies, "Vendre des tableaux—donner à lire," *DHK marchand, éditeur, écrivain*, Centre Pompidou, 1984.
13. Chavasse, op. cit.
14. Ibid.; DHK, *My Galleries*, p. 30; DHK, "Ein Selbstportrait"; Cabanne, *Lectures*.
15. DHK, *Confessions esthétiques* (Paris: Gallimard, 1963), p. 20.
16. Fernand Léger, *Functions of Painting* (New York: Viking, 1973).
17. DHK, Salut aux Indépendants, in "69e Salon des Indépendants 1906–1909 le carré des anciens," Grand Palais 1968.
18. Ibid.
19. DHK, "Ein Selbstportrait."
20. André Level, *Souvenirs d'un Collectionneur*, Alain Mazo, 1959, p. 17; Guy Habasque, "Quand on vendait la peau de l'ours," in *l'Oeil*, No. 15, March 1956.
21. DHK, *My Galleries*, p. 32.
22. Friedrich Ahlers-Hestermann, *Kunst und Kunstler*, 1916.
23. Statement by DHK in "Seize écrivains definissent le bilinguisme," *Le Figaro littéraire*, July 29, 1961.
24. DHK, *Juan Gris: His Life and Work* (New York: Curt Valentin, 1947), p. 58.
25. Chavasse, op. cit.
26. *Gil Blas*, October 17, 1905.
27. DHK, *My Galleries*, p. 27.
28. Interview with Gustave Kahnweiler, cit.
29. Quoted from DHK, *My Galleries*; Chavasse, op. cit.; Cabanne, *Lectures*.
30. Interview with DHK in *Mon programme radio-télé*, February 13, 1960.
31. DHK, *My Galleries*, p. 29.
32. Ibid., p. 88.
33. Letter from Eugène Reignier to DHK, not dated but probably from December 1906, GLL Archives.
34. Letter from Eugène Reignier, January 30, 1906, GLL Archives.

CHAPTER 3. THE KAHNWEILER GALLERY

1. GLL Archives.
2. DHK, *My Galleries*, p. 35.
3. Florent Fels, *Voilà*, Paris 1957, p. 23.
4. Interview with DHK by Hubert Juin, *Les Lettres Françaises*, June 1961, pp. 22–28.
5. Maurice Jardot, "DHK ou la morale d'un metier," in *DHK marchand, éditeur, et écrivain*, Centre Pompidou, 1984.
6. Interview with DHK by Hughes Delesalle, recording number 56, Collection "Hommes d'aujourd'hui," Alliance Française.
7. Interview (1958) with DHK by Raymonde Moulin, *Le Marché de la peinture en France*, Minuit, 1967, p. 100.
8. Interview with DHK by Hélène Parmelin, *L'Humanité*, 1954.

9. Henri-Pierre Roché, *Le courrier graphique*, July 1954.
10. DHK, "Ein Selbstportrait"; DHK, *My Galleries*, p. 35; Cabanne, *Lectures*.
11. DHK, "Ein Selbstportrait."
12. André Derain, *Lettres à Vlaminck* (Flammarion, 1955), p. 192.
13. DHK, "Ein Selbstportrait."
14. Ibid.; Chavasse, op. cit.
15. DHK, *Juan Gris*, p. 40.
16. Derain, op. cit., p. 192; DHK, *My Galleries*, p. 35.
17. Interview with DHK by Georges Bernier, "Du temps que les cubistes étaient jeunes," *L'Oeil*, No. 1, January 15, 1955.
18. DHK, preface to Gertrude Stein, *Painted Lace and Other Pieces* (New Haven, 1955); Program on Matisse, France-Culture, June 23, 1970, INA Archives.
19. Maurice de Vlaminck, *Portraits avant décès* (Flammarion, 1943).
20. Malcolm Gee, *Dealers, Critics and Collectors of Modern Painting: Aspects of the Parisian Art Market 1910–1930*, Ph.D., Courtauld Institute, University of London, 1977.
21. Théda Shapiro, *Painters and Politics: The European Avant-Garde and Society 1900–1925* (New York: Elsevier, 1976); David Cottington, *Cubism and the Politics of Culture in France 1905–1914*, Ph.D., (Courtauld Institute, University of London, 1985).
22. Cottington, op. cit., p. 181.
23. René Julian, "Un peintre et son marchand à Rome vers la fin du XVIème siècle," *Pour DHK*, ed. Werner Spies (Stuttgart: Gerd Hatje, 1965).
24. Krisztof Pomian, *Collectionneurs, amateurs et curieux, Paris–Venise XVIè–XVIIIè siècle* (Paris: Gallimard, 1987).
25. Nicholas Green, "Dealing in Temperaments: Economic Transformation of the Artistic Field in France during the Second Half of the Nineteenth Century," *Art History*, Vol. 10, No. 1, March 1987.
26. Albert Boime, "Les magnats américains à la conquête de l'art français," *L'Histoire*, No. 44, April 1982.
27. Henri Perruchot, "Le Père Tanguy," *L'Oeil*, No. 6, June 15, 1955.
28. DHK, *L'Arche*, No. 55, August–September 1961.
29. Interview with Francis Jourdain, *L'Oeil*, No. 21, September 1956.
30. Boime, op. cit.
31. S. N. Behrman, *Duveen* (New York: Random House, 1952); Raymonde Moulin, op. cit., p. 205.
32. Ambroise Vollard, *Souvenirs d'un marchand de tableaux* (Albin Michel, 1937); Ambroise Vollard, *En écoutant Cézanne, Degas, Renoir . . .* (Grasset, 1938); Fels, op. cit., p. 145.
33. Apollinaire, *Je dis tout*, October 26, 1907.
34. DHK, *L'Arche*, art. cit.
35. Camille Pissarro, *Lettres à son fils Lucien* (Albin Michel, 1950).
36. Cabanne, *Lectures*.
37. DHK, "Der Anfang des modernen Kunsthandels, *Standorte in Zeitsrom*, E. Forsthoff and R. Horstel (Frankfurt: Athenaum Verlag, 1974).
38. Jardot, op. cit.
39. GLL Archives.
40. Letter, DHK to Lascaux, June 10, 1931, GLL Archives.
41. DHK, *Les grandes collectionneurs*.
42. Spies, op. cit.
43. Francis Berthier, preface, *Catalogue de la donation Jean et Geneviève Masurel*, Musée d'art moderne de Villeneuve d'Ascq, Tourcoing, 1984.
44. Jean Grenier, "Un collectionneur pionnier," *L'Oeil*, No. 15, March 1956.

45. Interview with Jean Masurel, nephew of Roger Dutilleul.
46. Liliane Meffre, "DHK et Carl Einstein: les affinités électives," *DHK marchand, éditeur, écrivain*, Centre Pompidou, 1984.
47. Letter, DHK to Raymond Queneau, May 6, 1971, GLL Archives.
48. Gabrielle Linnebach, "Wilhelm Uhde, le dernier romantique," *L'Oeil*, No. 285, April 1979.
49. DHK, "Ein Selbstportrait."
50. Liliane Meffre, "DHK et Wilhelm Uhde: le marchand et l'amateur," from *DHK marchand, éditeur, écrivain*, Centre Pompidou, 1984.
51. DHK, *My Galleries*, p. 38; Cabanne, *Lectures*; Chavasse, op. cit.
52. DHK, *My Galleries*, p. 38; DHK, "Ein Selbstportrait."
53. Jeanine Warnod, *Le Bateau-Lavoir* (Mayer, 1986), p. 13.
54. Interview with Pierre Mac Orlan in Chavasse, op. cit.
55. Chavasse, op. cit.
56. Cabanne, *Lectures*.
57. Daniel Henry, "Der Kubismus," *Die Weissen Blatter*, Zurich, 1916, p. 212; Spies, art. cit.
58. DHK, *Juan Gris*, pp. 69–70.
59. Ibid.; DHK, *Confessions esthétiques*, pp. 22, 23.
60. Ibid.
61. DHK, *Picasso et le cubisme*, exhibition catalogue, Musée de Lyon, 1953.
62. DHK, *My Galleries*, p. 39.
63. Ibid.
64. Wilhelm Uhde, *Von Bismarck bis Picasso* (Zurich: Verlag Oprecht, 1938).
65. DHK, *My Galleries*, p. 59.
66. Pierre Cabanne, *Le siècle de Picasso*, Denoël, 1975, p. 245.
67. Chavasse, op. cit.

CHAPTER 4. THE HEROIC YEARS

1. André Dunoyer de Segonzac, "Souvenirs sur André Derain," *Le Figaro littéraire*, September 18, 1954.
2. Cabanne, *Lectures*.
3. Raymonde Moulin, op. cit., p. 112.
4. Letter, DHK to Togorès, December 23, 1925, GLL Archives.
5. Cabanne, *Lectures*; DHK, Crémieux, op. cit., p. 100.
6. Linnebach, op. cit.
7. Vlaminck, op. cit., p. 33.
8. *Paris-Journal*, 1911.
9. Ibid.
10. Letter, Vlaminck to DHK, December 18, 1919, GLL Archives.
11. Apollinaire, *Je dis tout*, October 26, 1907.
12. Gustave Coquiot, "Maurice de Vlaminck," *Peintres d'aujourd'hui*, 1914.
13. La Palette (pseud. André Salmon), "Portrait de Braque," *Paris-Journal*, October 13, 1911.
14. Chavasse, op. cit.
15. Dora Vallier, *L'intérieur de l'art*, Seuil, 1982, p. 42.
16. Chavasse, op. cit.
17. J. K. Huysmans, *L'art moderne*, 10/18, 1975, pp. 252–53.
18. Letter, DHK to Borès, November 29, 1939, GLL Archives.
19. *Montjoie*, April 4–6, 1914; cit. by Gee, op. cit.
20. Vollard, *Souvenirs*, pp. 204, 207.
21. *Gil Blas*, October 17, 1905.

22. Rewald, article in *Charivari*, op. cit., pp. 204, 207.
23. DHK, *Juan Gris*.
24. Chavasse, op. cit.
25. Jean Cassou, *Une vie pour la liberté* (Robert Laffont, 1981), p. 277.
26. Letter, Max Jacob to DHK, April 1913, *Correspondance de Max Jacob* (Éditions de Paris, 1953).
27. DHK, *My Galleries*, p. 45.
28. Otto Freundlich, "Journal," *Prisme des arts*, January 1957.
29. Camille Mauclair, *Les métèques contre l'art français* (Éditions de la Nouvelle Revue Critique, 1930), p. 121.
30. Adolphe Basler, *La peinture . . . religion nouvelle* (Librairie de France, 1926).
31. *Le Figaro*, October 3, 1911; *Gil Blas*, September 22, 1911.
32. Brassaï, *Conversations avec Picasso*, Gallimard, 1964, p. 34.
33. DHK, *Juan Gris,* p. 71.
34. Chavasse, op. cit.
35. Letters, DHK to Togorès, May 10, 1924 and November 12, 1928, GLL Archives.
36. Letter, Max Jacob to DHK, September 12, 1912, *Correspondance de Max Jacob*, p. 73.
37. Ibid., pp. 37–39.
38. Ibid., p. 40.
39. François Chapon, "Livres de Kahnweiler," *DHK marchand, éditeur, écrivain*, op. cit.
40. Chavasse, op. cit.
41. Chapon, op. cit.
42. Cabanne, *Lectures*.
43. Cabanne, "Le siècle de Picasso."
44. DHK, Note, 1952, GLL Archives.
45. DHK, *My Galleries*, pp. 39–40.
46. Ibid.
47. Beverly Whitney Kean, *All the Empty Palaces: The Merchant Patrons of Modern Art in Pre-Revolutionary Russia* (London: Barrie and Jenkins, 1983).
48. Serge Fauchereau, *Beaux-Arts Magazine,* November 1981.
49. Henri Matisse, *Écrits et propos sur l'art* (Hermann, 1972).
50. B. Whitney Kean, op. cit., p. 164.
51. Matisse, op. cit., p. 119.
52. GLL Archives.
53. DHK, "Souvenir du Dr. Vincenz Kramar," preface to exhibition catalogue, Prague, 1964.
54. Adolf Hoffmeister, article in "Catalogue of the Paris-Prague Exhibition," MNAM, 1966.
55. Marc Dachy, Catalogue, exhibition Gertrude Stein, Clos Poncet, Culoz, 1987; Gertrude Stein issue, *Europe*, August 1985; author interview with Joseph Barry and Edward Burns.
56. Linda Simon, *The Biography of Alice B. Toklas* (Garden City, N.Y.: Doubleday, 1977).
57. DHK in "Bonjour, Monsieur Léger," *L'art et la vie*, broadcast on France I, September 2, 1954, INA Archives; DHK, *My Galleries*, p. 68.
58. Chavasse, op. cit.
59. DHK, preface to catalogue, Manolo exhibition, Chalette Gallery, New York, 1957.
60. Chavasse, op. cit.; DHK, *My Galleries*, p. 48.
61. DHK, *Juan Gris*, p. 8.
62. DHK, *Confessions esthétiques*, p. 122.
63. Vallier, op. cit., p. 84.
64. *Livre et Image*, July 4, 1910.
65. Letter, Apollinaire to DHK, November 28, 1910, GLL Archives.
66. Letter, Derain to DHK, 1910, GLL Archives.
67. Letter, Max Jacob to DHK, 1910, *Correspondance de Max Jacob*, pp. 40, 41.
68. Ibid., p. 54.
69. DHK, Interview for tenth-anniversary memorial to Max Jacob,

broadcast on France I, March 8, 1954, INA Archives.

70. Yves Kobry, "Archimboldo, l'illusionniste," *Beaux-Arts Magazine*, No. 44, March 1987.

71. Pierre Daix, *Picasso créateur: la vie intime et l'oeuvre* (Seuil, 1987), p. 111; Michael Baxendall, *Patterns of Intention: On the Historical Explanation of Pictures* (Yale University Press, 1985), pp. 41–72.

72. Letter, DHK to Picasso, November 20, 1962, GLL Archives.

73. Roland Penrose, "Picasso's Portrait of Kahnweiler," *The Burlington Magazine*, No. 852, March 1974.

74. Letter, DHK to van Hecke, March 12, 1924, GLL Archives.

75. René Brimo, *L'évolution du goût aux États-Unis d'après l'histoire des collections* (Éditions James Fortune, Paris, 1938).

76. Ibid.

77. Chavasse, op. cit.

78. DHK, *Juan Gris*.

79. Vallier, op. cit., p. 34.

80. *Le petit phare*, Nantes, October 9, 1911.

81. *The Sunday Times*, October 1, 1911.

82. Letter, Max Jacob to DHK (n.d.), 1912, *Correspondance de Max Jacob*, pp. 80–85.

83. *Gil Blas*, February 9, 1912.

84. *Gil Blas*, March 19, 1912.

85. James Burckley, article in *L'assiette au Beurre*, February 17, 1912.

86. *L'Intransigeant*, January 6, 1912.

87. Jacques de Gachons, "La Peinture d'après-demain," *Je sais Tout*, April 15, 1912.

88. Author interview with André Masson.

89. Paul Klee, *Journal* (Paris: Grasset, 1959).

90. GLL Archives.

91. Fernande Olivier, *Picasso et ses amis* (Paris: Stock, 1933).

92. GLL Archives.

93. Letters, DHK to Picasso, June 6 and July 12, 1912, GLL Archives.

94. Letters, Picasso to DHK, June 12 and 17, 1912, GLL Archives.

95. Letter, Picasso to DHK, August 15, 1912, GLL Archives.

96. Letter, Braque to DHK, GLL Archives.

97. Ibid., summer 1912.

98. Ibid.

99. *DHK marchand, éditeur, et écrivain*, p. 111.

100. Vallier, op. cit., pp. 39, 40.

101. *L'Intransigeant*, October 1 and 3, 1912.

102. *Gil Blas*, October 21, 1912.

103. DHK, *Juan Gris*, p. 71.

104. DHK, *Confessions esthétiques*, p. 35.

105. Chavasse, op. cit.

106. DHK, *Confessions esthétiques*, p. 35.

107. DHK, "Ein Selbstportrait."

108. DHK, *Juan Gris*, p. 65.

109. Chavasse, op. cit.

110. René Gimpel, *Journal d'un collectioneur marchand de tableaux* (Paris: Calmann-Lévy, 1963), p. 84.

111. Vallier, op. cit., p. 43; *Amis de l'art*, No. 6, 1949.

112. *Excelsior*, October 2, 1911.

113. *Bulletin de la section d'or*, October 9, 1912.

114. Michael Baxendall, *L'Oeil du Quattrocento* (Paris: Gallimard, 1985).

115. Vincent van Gogh, *Lettres à Théo*, p. 271, quoted by Moulin.

116. Jean Ajalbert, *L'Humanité*, 1905.

117. Vollard, op. cit.

118. Letter, DHK to Philippe Vergnaud, December 9, 1958, GLL Archives.

119. DHK, *My Galleries*, p. 73.

120. Letter, DHK to Manolo, July 9, 1923, GLL Archives.

121. Philippe Vergnaud, *Les contrats conclus entre peintres et mar-*

chands de tableaux (Bordeaux: Rousseau, 1958), p. 83.

122. Contract letters drawn up by DHK to Picasso, Derain, Braque, December 18, 1912, GLL Archives.

123. Letter, Gris to DHK, February 20, 1913, GLL Archives.

124. Raymond Bachollet, "A la découverte de Juan Gris, déssinateur de presse," in *Hommage à Juan Gris,* Grand Orient de France, June 1987.

125. DHK, *Juan Gris.*

126. Ibid.

127. Ibid.

128. Chavasse, op. cit.

129. Wilhelm Uhde, *Picasso et la tradition française* (Paris: Les 4 Chemins, 1928), p. 83.

130. Letter, DHK to Hughes Delesalle, op. cit.

131. Letter, Vlaminck to DHK, March 2, 1934, GLL Archives.

132. Letter, Nadia Léger to DHK, December 9, 1958, GLL Archives.

133. Ibid.

134. Henri-Pierre Roché, "Adieu brave petite collection," *L'Oeil,* No. 51, March 1959.

135. Roché, *Le courrier graphique.*

136. Cabanne, *Lectures;* DHK, Crémieux, op. cit.

137. Letter, Picasso to DHK, April 11, 1913, GLL Archives.

138. Letters, Gris to DHK, September 29, 1913, October (n.d.), 1913, GLL Archives.

139. Letter, Braque to DHK, Summer 1913, GLL Archives.

140. *Gil Blas,* November 15, 1913.

141. Letter, DHK to Douglas Cooper, March 15, 1937, GLL Archives.

142. Letter, DHK to Halvorsen, April 7, 1922, GLL Archives.

143. Letter, DHK to Cooper, cit.

144. Christian Zervos, "Entretien avec Alfred Flechtheim," *Feuilles volantes,* supplement to *Cahiers d'Art,* No. 10, 1927.

145. Ibid.

146. Ibid.

147. Cabanne, *Le siècle de Picasso.*

148. Letter, DHK to Raymond Queneau, February 26, 1960, GLL Archives.

149. DHK, *Juan Gris,* p. 99.

150. Vallier, op. cit.

151. Apollinaire, *Les peintres cubistes* (Berg International, 1986), p. 75.

152. *L'Intransigeant,* March 18 and 22, 1913.

153. Chavasse, op. cit.; Levêque, op. cit.

154. Letter, Apollinaire to DHK (n.d.), spring 1913, GLL Archives.

155. Letter, DHK to Apollinaire, March 27, April 3, 1913, GLL Archives.

156. Letter, DHK to Picasso, March 4, 1913, GLL Archives.

157. Pierre Daix, *Journal du cubisme* (Lausanne: Skira, 1982), p. 115.

158. Letter, DHK to Gris, February 19, 1914, GLL Archives.

159. Shapiro, op. cit., p. 75.

160. Letter, DHK to Leo Stein, February 10, 1914, GLL Archives; Letter, DHK to Ivan Morozov, February 9, 1914, GLL Archives.

161. Letters, DHK to Sergei Shchukin, February 3, 9, 12, and 18, 1914, GLL Archives.

162. GLL Archives.

163. Daniel Henry, "Werkstatten," *Die Freude,* Oberfranken, Vol. 1, 1920.

164. *Gil Blas,* March 3, 1914.

165. Letters, DHK to Shchukin and Morozov, February 20, 1914, GLL Archives.

166. *Journal des débats,* March 2, 1914; *Paris-Midi,* March 1, 1914.

167. *Gil Blas,* March 3, 1914.

168. Guy Habasque, "Quand on vendait la peau d'ours," *L'Oeil,* No. 15, March 1956.

169. *L'homme libre,* March 3, 1914.

170. Delcour, "Avant l'invasion," *Paris-Midi*, March 3, 1914.
171. Dr. Artault, *La Revue sans titre*, quoted by Apollinaire in *Paris-Journal*, May 15, 1914.
172. *L'Intransigeant*, June 12, 1914.
173. Joseph Kessel, *Kisling* (Turin: Éditions Jean Kisling, 1971).
174. Gertrude Stein, *The Autobiography of Alice B. Toklas* (New York: Harcourt, Brace, 1933).
175. Chavasse, op. cit.
176. Letter, Derain to DHK, July 12, 1914, GLL Archives.
177. DHK, "Ein Selbstportrait."
178. Letter, DHK to Derain, September 6, 1919, GLL Archives.
179. DHK, *My Galleries*, pp. 49, 73; Chavasse, op. cit.; DHK, "Ein Selbstportrait."
180. Chavasse, op. cit.
181. Letter, Gris to DHK, August 1, 1914, GLL Archives.
182. DHK, *My Galleries*, p. 50.

INTERMISSION: EXILE (1915–1920)

1. Letter, DHK to Manolo, September 25, 1919, GLL Archives.
2. DHK, Les grands collectionneurs.
3. Chavasse, op. cit.
4. Yves Collart, *Le Parti socialiste suisse et l'Internationale 1914–1915* (Geneva: Droz, 1969), p. 208.
5. Frances Trezevant, *Un collectionneur suisse au XXème Siècle: Hermann Rupf*, Mémoire de licence, Université de Lausanne, 1975.
6. Letter, Max Jacob to DHK, September 22, 1914, *Correspondance de Max Jacob*.
7. Letter, Max Jacob to Maurice Raynal, September 23, 1914, *Correspondance de Max Jacob*.
8. Letters, Juan Gris to Maurice Raynal, February 15, 1915 and October 4, 1916, GLL Archives.
9. Maximilien Gauthier, "Derain," *Larousse mensuel*, November 1954.
10. Vallier, op. cit., p. 62.
11. Ibid.
12. Chavasse, op. cit.
13. Oskar Kokoschka, *My Life* (New York: Macmillan, 1974).
14. Police registers and reports from the canton of Bern. Lawyers' letters, January 28 and February 15, 1915. Testimonial by Hermann Rupf, February 22, 1915. Stadtarchiv, Bern, BB4.1.952.
15. Apollinaire, "Les inédits," *Revue de Paris,* January 1947.
16. Letter, Gris to DHK, March 26, 1915, GLL Archives; Douglas Cooper, ed. and trans., *Letters of Juan Gris, 1913–1927* (London, 1956).
17. Ibid.
18. Cabanne, *Lectures.*
19. Christian Derouet, "De la voix et de la plume: les émois cubistes d'un marchand de tableaux," *Europe,* No. 638, June 1982.
20. Chavasse, op. cit.
21. Letter, Gris to DHK, April 19, 1915, GLL Archives.
22. Gimpel, op. cit., p. 23.
23. Séance du 6 juillet 1915, document Bibliothèque Nationale.
24. Alfred Erich Senn, *The Russian Revolution in Switzerland, 1914–1917* (University of Wisconsin Press, 1971).
25. Ibid., p. 31.
26. John Willett, *Art and Politics in the Weimar Period: The New Sobriety, 1917–1933* (New York: Pantheon, 1978).
27. Tzara, quoted by Chavasse, op. cit.

28. Letter, DHK to Gris, August 22, 1919, GLL Archives.
29. Chavasse, op. cit.; DHK, Crémieux, op. cit.
30. Published for the first time in French, *Confessions esthétiques*.
31. Letter, DHK to René Leibowitz, February 20, 1942, GLL Archives.
32. Alois Riegl, *Spätromische Kunstindustrie*, 1906.
33. Maurice Raynal, *Les créateurs du cubisme*, Catalogue No. 13, Exposition de Beaux-Arts, March 1935.
34. DHK, *Maurice de Vlaminck* (Leipzig: Klinkhard et Biermann, 1920).
35. Letter, DHK to Masson, November 13, 1939, GLL Archives.
36. DHK, *Confessions esthétiques*.
37. Chavasse, op. cit.
38. DHK, *Confessions esthétiques*.
39. Letter, DHK to Masson, September 19, 1957, GLL Archives.
40. Stefan Zweig, *Journaux, 1912–1940* (Paris: Belfond, 1986).
41. Letters, DHK to Tristan Tzara, February 13 and August 29, 1917, Bibliothèque littéraire Jacques Doucet.
42. Chavasse, op. cit.
43. Félix Fénéon, *Oeuvres plus que complètes*, texts compiled and introduced by J. V. Halperin (Geneva: Droz, 1970).
44. Philippe Vatin, "La Vie artistique en 1917," *Images de 1917*, Musée d'histoire contemporaine, Catalogue BDIC, 1987.
45. Roland Ruffieux, *La Suisse de l'entre-deux-guerres* (Lausanne: Payot, 1974).
46. Letters, DHK to Tristan Tzara, November 30 and December 20, 1918, Bibliothèque littéraire Jacques Doucet.
47. Letter, DHK to Manolo, September 25, 1919, GLL Archives.
48. Letter, DHK to Tristan Tzara, November 30, 1918, Bibliothèque littéraire Jacques Doucet.
49. Pierre Reverdy, *Note éternelle du présent* (Paris: Flammarion, 1973).
50. Meffre, op. cit.
51. Letter, DHK to Braque, September 19, 1919, GLL Archives.
52. Letter, DHK to Vlaminck, September 23, 1919, GLL Archives.
53. Letter, Braque to DHK, September 17, 1919, GLL Archives.
54. Letter, DHK to Manolo, December 11, 1919, GLL Archives.
55. Letter, Gris to DHK, August 25, 1919, GLL Archives.
56. Letter, DHK to Gris, August 1919, GLL Archives.
57. Letter, Gris to DHK, September 3, 1919, GLL Archives.
58. Letters, DHK to Gris, September 17 and October 1, 1919, GLL Archives.
59. Letter, DHK to Gris, December 8, 1919, GLL Archives.
60. Letter, DHK to Braque, September 2, 1919, GLL Archives.
61. Ibid., September 19, 1919.
62. Ibid.
63. Letter, Braque to DHK, October 8, 1919, GLL Archives.
64. Letter, DHK to Braque, October 14, 1919, GLL Archives.
65. Letter, DHK to Braque, November 11, 1919, GLL Archives.
66. Letter, DHK to Braque, September 15, 1919, GLL Archives.
67. Letter, DHK to Derain, September 6, 1919, GLL Archives.
68. Letter, Derain to DHK, September 6, 1919, GLL Archives.
69. Letter, DHK to Derain, December 16, 1919, GLL Archives.
70. Letter, Derain to DHK, December 17, 1919, GLL Archives.
71. Letters, DHK to Vlaminck, September 9 and 11, 1919, GLL Archives.
72. Letters, DHK to Manolo, September 11 and 25, 1919, GLL Archives;

Letter, Manolo to DHK, October 6, 1919, GLL Archives.

73. Letter, DHK to Manolo, December 11, 1919, GLL Archives.
74. Letter, Léger to DHK, autumn 1919, GLL Archives.
75. Letter, DHK to Braque, November 11, 1919, GLL Archives.
76. Chavasse, op. cit.
77. DHK interview with unidentified Paris daily newspaper, November 13, 1966, GLL Archives.
78. Letter, DHK to Léger, October 13, 1919, GLL Archives; Letters, DHK

to Derain, December 16 and 26, 1919, GLL Archives; Letter, DHK to Vlaminck, December 16, 1919, GLL Archives.

79. Letter, Léger to DHK, October 9, 1919, GLL Archives.
80. DHK, *Confessions esthétiques*.
81. Ibid.
82. *Aux Écoutes*, January 2, 1953.
83. DHK, *Confessions esthétiques*.
84. Ibid.
85. Ibid.; DHK, *My Galleries*, p. 56; Chavasse, op. cit.
86. Chavasse, op. cit.

CHAPTER 5. FORGETTING DROUOT

1. Cabanne, *Lectures*.
2. DHK, manuscript notes, February 1920, GLL Archives.
3. Letter, van Dongen to DHK, April 8, 1920, GLL Archives.
4. Letters, Manolo to DHK, May 7 and 16, 1920, GLL Archives; letter, DHK to Manolo, May 2, 1920, GLL Archives.
5. Letter, DHK to Picasso, February 10, 1920, GLL Archives.
6. DHK, *Juan Gris*, p. 16.
7. DHK, manuscript notes, February 1920, GLL Archives.
8. Letter, Gris to DHK, February 17, 1920, GLL Archives.
9. Braque contract, May 11, 1920, GLL Archives.
10. Letter, Braque to DHK, June 30, 1920, GLL Archives.
11. Léon Degand, "DHK et la galerie Louise Leiris," *Aujourd'hui*, No. 13, June 1957.
12. Letter, Florent Fels to DHK, September 7, 1920, GLL Archives.
13. Letter, J. Gunzburg to DHK, April 2, 1920, GLL Archives.
14. Letter, DHK to the controller of di-

rect contributions to the Madeleine church, January 25, 1921, GLL Archives.

15. Letter, DHK to Stephan Bourgeois, October 21, 1921, GLL Archives.
16. Ambrogio Ceroni, "Memories of Lunia Czechowska," *Amédéo Modigliani* (Milan, 1958).
17. Letters, DHK to Zborowski, January 18 and February 5, 1921, GLL Archives.
18. Amédée Ozenfant, *Mémoires, 1886–1962* (Paris: Seghers, 1968).
19. Roland Penrose, *Picasso: His Life and Work* (New York: Harper & Row, 1971).
20. Derouet, *Europe*, op. cit.
21. Letter, DHK to Gris, December 23, 1920, GLL Archives.
22. Letters, Léger to DHK, November 9 and October 30, 1920, GLL Archives.
23. Letter, Kundig to DHK, November 20, 1920, GLL Archives.
24. Invoice, December 1920, GLL Archives.
25. Letter, Jacques Doucet to DHK, December 29, 1920, GLL Archives;

Letter, DHK to Jacques Doucet, December 31, 1920, GLL Archives.

26. Letter, DHK to Signac, November 12, 1920, GLL Archives.

27. Letter, DHK to Kundig, November 12, 1920, GLL Archives.

28. Letter, DHK to Braque, January 14, 1921, GLL Archives.

29. Letter, DHK to Derain, May 10, 1921, GLL Archives.

30. Miró, *Selected Writings and Interviews,* ed. Margit Rowell (London: Thames and Hudson, 1987).

31. Letter, DHK to Fernande Olivier, May 27, 1921, GLL Archives; Letters, Fernande Olivier to DHK, July 9 and 11, 1921, GLL Archives.

32. *L'Intransigeant,* May 31, 1921.

33. Meffre, op. cit.

34. Laurent, op. cit., p. 121.

35. Meffre, op. cit.

36. Derouet, *Europe,* op. cit.

37. Letter, Gris to DHK, May 18, 1921, GLL Archives.

38. Laurent, op. cit., p. 119; Ozenfant, op. cit.; *Echo de Paris,* June 13, 1921; Gertrude Stein, op. cit., p. 118; Georges Auric, *Quand j'étais là* (Paris: Grasset, 1979).

39. Cabanne, *Lectures.*

40. Tzara interview quoted in Chavasse, cit.

41. Ozenfant, op. cit., p. 119.

42. Letter, DHK to Manolo, June 25, 1921, GLL Archives.

43. DHK, interview in Gee, op. cit.; Wilhelm Uhde, *Von Bismarck bis Picasso* (Zurich: Verlag Oprecht, 1938).

44. *La Gazette de l'Hôtel Drouot,* March 19, 1921; *L'Écho de Paris,* June 13, 1921; *Comoedia,* June 15, 1921.

45. *Comoedia,* November 21, 1921.

46. Letter, DHK to Gris, November 15, 1921, GLL Archives.

47. Pinturicchio (Louis Vauxcelles), *Le Carnet de la semaine,* November 13, 1921.

48. Ibid., February 4, 1921.

49. *Comoedia,* November 21, 1921.

50. Letters, DHK to Derain, November 22 and December 2, 1921, GLL Archives.

51. Letter, DHK to Braque, November 22, 1921, GLL Archives.

52. Pinturicchio (Louis Vauxcelles), in *Le Carnet de la semaine,* November 27, 1921.

53. *L'Oeuvre,* November 17, 1921; *Le Journal,* November 18, 1921; *Bulletin de l'art ancien et moderne,* November 25, 1921.

54. Letter, Léonce Rosenberg to DHK, October 10, 1921, GLL Archives.

55. Letter, DHK to Léonce Rosenberg, October 11, 1921, GLL Archives.

56. Letter, Léonce Rosenberg to DHK, October 27, 1921, GLL Archives.

57. Letter, DHK to Léonce Rosenberg, October 28, 1921, GLL Archives.

58. Letter, DHK to Derain, October 17, 1921, GLL Archives.

59. Letter, DHK to Braque, October 4, 1921, GLL Archives.

60. Letter, Léonce Rosenberg to Alfred Flechtheim, November 3, 1921, GLL Archives.

61. Letter, DHK to Léonce Rosenberg, December 29, 1921, GLL Archives; Letter, DHK to Gris, November 25, 1921, GLL Archives; Letter, DHK to Derain, December 3, 1921, GLL Archives.

62. Letter, DHK to Gris, December 3, 1921, GLL Archives.

63. Letter, DHK to Derain, December 31, 1921, GLL Archives.

64. Letter, Joseph Brenner to DHK, December 28, 1921, GLL Archives.

65. Letters, DHK and Halvorsen, October and November 1921, GLL Archives.

66. GLL Archives.

67. Letters, Léonce Rosenberg to DHK,

April 15 and May 1, 1922, GLL Archives.

68. Letter, Léonce Rosenberg to DHK, January 12, 1922, GLL Archives.

69. Letter, Léonce Rosenberg to DHK, April 10, 1922, GLL Archives.

70. Letter, Léonce Rosenberg to DHK, April 27, 1922, GLL Archives.

71. Letters, DHK to Léonce Rosenberg, January 11 and 13, and April 19, 1922, GLL Archives.

72. *Le Carnet de la semaine*, November 20, 1921.

73. "Une sombre histoire," *Le Carnet de la semaine*, March 5, 1922.

74. Letter, DHK to Derain, September 21, 1922, GLL Archives.

75. Marie Laure, "Journal d'un peintre," *Cahiers des Saisons*, Summer 1964.

76. Alfred Richet, "Propos épars à l'occasion de l'exposition Collection André Lefèvre," *Pour DHK,* op. cit.

77. *Petit Larousse de la peinture*, ed. Michel Laclotte, 1979.

78. Letter, Léonce Rosenberg to DHK, September 19, 1922, GLL Archives.

79. Letter, Brenner to DHK, March 4, 1922, GLL Archives.

80. Letter, John Wanamaker to DHK, March 13, 1922, GLL Archives.

81. Accounts book, June 30, 1922, GLL Archives.

82. Letter, DHK to Samuel Katznelson, June 19, 1922, GLL Archives.

83. Letters, Gusta Olson to DHK, May 13, August 23, and September 16, 1922, GLL Archives.

84. Letter, Jacques de Gunzburg to DHK, January 22, 1922, GLL Archives.

85. Letter, DHK to Robert Delaunay, April 15, 1922, GLL Archives.

86. Letter, DHK to Jacques Doucet, January 23, 1922, GLL Archives.

87. Letters, DHK to Edmond Jaloux, January 30 and 31, 1922, GLL Archives.

88. Letter, DHK to M. Vautheret, June 30, 1922, GLL Archives.

89. Letter, DHK to Derain, September 21, 1922, GLL Archives.

90. Letter, DHK to Togorès, November 29, 1922, GLL Archives.

91. Letters, DHK to Manolo, May 30, June 27, and November 24, 1922, GLL Archives.

92. Letter, Vlaminck to DHK (n.d.), GLL Archives.

93. DHK, "Fernand Léger," *Europe*, September 1971.

94. Letter, DHK to Manolo, March 29, 1922, GLL Archives; Letter, Vauxcelles to DHK, March 22, 1923, GLL Archives.

95. Letter, DHK to Manolo, July 9, 1923, GLL Archives.

96. Letter, DHK to Manolo, July 16, 1923, GLL Archives.

97. Robert Desnos, *Écrits sur les peintres* (Paris: Flammarion, 1984).

98. Letter, DHK to Georges Aubry, May 9, 1923, GLL Archives.

CHAPTER 6. SUNDAYS IN BOULOGNE

1. Armand Salacrou, *Dans la salle des pas perdus* (Paris: Gallimard, 1974).

2. Ibid., p. 129.

3. Letter, DHK to Louis Dubos, February 10, 1926, GLL Archives.

4. Private source.

5. Salacrou, op. cit., p. 128.

6. Chavasse, op. cit.

7. Letter, DHK to René Leibowitz, March 10, 1950, GLL Archives.

8. DHK, *Juan Gris.*
9. Letter, DHK to Togorès, July 2, 1923, GLL Archives.
10. DHK, *Juan Gris,* p. 110.
11. Letter, DHK to Lascaux, June 1, 1923, GLL Archives.
12. Letter, Gris to DHK, December 9, 1923, GLL Archives.
13. Jean Lacouture, *Malraux: une vie dans le siècle* (Points Seuil, 1973); Pierre Lescure, *Album Malraux* (La Pléiade, 1986.)
14. Letter, DHK to André Simon, March 20, 1923, GLL Archives.
15. Lacouture, op. cit., p. 57.
16. Salacrou, op. cit., p. 133.
17. Letter, Antonin Artaud to DHK, July 1927, GLL Archives.
18. Letter, DHK to Masson, September 17, 1925, GLL Archives.
19. Salacrou, op. cit., p. 130.
20. Letter, DHK to Lugné-Poë, January 29, 1925, GLL Archives.
21. Fels, op. cit., p. 78.
22. Man Ray, *Self Portrait* (Boston: Little, Brown, 1988), p. 96.
23. Interview with Claude Laurens, quoted in Chavasse.
24. DHK, preface to Stein, *Painted Lace.*
25. Chavasse, op. cit.
26. Letter, DHK to Mollet, October 11, 1923, GLL Archives; Mollet, *Les mémoires du baron Mollet* (Paris: Gallimard, 1963).
27. Baudelaire, *Pour Delacroix* (Brussels: Editions Complexe, 1987), p. 771.
28. Emmanuel Bréon, "Juan Gris à Boulogne-Billancourt," *Hommage à Juan Gris.*
29. Letter, DHK to Breton, October 22, 1924, GLL Archives.
30. Letter, DHK to Masson, May 5, 1928, GLL Archives.
31. Chavasse, op. cit.
32. DHK, *My Galleries,* pp. 97, 102.
33. Georges Charbonnier, *Entretiens avec André Masson* (Paris: Juilliard, 1958), p. 26.
34. Ibid., p. 39.
35. Charbonnier, op. cit., p. 68.
36. Ibid.
37. Michel Leiris, interview with the author.
38. Michel Leiris, *Manhood: a journey from childhood into the fierce order of virility,* trans. Richard Howard (San Francisco: North Point Press, 1984); Madeleine Chapsal, "Entretien avec Pierre Loeb," *L'Express,* April 9, 1964.
39. Michel Surya, *Georges Bataille, La mort à l'oeuvre* (Paris: Seguier, 1987), p. 82.
40. Letter, Max Jacob to DHK, September 2, 1921, *Correspondance de Max Jacob,* p. 35.
41. Salacrou, vol. I, p. 124.
42. Ibid., p. 139.
43. Letter, DHK to Vlaminck, December 2, 1925, GLL Archives.
44. Letter, DHK to Delessale, cit.
45. Letter, DHK to Shchukin, June 9, 1923, GLL Archives.
46. Invoice, June 1923, GLL Archives; DHK, *Preface Kramar.*
47. Letter, DHK to H. P. Roché, October 17, 1923, GLL Archives.
48. Letter, DHK to H. P. Roché, October 1924, GLL Archives.
49. Letter, DHK to Gourgaud, April 12, 1926, GLL Archives.
50. Letter, DHK to Noailles, January 20, 1926, GLL Archives.
51. Salacrou, op. cit., pp. 135, 136.
52. Letter, DHK to Robert Brussel, November 14, 1925, GLL Archives.
53. Letter, DHK to Baum, April 2, 1925, GLL Archives.
54. Letter, Paul Rosenberg to DHK, June 12, 1926, GLL Archives.
55. Letter, DHK to Vauxcelles, December 11, 1923, GLL Archives.

56. Letter, DHK to Plandiura, January 27, 1926, GLL Archives.
57. Letter, Gunzburg to DHK, February 2, 1925, GLL Archives.
58. Letter, Banque Franco-Japonaise to DHK, April 21, 1926, GLL Archives.
59. Salacrou, op. cit.
60. Letter, DHK to Togorès, September 14, 1926, GLL Archives.
61. Letter, DHK to Togorès, February 1, 1926, GLL Archives.
62. Letter, DHK to Togorès, January 27, 1926, GLL Archives.
63. Louise and Michel Leiris, interview with the author.
64. Derain, op. cit.
65. Letter, Derain to DHK, February 28, 1924, GLL Archives.
66. Christian Derouet, "Le premier accrochage de 'La Lecture' par Fernand Léger," *Cahiers du Musée national d'art moderne*, 1986, pp. 17–18.
67. Letter, DHK to Crémieux, op. cit., p. 110.
68. Letter, Raoul La Roche to DHK, July 25, 1923, GLL Archives.
69. DHK, *Juan Gris*, p. 30.
70. Letters, DHK to Gris, December 5, 14, and 27, 1923, GLL Archives.
71. Letter, DHK to Jouhandeau, March 19, 1927, GLL Archives.
72. E. Tériade, "Nos enquêtes: entretien avec DH Kahnweiler," *Feuilles Volantes*, supplement to *Cahiers d'Art*, No. 2, February 1927.
73. Letter, DHK to Georges Limbour, April 29, 1926, GLL Archives.
74. Telegram, Gris to DHK, January 22, 1927, and correspondence between Gris and DHK, January 1927, GLL Archives.
75. DHK, *Juan Gris*, pp. 35–36.
76. Ibid., p. 45.
77. Stein, op. cit.
78. Cabanne, *Le siècle de Picasso*, II, p. 212.
79. Stein, op. cit., p. 27 (collection L'imaginaire).
80. *Hommage à Juan Gris pour le centenaire de naissance*, Grand Orient de France, 1987.
81. Golding, op. cit., p. 117.
82. DHK, *Juan Gris*, pp. 36, 134; DHK, *Confessions esthétiques*, chapter V.

CHAPTER 7. SURVIVING THE CRASH

1. Bernard Droz and Anthony Rowley, *Histoire générale du XXe siècle* I (Paris: Editions du Seuil, 1986), p. 117.
2. Durand-Robert, "Le marché de la peinture cubiste: evolution de la cote depuis 1907," *Perspectives*, January 6, 1962.
3. Letter, DHK to Salacrou, January 15, 1932, GLL Archives.
4. *Cahiers d'Art*, No. 10, 1928.
5. Letter, DHK to Anon., January 26, 1927, GLL Archives.
6. Letter, DHK to Alphonse Bellier, July 2, 1932, GLL Archives.
7. Letter, DHK to Pierre Matisse, June 16, 1931, GLL Archives.
8. Letter, DHK to Togorès, July 11, 1925, GLL Archives.
9. Moulin, op. cit., p. 40.
10. DHK, *My Galleries*, p. 133.
11. Letters, DHK to the Duchess de Clermont-Tonnerre, February 1 and 3, 1930, GLL Archives.
12. Letter, DHK to the Princess de Bassiano, July 29, 1932, GLL Archives.

13. Georges Charensol, *D'une rive à l'autre* (Paris: Mercure de France, 1973).
14. Letter, Alphonse Kann to DHK, June 1, 1937, GLL Archives.
15. Letter, DHK to "Mon cher vieux" (probably André Simon), January 14, 1930, GLL Archives.
16. Letter, DHK to Banque Franco-Japonaise, December 22, 1930, GLL Archives.
17. Letter, DHK to "Mon cher vieux" (probably André Simon), January 30, 1931, GLL Archives.
18. Letter, DHK to Banque Franco-Japonaise, June 16, 1931, GLL Archives.
19. Interview with Gustave Kahnweiler.
20. July–August 1932, GLL Archives.
21. Correspondence between DHK and Neumann, *Dossier Londres 1931–1933*, GLL Archives.
22. Letter, DHK to Suzanne Roger, June 27, 1932, GLL Archives.
23. Letter, Manolo to DHK, October 10, 1928, GLL Archives.
24. Letter, DHK to Manolo, March 16, 1932, GLL Archives.
25. Letter, DHK to Togorès, October 31, 1931, GLL Archives.
26. Letters, DHK to Togorès, November 16 and 30, 1931, GLL Archives; Letter, Togorès to DHK, November 23, 1931, GLL Archives.
27. Letter, DHK to the Princess de Bassiano, July 17, 1929, GLL Archives.
28. Letters, DHK to Masson, July 9, December 8 and 10, 1930, July 27, 1933, GLL Archives; Letter, Masson to DHK, June 5, 1930, GLL Archives; Letter, DHK to Michel Leiris, November 5, 1932, GLL Archives; Letter, DHK to Georges Wildenstein, July 27, 1933, GLL Archives.
29. Derouet, "L'accrochage."
30. Cogniat, op. cit.
31. Letter, DHK to Picasso, January 18, 1929, GLL Archives.
32. Letter, DHK to Michel Leiris, March 19, 1932, GLL Archives.
33. DHK, preface to Werner Hoffman, *Henri Laurens Sculptures* (Teufen, 1970).
34. Letter, DHK to Manolo, December 1, 1924, GLL Archives.
35. Letter, DHK to Masson, May 24, 1929, GLL Archives.
36. Letter, DHK to Kann, February 28, 1929, GLL Archives.
37. Letter, DHK to Michel Leiris, June 6, 1931, GLL Archives; Letter, DHK to Fernande Olivier, December 21, 1933, GLL Archives.
38. Letter, DHK to Michel Leiris (n.d., circa 1929), GLL Archives.
39. Letter, DHK to Malraux, October 3, 1928, GLL Archives.
40. Letter, DHK to Hemingway, July 24, 1930, GLL Archives.
41. Letter, DHK to Michel Leiris, December 11, 1931, GLL Archives; Letter, DHK to Masson, May 5, 1928, GLL Archives.
42. Gee, op. cit.
43. Léonce Rosenberg, "Cubisme et empiricisme," *Bulletin de l'Effort moderne*, Nos. 29, 30, etc.
44. *Bulletin de l'Effort moderne*, No. 34, 1927.
45. Moulin, op. cit., p. 117.
46. Charensol, op. cit., p. 103.
47. Emmanuel Mounier, quoted by Laurence Bertrand-Dorléac, *Histoire de l'art, Paris 1940–1944: ordre national, traditions et modernités*, Publications de la Sorbonne, 1986.
48. Chapsal, op. cit.
49. Uhde, *Picasso*, p. 81.
50. *L'ami du peuple*, September 18, 1932, quoted by Ralph Schor, *L'opinion française et les étrangers 1919–1939*, Publications de la Sorbonne, 1985.

51. Gustave Kahnweiler, interview with the author.
52. Kokoschka, op. cit.
53. Robert Musil, *Lettres* (Seuil, 1987).
54. Adolf Hitler, *Mein Kampf.*
55. Ibid., p. 257.
56. Jimmy Ernst, *A Not-So-Still Life* (New York: St. Martin's, 1984).
57. Letters, DHK to Malraux, October 1 and 11, 1933, GLL Archives.
58. Letter, DHK to Georges Wildenstein, November 29, 1935, GLL Archives.
59. DHK, answer to questionnaire by *Numero,* Florence, October 1925; DHK, "Paul Klee, curieux homme," preface to exhibition catalogue, Musée Cantini, Marseilles 1967; DHK, *Confessions esthétiques,* op. cit., p. 196; Will Grohman, *Paul Klee,* Flinker, 1954; Correspondence, DHK-Klee, 1934–1940, GLL Archives.
60. Letter, DHK to Artaud, March 30, 1933, GLL Archives.
61. Letter, DHK to Masson, July 2, 1934, GLL Archives.
62. Letter, Leo Swane to DHK, November 15, 1934, GLL Archives; Letter, DHK to Leo Swane, November 17, 1934, GLL Archives; Letter, DHK to Braque, December 7, 1934, GLL Archives.
63. Letter, DHK to Pierre Matisse, December 13, 1935, GLL Archives.
64. Letter, DHK to Pierre Matisse, November 6, 1934, GLL Archives.
65. Letter, DHK to G. L. Roux, December 21, 1933, GLL Archives.
66. Letter, DHK to Masson, May 9, 1935, GLL Archives.
67. Letter, DHK to Salacrou, May 9, 1935, GLL Archives.
68. Letter, DHK to Miró, April 16, 1935, GLL Archives.
69. Letter, DHK to Salacrou, May 19, 1935, GLL Archives.
70. Letter, DHK to G. L. Roux, December 17, 1932, GLL Archives.
71. Letter, DHK to Togorès, June 15, 1929, GLL Archives.
72. Letter, DHK to Douglas Cooper, November 6, 1934, GLL Archives.
73. Letter, DHK to Pierre Matisse, June 24, 1935, GLL Archives.
74. Letter, Herbert Read to DHK, June 18, 1934, GLL Archives.
75. Letter, DHK to Malraux, June 9, 1933, GLL Archives.
76. Letter, DHK to Malraux, July 9, 1935, GLL Archives.
77. Letter, DHK to Malraux, March 24, 1933, GLL Archives.
78. Letter, Malraux to DHK, March 22, 1932, GLL Archives; Letter, DHK to Malraux, March 24, 1932, GLL Archives.
79. *Le Point,* No. 42, October 1952.
80. Ibid.
81. Letter, Vlaminck to DHK, March 2, 1934, GLL Archives.
82. Letter, DHK to Vlaminck, March 8, 1934, GLL Archives.
83. Letter, Vlaminck to DHK, March 8, 1934, GLL Archives.
84. Letter, DHK to Masson, April 20, 1935, GLL Archives.
85. Letter, DHK to Masson, May 9, 1935, GLL Archives.

CHAPTER 8. COME WHAT MAY

1. Letter, DHK to Masson, January 22, 1936, GLL Archives.
2. Letter, Kann to DHK, April 16, 1936, GLL Archives.
3. Letter, DHK to Masson, May 7, 1936, GLL Archives.
4. Letters, DHK to Malraux, May 17 and June 11, 1936, GLL Archives; Letters, Malraux to DHK, June 4 and 6, 1936, GLL Archives.
5. Letter, DHK to Douglas Cooper, September 30, 1936, GLL Archives.
6. Letter, DHK to Douglas Cooper, May 19, 1936, GLL Archives.
7. Letter, DHK to Douglas Cooper, April 1, 1936, GLL Archives.
8. Letter, Douglas Cooper to DHK, April 2, 1936, GLL Archives.
9. Letter, DHK to Douglas Cooper, April 3, 1936, GLL Archives.
10. Letter, Douglas Cooper to DHK, April 5, 1936, GLL Archives.
11. Letter, DHK to Douglas Cooper, April 7, 1936, GLL Archives.
12. Letter, DHK to Picasso, May 3, 1936, GLL Archives.
13. Letter, DHK to Masson, June 11, 1936, GLL Archives.
14. Letter, Miró to DHK, July 13, 1936, GLL Archives.
15. Letter, DHK to Masson, September 11, 1936, GLL Archives.
16. Letter, DHK to Masson, December 14, 1936, GLL Archives.
17. Letter, DHK to Lascaux, September 18, 1937, GLL Archives.
18. Letter, DHK to Masson, February 24, 1937, GLL Archives.
19. Letter, DHK to Klee's wife, March 9, 1940, GLL Archives.
20. Michel Leiris, interview with the author, op. cit.
21. Letters, DHK to Borès, July 31 and November 29, 1939, GLL Archives.
22. Letter, DHK to Oppenheimer, Nathan, Vandyck and Mackay, September 30, 1937, GLL Archives.
23. Letter, DHK to Douglas Cooper, February 13, 1937, GLL Archives.
24. Letter, DHK to Douglas Cooper, November 23, 1937, GLL Archives.
25. Letter, DHK to Tzara, March 5, 1937, GLL Archives.
26. Pierre Broué.
27. Letter, DHK to Douglas Cooper, February 13, 1937, GLL Archives.
28. Léger, op. cit., p. 124.
29. Vallier, op. cit., p. 81.
30. DHK, *Confessions esthétiques*.
31. Ibid.
32. Interview with Paul Belmondo, in Bertrand-Dorléac, op. cit.
33. Ernst, op. cit.
34. Marie-Hélène Delpeuch, Preface to the inventory of the Carré collection; Irmelin Lebeer, interview with Louis Carré, July 24, 1967, National Archives 389 AP 1.
35. Letter, DHK to Berger, January 7, 1938, GLL Archives.
36. Letter, DHK to Pierre Matisse, April 2, 1938, GLL Archives.
37. Letter, DHK to Borès, August 31, 1938, GLL Archives.
38. Letters, DHK to Masson, April 7 and September 29, 1938, GLL Archives.
39. Letter, DHK to Borès, July 31, 1939, GLL Archives.
40. Letter, Theodore Fischer to DHK, June 1, 1939, GLL Archives.
41. Ernst, op. cit.
42. DHK, *Klee* (New York: E. S. Hermann, 1950); DHK, *Klee: curieux homme*.
43. DHK, *Juan Gris*.
44. Colin Simpson, *The Partnership: The Secret Association of Bernard Beren-*

son and Joseph Duveen (London: The Bodley Head, 1987).

45. Martin Fabiani, *Quand j'étais marchand de tableaux* (Paris: Juilliard, 1976).

46. Letter, DHK to Gustave Kahnweiler, September 15, 1939, GLL Archives.

47. Letters, DHK to Lascaux, August 31 and September 15, 1939, GLL Archives; Letter, DHK to his sister Gustie, September 22, 1939, GLL Archives; Letter, DHK to Gustave Kahnweiler, September 15, 1939, GLL Archives.

48. Letter, DHK to Kermadec, December 27, 1939, GLL Archives.

49. Letter, Rupf to DHK, October 22, 1939, GLL Archives.

50. Salacrou, op. cit.; Letter, DHK to Kermadec, October 2, 1939, GLL Archives.

51. Letter, DHK to his sister, April 29, 1940, GLL Archives.

52. Letter, DHK to Rupf, December 21, 1939, GLL Archives.

53. Letter, DHK to unknown correspondent, December 1, 1939, GLL Archives.

54. Man Ray, op. cit., p. 194.

55. DHK, preface to Stein, op. cit.

56. Letter, DHK to Masson, November 15, 1939, GLL Archives.

57. Letter, DHK to Kermadec, October 31, 1939, GLL Archives.

58. Letter, DHK to Borès, September 6, 1939, GLL Archives.

59. Letter, DHK to Masson, August 18, 1939, GLL Archives.

60. Letter, DHK to Masson, November 27, 1939, GLL Archives.

61. Letter, DHK to his sister, January 23, 1940, GLL Archives.

62. Letter, DHK to Queneau, January 9, 1940, GLL Archives.

63. Letter, DHK to unknown correspondent, February 19, 1940, GLL Archives.

64. Correspondence between DHK and Olson, January–March 1940, GLL Archives.

65. Letter, DHK to his sister, April 29, 1940, GLL Archives.

66. Letter, Rupf to DHK, March 25, 1940, GLL Archives; Letter, DHK to Rupf, April 22, 1940, GLL Archives.

67. Peggy Guggenheim, *Out of This Century: Confessions of an Art Addict* (New York: Universe Books, 1979).

68. Letter, DHK to Picasso, June 5, 1940, GLL Archives.

69. Bertrand-Dorléac, op. cit.

70. Letter, DHK to Marie Cuttoli, February 27, 1940, GLL Archives.

71. Charles Lapicque, interviewed by the author.

72. National Archives, F 21 3972, Dossier 1b.

73. Letter, DHK to Braque, May 10, 1940, GLL Archives.

74. Ibid.

75. Letter, DHK to unknown correspondent, June 8, 1940, GLL Archives.

76. Letter, Masson to DHK, undated (June 1940), GLL Archives.

77. Letter, DHK to Marcel Moré, June 17, 1940, Patrick-Gilles Persin Archives.

INTERMISSION: INTERNAL EXILE (1940–1944)

1. Letter, DHK to René Leibowitz, August 8, 1940, GLL Archives.

2. Georges-Emmanuel Clancier, in an interview, G. E. Clancier, "Queneau," *L'Herne*, No. 29, 1976.

3. Ibid.

4. Article on St. Léonard-de-Noblat during the occupation, in *Auvergne-Magazine* (Limoges), March 1973.
5. Clancier interview, op. cit.
6. Letter, DHK to Marcel Moré, July 9, 1940, P. G. Persin Archives.
7. Letter, DHK to Marcel Moré, July 20, 1940, P. G. Persin Archives.
8. Letter, Antonin Artaud to DHK, December 14, 1940, *Pour DHK*, op. cit.
9. Bertrand-Dorléac, op. cit., pp. 86, 87, 104.
10. Ibid., p. 308.
11. Letter, DHK to Max Jacob, November 27, 1936, in *DHK marchand, éditeur, écrivain*, p. 150.
12. Rose Valland, *Le front de l'art: défense des collections françaises, 1939–1945* (Paris: Plon, 1961).
13. Ibid.
14. Ibid.
15. Arno Brecker, interview in Bertrand-Dorléac.
16. *Les chefs-d'oeuvre des collections privées françaises retrouvées en Allemagne*, Orangerie des Tuileries, June–August 1946, Ministère de l'Éducation nationale.
17. *L'art français* (clandestine), No. 5, March 1944, quoted in Bertrand-Dorléac, op. cit.
18. "Dossier Wildenstein," National Archives, AJ 40 610.
19. Fabiani, op. cit.
20. Letter, Louis Carré to André Weil, 1940, National Archives, 389 AP 35.
21. "Verzeichnis der erfassten Judischen Kunstammlungen," Centre de documentation Juive contemporaine, XIII–45.
22. Letter, Louis Carré to Léonce Rosenberg, February 26, 1941, National Archives, 389 AP 33.
23. Pierre Loeb, *Voyages à travers la peinture* (Bordas, 1945).
24. Louise Leiris, interview with the author.
25. Archives du Registre de Commerce.
26. Duret-Robert, op. cit.
27. Bertrand-Dorléac, op. cit.
28. Invoice, April 10, 1941, GLL Archives.
29. Mary-Margaret Goggin, *Picasso and His Art during the German Occupation, 1940–1944*, thesis, Stanford University, August 1985.
30. Letter, DHK to Walter Pach, July 19, 1947, GLL Archives.
31. List of August 24, 1942, quoted by Goggin, p. 23.
32. Henri Colas, Paris, 1940.
33. Ibid.
34. *Comoedia*, May 23, 1942.
35. Letter, DHK to Marcel Moré, January 11, 1943, P. G. Persin Archives.
36. Letter, DHK to Marcel Moré, 1942, P. G. Persin Archives.
37. Letter, DHK to René Leibowitz, October 10, 1940, GLL Archives.
38. Ernst Jünger, *Second journal parisien III* (Paris: Christian Bourgois, 1980).
39. DHK, Crémieux, op. cit.
40. Interview with Michel Leiris.
41. Ibid.
42. Ibid.
43. Camille Mauclair, *La crise de l'art moderne*, CEA, 1944.
44. Rose Valland, op. cit.
45. Man Ray, op. cit.
46. Bertrand-Dorléac, op. cit.
47. DHK, interview with Hélène Parmelin, *L'Humanite*, op. cit.
48. *Le Point* (Souillac), art. cit.
49. Letter, DHK to Masson, December 2, 1944, GLL Archives.
50. Bernard Dorival, interview quoted in Bertrand-Dorléac, op. cit.
51. Note of the inspector of direct contributions, February 17, 1949, National Archives 389 AP 29.
52. Goggin, op. cit.
53. André Combes et al., *Nazisme et antinazisme dans la littérature et l'art*

allemands 1920–1945, Publications Universitaires de Lille, 1986.

54. Letter, DHK to Curt Valentin, December 2, 1944, GLL Archives.

55. Letter, DHK to Thannhauser, September 12, 1945, GLL Archives.

CHAPTER 9. THE ACKNOWLEDGED MASTER

1. Michael Hertz, *Erinnerung an D. H. Kahnweiler* (Verlabt, 1980, Bremen, 1987).
2. *Paroles Françaises,* August 31, 1946; *Combat,* August 16, 1946; *Sachez Tout,* August 31, 1946.
3. *L'Oeil,* No. 1, January 15, 1955.
4. *Carrefour,* November 14, 1951.
5. *Revue d'esthétique,* Vol. 5, January–March 1952.
6. Letter, Aimé Maeght to DHK, May 14, 1946, GLL Archives; Letter, DHK to Aimé Maeght, June 4, 1946, GLL Archives.
7. Michael Hertz, op. cit.
8. Ibid.
9. Pomian, op. cit.
10. Letter, Berggruen to DHK, January 8, 1959, GLL Archives.
11. Note, DHK, May 16, 1962, GLL Archives.
12. Note, DHK, October 1958, GLL Archives.
13. Letter, DHK to Bellier, July 2, 1949, GLL Archives.
14. Gustave Kahnweiler, interview with the author.
15. Letter, DHK to Picasso, June 27, 1963, GLL Archives.
16. Nora Coste, "Les faux tableaux," *Spectacles du monde,* April 1979.
17. *France Soir,* October 27, 1967.
18. Letter, DHK to Picasso, August 28, 1963, GLL Archives.
19. Pierre Schneider, "Toujours le scandale des faux," *L'Express,* July 3–9, 1967.
20. *Libération,* July 7, 1954.
21. Letter, John Rewald to DHK, June 1, 1946, GLL Archives; Letter, DHK to John Rewald, July 3, 1946, GLL Archives.
22. Letter, DHK to Gaston Gallimard, May 23, 1924, GLL Archives.
23. GLL Archives.
24. Letter, Jacques Lipchitz to DHK, May 27, 1947, GLL Archives.
25. Yves-Alain Bois, op. cit.
26. Michael Hertz, op. cit.
27. Ibid.
28. Letter, DHK to Masson, April 16, 1947, GLL Archives.
29. DHK, "Der Anfgang."
30. *The Washington Reporter,* April 13, 1949; *The New York Times,* January 10, 1949.
31. Michael Hertz, op. cit.
32. Letter, DHK to Frantisek Dolezal, September 2, 1964, GLL Archives.
33. Letter, Maurice Jardot to DHK, July 18, 1947, GLL Archives; Maurice Jardot, interview with the author.
34. Letter, DHK to J. K. Thannhauser (New York), September 12, 1945, GLL Archives.
35. Letter, DHK to Mourlot, February 15, 1947, GLL Archives.
36. Michael Hertz, op. cit.
37. Ibid.
38. Letter, DHK to Picasso, May 15, 1956, GLL Archives.
39. Alexander Watt, "Daniel-Henry Kahnweiler," *The Studio,* July 1958, London and New York.
40. Letter, DHK to Masson, August 12, 1947, GLL Archives.

41. DHK, *L'Oeil*, No. 1, op. cit.
42. DHK, preface to *Henri Laurens* by Werner Hoffman, Hatje 1970.
43. Letter, DHK to Picasso, September 8, 1954, GLL Archives.
44. Letter, DHK to Rouvre, September 8, 1955, GLL Archives.

45. Letter, Nadia Léger to DHK, December 22, 1973, GLL Archives.
46. Maurice Jardot, *Pour DHK*, op. cit.
47. DHK, *Dernières nouvelles d'Alsace* (Colmar, 1966).

CHAPTER 10. KAHNWEILER AND PICASSO

1. Letter, DHK to Picasso, April 15, 1970, GLL Archives.
2. Isabelle Monod-Fontaine, "Picasso," *Catalogue de la donation Louise et Michel Leiris*, Centre Pompidou, 1984.
3. Cabanne, *Le siècle de Picasso*, IV.
4. DHK, preface to catalogue, *Pour les 80 ans de Picasso*, Los Angeles, UCLA Art Galleries, 1961.
5. DHK, *Picasso: Ceramics* (Hanover: Fackeltrager Verlag, 1957).
6. DHK, "Pour le bonheur des hommes," *Les Lettres Françaises*, October 21–27, 1965; DHK, Crémieux, interview 1971, INA Archives.
7. Cabanne, op. cit.
8. Françoise Gilot and Carlton Lake, *Life with Picasso* (New York: McGraw-Hill, 1964).
9. Ibid.
10. DHK, interview with an unidentified Paris daily, November 13, 1966.
11. Marie-Andrée de Sardi, "Kahnweiler, le marchand des cubistes," *Jardin des Arts*, No. 96, November 1962.
12. Gilot, op. cit.
13. Ibid.
14. Letter, DHK to Curt Valentin, January 25, 1947, GLL Archives.
15. Letter, Curt Valentin to DHK, January 30, 1947, GLL Archives.

16. DHK, Delesalle, op. cit.
17. Maurice Jardot, interview with the author.
18. Paul Waldo Schwartz, *The New York Times*, June 26, 1964.
19. Letter, DHK to Picasso, December 29, 1964, GLL Archives.
20. Letter, DHK to Picasso, March 21, 1967, GLL Archives.
21. Letter, DHK to Picasso, October 11, 1958, GLL Archives.
22. Letter, DHK to Picasso, November 4, 1966, GLL Archives.
23. Letter, DHK to Picasso, March 19, 1958, GLL Archives.
24. Letter, DHK to Picasso, July 6, 1960, GLL Archives.
25. Gerald MacKnight, *Bitter Legacy: Picasso's Disputed Millions* (London: Bantam, 1987).
26. Mary Blume, "Alive and Well: The Woman Picasso Sought to Annihilate," *The International Herald Tribune*, October 5, 1987.
27. DHK, *Gris*.
28. Letter, DHK to Picasso, November 30, 1949, GLL Archives.
29. DHK, Sardi, op. cit.
30. Letter, DHK to Douglas Cooper, May 5, 1939, GLL Archives.
31. Letter, DHK to Picasso, December 2, 1960, GLL Archives.
32. Letter, DHK to Léo Hamon, November 8, 1956, GLL Archives.

33. DHK, note of December 27, 1937, GLL Archives.
34. DHK, Notes, January 1955, in *Aujourd'hui, art and architecture*, September 1955.
35. Letter, DHK to Margo Barr, June 12, 1973, GLL Archives.
36. *L'Humanité-Dimanche*, January 17, 1979.

CHAPTER 11. DOWN WITH ABSTRACT ART!

1. DHK, Delesalle, op. cit.
2. DHK, Crémieux, 1971, INA Archives.
3. DHK, Delesalle, op. cit.
4. "Aimé Maeght renouvelle ses cadres," *L'Express*, July 11–17, 1966.
5. Letter, DHK to Fernand Graindorge (Liège), November 5, 1946, GLL Archives.
6. DHK, Crémieux, op. cit.
7. Nigel Gosling, "DHK in interview," *Art and Artists*, No. 64, July 1971; DHK, Cabanne, *Lectures*, art. cit.
8. DHK, *Gris*.
9. DHK, Cabanne, op. cit.
10. DHK, *Juan Gris*.
11. DHK, *My Galleries*, pp. 104, 105.
12. DHK, Afterword, American edition *My Galleries*.
13. "A bâtons rompus avec DHK," Exposition Léger, Dernières nouvelles d'Alsace, July 23, 1966.
14. Chavasse, op. cit.
15. *Almanach Flinker*, op. cit.
16. Letter, DHK to Meyer Shapiro, July 19, 1962, GLL Archives.
17. DHK, *My Galleries*, p. 96.
18. DHK, *Juan Gris*.
19. Letter, DHK to Fernand Graindorge (Liège), November 5, 1946, GLL Archives.
20. DHK, interviewed in "Enquête de Georges Boudaille and Guy Weelen sur un musée d'art moderne," *Les Lettres Françaises*, April 7–13, 1966.

CHAPTER 12. A WISE MAN WHO HAS NO DOUBTS

1. Georges Limbour, "Les grandes collections: DHK," *Plaisir de France*, July 1969.
2. Ibid.
3. Letter, DHK to George Weidenfeld, February 27, 1958, GLL Archives.
4. Letter, Jean Lacouture to DHK, May 22, 1975, GLL Archives.
5. Letter, DHK to Jean Lacouture, May 23, 1975, GLL Archives.
6. DHK's answers to the *Almanach Flinker*, op. cit.
7. Fabiani, op. cit.
8. DHK, Afterword to the American edition of *My Galleries*.
9. Letter, DHK to Raymond Queneau, December 6, 1960, GLL Archives.
10. Letter, DHK to Jean-Pierre Rosier, Gallimard, May 10, 1961, GLL Archives.
11. DHK, Afterword to the American edition of *My Galleries;* DHK, interview with Crémieux, 1971, INA Archives.
12. Michael Hertz, op. cit.
13. Ibid.

14. *Nouvelle Gauche,* November 9–22, 1957; *Le Monde,* August 26 and October 24, 1968; *L'Humanité-Dimanche,* April 2, 1967; *L'Aurore,* May 8, 1967; *L'Humanité,* December 17, 1970; *Le Monde,* June 14, 1972; *Les Lettres Françaises,* January 6, 1971.
15. *Le Monde,* November 3, 1973.
16. Gilot, op. cit.
17. Pierre Daix, *La vie de peintre de Pablo Picasso,* Seuil, 1977; *Picasso créateur,* Seuil, 1987.
18. DHK, *My Galleries,* p. 77
19. Letters, DHK to Léo Hamon, September 19 and October 10, 1956, GLL Archives.
20. Letter, DHK to Picasso, September 5, 1963, GLL Archives.
21. Letter, DHK to Malraux, June 25, 1959, GLL Archives.
22. *Le Moniteur du Commerce International,* July 1970.
23. Letter, DHK to Picasso, December 2, 1964, GLL Archives.
24. Gilles Lapouge, "Les marchands devant la crise," *Le Figaro littéraire,* December 16, 1965.
25. Letter, DHK to Marcel Moré, August 13, 1967, P. G. Persin Archives.
26. Ibid.
27. *Carrefour,* February 8, 1956.
28. DHK, Cabanne, op. cit.

D. H. Kahnweiler: The monographs, prefaces, articles by and interviews of D. H. Kahnweiler are too numerous to be listed here. The definitive bibliography was established by Claude Laugier in *Daniel-Henry Kahnweiler marchand, éditeur, écrivain*. The following texts by Kahnweiler are quoted in this biography:

The Rise of Cubism [1916] (New York: Wittenborn, Schultz, 1949).
Maurice de Vlaminck (Leipzig: Klinkhardt and Bierman, 1920).
André Derain (idem).
Juan Gris (idem, 1929).
Juan Gris: his life and work [1946]. Trans. Douglas Cooper (New York: Curt Valentin, 1947; revised ed., 1969).
Les sculptures de Picasso (Paris: Editions du Chêne, 1949).
Klee (New York: E. S. Hermann, 1950).
My Galleries and Painters. Interviews with Francis Crémieux [1961]. Trans. Helen Weaver (New York: Viking, 1971).
Confessions esthétiques (Paris: Gallimard, 1963).
"Ein Selbstportrait," in *Das Selbstportrait: Grosse Kunstler und Denker unserer Zeit erzahlen von ihrem Leben und ihrem Werk* (Hamburg: Christian Wegner Verlag, 1967).
"Der Anfang des modernen Kunsthendels," in E. Forsthoff and R. Horstel, *Standorte im Zeitsrom* (Frankfurt: Athenaum Verlag, 1974).

CENTERS FOR RESEARCH

PARIS

Galerie Louise Leiris, personal archives and the archives of the gallery from 1907 to 1979.
Musée Picasso.
Centre de documentation of the Musée National d'Art Moderne.
Bibliothèque littéraire Jacques Doucet.
Bibliothèque d'Art et d'Archéologie Jacques Doucet.
Bibliothèque Nationale.

Archives Nationales. Louis Carré Archives.
Centre de Documentation Juive Contemporaine (Aryanization 1940–1944).
Institut National de l'Audiovisuel.
Patrick-Gilles Persin Archives. Marcel Moré Foundation.

LONDON

Courtauld Institute.
Warburg Institute.

BERN

State Archives.
Municipal Archives.
Federal Archives.

BOOKS

Abastado, Claude, *Introduction au surréalisme* (Paris: Bordas, 1986).
Ajalbert, Jean, *Une enquête sur les droits de l'artiste* (Paris: Stock, 1905).
Apollinaire, Guillaume, *Apollinaire on Arts Essays and Reviews, 1902–1918* (New York: Viking, 1972).
————, *The Cubist Painters* (New York: Wittenborn, Schultz, 1949).
Auric, Georges, *Quand j'étais là* (Paris: Grasset, 1979).
Barr, Alfred H., *Cubism and Abstract Art* (New York: Museum of Modern Art, 1936).
Basler, Adolphe, *La Peinture, religion nouvelle* (Paris: Librarie de France, 1926).
Bauquier, Georges, *Fernand Léger: Vivre dans le vrai* (Paris: Maeght, 1987).
Baxandall, Michael, *Patterns of Intention: On the Historical Explanation of Pictures* (New Haven: Yale University Press, 1985).
Bazin, Germain, *Histoire de l'histoire de l'art de Vasari à nos jours* (Paris: Albin Michel, 1986).
Behrman, N. S., *Duveen* (New York: Random House, 1952).
Bernier, Georges, *L'art et l'argent. Le marché de l'art au XXe siècle* (Paris: Robert Laffont, 1977).
Bertrand-Dorléac, Laurence, *Histoire de l'art. Paris 1940–1944. Ordre national, traditions et modernités* (Paris: Publications de la Sorbonne, 1986).
Blot, E., *Histoire d'une collection de tableaux modernes* (Paris, 1934).
Blunt, Anthony, *Souvenirs* (Paris: Christian Bourgois, 1985).
Brassaï, *Picasso* (New York: Doubleday, 1966).
Brimo, René, *L'évolution de goût aux États-Unis d'après l'histoire des collections* (Paris: Éditions James Fortune, 1938).
Cabanne, Pierre, *Le roman des grands collectionneurs* (Paris, 1963).
————, with Pierre Restany, *L'avant-garde au XXe siècle* (Paris: André Balland, 1969).
————, *Le siècle de Picasso* (Paris: Denoël, 1975).
————, *Le cubisme* (Paris: PUF, 1982).
————, *L'épopée du cubisme* (Paris: La Table Ronde, 1963).
Cassou, Jean, *Le pillage par les Allemands des oeuvres d'art et des bibliothèques appartenant à des juifs en France* (Paris: Éd. du Centre, 1947).

————, *Une vie pour la liberté* (Paris: Robert Laffont, 1981).

Ceroni, Ambrogio, *Amédéo Modigliani* (Milan: Edizione del Milione, 1958).

Chapon, François, *Mystère et splendeurs de Jacques Doucet 1853–1929* (Paris: J.-C. Lattès, 1984).

————, *Le peintre et le livre* (Paris: Flammarion, 1987).

Charbonnier, Georges, *Entretiens avec André Masson* (Paris: Julliard, 1958).

Combes, André et al., *Nazisme et antinazisme dans la littérature et l'art allemands 1920–1945* (Lille: Presses Universitaires de Lille, 1986).

Cooper, Douglas, *The Cubist Epoch* (Oxford: Phaidon Press, 1970).

Coppet, Laure de, and Alan Jones, *The Art Dealers* (New York: Clarkson Potter, 1984).

Crespelle, Jean-Paul, *La vie quotidienne à Montmartre au temps de Picasso 1900–1910* (Paris: Hachette, 1978).

Daix, Pierre, *Journal du cubisme* (Lausanne: Skira, 1982).

————, *Picasso* (New York: Praeger, 1965).

————, *Picasso créateur. La vie intime et l'oeuvre* (Paris: Seuil, 1987).

————, *L'ordre et l'aventure. Peinture, modernité et répression totalitaire* (Paris: Arthaud, 1984).

Decaudin, Michel, *Apollinaire* (Paris: Séguier, 1986).

Delevoy, Robert, *Léger* (Geneva: Skira, 1962).

Derain, André, *Lettres à Vlaminck* (Paris: Flammarion, 1955).

Desnos, Robert, *Écrits sur les peintres* (Paris: Flammarion, 1984).

Diehl, Gaston, *La peinture moderne dans le monde* (Paris: Flammarion).

Dorival, Bernard, *Les étapes de la peinture française contemporaine* (Paris: Gallimard, 1944).

Einstein, Carl, *Die Kunst des 20. Jahrhunderts* (Berlin: Propylaen, 1931).

Ernst, Jimmy, *A Not-So-Still Life* (New York: St. Martin's Press, 1984).

Fabiani, Martin, *Quand j'étais marchand de tableaux* (Paris: Julliard, 1976).

Fage, André, *Le collectionneur de peintures modernes. Comment acheter, comment vendre* (Paris: Les Éditions pittoresques, 1930).

Fauchereau, Serge, *Braque* (Paris: Albin Michel, 1987).

Fels, Florent, *Voilà* (Paris, 1957).

Fénéon, Félix, *Oeuvres plus que complètes. Textes réunis et présentés par J.U. Halperin* (Geneva: Droz, 1970).

————, *Au-delà de l'impressionnisme* (Geneva: Hermann, 1966).

Francastel, Pierre, *Nouveau dessin, nouvelle peinture. L'école de Paris* (Paris: Librarie de Médicis, 1946).

Fry, Edward, *Le cubisme* (Paris: La Connaissance Bruxelles, 1966).

Gagliardi, Jacques, *Les trains de Monet ne conduisent qu'en banlieue* (Paris: PUF, 1987).

Gimpel, René, *Journal d'un collectionneur-marchand de tableaux* (Paris: Calmann-Lévy, 1963).

Gilot, Françoise, with Carlton Lake, *Life with Picasso* (New York: McGraw-Hill, 1964).

Glimcher, Arnold, and Mark Glimcher, *Je Suis le Cahier: The Sketchbooks of Picasso* (New York: Atlantic Monthly Press, 1986).

Golding, John, *Cubism: A History and an Analysis, 1907–1914* (London, 1968).

Gray, Camilla, *The Great Experiment: Russian Art, 1863–1922* (London: Thames and Hudson, 1962).

Green, Christopher, *Cubism and Its Enemies: Modern Movement and Reaction in French Art, 1916–1928* (New Haven: Yale University Press, 1987).

Grohmann, Will, *Paul Klee* (New York: Abrams, 1985).

Guggenheim, Peggy, *Out of the Century: Confessions of an Art Addict* (revised ed., New York: Universe Books, 1986).

Guyot, Adelin, and Patrick Restellini, *L'art nazi* (Brussels: Complexe, 1983).

Haskell, Francis, *Rediscoveries in Art: Some Aspects of Taste, Fashion, and Collecting in France* (Ithaca, NY: Cornell University Press, 1980).

Hemming Fry, John, *Art décadent sous le règne de la démocratie et du communisme* (Paris: Henri Colas, 1940).

Hertz, Michael, *Erinnerung an D. H. Kahnweiler* (Bremen, 1987).

Huysmans, J.K., *L'art moderne* (Paris: 10/18, 1975).

Jacob, Max, *Correspondance générale* (Paris: Éditions de Paris, 1953).

Jardot, Maurice, *Fernand Léger* (Paris: Hazan, 1956).

————, with Kurt Martin, *Les maîtres de la peinture française contemporaine* (Baden-Baden: Woldemar Klein, 1948).

Jourdain, Francis, *Sans remords ni rancune* (Paris, 1953).

Klee, Paul, *Diaries* (Berkeley: University of California Press, 1988).

Laclotte, Michel, ed., *Dictionnaire de la peinture* (Paris: Larousse, 1980).

Laurent, Jeanne, *Arts et pouvoirs* (Paris: Université de Saint-Étienne, CIEREC, 1983).

Léger, Fernand, *Fonctions de la peinture* (Paris: Denoël-Méditations, 1965).

Leiris, Michel, *L'Afrique fantôme* (Paris: Gallimard, 1934).

————, *Manhood: A Journey from Childhood into the Fierce Order of Virility* (San Francisco: North Point Press, 1984).

————, *Au verso des images* (Montpellier: Fata Morgana, 1980).

Level, André, *Souvenirs d'un collectionneur* (Paris: Alain Mazo, 1959).

Lévy, Pierre, *Des artistes et un collectionneur* (Paris: Flammarion, 1976).

Loeb, Pierre, *Voyages à travers la peinture* (Paris: Bordas, 1945).

Mac Knight, Gerald, *Bitter Legacy: Picasso's Disputed Millions* (London: Bantam Press, 1987).

Maillard, Robert, ed., *Dictionnaire de l'art et des artistes* (Paris: Hazan, 1982).

————, with Franck Elgar, *Picasso* (Paris: Hazan, 1955).

Matisse, Henri, *Écrits et propos sur l'art* (Paris: Hermann, 1972).

Mauclair, Camille, *La farce de l'art vivant* (Paris, 1929).

————, *La crise de l'art moderne* (Paris, 1944).

Mellow, James, R., *Charmed Circle: Gertrude Stein and Cie* (New York: Praeger, 1974).

Metzinger, Jean, *Le cubisme était né,* (Chambéry: Présence, 1972).

————, with Albert Gleizes, *Du cubisme* (Paris: Figuière, 1912).

Mirbeau, Octave, *Des artistes* (Paris: 10/18, 1986).

Miró, Joan, with Margit Rowell, ed., *Selected writings and interviews* (London: Thames and Hudson, 1987).

Les Mémoires du baron Mollet (Paris: Gallimard, 1963).

Monneret, Sophie, *L'impressionnisme et son époque* (Paris: Laffont, 1987).

Moulin, Raymonde, *Le marché de la peinture en France* (Paris: Minuit, 1967).

Olivier, Fernande, *Picasso and His Friends* (London: Heinemann, 1964).

Ozenfant, Amédée, *Mémoires, 1886–1962* (Paris: Calmann-Lévy, 1968).

Palmier, Jean-Michel, *Weimar en exil* (Paris: Payot, 1987).

Penrose, Roland, *Portrait of Picasso* (New York: Museum of Modern Art, 1971).

Pignon, Édouard, *La quête de la réalité* (Paris: Denoël-Méditations, 1966).

Pissarro, Camille, *Lettres à son fils Lucien* (Paris: Albin Michel, 1950).

Pomian, Krzysztof, *Collectionneurs, amateurs et curieux. Paris, Venise XVIe–XVIIIe siècle* (Paris: Gallimard, 1987).

Pradel, Jean-Louis, ed., *La peinture française* (Paris: Le Robert, 1983).

Raphael, Max, *Von Monet zu Picasso* (Munich: Delphin Verlag, 1913).

Ray, Man, *Self Portrait* (Boston: Little, Brown, 1988).

Read, Herbert, *The Origins of Form in Art* (New York: Horizon Press, 1965).

Reitlinger, Gerard, *The Economics of Taste* (London: Barrie and Rockliff, 1961).

Reverdy, Pierre, *Note éternelle du présent* (Paris: Flammarion, 1973).

Rewald, John, *The History of Impressionism*, 4th ed. (New York: Museum of Modern Art, 1973).

Rheims, Maurice, *Les collectionneurs* (Paris: Ramsay, 1981).

Rosenberg, Léonce, *Cubisme et tradition* (Paris: L'Effort moderne, 1920).

————, *Cubisme et empirisme* (Paris: L'Effort moderne, 1921).

Rosenblum, Robert, *Cubism and Twentieth Century Art* (New York: Abrams, 1976).

Sachs, Maurice, *Au temps du Boeuf sur le toit* (Paris: Grasset, 1987).

Salacrou, Armand, *Dans la salle des pas perdus*, I and II (Paris: Gallimard, 1974 and 1976).

Salmon, André, *Souvenirs sans fin*, I, II, III (Paris: Gallimard, 1955, 1956, 1961).

Secrest, Meryle, *Being Bernard Berenson* (London: Weidenfeld and Nicolson, 1979).

Shapiro, Theda, *Painters and Politics: The European Avant-Garde and Society 1900–1925* (New York: Elsevier, 1976).

Simon, Linda, *The Biography of Alice B. Toklas* (New York: Doubleday, 1979).

Simpson, Colin, *The Partnership: The Secret Association of Bernard Berenson and Joseph Duveen* (London: The Bodley Head, 1987).

Stein, Gertrude, *The Autobiography of Alice B. Toklas* (New York: Harcourt Brace and Co., 1933).

Surya, Michel, *Georges Bataille, La mort à l'oeuvre* (Paris: Séguier, 1987).

Sverini, Gino, *Dal cubismo al classicismo* (Florence: Marchi et Bertolli, 1972).

Tollet, Tony, *De l'influence de la corporation judéo-allemande des marchands de tableaux de Paris sur l'art français* (Paris: Communication à l'Académie des sciences et belles-lettres et Arts de Lyon, Bibliothèque Nationale, July 6, 1915).

Uhde, Wilhelm, *Picasso et la tradition française* (Paris: Les 4 chemins, 1928).

————, *Von Bismarck bis Picasso* (Zurich: Uprecht, 1938).

Vaisse, Pierre, *La IIIe République et les peintres* (Paris: 1980).

Valland, Rose, *Le front de l'art* (Paris: Plon, 1967).

Vallentin, Antonina, *Pablo Picasso* (Paris: Albin Michel, 1957).

Vallier, Dora, *L'intérieur de l'art* (Paris: Seuil, 1982).

Van Gogh, Vincent, *Lettres à son frère Théo* (Paris: Gallimard, 1956).

Vergnaud, Philippe, *Les contrats conclus entre peintres et marchands de tableaux* (Bordeaux: Rousseau, 1958).

Vlaminck, Maurice de, *Portraits avant décès* (Paris: Flammarion, 1943).

Vollard, Ambroise, *Souvenirs d'un marchand de tableaux* (Paris: Albin Michel, 1937).

————, *En écoutant Cézanne, Degas, Renoir* (Paris: Grasset, 1938).

Warnod, Jeanine, *Le Bateau-Lavoir* (Paris: Mayer, 1986).

Westheim, Paul, ed., *Kunstlerbekenntnisse* (Berlin: Propylaen, 1925).

Whitney Kean, Beverly, *All the Empty Palaces: The Merchant Patrons of Modern Art in Pre-Revolutionary Russia* (London: Barrie and Jenkins, 1983).

Will-Levaillant, Françoise, *André Masson, Le rebelle du surréalisme* (Paris: Hermann, 1976).

Willett, John, *The New Sobriety: Art and Politics in the Weimar Period 1917–1933* (London: Thames and Hudson, 1978).

Zilczer, Judith, *The Noble Buyer: John Quinn, Patron of the Avant-garde* (Washington: Smithsonian Institution Press, 1978).

ARTICLES

Breerette, Geneviève, "Le marchand pêcheur d'hommes," in *Le Monde*, November 22, 1984.

Boime, Albert, "Les magnats américains à la conquête de l'art français," in *L'Histoire*, no. 44, April 1982.

Bois, Yves-Alain, "Kahnweiler's Lesson," in *Representations 18*, Spring 1987, University of California Press.

Bouillon, Jean-Paul, "L'énigme cubiste," in *Beaux-Arts Magazine*, no. 2, May 1983.

Cabanne, Pierre, "DHK le marchand de Picasso. Interview," in *Lectures pour tous*, no. 190, November 1969.

———, "DHK le divin marchand," in *Le Matin*, November 24, 1984.

Castro, Carmen, "DHK el marchante de Picasso en Madrid," in *Vida mundial*, February 18, 1961.

Chapsal, Madeleine, "Entretien avec Pierre Loeb," in *L'Express*, April 9, 1964.

Charensol, Georges, "Chez Fernand Léger," in *Paris-Journal*, December 1924.

Chevalier, Denys, "Les animateurs," in *XXe siècle Cahiers d'art*, no. 17, 1961.

Clancier, Georges-Emmanuel, article in *Auvergne-magazine*, Limoges, March 1973.

———, "Queneau," in *L' Herne*, no. 29, 1976.

Cogniat, Raymond, "Art et commerce," in *Beaux-Arts*, no. 42, October 20, 1933.

———, "DHK et les débuts du cubisme," in *Beaux-Arts*, August 11, 1933.

———, "Une visite à l'atelier de Léger," in *Beaux-Arts*, April 21, 1933.

Cooper, Douglas, "Fernand Léger," in *L'Oeil*, no. 204, December 1971.

Courthion, Pierre, "Le passe-temps de Crésus. Le marché international des oeuvres d'art," in *Preuves*, December 1956.

Daix, Pierre, "DHK et les débuts du cubisme," in *Beaux-Arts Magazine*, no. 19, December 1984.

———, "L'aventurier du cubisme," in *Le Nouvel Observateur*, January 22, 1979.

———, "DHK un marchand pas comme les autres," in *Le Quotidien de Paris*, November 21, 1984.

Degand, Léon, "DHK et la galerie Louise Leiris," in *Aujourd'hui*, June 1957.

Derouet, Christian, "Quand le cubisme était un bien allemand," in *Paris-Berlin 1900–1933*, Centre Pompidou, 1978.

———, "De la voix et de la plume. Les émois cubistes d'un marchand de tableaux," in *Europe*, no. 638, June 1982.

———, "Le premier accrochage de La lecture, par Fernand Léger," in *Cahiers du Musée national d'art moderne 17–18*, 1986.

Dorival, Bernard, "La donation André Lefèvre au MNAM," in *Revue du Louvre et des musées de France*, no. 1, 1964.

———, "Le legs Gourgaud," in *Revue du Louvre et des musées de France*, no. 2, 1967.

Duret-Robert, F., "Le marché de la peinture cubiste. Évolution de le cote depuis 1907," in *Perspectives*, January 6, 1962.

Einstein, Carl, "La sculpture nègre," in *Médiations*, no. 3, 1961.

Fauchereau, Serge, "Matisse dans les collections russes," in *Beaux-Arts Magazine*, November 1981.

Franck, Herbert, "DHK unvekäufliche Bilder," in *Schöner Wohnen*, March 3, 1961.

Göpel, Ehrard, article in *Frankfurter Allgemeine*, July 23, 1964.

Gosling, Nigel, "DHK in interview," in *Art and Artists*, no. 64, London, July 1971.

Green, Nicholas, "Dealing in temperaments: economic transformation of the artistic field in France during the second half of the nineteenth century," in *Art History*, vol. 10, no. 1, March 1987.

Grenier, Jean, "Un collectionneur pionnier," in *L'Oeil*, no. 15, March 1956.

Guicheteau, M., "Essai sur l'esthétique spontanée du marchand de tableaux," in *Revue d'esthétique*, vol. V, part 1.

Habasque, Guy, "Quand on vendait la peau de l'ours," in *L'Oeil*, no. 15, March 1956.

Hahn, Otto, "Comment on fabrique la cote des peintres," in *Investir*, November 9, 1985.

———, "Le marchand sans galerie," in *L'Express*, November 23, 1984.

Jourdain, Francis, interview in *L'Oeil*, no. 21, September 1956.

Lapouge, Gilles, "Les marchands devant la crise," in *Le Figaro littéraire*, December 16, 1965.

Laude, Jean, "L'esthétique de Carl Einstein," in *Médiations*, no. 3, 1961.

Lemaire, Gérard-Georges, "Carlo Carra un futurise repenti," in *Beaux-Arts Magazine*, no. 46, May 1987.

Lévêque, Jean-Jacques, "DHK l'art pour une élite?" in *Les Nouvelles littéraires*, January 18, 1979.

Limbour, Georges, "Les grands collectionneurs: DHK," in *Plaisir de France*, July 1969.

Linnebach, Gabrielle, "W. Uhde, le dernier romantique," in *L'Oeil*, no. 285, April 1979.

Masson, André, "Le surréalisme et après," in *L'Oeil*, no. 15, May 1955.

Michel, Jacques, "DHK le marchand des cubistes," in *Le Monde*, January 13, 1979.

Parmelin, Hélène, interview with DHK, in *L'Humanité*, July 4, 1954.

Penrose, Roland, "Picasso's portrait of Kahnweiler," in *The Burlington Magazine*, no. 852, March 1974.

Perruchot, Henri, "Scandale au Luxembourg," in *L'Oeil*, no. 9, September 1955.

———, "Le père Tanguy," in *L'Oeil*, no. 6, June 1955.

Pia, Pascal, "A. Vollard marchand et éditeur," in *L'Oeil*, no. 3, March 1955.

Read, Herbert, "Le dilemme du critique," in *L'Oeil*, no. 72, December 1960.

Revel, Jean-François, "Paul Guillaume par lui-même," in *L'Oeil*, no. 135, March 1966.

Richardson, John, "Au château des cubistes," in *L'Oeil*, no. 4, April 15, 1955.

Roché, Henri-Pierre, article in *Le Courrier graphique*, July 1954.

———, "Adieu brave petite collection," in *L'Oeil*, no. 51, March 1959.

Russell, John, "The Man Who Invented Modern Art Dealings," in *Vogue*, September 15, 1965.

Sachko Macleod, Dianne, "Art Collecting and Victorian Middle Class Taste," in *Art History*, vol. 10, no. 3, September 1987.

Segonzac, Dunoyer de, "Souvenirs sur André Derain," in *Le Figaro littéraire*, September 18, 1954.

Spies, Werner, "En URSS avec l'exposition Léger. Entretien avec DHK," in *Preuves*, no. 151, September 1963.

——————, Article in honor of DHK's eightieth birthday in *Neue Zurcher Zeitung*, June 25, 1964.

Steiner, Wendy, "Resemblance exacte à: les portraits littéraires de Gertrude Stein," in *Europe*, August 1985.

Tériade, "Entretien avec DHK," in *Cahiers d'art*, no. 2, 1927.

Watt, Alexander, "Art dealers of Paris: DHK," in *The Studio*, London, vol. 156, no. 784, July 1958.

Zervos, Christian, "Entretien avec Alfred Flechtheim," in *Cahiers d'art*, no. 10, 1927.

CATALOGUES

Cooper, Douglas, and Gary Tinterow, *The Essential Cubism 1907–1920*, The Tate Gallery, London, 1983.

Laugier, Claude, and Michèle Richet, *Léger*, Centre Pompidou, 1981.

L'aventure de Pierre Loeb. La galerie Pierre 1924–1964. Musée d'art moderne, 1979.

Monod-Fontaine, Isabelle, *DHK marchand, éditeur, écrivain* (with Claude Laugier and Sylvie Warnier), Centre Pompidou, 1984.

——————, *Donation Louise et Michel Leiris, collection Kahnweiler-Leiris* (with Agnes Angliviel de La Baumelle, Claude Laugier, Sylvie Warnier and Nadine Pouillon), Centre Pompidou, 1984.

Pouillon, Nadine, *Braque* (with the cooperation of Isabelle Monod-Fontaine), Centre Pompidou, 1982.

Valentin, Curt (in memory of), *Modern Masterpieces Lent by American Museums*, New York, October 1954.

Vatin, Philippe, "La vie artistique en 1917," in *Images de 1917*, Musée d'histoire contemporaine BDIC-Nanterre, 1987.

Wilson, Sarah, "Fernand Léger, Art and Politics 1935–1955," in *Léger: The Later Years*, Whitechapel Art Gallery, London 1987.

THESES

Berthier, Francis, *La collection Roger Dutilleul*. Sorbonne, 1977.

Cottington, David, *Cubism and the Politics of Culture in France 1905–1914*, University of London, 1985.

Gee, Malcolm, *Dealers, Critics and Collectors of Modern Painting: Aspects of the Parisian Art Market 1910–1930*, University of London, 1977.

Goggin, Mary-Margaret, *Picasso and His Art During the German Occupation 1940–1944*, Stanford University, 1985.

Trezevant, France, *Un collectionneur suisse au XXe siècle: Hermann Rupf*, Université de Lausanne, 1975.

INDEX

. . .

ABOUT THE AUTHOR

Pierre Assouline is a staff reporter for the French magazine *Lire* and a frequent contributor to *L'Histoire*. His previous books include *Gaston Gallimard: A Half-Century of French Publishing*, as well as biographies of Marcel Dassault, Jean Jardin, and Albert Londres. Mr. Assouline lives in Paris.

ABOUT THE TRANSLATOR

Charles Ruas, critic and essayist on art and literature, is the translator of Michel Foucault's *Death and the Labyrinth: The World of Raymond Roussel*. He is also the author of *Conversations with American Writers* and is currently working on a novel. Mr. Ruas lives in New York.